# Management Science with Spreadsheet Modeling

**THIRD EDITION**

Revised Printing

PATRICK JOHANNS

**Kendall Hunt**

publishing company

Cover image courtesy of Patrick Johanns

**Kendall Hunt**
publishing company

www.kendallhunt.com
*Send all inquiries to:*
4050 Westmark Drive
Dubuque, IA 52004-1840

Printed in the United States of America
10 9 8 7 6 5 4 3

To Barbara, Gwendolyn, Rebecca, and David

# Contents

# Preface

This workbook is intended to introduce you to the field of management science. It will provide the practical knowledge and skills to enable you to construct valid mathematical and spreadsheet models for business applications, quantitatively analyze the models to arrive at a solution, and critically assess alternative solutions. The power of the personal computer gives managers the unprecedented ability to create spreadsheet models. A major goal of this workbook is to assist you in developing spreadsheet modeling skills that can be successfully applied to real world problems.

Microsoft Excel is a staple in the workplace. It will be used as a platform for model building. Special add-ins to Excel will be implemented to aid in the finding of solutions to business problems. The best solution to the optimization problems found throughout the book will be identified using Excel Silver. Palisade's @RISK and PrecisionTree will be utilized in simulation modeling and decision tree analysis. Palisade's DecisionTools Suite, which includes these add-ins, can be downloaded for free with the purchase of this book.

Each chapter will contain the following features:

1. Chapter Objectives: These are intended to alert you to important topics in the chapter and the business questions it will be addressing.
2. Examples: Each chapter will contain worked examples to illustrate the concepts and serve as a reference for examples that we will solve together in class or assign as homework.
3. Key Terms: Important terms presented in the chapter will be provided at the end of each chapter.
4. Exercises: At the end of each chapter will be a set of problems to allow you to practice the techniques covered and test your comprehension.

CHAPTER 1

# Introduction to Management Science

## ▣ CHAPTER OBJECTIVES

- Show the range of management science tools and areas where these tools have been successfully applied.
- Define the characteristics of a management science model.
- Describe the model building and quantitative analysis process.
- Demonstrate how to develop a mathematical model.
- Explore feasible and optimal solutions.
- Discuss methods and software to optimally solve mathematical models.

## Introduction

The ability to make well reasoned decisions is the hallmark of a successful manager. When problems are familiar, simple, and do not involve great costs, managers will generally use a qualitative approach to arrive at a solution. However, when the stakes are higher and the problems more complex, managers tend to use the more quantitative approach offered through Management Science. Management science tools, techniques, and concepts have significantly changed the way business decisions are made in finance, manufacturing, service operations, marketing, and consulting, and have led to increased profits across all industries. The study of management science combines the quantitative tools of Operations Research with the more qualitative field of Decision Analysis.

Some of the management science tools and techniques that have proved their value in real world applications are:

- Optimization;
- Decision analysis;
- Simulation;
- Forecasting;
- Network models;
- Data mining;
- Resources allocation; and
- Project management.

Management science models and tools span across the typical business functional areas and have the power to enhance the competitiveness of almost any company or enterprise. Modeling and optimization techniques have been used successfully in:

- Marketing;
- Finance;

- Facility design and location;
- Human resource management;
- Transportation and distribution;
- Production scheduling;
- Supply chain management;
- Inventory control; and
- Project management.

This book will:

- Familiarize you with quantitative modeling techniques and solution algorithms which aid in managerial decision-making;
- Help you formulate business models, apply optimization and simulation techniques, and use sensitivity analysis to assess decision alternatives;
- Develop your expertise in solving business problems in a variety of areas using spreadsheet models on a personal computer; and
- Give you experience in building models, analyzing results, and making decisions using the end of chapter exercises.

## What Is a Model?

Models are a simplified representation of the real objects or situation. Automobile and airplane designers build scale models that they test in wind tunnels. These physical models are used to gather information about the final design in an efficient and cost effective manner. In management science, we use mathematical and spreadsheet models to create simplified representations of business problems. Mathematical equations are used to express the desired goal and the restrictions that have to be addressed. Quantitative analysis is then applied to arrive at the best solution and assess alternatives.

## The Modeling Process

The model building process starts with assessing the problem faced and asking a series of questions to determine the information available and the important parameters of the problem. The modeling process is summarized in Figure 1.1.

### What Is Important?

It may not seem necessary to say it, but too many times people lose track of the purpose of the model in the chaos of the data available. The objective of the model needs to be stated. It could be to maximize profit, throughput, return on investment, or productivity. Alternatively, the goal may be to minimize cost, risk, completion time, or inventory. There needs to be a quantifiable objective for the model.

Likewise, it is essential to identify which factors can be controlled or influenced. The manager may have control over the projects selected, quantity produced, or resources allocated, but may not have control over the budget, labor hours available, or time deadlines. Government regulations and contracts with unions and other companies will also restrict the options available. A good model will help the decision maker determine the best values for controllable factors and take into account constraints posed by the uncontrollable ones.

**Model Building/Formulation**
- What is important?
- Can things be quantified?
- What is a good representation of the problem?

**Quantitative Analysis**
- Does model correspond to reality?
- How do changes in the inputs affect the optimal solution?

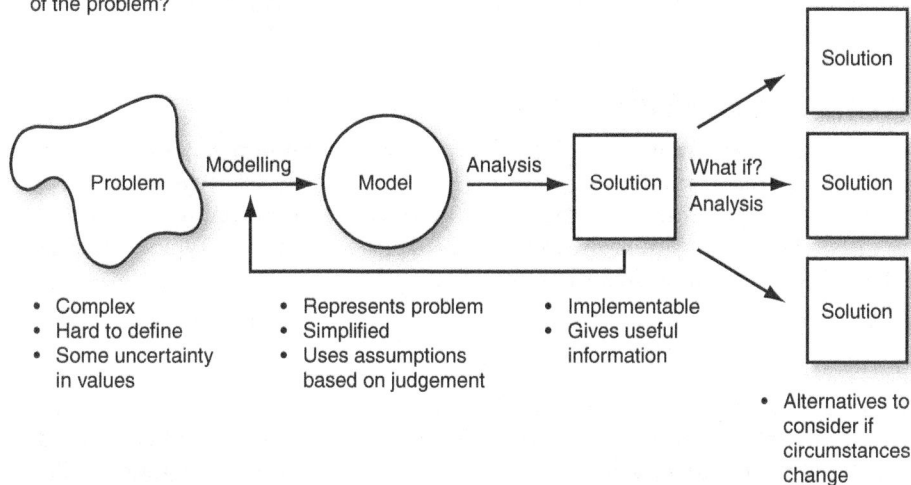

■ FIGURE 1.1

The Modeling and Analysis Process

Problem → Modelling → Model → Analysis → Solution → What if? Analysis → Solution / Solution / Solution

- Complex
- Hard to define
- Some uncertainty in values

- Represents problem
- Simplified
- Uses assumptions based on judgement

- Implementable
- Gives useful information

- Alternatives to consider if circumstances change

The focus of this book is the use of spreadsheet models as an aid in business decision making. As such, it is essential to be able to quantifiably measure inputs and outputs of the model. It is a common business adage that "If you can't measure it, you can't manage it." The quality of the models you build will depend on the quality of the data you use in them. As parameters that we cannot reliably assign a value to can often affect our results, we will explore methods of considering the impact of uncertainty and variability in the models we build.

## What Is a Good Representation of the Problem?

Throughout this book, we will be exploring different ways of representing business problems to yield usable solutions. These techniques will include mathematical models used in linear and nonlinear optimization, simulation, and decision analysis. A good model will take into account the quantity and quality of input data, the objective function, and the type of problem being posed.

## Does the Model Correspond with Reality?

Building a model is only the start of the process. Models should be verified and validated before major decisions are based on the results. Does the solution suggested by the model reflect reality? Does the distribution of values generated correspond to the distribution you used to build the model? Does the solution give results that are useful and can be implemented? Have the assumptions that the model was based on changed? The model may need to be modified in consideration of these issues.

## How Do Changes in the Inputs Affect the Optimal Solution?

Models are built because problems are complex and there exists uncertainty and variability. Assumptions often have to be made in the construction of the model. Sensitivity analysis is an important step in the decision making process. It is valuable to the decision maker to know if the solution suggested by the model is sensitive to small changes in the inputs used to build the model. For example, in planning production of a new product, we may have estimated that 60% of consumers would prefer our product to our competitors. What if the percentage was actually 20% higher or lower? Would the solution change? Solutions that do not change over a wide range of values are called **robust solutions.** Sensitivity Analysis can also identify which inputs require close measurement and monitoring as changes in them could lead to a different solution.

# Mathematical Models

In mathematical modeling, we seek to either maximize or minimize an **objective function** subject to **constraints** which limit the values of our **decision variables.** Typical objectives might be to minimize the time, risk, or cost of a project. Alternatively, you might be seeking to maximize the capacity, productivity, or profit. Typical constraints are limits in budgets, time, materials, etc.

## Inputs

Many inputs can impact the model and the solution. Inputs can be parameters that we do not have control over or decision variables. Some examples of parameters could be production time per item, selling price, materials required, and labor hours available. Inputs that we do have the ability to set the value for are called decision variables. Decision variables are often such things as the quantity of each item to produce or order, number of employees to assign to each shift, amount of money to invest in each stock, etc.

## Objective Function

In every business decision there is a goal to be pursued. The manager may have as an objective to maximize profit, return on investment, or number of customers served. On the other hand, the desired outcome may be to minimize the total cost of a project, risk of a portfolio, or time to complete a task.

## Constraints

In every decision there will be limits on the possible values of the decision variables. Limitation of available resources like raw materials, labor hours, money, or machines are common constraints placed on the decision process. Other constraints might be due to contracts, capacity, or corporate strategy.

# Example 1: Building a Mathematical Model for Down to Earth Pottery

Mary Alexander runs Down to Earth Pottery and she is planning how many vases and sets of bowls to make this week. Each vase requires 3 pounds of clay and each set of bowls requires 2 pounds of clay. She has 60 pounds of clay to use. Normally she spends 40 hours per week at her pottery wheel. The vases she makes are large and ornate and each takes one hour to make. Each bowl set takes an hour and a half to make. Mary has an order for 8 sets of bowls that she must fill this week. Several local businesses sell her productions and she earns a profit of 12 dollars for each vase and 15 dollars for each set of bowls. She would like to maximize her profit for the week. How many vases and sets of bowls should she make?

Writing a mathematical model for a problem requires a good understanding of the problem. In this problem there are a number of uncontrollable inputs: Profit per item, amount of clay used for each vase and bowl set, amount of clay available, and time to make each item. While they are uncontrollable, they are important in understanding and building the mathematical model.

There are three main steps to building a mathematical model for this problem.

1. **Define the Decision Variables.** What fundamental decisions need to be made to arrive at a solution? Mary needs to determine how many vases and bowl sets to make. Note that units are important in your definition. For Down to Earth Pottery, we will define the following decision variables:

   Let $V$ be the number of vases made this week.
   Let $B$ be the number of bowl sets to make this week.

2. **State the objective function in terms of the decision variables.** It often helps to state the objective function verbally first. Then write it as an equation that needs to be maximized or minimized using the decision variables, $V$ and $B$, defined in step 1. In this case, the objective function is to maximize profit. It would be written mathematically as:

$$\text{MAX: Profit} = 12V + 15B$$

3. **State the constraints in terms of the decision variables.** As stated before, there are limitations placed on the values that the decision variables may take. These limitations need to be identified and written as equations using the decision variables. We will write these constraints in **standard form.** In standard form, all of the variables with their coefficients appear on the **left hand side (LHS)** of the equation while the **right hand side (RHS)** of the equation consists only of a numerical value.

Clay—Mary has only 60 pounds of clay. Each vase takes 3 pounds of clay and each bowl set takes 2 pounds. This can be written as:

$$3V + 2B \leq 60$$

Labor—Mary limits her time at the potter's wheel to a maximum 40 hours per week. It takes her an hour to make a vase and 1.5 hours to make a bowl set. Mathematically this is:

$$1V + 1.5B \leq 40$$

Bowl Set Order—Mary has orders for 8 sets of bowls so she needs to make at least 8 to fill the orders. This requirement can be written as:

$$B \geq 8$$

Non-Negativity—In a majority of mathematical models like this one, it does not make sense for the variables to take on a negative value. A lower limit of 0 for the variables needs to be added to problems. These are called non-negativity constraints and can be written as:

$$V \geq 0$$
$$B \geq 0$$

Example 1 illustrates a mathematical model that could be used to determine the optimal number of vases and bowl sets for Mary to make. As can be seen, all of the decision variables in the objective function and constraints are of the first power (no squares, square-roots, etc.) and none of the decision variables are multiplied or divided by each other. When these conditions are met, this type of mathematical model is called a **linear program** or a **LP model.** LP models are easy to lay out on a spreadsheet, explain, and understand. They can also be solved efficiently to optimality using the Simplex Method. In Chapter 2, we will look at formulating this example on a spreadsheet.

## Summary of Down to Earth Pottery LP Model

The complete LP model for Down to Earth Pottery can be written as:

Let $V$ be the number of vases to make this week.
Let $B$ be the number of bowl sets to make this week.

$$
\begin{array}{llll}
\text{MAX:} & 12V & + 15B \\
\text{Subject to:} \\
& 3V & + 2B & \leq & 60 & \text{Available clay} \\
& 1V & + 1.5B & \leq & 40 & \text{Labor} \\
& & B & \geq & 8 & \text{Bowl set order} \\
& V, & B & \geq & 0 & \text{Non-negativity}
\end{array}
$$

During the modeling process, the problem is generally simplified by making certain assumptions for ease of obtaining solutions, often at the expense of representing the "real-life" problem accurately. In **deterministic models,** it is assumed that all input data are known precisely and there is no variation in the values. These models can often generate reasonable and useful solutions. The accuracy and validity of such models depends on the ability to estimate values of the input data and the amount of variation that naturally occurs in processes. The Down to Earth Pottery example is classified as a deterministic model. **Stochastic models,** on the other hand, recognize that inputs are often subject to variation and are set up to accommodate these variations. In Chapter 7 we will investigate simulation modeling which allows the inclusion of variation in values and the likelihood of events.

## Determining Model Solutions

The goal of the manager is to arrive at the best possible solution for the problem. That is, to identify the values of the decision variables that provide the best output for the model. There may be many **feasible solutions** to the model such that the values of the decision variables satisfy *all* the constraints. By satisfy, we mean that when the values of the decision variables are calculated in a constraint it yields a valid equation. For example, a feasible solution for Down to Earth Pottery would be to make 10 vases and 10 bowl sets. If we set $V = 10$ and $B = 10$, into the objective function, we find:

$$12(10) + 15(10) = \$270.$$

Looking at our constraints, we can see that all are satisfied:

$$
\begin{array}{lll}
3(10) + 2(10) = 50 & \leq 60 & \text{Clay} \\
1(10) + 1.5(10) = 25 & \leq 40 & \text{Labor} \\
\hspace{2.2cm} 10 & \geq 8 & \text{Bowl Set Order}
\end{array}
$$

Thus, making 10 vases and 10 bowl sets is a feasible solution but is it the best solution? Obviously not. We can see that there are 10 pounds of unused clay and 15 hours of labor still available. If we were to use all of the extra clay in making bowl sets, we would arrive at the solution to make 10 vases and 15 bowl sets. Setting $V = 10$ and $B = 15$ we find the objective function equals:

$$12(10) + 15(15) = \$345.$$

Looking at our constraints, we can again see that all are satisfied:

$$
\begin{array}{lll}
3(10) + 2(15) = 60 & \leq 60 & \text{Clay} \\
1(10) + 1.5(15) = 32.5 & \leq 40 & \text{Labor} \\
\qquad\qquad\quad 15 & \geq 8 & \text{Bowl Set Order}
\end{array}
$$

This solution is an improvement, but is it the best? The feasible solution that provides the best objective function value is called the **optimal solution.** Learning how to model business problems and finding the optimal solution is one of the primary goals of this book. For linear programs like this example, there is a sophisticated technique we could use to solve this problem called the **simplex method**. Detailed knowledge of doing the simplex method by hand is not covered in this book. Fortunately, software exists that will implement the simplex method to help us solve these problems.

For problems with a large number of decision variables and constraints, special optimization software packages like CPLEX or MINOS are implemented, or modeling languages like GAMS or AMPL are used to write a program to solve the model. These programs and languages are only really needed in situations where the problems contain hundreds or thousands of variables and constraints. For smaller problems, Microsoft Excel comes with an add-on called Solver that can optimally solve problems with up to 200 variables and 200 constraints. In Chapter 3 we will learn how to find the optimal solution to a two-variable problem using a graphical analysis. We will also explore finding the optimal solutions to LP models using Excel Solver.

## Optimal Solution for Down to Earth Pottery

If Down to Earth Pottery is solved to optimality it yields a solution of 4 vases and 24 bowl sets resulting in the maximum total profit of $408.

$$12(4) + 15(24) = \$408.$$

Looking at our constraints, we can again see in this solution that all of the clay is used, as well as the available time. The 24 bowl sets produced exceeds the minimum required of 8. No other feasible solution yields a greater profit.

$$
\begin{array}{lll}
3(4) + 2(24) = 60 & \leq 60 & \text{Clay} \\
1(4) + 1.5(24) = 40 & \leq 40 & \text{Labor} \\
\qquad\qquad\quad 24 & \geq 8 & \text{Bowl Set Order}
\end{array}
$$

## SUMMARY

Decision making is the daily part of being a manager. The study of management science will improve your ability to make better decisions through the building of mathematical and spreadsheet models. These models allow the simplification of complex business situations to focus on the important parameters in the problem. Spreadsheets allow the changing of values to explore how the outcomes change with changes in decision variables and uncontrollable inputs. Specialized software like the add-in to Excel called Solver can find the optimal solutions to linear models.

## KEY TERMS

**Constraint** A limitation placed on the possible values for the decision variables in a feasible solution. In mathematical modeling it takes the form of an equation or inequality.

**Decision Variable** An input to the model over which the decision maker has control.

**Deterministic Model** A model where the inputs are each assigned a point estimate, usually the most likely value. Deterministic models ignore the uncertainty that can occur in these values.

**Feasible Solution** A set of values for the decision variables that satisfy all constraints.

**LHS** The left hand side of a constraint in standard form.

**Linear Program (LP) Model** A mathematical model used to determine the optimal solution to a business situation in which all of the decision variables in the objective function and constraints are of the first power (no squares, square-roots, etc.) and none of the decision variables are multiplied or divided by each other.

**Objective Function** An equation to be maximized or minimized representing the goal of a mathematical model.

**Optimal Solution** The set or sets of values for the decision variables that yield the best value for the objective function.

**Parameters** Uncontrollable inputs that are constants in a model.

**RHS** The right hand side of a constraint in standard form.

**Robust Solutions** When the choice of decision alternatives stays the same despite changes in the input variables it is called a robust solution.

**Simplex Method** A method for solving linear programs used as the basis for many optimization software packages.

**Standard Form.** A constraint in standard form will only have variables with their coefficients on the left hand side (LHS) of the equation while the right hand side (RHS) of the equation consists only of a numerical value.

**Stochastic Model** A model which contains one or more random variables and determines the probabilities of different outcomes occurring.

# EXERCISES

1. What is the difference between a deterministic model and a stochastic model? Which type of model is linear programming?

2. What is feasible solution? What is optimal solution? What is robust solution? What is the relationship between a feasible solution and an optimal solution?

3. What are the steps in formulating a mathematical model?

4. Indicate whether the following statements are TRUE or FALSE. If it is not true, why?

   a. Formulation, solution, and implementation are the three major steps involved in decision modeling.

   b. Changing input values of decision variables always changes the value of objective function.

   c. Deterministic models assume all relevant input data are known with certainty.

   d. A constraint should be an equation.

   e. *Minimize: Cost* = $2X - 3Y + 0.5XY$ is a valid linear programming objective function.

5. Natalya Dunovich manages Organic Greenhouses. They supply organically grown vegetables year-round to the local markets. Their greenhouses enclose 12 acres of growing space that they use to raise peppers and tomatoes. They employ 30 people. Each acre of pepper plants requires 1.5 workers to tend and harvest the plants and each acre of tomatoes requires 3 workers. Peppers require a special watering system limiting production to 6 acres of peppers. Organic Greenhouses earns a profit of $30,000 per acre of peppers and $40,000 per acre of tomatoes. Formulate a linear program to help Organic Greenhouses maximize their profit.

   a. Decision variables:

   b. Objective function:

   c. Constraints:

6. Kate Kelly, owner of Kelly Moving Company (KMC) plans to purchase some new trucks with a budget of $1,500,000. There are three different truck sizes in the market: large, medium, and small, with a price of $60,000, $45,000, and $30,000, respectively, and the annual profit from these trucks is $20,000, $16,000, and $9,000. Due to the current labor force limitation, KMC will buy at most 40 extra new trucks. Formulate a linear program to help KMC Moving Co. maximize their annual profit.

a. Decision variables:

b. Objective function:

c. Constraints:

7. TaxHunter faces an insufficient labor force to prepare 24,000 tax return forms for its customers during a 6-week period in March and April this year. TaxHunter plans to hire additional full-time and part-time employees that work 40 hours a week as full-time or 20 hours a week as part-time before March. TaxHunter pays full-time employees $800 per week and part-time employees $300 per week. For each form, it takes 40 minutes on average for a full-time employee and 60 minutes on average for a part-time employee to collect and process the information. The number of part-time employees cannot exceed 60% of the total employees . Formulate an LP model to minimize the expense and cover the workload during a 6-week period in March and April. (Define decision variables and write the objective function and constraints.)

8. Tom Peterson is starting a car rental company and has a budget of $2,000,000. He plans to buy automobiles, SUVs, and trucks to satisfy client's demands. The estimated costs are as follows:

Price of an automobile: $35,000
Price of a SUV: $40,000
Price of a truck: $60,000

He expects to earn $2,000 profit from an automobile, $4,500 from an SUV and $3850 from a truck per month. He wants to buy at least two vehicles of each type. In addition, because the demand of automobiles is much higher than SUVs and trucks, automobiles should comprise at least 2/3 of his fleet.

Formulate a linear program model to help Tom maximize his monthly profit. (Define decision variables and write the objective function and constraints.)

9. The Top-Humid Company manufactures water containers for commercial humidifiers and vaporizers. The production processes for each product are similar but they require a different amount of time for blending and molding. For a humidifier, it takes 5 hours of blending and 2.5 hours of molding. For a vaporizer, it takes 12 hours of blending and 3 hours of molding.

There are up to 900 blending hours and 300 molding hours available for the coming production period. In particular, to ensure sufficient supplies, the company decides to manufacture at least 40 humidifier and 20 vaporizer water containers. The company will earn a profit of $15 per humidifier and $23 per vaporizer.

Formulate a linear program model to maximize the profit during the next production period. (Define decision variables and write the objective function and constraints.)

10. Polly Woodsides is planning to invest her savings of $100,000 into three stocks: ABC, PQR, and XYZ. For each dollar invested, she can expect to get 4%, 6.5%, and 7.5%, respectively. Her investment policy is that:

   (a) She would invest at most 40% of her money in any one stock.
   (b) The amount of money invested in ABC should be at least as much as the amount invested in XYZ.
   (c) At least 25% of her money should be invested in PQR.

   Formulate an LP to maximize the total return on Polly's investment.

# CHAPTER 2

# Spreadsheet Model Design in Excel

◻CHAPTER OBJECTIVES

- Understand and apply the concepts of good spreadsheet design.
- Use fixed and relative addresses in formulas.
- Name ranges to fix addresses to an array of cells in a spreadsheet.
- Implement Excel shortcuts like auto-fill to create series and copy formulas.

## Introduction

For hundreds of years, accountants have used spreadsheets to organize all of the costs, income, taxes, and other related data on a single sheet of paper for the business manager to assess the health of the business and consult when making decisions. However, their use was limited until the development of computerized spreadsheets with the ability to automatically carry out specified calculation. In 1979, Dan Bricklin and Bob Frankston created the first spreadsheet software program called VisiCalc.

The growing popularity of the personal computer in business during the last 25 years has gone hand in hand with the use of electronic spreadsheets to crunch and present data. The use of spreadsheets has evolved too. Starting as a tool for tracking current financial status, they now have taken on an expanded role in analyzing "what if?" scenarios, asking questions like: What will happen to payments if the interest rate goes up? What will happen to profit if overtime labor is used? What if the probability of winning the contract is lower than we estimate?

In this chapter we will discuss how to design spreadsheets to model business situations. An intelligently designed spreadsheet will be comfortable to work with and make it easy to answer the questions you want to ask. It will also be easier for others to understand your model and the conclusions that can be drawn from it.

## Spreadsheet Design

Good design doesn't just mean making your spreadsheet look good—although spreadsheet appearance can definitely aid in usability and readability. Good spreadsheet design consists of organizing your data logically and ensuring that all your formulas are correct. A good spreadsheet design makes it easy to:

- Read the data;
- Identify the intent of the spreadsheet;
- Spot the important parts quickly;
- Copy frequently used formulas to other cells;

- Use information generated;
- Update calculations as parameters change; and
- Convey the results to a user.

## Spreadsheet Formatting Tips

To improve the appearance and readability of your spreadsheet models, use the following tips:

- **Construct a data table for numeric constants.** Placing constants in a data table clearly indicates the values used and permits easy sensitivity analysis and changing of the values throughout the spreadsheet. Later when you enter a formula, if you reference a numeric constant found in the data table instead of placing it directly in the formula, you will be able to modify the spreadsheet faster and more reliably.
- **Physically locate things close together that are logically related to each other.** Use columns and rows to further orient your model. For example, when you look at an accounting spreadsheet, the income is grouped together, the expenses are grouped together, and columns represent years. When possible, a formula should refer only to the cells above it.
- **Vertically organize your spreadsheet.** Try to use only one or two screens of columns but as many rows as needed. Vertical layouts allow a clearer flow of calculations. Start with the raw data in a table at the top (or on another worksheet if the dataset is large) and progress with calculations down the page.
- **Use boldface column labels.** They draw the attention of the reader and help signal the layout of the spreadsheet.
- **Use shading, background color, and borders to highlight results that are important to the user of the model.** Formatting techniques like these will increase the readability and understanding of the spreadsheet. Keep in mind how the spreadsheet will look both on the screen and printed. Some color schemes are hard to interpret when printed on a non-color printer. See Table 2.1 for the formatting used in this book.
- **Use text boxes and cell comments to provide additional information.** Text boxes and cell comments provide extra information and greater detail about the model that can be helpful to others who use your spreadsheet or to yourself if it is a spreadsheet that you only use periodically. Text boxes can be added using the drawing menu. Comments can be added to a cell by highlighting the cell and using the **Insert/Comment** menu command.
- **Avoid unnecessary blank rows and columns.** Blank rows and columns are a good idea to separate different segments of the spreadsheet but blank rows should be avoided in the data area of your spreadsheet. Many Excel features assume that a blank row or column signals the end of your data so it is best to avoid them in your data table.

☐ TABLE 2.1 Recommended Spreadsheet Formatting

| CELL CONTENTS | FILL COLOR | FONT FORMATTING | BORDERS |
|---|---|---|---|
| Column heading | None | Bold | Optional |
| Parameter/numeric constant | Gray | None | Optional |
| Decision variable | Yellow | Bold | Bold Box |
| Intermediate calculation or low value output | Blue | None | Optional |
| High vlaue output | Green | Bold | Bold Box |

# Using Excel

Microsoft Excel is widely used by business around the world. While this book assumes a basic knowledge of Excel, skill levels will vary. While some aspects of Excel will be covered in detail, others will not be covered in the same depth. Learning to use Excel's Help menu will prove to be valuable in getting more information on how to use the wide range of Excel functions. The Help menu can be found on the right side of the menu bar.

## Using Formulas in Excel

The ability to put formulas in cells that automatically calculate desired values is one of the greatest advantages of using spreadsheet models. Formulas can get the values it needs for its calculations through the use of cell addresses or direct entry of the value in the formula. Any time you change the content of a cell *referenced* by that formula, the content of the cell containing the formula will be updated to show the new result. Each cell in the spreadsheet can be uniquely identified by its **cell address,** which is the intersection of the column and row. Cell addresses can be relative or fixed and this difference is extremely important when formulas are copied to another cell. Exhibit 2.1 shows how we can use relative and fixed addresses in an efficient manner so that formulas can be copied down the spreadsheet. In cell B7 is the formula C6*$C$3. C6 is a relative address. Cell C6 is located left one column and up one row from B7, the cell the formula is entered in. When **relative cell addresses** in a formula are copied to another cell, Excel adjusts them to reflect the cell address with the same relative position to the original cell. As you can see when cell B7 is copied down the column, the cell address for C6 is increased by one row each time. The address, $C$3, found in the same cell, is an example of a **fixed** or **absolute address.** The dollar signs in front of the row and column designation tells Excel to not change the row or column when this formula is copied to another cell.

You can also refer to a range of cells by specifying the first and last cells in the range, separated by a colon. In Exhibit 2.1, the sum function is used with the range B7:B11 which refers to the range of cells starting in cell B7 and extending down to cell B11. To select a range of cells, left click in the first cell and while keeping the mouse button depressed, drag the mouse pointer to the last cell you want to select. Then release the mouse button. The address of the selected range will appear in the address box which is on the left side of the input line of Excel.

| | A | B | C | D |
|---|---|---|---|---|
| 1 | **Using Cell Addresses in Formulas** | | | |
| 2 | | | | |
| 3 | | Interest Rate = | 5% | |
| 4 | | | | |
| 5 | Year | Interest Earned | Balance | |
| 6 | Starting | | $    1,000.00 | |
| 7 | 1 | $    50.00 | $    1,050.00 | |
| 8 | 2 | $    52.50 | $    1,102.50 | |
| 9 | 3 | $    55.13 | $    1,157.63 | |
| 10 | 4 | $    57.88 | $    1,215.51 | |
| 11 | 5 | $    60.78 | $    1,276.28 | |
| 12 | | | | |
| 13 | Total | $    276.28 | | |
| 14 | | | | |

| | A | B | C | D |
|---|---|---|---|---|
| 1 | **Using Cell Addresses in Formulas** | | | |
| 2 | | | | |
| 3 | | Interest Rate = | 0.05 | |
| 4 | | | | |
| 5 | Year | Interest Earned | Balance | |
| 6 | Starting | | 1000 | |
| 7 | 1 | =C6*$C$3 | =C6+B7 | |
| 8 | 2 | =C7*$C$3 | =C7+B8 | |
| 9 | 3 | =C8*$C$3 | =C8+B9 | |
| 10 | 4 | =C9*$C$3 | =C9+B10 | |
| 11 | 5 | =C10*$C$3 | =C10+B11 | |
| 12 | | | | |
| 13 | Total | =SUM(B7:B11) | | |
| 14 | | | | |

◻ **EXHIBIT 2.1**

**Relative and Fixed Cell Addresses**

On the left you can see a small spreadsheet showing the end of year balances of $1000 invested at 5% interest for five years. On the right you can see the formulas used to calculate this spreadsheet. A fixed address was used in the calculation of interest earned for the interest rate ($C$3). Relative addresses were used for other cell references.

## Range Names

**Range names** are another method of fixing addresses for copying in formulas. They also have the added advantage of allowing you to apply a meaningful name to a cell or range of cells. To name a cell or range of cells, select the cell or range to be named and then type the desired name in the address portion on the left side of the input line. In Exhibit 2.2, cell C3 has been named *Rate*. When the formula for B7 was entered the word *Rate* was typed in the formula instead of $C$3. The formula was then copied down to cells B8 to B11. In Exhibit 2.2, the range of cells from B7 to B11 was named *Interest* and used in the formula found in cell B13 to determine the total interest accumulated over the five-year period.

## Copying Shortcuts

Spreadsheets are wonderful at eliminating repetitive work. Shortcuts have been created to make copying formulas or series down a column or across a row. For instance, to place the series of numbers in the first column (cells A7 to A11) in Exhibit 2.2, type the number 1 in cell A7. Then click-and-drag the 'handle' in the bottom right corner of cell A7 down to A11. An auto-fill menu will appear when you let up on the mouse button. Click on this menu button and then select *Fill Series*. The same technique was used to copy the formula in cell B7 to cells B8 to B11 in Exhibit 2.2 with *Copy Cells* selected from the auto fill menu.

| | Rate | ▼ | *fx* | 5% | | | |
|---|---|---|---|---|---|---|---|
| | A | B | C | D | E | F | G |
| 1 | **Using Cell Addresses in Formulas** | | | | | | |
| 2 | | | | | | | |
| 3 | | Interest Rate = | 0.05 | | | | |
| 4 | | | | | | | |
| 5 | Year | Interest Earned | Balance | | | | |
| 6 | Starting | | 1000 | | Range Names | Cells | |
| 7 | 1 | =C6*Rate | =C6+B7 | | Interest | =Addresses!$B$7:$B$11 | |
| 8 | 2 | =C7*Rate | =C7+B8 | | Rate | =Addresses!$C$3 | |
| 9 | 3 | =C8*Rate | =C8+B9 | | | | |
| 10 | 4 | =C9*Rate | =C9+B10 | | | | |
| 11 | 5 | =C10*Rate | =C10+B11 | | | | |
| 12 | | | | | | | |
| 13 | Total | =SUM(Interest) | | | | | |
| 14 | | | | | | | |

☐ **EXHIBIT 2.2**

**Naming Ranges in Excel**

Cell C3 has been named *Rate* as can be seen in the address portion of the Excel Input line shown in the top of the exhibit. It contains the value of 0.05 or 5%. The range of cells from B7 to B11 has been named *Interest* and is used in the sum function in cell B13.

| | A | B | C | D | E | F | G | H | I |
|---|---|---|---|---|---|---|---|---|---|
| 1 | **Down to Earth Pottery** | | | | | | | | |
| 2 | | | | | | | | | |
| 3 | Data Table | | | | | | | | |
| 4 | | Vases | Bowl Sets | Limitation | | | | | |
| 5 | Clay(lbs) | 3 | 2 | 50 | | | | | |
| 6 | Time(hours) | 1 | 1.5 | 40 | | | | | |
| 7 | Bowl Set Order | 0 | 1 | 8 | | | | | |
| 8 | Profit (dollars) | 12 | 15 | | | | | | |
| 9 | | | | | | | | | |
| 10 | Number to Make | 0 | 25 | | | | | | |
| 11 | | | | | | | | | |
| 12 | Use of Resources | LHS | | RHS | | | | | |
| 13 | Clay(lbs) | 50 | <= | 50 | | | | | |
| 14 | Time(hours) | 37.5 | <= | 40 | | | | | |
| 15 | Bowl Set Order | 25 | >= | 8 | | | | | |
| 16 | | | | | | | | | |
| 17 | Total Profit | 375 | | | | | | | |
| 18 | | | | | | | | | |

Let V be the number of vases to make this week.
Let B be the number of bowl sets to make this week.
MAX: 12V + 15B
Subject to:
$3V + 2B \le 60$    (Clay available)
$1V + 1.5B \le 40$    (Labor hours available)
$B \ge 8$    (Bowl set contract)
$V, B \ge 0$    (Non-Negativity)

**Formatting Suggestion:**
Shade your decision variables in yellow and use a border to draw attention to them

☐ **EXHIBIT 2.3**

**Down to Earth Pottery**

## Using Test Data

When entering formulas it pays to check and double-check the row and column coordinates. It will be easier to check your formulas if you enter some test data in your spreadsheet, confirm the results, alter the test data, and re-check the results. Errors in cell addresses or formulas will frequently be revealed in this fashion.

# Example: Down to Earth Pottery

Let's take a look at the Down to Earth Pottery spreadsheet model (Exhibit 2.3) and see how the different aspects of good spreadsheet design are implemented in it.

- **Construct a data table for numeric constants.** The data table for Down to Earth Pottery is at the top of our spreadsheet just below the title. The values have been shaded in gray to identify them as input data.

- **Physically locate things close together that are logically related to each other.** The data is organized in columns for vases and bowl sets. Each row represents a different aspect of the problem. We have rows representing the clay, time, and order constraints, in addition to the profit for vases and bowl sets. Looking further down the spreadsheet we can see the decision variables, the constraints, and the objective function all located in groups with blank lines separating them.
- **Vertically organize your spreadsheet.** As we progress down the spreadsheet we go from raw data logically through the calculations needed to conduct this optimization. Everything fits on a single screen.
- **Use boldface column labels.** The labels for the columns are easy to see and inform as to the contents of the column.
- **Use shading, background color, and borders to highlight results that are important to the user of the model.** The decision variable cells, left hand side (LHS) of the constraints, and the objective function values are all separated from the rest of the spreadsheet using borders. They are also shaded to draw further attention to their values. In this spreadsheet the following shadings are used:
  - Gray shading to indicate input data;
  - Yellow shading to indicate decision variables;
  - Blue for the LHSs of constraints; and
  - Green to indicate the objective function value.
- **Use text boxes and cell comments to provide additional information.** The text box in the upper left hand corner shows the formulation of our problem. Cell C10 shows an example of a comment box. These can be displayed as you see here or set to display only when you put your cursor over the red triangle in the upper left hand corner of the cell.
- **Avoid unnecessary blank rows and columns.** Single blank rows are used to separate the decision variables, the constraints, and the objective function.

## Use of Cell Formulas

The Down to Earth Pottery spreadsheet (Exhibit 2.3) uses name ranges and cell formulas (see Exhibit 2.4) that make it easy to copy the formulas to other cells. Cells B10 and C10 have been give the range name *Number*. In Cell B13, the formula '=SUMPRODUCT(B5:C5,Number)' has been entered. The **SUMPRODUCT** function multiplies corresponding cells in arrays of the same size and shape together and then adds them together. In this case, cell B5 is multiplied by the first cell in the range named *Number*, B10, and adds it to the product of cell C5 and the second cell in the range named *Number*, C10. Thus, the impact is the same as the formula '= B5 * $B$10 + C5 * $C$10'. The SUMPRODUCT command will be extremely useful in the spreadsheets throughout this book. The formula in cell B13 is copied down to cells B14 and B15.

| ⬚ | A | B | C | D | E |
|---|---|---|---|---|---|
| 1 | Down to Earth Pottery | | | | |
| 2 | | | | | |
| 3 | Data Table | | | | |
| 4 | | Vases | Bowl Sets | Limitation | |
| 5 | Clay(lbs) | 3 | 2 | 50 | |
| 6 | Time(hours) | 1 | 1.5 | 40 | |
| 7 | Bowl Set Order | 0 | 1 | 8 | |
| 8 | Profit (dollars) | 12 | 15 | | |
| 9 | | | | | |
| 10 | Number to Make | 0 | 25 | | |
| 11 | | | | | |
| 12 | Use of Resources | LHS | | RHS | |
| 13 | Clay(lbs) | =SUMPRODUCT(B5:C5,Number) | <= | =D5 | |
| 14 | Time(hours) | =SUMPRODUCT(B6:C6,Number) | <= | =D6 | |
| 15 | Bowl Set Order | =SUMPRODUCT(B7:C7,Number) | >= | =D7 | |
| 16 | | | | | |
| 17 | Total Profit | =SUMPRODUCT(B8:C8,Number) | | | |
| 18 | | | | | |

⬚ **EXHIBIT 2.4**

Down to Earth Pottery

## Seeing and Printing Formulas in Excel

Throughout this chapter there have been exhibits that display the formulas and functions used in spreadsheet models. Ctrl-~ toggles your spreadsheet back and forth between formulas and values in each cell. To print a copy of your spreadsheet showing the formulas simply use the print command while formulas are displayed. To switch back to displaying values, press Ctrl-~ again.

# SUMMARY

Spreadsheets are a powerful tool for managers and business analysts to use for model building and problem analysis. Using good design techniques when building a spreadsheet model will increase its readability, decrease errors, and convey information more quickly. Following the recommendations in this chapter will improve the quality of your spreadsheet models.

# KEY TERMS

**Cell address** A unique cell identifier that is the intersection of the column and row (e.g., the cell at the intersection of column B and row 5 has the address B5). When a cell address is used in an Excel formula, the value found at that cell address is used in the calculation.

**Fixed cell address** A cell address that does not change when the formula in that cell is copied to another cell. It is also called an absolute address. Dollar signs are used to fix the column and/or row. The fixed address for cell B5 is $B$5.

**Range Names** A name given to a fixed array of cells. The range name can be used in formulas and copied to other cells. The range name will always refer to the same array of cells even when it is copied.

**Relative cell address** When a relative cell address in a formula is copied to another cell, Excel adjusts them to refer to a cell address with the same relative position to the original cell.

**SUMPRODUCT** SUMPRODUCT is an Excel function that multiplies two or more arrays of numbers together.

## BIBLIOGRAPHY

Power, D. J. "A Brief History of Spreadsheets," DSSResources.COM, http://dssresources .com/ history/sshistory.html, version 3.6, 08/30/2004.

# EXERCISES

1. In Chapter 1 we formulated the following linear program for Organic Greenhouses (Problem 5):
Let *P* be the number of acres of peppers planted.
Let *T* be the number of acres of tomatoes planted.
Max: $30{,}000P + 40{,}000T$
st.

| | |
|---|---|
| $1P + 1T \leq 12$ | Land |
| $1.5P + 3T \leq 30$ | Labor |
| $1P \leq 6$ | Max Acres of Pepper |
| $P, T \geq 0$ | Non-negativity |

Implement this chapter's concepts to build a spreadsheet model for Organic Greenhouses. Add borders and shading to your spreadsheet as needed. Include the following:

  - Title
  - Data table
  - Decision variables
  - Constraints
  - Objective function

   a. Write formulas that can be copied down where appropriate.

   b. Print the Excel spreadsheet showing the values. Print it again showing the formulas used.

2. Gregory Smith, a senior in management, has devised a way to get through Fridays just eating the 5 basic food groups: beer, pizza, coffee, diet soda, and sandwiches. Consider the following information regarding his 5 basic food groups:

|  | BEER | PIZZA | COFFEE | DIET SODA | SANDWICH |
|---|---|---|---|---|---|
| CALORIES | 84.5 | 338 | 67 | 4 | 245 |
| FAT | 0.5 | 12 | 3 | 0 | 5 |
| CARBOHYDRATES | 20 | 50 | 10 | 1 | 35 |
| PROTEIN | 0 | 7.5 | 0 | 0 | 15 |
| ALCOHOL | 1 | 0 | 0 | 0 | 0 |
| CAFFEINE | 0 | 0 | 10 | 7.5 | 0 |
| PRICE | $ 1.75 | $ 1.50 | $ 0.95 | $ 0.60 | $ 3.25 |

Greg has learned that he can have no more than 2,000 calories per day in order to avoid repeating the "freshman fifteen" weight gain from each of the last 3 years.

Greg would like to keep the following nutritional content:

- less than or equal to 55 grams of fat per day;
- at least 300 grams of carbohydrates;
- at least 45 grams of protein.

Greg plans to consume *at least* 4 beers at Harry's and requires a food consumption plan to allow for that. Greg has gotten used to consuming either 3 coffees or 4 diet sodas per day in order to stay awake in Accounting class. He also has learned from Accounting class that it is critical to minimize his expenses in order to fulfill this routine every Friday.

**Decision variables:**

$B$ = number of beers consumed per Friday
$P$ = number of slices of pizza consumed per Friday
$C$ = number of cups of coffee consumed per Friday
$D$ = number of cans of diet soda consumed per Friday
$S$ = number of sandwiches consumed per Friday

Design a spreadsheet model for this problem with well-defined Title, Data Table, Decision Variables, Constraints, and Objective Function. The LP model is given as follows:

MIN $1.75B + 1.50P + 0.95C + 0.60D + 3.25S$
s.t.

| | |
|---|---|
| $84.5B + 338P + 67C + 4D + 245S \leqslant 2{,}000$ | (Calories) |
| $0.5B + 12P + 3C + 5S \leqslant 55$ | (Fat) |
| $20B + 50P + 10C + 1D + 35S \geqslant 300$ | (Carbohydrates) |
| $7.5P + 15S \geqslant 45$ | (Protein) |
| $1B \geqslant 4$ | (Beer Consumption) |
| $10C + 7.5D \geqslant 30$ | (Caffeine) |
| $B, P, C, D, S \geqslant 0$ | |

Turn in printouts showing the formulas and values in each cell.

3. Anadol is an automobile manufacturer that produces and sells 4 different cars: *Metra*, a 2-door economy car with a unit profit of $1,000; *Ego*, a 4-door economy car with a unit profit of $1,400; *Civil*, a 2-door mid-size car with a unit profit of $2,200; and *Corona*, a 4-door mid-size car with a unit profit of $3,000. These cars share labor time, advertising budget, and the same doors and 1.6 L engines.

Let $X_1$, $X_2$, $X_3$, $X_4$ represent the number of *Metra*, *Ego*, *Civil*, and *Corona* cars that are produced. The LP (Linear Programming) model is given as follows:

Max $1{,}000\, X_1 + 1{,}400\, X_2 + 2{,}200\, X_3 + 3{,}000\, X_4$    (maximize total profit)

s.t.

| | |
|---|---|
| $4\, X_1 + 7.5\, X_2 + 9\, X_3 + 10\, X_4 \leqslant 4{,}500$ | (Constraint 1: labor time of 4,500 hours) |
| $200\, X_1 + 500\, X_2 + 600\, X_3 + 900\, X_4 \leqslant 400{,}000$ | (Constraint 2: advertising budget of $400,000) |
| $X_1 + X_2 + X_3 + X_4 \leqslant 750$ | (Constraint 3: 750 available engines) |
| $2\, X_1 + 4\, X_2 + 2\, X_3 + 4\, X_4 \leqslant 1{,}800$ | (Constraint 4: 1,800 available doors) |
| $X_1 \geqslant 200$ | (Constraint 5: contract for *Metra* production) |
| $X_2 \leqslant 700$ | (Constraint 6: capacity for *Ego* production) |
| $X_3 \leqslant 600$ | (Constraint 7: capacity for *Civil* production) |
| $X_4 \geqslant 150$ | (Constraint 8: contract for *Corona* production) |
| $X_1, X_2, X_3, X_4 \geqslant 0$ | (non-negativity) |

Design a spreadsheet model for this problem and print out your Excel worksheet with well-defined Title, Data Table, Decision Variables, Constraints, and Objective Function. Print and turn in spreadsheets showing the formulas and the values in each cell.

Print and turn in spreadsheets showing the formulas and the values in each cell.

4. Build a spreadsheet model for Top-Humid Company (Question 9 from Chapter 1) with well-defined Title, Data Table, Decision Variables, constraints, and Objective Function. Turn in the printouts showing both the formulas and the values in each cell.

5. Bartlett's Greenhouse produces two types of specialty fertilizers: one for roses and the other for tomatoes. The three main ingredients in both fertilizers are Nitrogen, Phosphorus, and Potassium.

   Fertilizers are sold in bags. A 1 kilo bag of rose fertilizer contains 200 grams of Nitrogen, 120 grams of Phosphorus, and 80 grams of Potassium. A bag of tomato fertilizer contains 240 grams of Nitrogen, 70 grams of Phosphorus, and 90 grams of Potassium. They have 100 kilograms of a Nitrogen compound, 60 kilograms of a Phosphorus compound, and 50 kilograms of a Potassium compound available for use.

   Bartlett's Greenhouse earns a profit of $3.00 for each bag of rose fertilizer it sells and $2.00 for each bag of tomato fertilizer it sells. Experience tells them that they can sell all of the fertilizer they can produce but they would like to produce at least 75 bags of each type so customers have a choice.

   a. Formulate an LP to maximize their profit. (Define decision variables and write the objective function and constraints.)

   b. Build a spreadsheet model for Bartlett's Greenhouse and print out your Excel worksheet with well-defined Title, Data Table, Decision Variables, constraints, and Objective Function.

6. Widespread is a marketing company which helps clients design ads for their products. One of its clients is now asking Widespread to allocate the marketing budget of $10,000 per month among four promotional media: TV ads, magazines ads, newspaper ads, and direct mailing. The goal of the client is to reach the maximum number of potential buyers through various promotional media. The estimated cost and reachable audience for each medium is given as follows:

| MEDIUM | COST PER AD | BUYERS REACHED PER AD | MAXIMUM ADS PER MONTH |
|---|---|---|---|
| TV ADS | $1,500 | 20,000 | 30 |
| MAGAZINE ADS | $700 | 6,000 | 150 |
| NEWSPAPER ADS | $400 | 2,500 | 300 |
| DIRECT MAILING | $200 | 400 | no limit |

The client requires that at least 4 TV ads and 8 newspaper ads be placed every month. The client also requires that at least 20% of budget should be on magazine ads and no more than 15% of budget be spent on direct mailing.

a. Formulate a linear program to maximize the total potential buyers reached.

b. Build a spreadsheet model for Widespread and print out your Excel worksheet with well-defined Title, Data Table, Decision Variables, constraints, and Objective Function.

# CHAPTER 3

# Optimization of Linear Models

■CHAPTER OBJECTIVES

- Find the optimal solution to a two variable linear program using graphical analysis.
- Use Solver to identify the optimal solution to an LP formatted on a spreadsheet.
- Interpret Solver output.
- Perform an LP sensitivity analysis to determine the impact of changes to the problem inputs.

## Introduction

After building a mathematical or spreadsheet linear model, we would like to determine what would be the best values for our decision variables. As we discussed in Chapter 1, there may be many feasible solutions to a linear program. The challenge is finding the optimal solution. In this chapter we will examine the graphical solving of two variable problems as it provides valuable insights into the structure of solutions. While it is possible to solve problems with more than two variables by hand, the use of optimization software like Excel Solver can help us quickly find the optimal solution for problems with hundreds of variables. Our analysis does not end with an optimal solution. Since there may be uncertainty in the parameters used in building the model or the situation changes, sensitivity analysis is essential. Excel Solver generates sensitivity reports that can be used to answer "What if?" questions.

## Graphical Solution to Two Variable Linear Programs

If there are only two decision variables, the linear program can be solved graphically. The first step in this process is to plot the constraints on an *x-y* axis to determine the set of feasible solutions. The set of feasible solutions to a problem is called the **feasible region.** Then we will evaluate the objective function within the feasible region to determine the values of the decision variables which yield the best value for the objective function.

### Determining the Feasible Region

Identifying the feasible region begins with plotting each of the constraints on an axis. The following steps can be followed to plot a constraint:

- Write the constraint as an equality equation.
- A common approach to plotting a line is to determine two points that satisfy the equality. Often this is easily done by setting one of the variables equal to 0 and solving for the other variables to give

one point, then repeating the process by setting the other variable equal to 0. (Alternatively, you could plot the line by identifying one point on the line and using the slope of the equation to plot the constraint.)

- Determine which side of the line satisfies the constraint (makes it a true statement). Do this by selecting a point not on the line and plugging it into the original constraint. If it satisfies the constraint, then the feasible region for this constraint is on the side of the line containing the point selected. If not, then the feasible region for the constraint is on the other side of the line.

When all of the constraints have been plotted, the region of the graph which satisfies all of the constraints is the feasible region and should be shaded in. The shaded region may be:

- Non-existent—no set of points satisfies all of the constraints. The problem is **infeasible.** One or more of the constraints will have to be removed or changed for a solution to be found.
- A point—Only one set of values for the decision variables satisfies all of the constraints.
- A line—The set of feasible solutions forms a line.
- A polygon—The feasible region is bounded on all sides by constraints.
- Unbounded—The set of feasible points is not bounded completely by the constraints. One or more decision variables can have values to infinity.

## Determining the Optimal Solution

If the plot of the constraints yields a feasible region, the next step is to plot the objective function line. One method of doing this is to set the objective function as being equal to an arbitrary value and plotting this line. The line that results is called an **isocost line** in the case of a minimization problem and an **isoprofit line** in maximization problems. All points on the line will have the same objective function value.

Setting the objective function equal to different value would result in an isocost or isoprofit line parallel to the first one drawn. The slope of the objective function line, $ax_1 + bx_2$, can be determined with the equation, slope $= -a/b$. All isocost or isoprofit lines will have the same slope. In one direction perpendicular to the objective function lines the objective function value will be increasing and in the other direction decreasing. Determine the direction which improves the objective function (decreasing for minimization problems and increasing for maximization problems).

Move your objective function line through the feasible region in the direction of improvement until it leaves the feasible region. The last point it touches on the feasible region before it leaves is the optimal solution. Thus, the optimal solution will exist at a corner of the feasible region. The values of our decision variable at this corner can be found by determining the intersection of the two constraints that comprise this corner.

# Graphical Analysis of the Down to Earth Pottery Model

Let $V$ be the number of vases to make this week.
Let $B$ be the number of bowl sets to make this week.
MAX:     $12V + 15B$
Subject to:

| | | | | |
|---|---|---|---|---|
| $3V$ | $+ 2B$ | $\leq$ | $60$ | Available clay |
| $1V$ | $+ 1.5B$ | $\leq$ | $40$ | Labor |
| | $B$ | $\geq$ | $8$ | Bowl set order |
| $V,$ | $B$ | $\geq$ | $0$ | Non-negativity |

## Plotting the Feasible Region

We determine the feasible region for the model by plotting each of the constraints. Starting with the available clay constraint:

$$3V + 2B \leq 60$$

Convert it to an equality equation:

$$3V + 2B = 60$$

Set $V = 0$ and solve for $B$:

$$3(0) + 2B = 60$$
$$B = 30$$

This gives one point on this line (0, 30). Now set $B = 0$ and solve for $V$.

$$3V + 2(0) = 60$$
$$V = 20$$

This gives a second point on this line (20, 0). With two points we can draw it on our graph (Figure 3.1).

As the constraint, $3V + 2B = 60$, is an inequality, the set of points that satisfy this constraint will be on one side of it. To determine which side, select a point not on the line and plug it into the inequality. If it forms a true statement, the set of feasible points is on that side of the line. If not, the set of feasible points is on the other side of the line. Selecting the point (1, 1), test this inequality:

$$3(1) + 2(1) \leq 60$$

Since this statement is true, 5 is less than 60, the set of feasible points for this constraint is on that side of the line. The feasible region for the clay constraint is shaded in Figure 3.1.

Plotting the other constraints and determining the set of points which satisfy all of the constraints, we find our feasible region and shade it in. See Figure 3.2.

## FIGURE 3.1

Plot of clay constraint with the feasible region for it shaded.

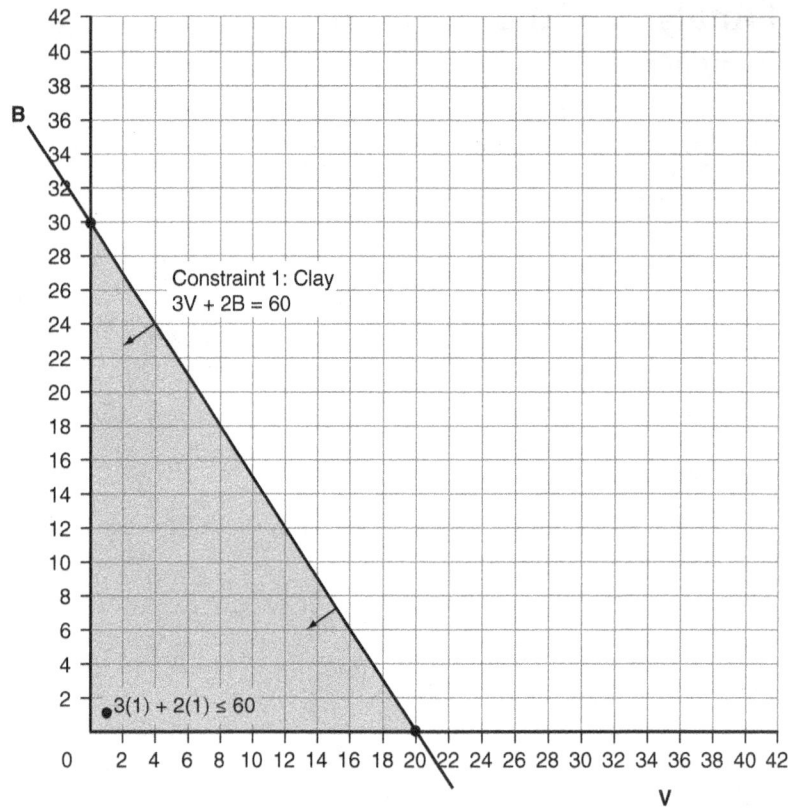

Constraint 1: Clay
$3V + 2B = 60$

$3(1) + 2(1) \leq 60$

## FIGURE 3.2

Plot of feasible region for Down to Earth Pottery problem. The set of values for $V$ and $B$ that satisfy all constraints is shaded. The feasible region for this model is a polygon.

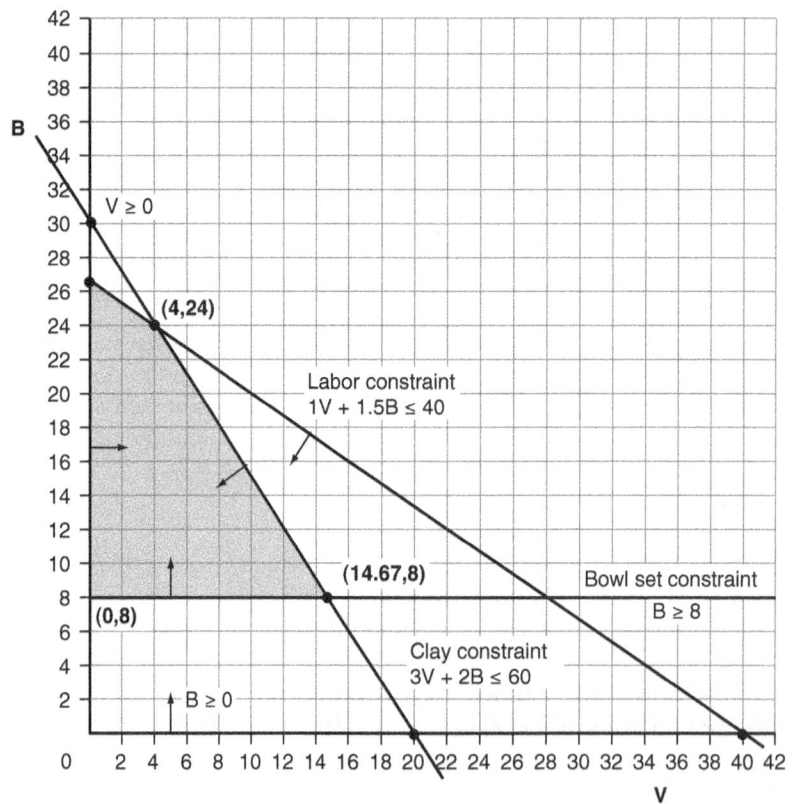

$V \geq 0$

(4,24)

Labor constraint
$1V + 1.5B \leq 40$

(14.67,8)

Bowl set constraint
$B \geq 8$

(0,8)

Clay constraint
$3V + 2B \leq 60$

$B \geq 0$

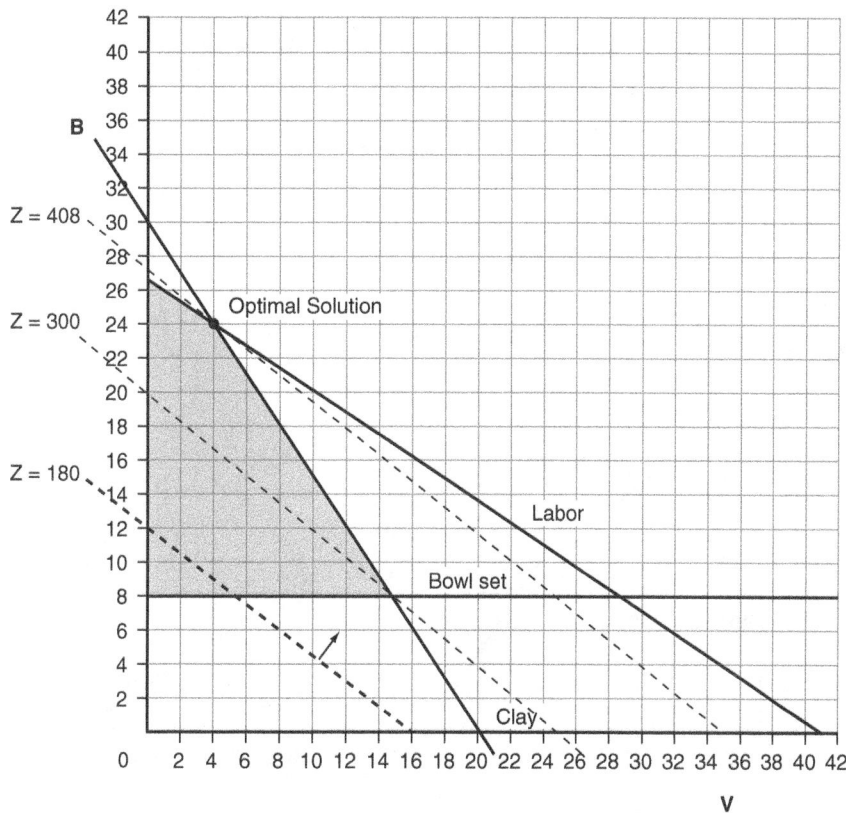

Plot of objective function lines. The objective function value, $Z$, increases as we move the line away from the origin.

## Plotting the Objective Function

In the Down to Earth Pottery example, the objective function is MAX: $12V + 15B$. Using the variable, $Z$, to represent the objective function value gives the equation $12V + 15B = Z$. We arbitrarily select a value for $Z$. Setting the objective function equal to a common multiple of the coefficients, 12 and 15, will give an easy set of intercept points to plot. In this example, we will set $Z = (12)(15) = 180$ for the equation $12V + 15B = 180$ and plot this line on the graph. Setting $V = 0$ gives the point $(0, 12)$. Setting $B = 0$ yields $(15, 0)$. The slope of this line is $-12/15$ or $-0.8$.

Selecting a parallel isoprofit line going through the point $(25, 0)$ has a value of $12(25) + 15(0) = 300$. As the value for Z increases for this new line, it can be seen that the objective function line value improves moving away from the origin. The optimal solution can be seen on the graph below. Moving the objective function line through the feasible region in the direction of improvement until it leaves the feasible region, it last touches the region at a corner. This corner is the optimal solution.

## Calculating the Optimal Solution and Value

The optimal solution occurs at the intersection of the clay and labor constraints.

$$
\begin{array}{llll}
3V & + 2B & \leq & 60 & \text{Available clay} \\
1V & + 1.5B & \leq & 40 & \text{Labor}
\end{array}
$$

Changing them to equalities and solving for $V$ and $B$ shows that they intersect at the point $(4, 24)$. The optimal solution is to make 4 vases and 24 bowl sets. Plugging these values in the objective function $12(4) + 15(24)$ yields the optimal value of 408. If Down to Earth Pottery implements the optimal solution of 4 vases and 24 bowl sets it will have a profit of \$408.

□ FIGURE 3.4

Extreme points of Down to
Earth Pottery example. The
largest Z value, 408, exists at
the corner (4, 24). This is the
optimal solution.

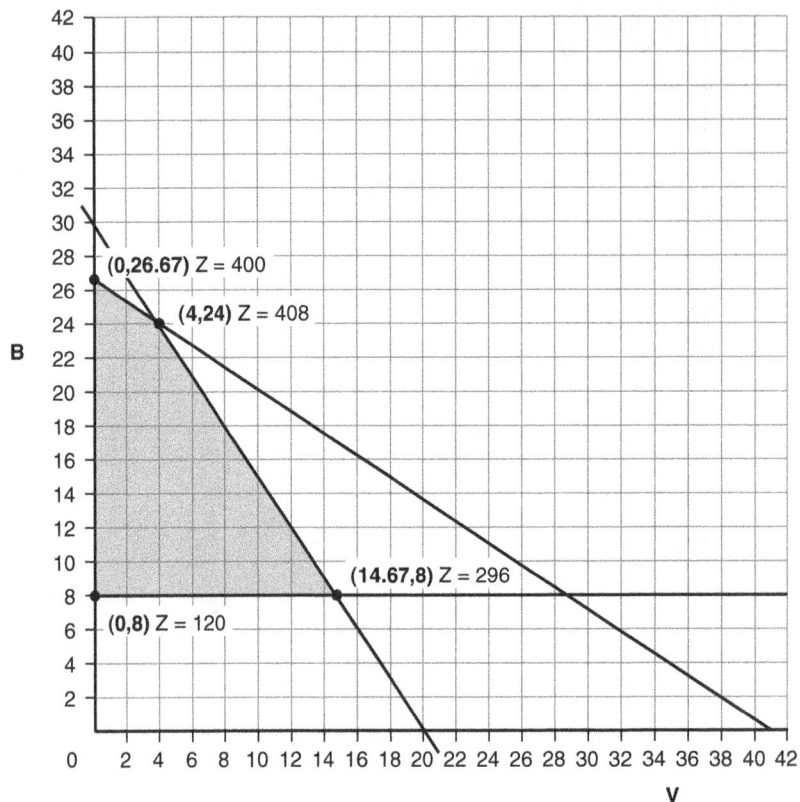

In this example clay and labor are **binding constraints.** The LHS of each equation
equals the RHS for both of these constraints at the optimal solution. All of the available clay and labor hours are used. Binding constraints will always have a slack or surplus of zero. It is also interesting to note that the slope of the objective function line
falls between the slopes of the binding constraints. In this case the slope of the clay
constraint is $-3/2$ or $-1.5$ and the slope of the labor constraint is $-1/1.5$ or $-0.67$.

$$-1.5 \leq -0.8 \leq -0.67$$

The bowl set constraint, on the other hand, is a **non-binding constraint.** The LHS
of this constraint at the optimal solution equals 24 while the RHS is 8. A surplus of
16 bowl sets is produced.

## Alternate Method of Determining the Optimal Solution

As was noted before the optimal solution exists at an extreme point (corner) of the feasible region. Therefore if the coordinates of each corner are determined and the objective function value calculated, the optimal solution can be identified as shown in
Figure 3.4.

## Optimal Solutions

Depending on the feasible region and the objective function line, there may exist zero, one, or many optimal solutions. If the feasible region is empty, there are no optimal solutions. If the objective function line leaves the feasible region in the direction of improvement at a single extreme point, there is a unique optimal solution. If there is a boundary constraint with the same slope as the objective function line and it is in the direction of improvement for the objective function, the objective function line will have the same value at all points along that boundary constraint and all will be optimal solutions.

## Impact of Adding Constraints

When constraints are added to a solved problem, they may further restrict the feasible region and make it smaller. If the new feasible region no longer contains the original optimal solution, then a new optimal solution and value will have to be determined. The new optimal value will not be as good as the original (larger value for a minimization problem and smaller for a maximization problem). If the new feasible region still contains the original optimal solution, the optimal solution and value stay the same. If the feasible region is unbounded, the optimal solution may be at the intersection of two constraints or be unbounded. The solution is unbounded if the objective function is moved in the direction of improvement and does not exit the feasible region.

## Impact of Removing Constraints

When constraints are removed from a solved problem, the feasible region may become larger. If the constraint removed is a non-binding constraint, it will not affect the optimal solution or value. However, if a binding constraint is removed, a new optimal solution and value will have to be calculated. When a constraint is removed from a solved problem, the new solution will be at least as good as the solution to the original problem. If the feasible region is unbounded, the optimal solution may be at the intersection of two constraints or be unbounded. The solution is unbounded if the objective function is moved in the direction of improvement and does not exit the feasible region.

## Solving Linear Programs Using Excel with the Solver Add-in

While solving linear programs using a graphical method provides valuable insights into the mathematics and properties of them it is rarely done outside an academic setting and is impractical for problems with more than two variables. Fortunately, Excel comes with an optimization add-in called Solver that uses the simplex method to find the optimal solution to linear programs. If you used the spreadsheet format described in Chapter 2 to lay out your linear program, then you are ready to use Solver.

Solver can be found under Data tab in Excel. If it is not displayed on the Data tab, follow the Excel Help instructions to add it in.

Let's go through the process of using Solver to find the optimal solution for the Down to Earth Pottery Example. (Exhibit 3.1). When Solver is selected, a dialogue box

□ EXHIBIT 3.1

Down to Earth Pottery
Spreadsheet Model

| | A | B | C | D | E |
|---|---|---|---|---|---|
| 1 | Down to Earth Pottery | | | | |
| 2 | | | | | |
| 3 | | Vases | Bowl Sets | Limitation | |
| 4 | Clay(lbs) | 3 | 2 | 60 | |
| 5 | Time(hours) | 1 | 1.5 | 40 | |
| 6 | Bowl Set Order | 0 | 1 | 8 | |
| 7 | Profit (dollars) | 12 | 15 | | |
| 8 | | | | | |
| 9 | Number to Make | 1 | 2 | | |
| 10 | | | | | |
| 11 | Use of Resources | LHS | | RHS | |
| 12 | Clay(lbs) | 7 | <= | 60 | |
| 13 | Time(hours) | 4 | <= | 40 | |
| 14 | Bowl Set Order | 2 | >= | 8 | |
| 15 | | | | | |
| 16 | Total Profit | 42 | | | |
| 17 | | | | | |

Let V be the number of vases made this week.
Let B be the number of bowl sets to make this week.
MAX:  12V + 15B
  Subject to:
  3V + 2B ≤ 60     (Clay available)
  1V + 1.5B ≤ 40    (Labor hours available)
         B ≥ 8     (Bowl set contract)
      V, B ≥ 0     (Non- Negativity)

(Exhibit 3.2) opens to allow you to identify the important parts of your spreadsheet model: the objective function cell, the decision variables, and the constraints.

### The Objective Function

Start with the **Set Objective** box. This is asking you to indicate the objective function value cell. In our Down to Earth Pottery example it is cell B16 (which we shaded green). You can simply left click on this cell to select it. Then indicate whether the goal is to maximize or minimize by selecting the appropriate option below the Set Target Cell box. In this case we wish to maximize total profit so Max is selected.

### Decision Variables

Solver needs to have the cells containing the decision variables identified in the **By Changing Variable Cells** section of the dialogue box. The range of cells containing our decision variables for Down to Earth Pottery, B10:B11, have been named Number. Indicate the location of the decision variables by either selecting cells B10 and B11 using the left button on your mouse or simply type the word "Number" in the appropriate box. Solver will adjust the values in these cells when it runs to the optimal solution.

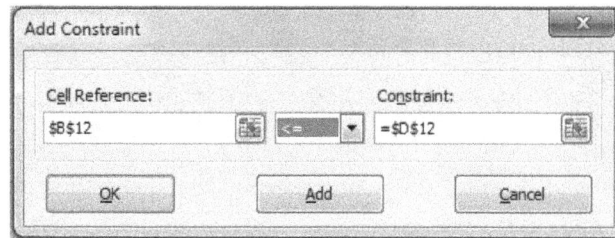

☐ EXHIBIT 3.2

Solver's Dialogue Box with
Model Entered

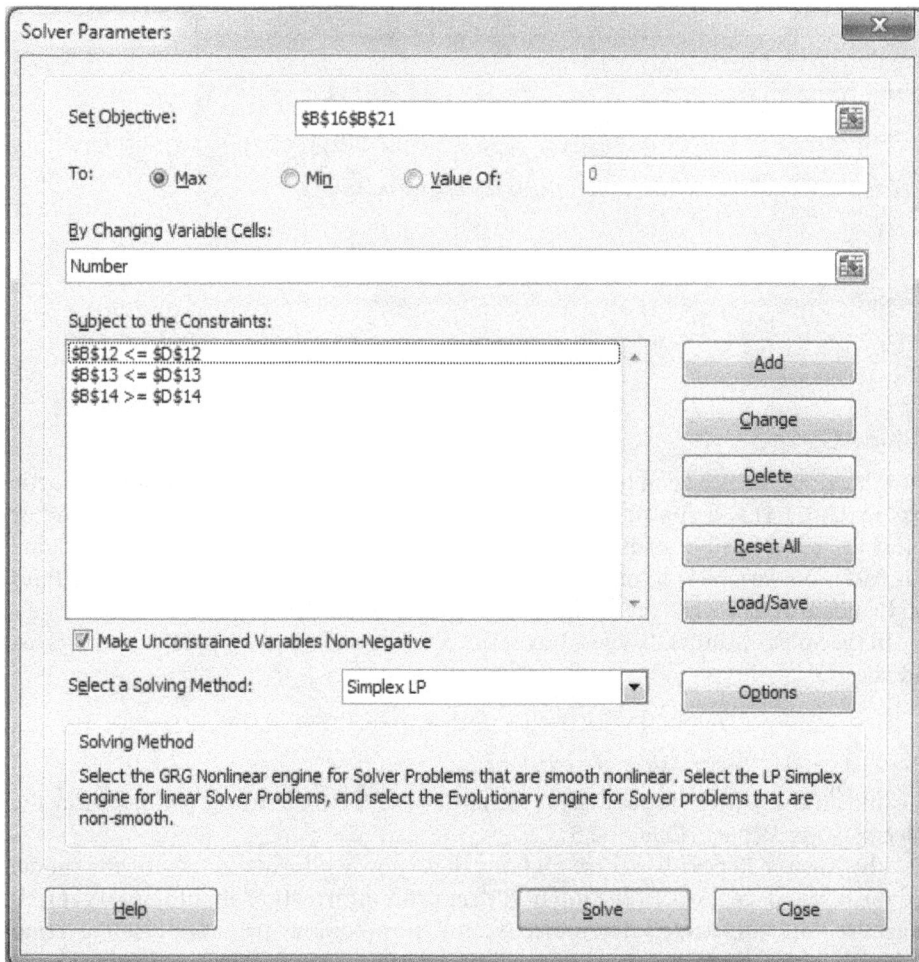

☐ EXHIBIT 3.3

Solver's Add Constraint
Dialogue Box
The first constraint in the model is
ready to add.

## Constraints

The **Subject to the Constraint** section is where the constraints are entered. Left click
on the Add button to get the Add Constraint dialogue box (Exhibit 3.3).

The first constraint is shown being added to the model by placing the cell address
of the LHS value of the Clay constraint in the **Cell Reference** box. The RHS of the constraint is placed in the **Constraint** box. A pull down menu between these two allows
us to select whether the relationship is less than or equal to, greater than or equal to,
or equal to. Clicking on the **Add** button adds this constraint to the model and returns
us to the **Add Constraint** dialogue box so another constraint can be added. Click on
**OK** when the last constraint has been added. Non-negativity constraints are added by
ticking the **Make Unconstrained Variables Non-Negative Box.**

We will use the Simplex LP method to solve this model.

**Optimal Solution with Solver Results Dialogue Box**
Select answer and sensitivity reports.

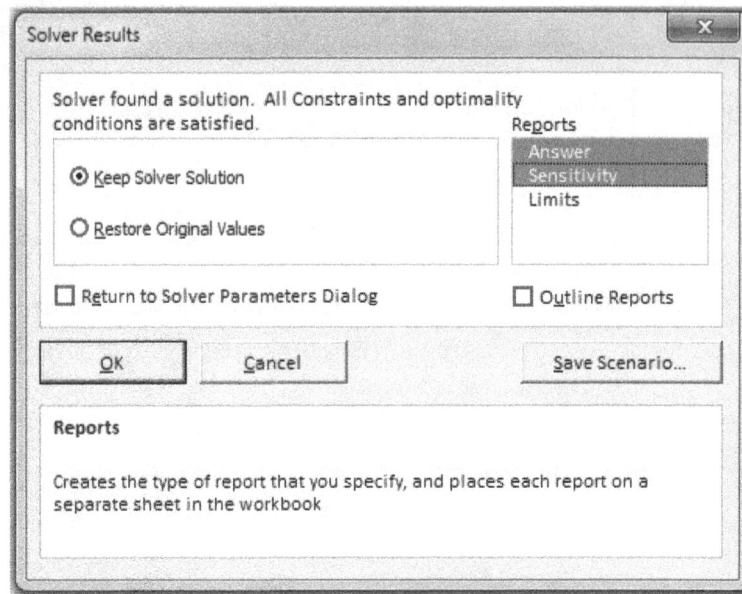

## Solver Output

With the model entered and options selected, click on **Solve.** A **Solver Results** dialogue box (Exhibit 3.4) will appear telling whether the optimal solution has been found or not. If there is a feasible solution, Solver will have changed the values in the changing cells (decision variables) to indicate the optimal solution. The LHS of each constraint will be updated as well as the optimal value displayed in the target cell.

In the **Solver Results** dialogue box select **Answer** and **Sensitivity** in the reports list and click **OK**.

## Interpreting the Answer Report

Clicking on the Answer Report tab at the bottom of the Excel window will display the Solver Answer Report (Exhibit 3.5).

The Answer Report has three sections that convey information about the model and the optimal solution. At the top of the report is information about the **Target Cell** (objective function value.) The objective function column with the heading **Final Value** contains the optimal value. The column next to it labeled **Original Value** shows the objective function value using the starting values we entered in the changing cells. As the starting values entered in the changing cells are often arbitrary numbers, the value generated by them is relatively meaningless.

The second section of the **Answer Report** shows value of the decision variables. The column with the heading **Final Value** shows the optimal solution reached by Solver. The Original Value column shows the numbers entered when the spreadsheet was prepared.

The third section relates information about the constraints at the optimal solution. The column with the heading **Cell Value** displays the LHS of each constraint at the optimal solution. The **status** column tells whether the constraint is a binding constraint or not. The final column with the heading **Slack** indicates the slack or surplus for each constraint.

Objective Cell (Max)

| Cell | Name | Original Value | Final Value |
|---|---|---|---|
| $B$16 | Total Profit LHS | 42 | 408 |

Variable Cells

| Cell | Name | Original Value | Final Value | Integer |
|---|---|---|---|---|
| $B$9 | Number to Make Vases | 1 | 4 Contin | |
| $C$9 | Number to Make Bowl Sets | 2 | 24 Contin | |

Constraints

| Cell | Name | Cell Value | Formula | Status | Slack |
|---|---|---|---|---|---|
| $B$12 | Clay(lbs) LHS | 60 | $B$12<=$D$12 | Binding | 0 |
| $B$13 | Time(hours) LHS | 40 | $B$13<=$D$13 | Binding | 0 |
| $B$14 | Bowl Set Order LHS | 24 | $B$14>=$D$14 | Not Binding | 16 |

**EXHIBIT 3.5**

**Down to Earth Pottery Answer Report**

The answer report shows that the maximun profit is achieved when 4 vases and 24 bowl sets are made.

In the Down to Earth Pottery example, the Answer Reports shows that the maximum profit of $408 per week is reached when 4 vases and 24 bowl sets are made. All 60 pounds of clay are used as well as all 40 hours of labor that were available. Twenty-four bowl sets were produced exceeding the minimum required by 16.

# Sensitivity Analysis

Business models provide a simplified representation of the real world. Values used in the model are often estimated or changed through time. Since the inputs are uncertain or can change, the solutions derived from the use of these models have some uncertainty. The process of reviewing the output of a model to determine how changes to inputs affect the proposed solution is called **sensitivity analysis.**

With linear program models, we will focus on determining the impact of changes to the coefficients in the objective function and changes to the right hand sides of constraints on the optimal solution and value.

## Changes to Objective Function Coefficients

The coefficients to terms in the objective function often change due to modifications to processes or demand. These changes will frequently change the optimal value of the objective function. However, the optimal solution is not always changed. When conducting the sensitivity analysis of a linear program, it is important to identify the

**EXHIBIT 3.6**

**Down to Earth Pottery Sensitivity Report**

Adjustable Cells

| Cell | Name | Final Value | Reduced Cost | Objective Coefficient | Allowable Increase | Allowable Decrease |
|---|---|---|---|---|---|---|
| $B$10 | Number to Make Vases | 4 | 0 | 12 | 10.5 | 2 |
| $C$10 | Number to Make Bowl Sets | 24 | 0 | 15 | 3 | 7 |

Constraints

| Cell | Name | Final Value | Shadow Price | Constraint R.H. Side | Allowable Increase | Allowable Decrease |
|---|---|---|---|---|---|---|
| $B$13 | Clay(lbs) LHS | 60 | 1.2 | 60 | 40 | 6.666666667 |
| $B$14 | Time(hours) LHS | 40 | 8.4 | 40 | 5 | 13.33333333 |
| $B$15 | Bowl Set Order LHS | 24 | 0 | 8 | 16 | 1E+30 |

**range of optimality** for each coefficient in the objective function. The range of values that the coefficient can assume without the optimal solution changing is called the range of optimality. This range assumes that all other things in the model are held constant.

## Range of Optimality for Down to Earth Pottery

Looking at the Adjustable Cells portion of the sensitivity report from Solver in Exhibit 3.6, the optimal solution is shown to be 4 vases and 24 bowl sets. The present value of the objective coefficients is $12 for vases and $15 for bowl sets. The last two columns provide the information to calculate the range of optimality for each coefficient. The allowable increase in the vase coefficient is 10.5. This tells us that the profit for vases can increase by 10.5 to $22.50 per vase before our optimal solution will change from making 4 vases and 24 bowl sets. The allowable decrease for vases is 2. The profit for vases can decrease to $10 per vase before the optimal solution will change. The range of optimality for the vase coefficient is from $10 to $22.50 if all other inputs are held constant.

If the profit for vases went from $12 to $14, the optimal solution (4 vases and 24 bowl sets) would stay the same as the change is within the range of optimality. However, the optimal value would go up by $2 per vase or a total of 4($2) = $8. The new optimal solution would be $416.

If the profit for vases increases by $14 per vase from $12 to $26, the change would be outside of the allowable increase. The coefficient would have to be changed on our spreadsheet and Solver re-run to determine the new optimal solution and value. Inferences can be drawn on the new optimal value though. The old optimal solution is still a feasible solution despite it not being the optimal solution. If it were followed, 4(26) + 24(15) = $464 would be the resultant profit. However, there is a better solution at the new optimal solution with a greater profit. $464 gives a lower limit on the new optimal value.

## Changes to the Right Hand Side of a Constraint

Changes to the right hand side of a constraint happen frequently—more raw materials may become available, the use of overtime may permit more labor hours, or demands for the product or service may change. These changes may affect the optimal solution and value. To determine the impact, start by looking at the **Shadow Price** found in the Constraints section of the Sensitivity Report. The shadow price indicates the change in the optimal value that results from increasing the RHS of that constraint by one unit with everything else held constant. The shadow price can be used to calculate the new value for the objective function by multiplying the amount of the change by the shadow price and adding this product to previous optimal value. The shadow price is only valid for a limited range of changes to the RHS of the constraint. The range of values for the RHS of the constraint for which the shadow price is valid is called the **range of feasibility.** The range of feasibility can be calculated by RHS of the constraint (found in the column next to the shadow price) and adding to it the value found in the **Allowable Increase** column to get an upper limit to the range and subtracting from it the value found in the **Allowable Decrease** column.

## Range of Feasibility and Shadow Price for Down to Earth Pottery

Suppose Mary at Down to Earth Pottery opens a 5 pound box of clay and finds that it is the wrong type and she cannot use it. What impact will this have on her profit for the week and the number of vases and bowl sets she makes?

The optimal profit was derived assuming there was 60 pounds of clay. The range of feasibility of the clay constraint is 53.333 to 100 pounds (60 − 6.667 to 60 + 40.) The decrease of 5 pounds is less than 6.667, the allowable decrease for the clay constraint. Therefore the shadow price of 1.2 is valid. The expected profit will change by (−5)(1.2) or a decrease of $6 from $408 to a new optimal value of $402. With less clay it should be obvious that the solution of 4 vases and 24 bowl sets is no longer feasible. The RHS of the constraint will have to be changed to 55 and Solver re-run to determine the new optimal solution.

What would be the impact if the decrease in usable clay was 10 pounds instead of 5 pounds? This change is beyond the allowable decrease. The RHS of the clay constraint would have to be changed to 50 in the spreadsheet model and the linear program re-run in Solver to determine the new optimal solution and value. However, some observations can be made about the new optimal value. When the decrease in clay goes below 6.667 pounds, the shadow price goes up. Because of the scarcity of the clay each pound has greater value beyond the allowable decrease. Therefore, the minimum change in the objective function value will be (−10)(1.2) or a decrease of $12. The new optimal value will be less than or equal to $396 (= 408 − 12.)

## SUMMARY

Linear programming can be a powerful tool for finding the best values for decision variables. The development of spreadsheet models coupled with optimization software has allowed companies to save millions of dollars in costs and maximize their profits. We will see throughout the rest of this book a wide range of problems to which we can apply optimization modeling and find solutions on a PC. Learning how to use optimization software will serve you well in a wide variety of careers and will be a valuable addition to your resume.

## KEY TERMS

**Binding Constraints** A constraint is binding if the RHS of the constraint equals the LHS when evaluated for a solution. The slack or surplus of a binding constraint equals zero. Removal of a binding constraint will result in a change in the optimal solution and a new optimal solution and value will have to be determined.

**Boundary Constraints** Constraints that form a border of the feasible region. Removal of a boundary constraint will cause the feasible region to increase in size.

**Changing Cells** The cells in an Excel spreadsheet that contain the values for the decision variables are called the changing cells when using Solver.

**Feasible Region** The set of values for the decision variables that satisfy all of the constraints.

**Infeasible Problem** A problem that does not have a solution that satisfies all of the constraints is infeasible.

**Isocost Line** An objective function line for a minimization problem. All points on this line yield the same value when plugged into the objective function.

**Isoprofit Line** An objective function line for a maximization problem. All points on this line yield the same value when plugged into the objective function.

**Non-binding Constraints** A constraint is non-binding for a solution if the LHS of a constraint does not equal the RHS.

**Range of Feasibility** The range of values that the RHS of a constraint can assume for which the shadow price for that constraint is valid.

**Range of Optimality** The range of values that an objective function coefficient can assume for which the optimal solution stays optimal. When the coefficient assumes a value outside of this range the problem will have to be resolved to determine a new optimal solution and value.

**Redundant Constraint** A redundant constraint does not restrict the set of feasible solutions. Removal of a redundant constraint will not affect the feasible region, optimal solution, or optimal value.

**Shadow Price** The change in the optimal value that would result from an increase of one unit to the RHS of a constraint assuming that the binding constraints did not change and all other inputs are held constant.

**Slack** The amount that the LHS of a less than or equal constraint is less than the RHS at a solution. Slack is always a non-negative number. The slack of a binding constraint is zero.

**Solver Parameters**  A spreadsheet model is entered into Solver using the Solver Parameters Dialogue box.

**Surplus** The amount that the LHS of a greater than or equal constraint is more than the RHS at a solution. Surplus is always a non-negative number. The surplus of a binding constraint is zero.

**Target Cell** The cell in an Excel spreadsheet that contains the formula for the objective function value is called the target cell when using Solver.

# EXERCISES

1. PCExpress is a small computer company that assembles and sells computers. Besides a desktop model that's been offered for a long time, PCExpress has recently started offering a laptop model. The company earns a profit of $600 on each desktop computer, and it is planning to price the laptop for a unit profit of $900. Knowing with fair certainty that PCExpress can sell all the assembled computers, PCExpress wants to determine the best combination of the two models assembled per month to maximize total profit. Each month PCExpress needs to supply at least 30 desktops to a local customer by contract.

   For each computer, PCExpress first assembles it, and then installs software and makes a final quality check. With the current resources, it takes 3 hours to assemble a desktop and 6 hours to assemble a laptop. For software installation and quality checking, it takes 1.5 hours for a desktop and 1 hour for a laptop. PCExpress wants to ensure that the total assembly time per month is at least 150 hours and at most 300 hours, and the total time for software installation and quality checking is at most 90 hours.

   a. How many desktops and laptops should PCExpress assemble to maximize total profit? What is the maximum profit? Model the problem as an LP and solve it by graphical solution approach. Do not use Excel Solver.

2. Consider the following linear program:

$$\text{Max } X + Y$$
$$\text{s.t. } 6X - 2Y \geq -2 \text{ (Constraint 1)}$$
$$2X - Y \quad \leq \quad 4 \text{ (Constraint 2)}$$
$$4X + 8Y \quad \leq 48 \text{ (Constraint 3)}$$
$$X, Y \quad \quad \geq \quad 0$$

a. What are the optimal solution and optimal objective function values? You may use the given graph with the objective function line and the constraints plotted. *Do not use Excel Solver. Show your graphical solution work.*

b. Input the LP model into the Excel worksheet and use Excel Solver to solve the model. What is the range of optimality for each variable? What is the range of feasibility for each constraint? Briefly interpret their meanings.

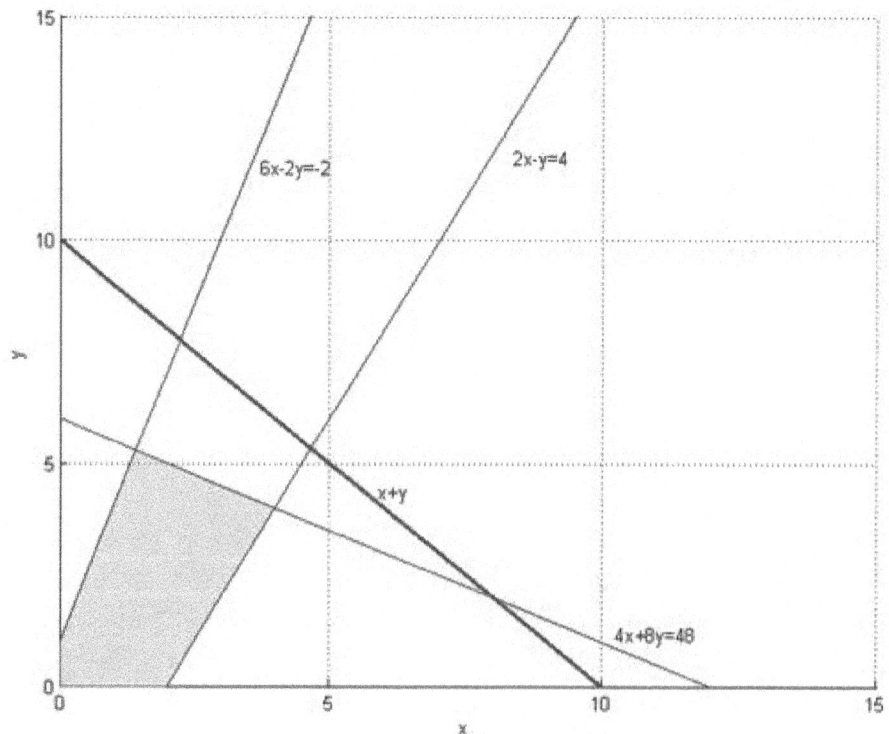

3. The formulation of the Organic Greenhouses problem and its graph is shown.

Let $P$ be the number of acres of peppers planted.
Let $T$ be the number of acres of tomatoes planted.

Max: $30,000P + 40,000T$
st.
$1P + 1T \leq 12$ Land
$1.5P + 3T \leq 30$ Labor
$1P \leq 6$ Max Acres of Pepper
$P, T \geq 0$ Non-negativity

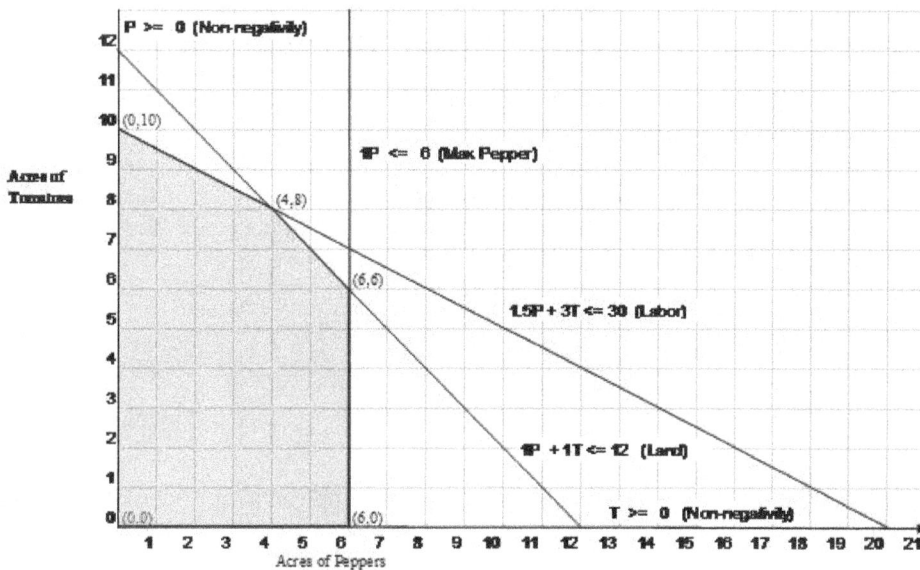

a. What is the value of the objective function for each of the extreme points?

(0,0)

(0,10)

(4,8)

(6,6)

(6,0)

b. What is the optimal solution?

c. Draw an isoprofit line through the point (0,3). What is the objective function value for this line?

d. Draw an isoprofit line through the point (0,6). What is the objective function value for this line?

e. In which direction does the isoprofit line improve in its objective function value?

f. Draw an isoprofit line through the optimal solution. What is the objective function value for this line?

4. Adding and Removing Constraints

Consider the formulation and graph in problem 3.

Four acres of peppers and eight acres of tomatoes is the optimal solution generating a profit of $440,000.

Consider each of the following conditions independently from the others. For each, will the feasible region stay the same, increase, or decrease? Will the optimal value stay the same, increase, or decrease?

a. Market research shows that there is a maximum demand of 11 acres of tomatoes.

b. Organic has signed a contract promising to supply at least 5 acres of tomatoes.

c. The watering system had to be replaced. The new system will only be able to provide water to a maximum of seven acres of tomatoes. Pepper production is not affected.

d. The ability to produce peppers has been increased from six acres to eight.

e. The workforce has been decreased to 28.

f. Tomato prices have increased the profit per acre to $50,000.

## 5. Interpreting Computer Output

### Spreadsheet

| | A | B | C | D | E | F | G | H | I |
|---|---|---|---|---|---|---|---|---|---|
| 1 | **Organic Greenhouses** | | | | | Let P be the number of acres of peppers planted. | | | |
| 2 | | | | | | Let T be the number of acres of tomatoes planted. | | | |
| 3 | | Peppers | Tomotoes | | | | | | |
| 4 | Land | 1 | 1 | 12 | | Max: 30,000P + 40,000T | | | |
| 5 | Labor | 1.5 | 3 | 30 | | | | | |
| 6 | Max Pepper | 1 | 0 | 6 | | st. | | | |
| 7 | Profit per Acre | 30000 | 40000 | | | 1P  + 1T <= 12  Land | | | |
| 8 | | | | | | 1.5P + 3T <= 30  Labor | | | |
| 9 | Acres Planted | 4 | 8 | | | 1P       <=  6  Max Pepper | | | |
| 10 | | | | | | P, T    >=  0  Non-negativity | | | |
| 11 | Total Profit | 440000 | | | | | | | |
| 12 | | | | | | | | | |
| 13 | | LHS | | RHS | | | | | |
| 14 | Land | 12 | <= | 12 | | | | | |
| 15 | Labor | 30 | <= | 30 | | | | | |
| 16 | Max Pepper | 4 | <= | 6 | | | | | |
| 17 | | | | | | | | | |

### Answer Report

Target Cell (Max)

| Cell | Name | Original Value | Final Value |
|---|---|---|---|
| $B$11 | Total Profit Peppers | 0 | 440000 |

Adjustable Cells

| Cell | Name | Original Value | Final Value |
|---|---|---|---|
| $B$9 | Acres Planted Peppers | 0 | 4 |
| $C$9 | Acres Planted Tomotoes | 0 | 8 |

Constraints

| Cell | Name | Cell Value | Formula | Status | Slack |
|---|---|---|---|---|---|
| $B$14 | Land LHS | 12 | $B$14<=$D$14 | Binding | 0 |
| $B$15 | Labor LHS | 30 | $B$15<=$D$15 | Binding | 0 |
| $B$16 | Max Pepper LHS | 4 | $B$16<=$D$16 | Not Binding | 2 |

a. What is the optimal solution?

b. What is the optimal value?

c. Which constraints are binding?

d. How much slack do we have in the Max Pepper constraint?

## 6. Interpreting Sensitivity Report

Adjustable Cells

| Cell | Name | Final Value | Reduced Cost | Objective Coefficient | Allowable Increase | Allowable Decrease |
|---|---|---|---|---|---|---|
| $B$9 | Acres Planted Peppers | 4 | 0 | 30000 | 10000 | 10000 |
| $C$9 | Acres Planted Tomotoes | 8 | 0 | 40000 | 20000 | 10000 |

Constraints

| Cell | Name | Final Value | Shadow Price | Constraint R.H. Side | Allowable Increase | Allowable Decrease |
|---|---|---|---|---|---|---|
| $B$14 | Land LHS | 12 | 20000 | 12 | 1 | 2 |
| $B$15 | Labor LHS | 30 | 6666.666667 | 30 | 6 | 3 |
| $B$16 | Max Pepper LHS | 4 | 0 | 6 | 1E+30 | 2 |

*Provide as much information as you can for each of the questions without re-solving the LP. Consider each question independent of the others.*

a. What minimum profit per acre should Organic consider planting more tomatoes?

b. The profit per acre of tomatoes has dropped to $35,000. How will this affect the optimal solution? Total profit?

c. The profit per acre of peppers has dropped to $15,000. How will this affect the optimal solution? Total profit?

d. The workforce has been reduced by 3. How will this affect the optimal solution? Total profit?

e. Two more acres of the 12 acres can be converted to produce peppers at a cost of $20,000. Should they make the conversion?

f. The nearby community college wants to rent a 2-acre greenhouse for $35,000 per year. Should they do it? Why or why not?

7. Joshua Bozin gets his gold ore to use in his processing plant from three sources: the Abracadabra, and the Busted Flush Mine, and the Castle Mine. In order to keep his plant running, at least three tons of ore must be processed each day. Ore from the Abracadabra Mine costs $200 per ton to process, and ore from the Busted Flush and the Castle Mines costs $100 per ton to process. Costs must be kept to less than $800 per day. Moreover, Federal Regulations require that the amount of ore from the Busted Flush Mine cannot exceed twice the amount of ore from the Abracadabra Mine. Ore from the Abracadabra Mine yields 2 oz. of gold per ton, ore from the Busted Flush Mine yields 3 oz. of gold per ton, and ore from the Castle Mine yields 1 oz. of gold per ton.

Here is the formulation of the problem.

Let $A$ = the number of tons of ore from the Abracadabra Mine.
Let $B$ = the number of tons of ore from the Busted Flush Mine.
Let $C$ = the number of tons of ore from the Castle Mine.

Max (gold extracted) = $2A + 3B + C$

st.

| | | | | | |
|---|---|---|---|---|---|
| $200A$ | $+ 100B$ | $+ 100C$ | $\leq 800$ | Cost constraint |
| $2A$ | $- B$ | | $\geq 0$ | Federal Regulation constraint |
| $A$ | $+ B$ | $+ C$ | $\geq 3$ | Minimum ore required constraint |
| $A,$ | $B,$ | $C$ | $\geq 0$ | Non-Negativity constraint |

Use Solver on this LP problem to determine the maximum gold produced.

a. What is the optimal solution?

b. What is the optimal value?

c. What is the reduced cost value for the Castle Mine?

8. Louise Mazzone, Production Manager for Stick to Your Knitting Inc., has just signed a contract to supply 1,000 hats and 2,000 scarves to the local Christmas market for $15,000. Each hat requires 50 meters of yarn and each scarf requires 100 meters. She has 50,000 meters of yarn available and an Acme knitting machine which can knit a hat in 8 minutes and a scarf in 10 minutes. 160 machine hours (9,600 minutes) are available. It costs $2 to make a hat and $1.50 to make a scarf. Louise also has the option to subcontract production at a cost of $3 per hat and $2 per scarf.

Here is the formulation of the problem.

Let $M_H$ be the number of hats made.
Let $M_S$ be the number of scarves made.
Let $B_H$ be the number of hats bought.
Let $B_S$ be the number of scarves bought.

Min Cost: $2M_H + 1.5M_S + 3B_H + 2B_S$

st.

| | | |
|---|---|---|
| $50M_H + 100M_S$ | $\leqslant 50{,}000$ | Available Yarn |
| $8M_H + 10M_S$ | $\leqslant 9{,}600$ | Machine Time |
| $M_H + B_H$ | $\geqslant 1{,}000$ | Hats Needed |
| $M_S + B_S$ | $\geqslant 2{,}000$ | Scarves Needed |
| $M_H, M_S, B_H, B_S$ | $\geqslant 0$ | Non-Negativity constraint |

Use Solver on this LP problem to determine the minimum cost of completing the contract.

a. What is the optimal solution?

b. What is the optimal value?

c. It will cost $20 to add an additional 5 hours of machine time. Is this a good business decision? What would be the total cost of completing the contract if the hours are added?

9. Jessica Lyell is the new owner of Coffee Country Roasters. They roast and blend coffee to sell on the internet. Their best sellers are "Best Blend" and "Economy Blend" coffee. Both are blended from three basic grades of coffee:

Best blend: 50% grade A, 20% grade B, and 30% grade C
Economy: 20% grade A, 50% grade B, and 30% grade C

The market prices are $790/ton for Best and $700/ton for Economy. The firm is given the option of buying up to 100 tons of grade A at $800/ton, 100 tons of grade B at $600/ton, and 75 tons of grade C at $400/ton. The profit on the Best Blend is $150 per ton and the profit on the Economy Blend is $120 per ton.

Jessica would like to maximize her profit.

a. Formulate this problem as a linear program.

b. Solve this problem using Excel Solver. (Turn in a copy of your spreadsheet and the formulas used in it.)

   *Using the sensitivity report from Solver, answer parts c–e. Do not resolve the problem to answer these questions. Treat each question separate from the others.*

c. The profit on Economy Blend coffee has dropped by $10 due to a bad economy. What impact will this have on our production plan and total profit?

d. The bean broker just called to tell you that due to some flooding only 80 tons of grade B beans are available. How will this affect your production plan and profit?

e. After you signed the contract for the purchase of beans according to your LP, another broker sent you an e-mail offering 12 tons of grade C coffee beans for a total of $3,000. You cannot buy less than 12 tons for this deal. Will you take this deal? Will this affect your production plan and profit? YES / NO

10. BathBros Inc. produces tubs and showers. Each product requires manufacturing and testing. Tubs require 18 minutes for manufacturing and 9 minutes for testing. Showers require 9 minutes for manufacturing and 18 minutes for testing. The capacity of the facility is 9,090 minutes of manufacturing and 7,110 minutes of testing. The unit profit from tubs and showers are $200 each.

a. *Formulate the LP model.*

b. *Solve this problem graphically. Do not use Excel Solver.*

How many of each should BathBros Inc. produce to maximize profit?

tubs =         showers =

What is the maximum profit?

*For parts c–e, set up a spreadsheet model and use Solver to find the optimal solution. Use the Solver output and sensitivity reports to answer the questions. Answer d and e independent of each other without resolving the problem. Turn in your spreadsheet model and reports.*

c. How many of each type should BathBros Inc. produce to maximize profit?

tubs =     showers =

What is the maximum profit?

d. Due to a change in marketing strategy, showers are priced differently such that the unit profit changed to $250.

Would the optimal product mix change?

How will this affect the optimal value?

At what minimum increased profit for showers would the company consider changing its production plan?

e. An electrical outage in one of the testing bays has reduced the available testing time to 6,000 minutes. Without resolving the problem:

Will the optimal solution change?

How will this affect the optimal value?

11. TVGuru Inc. manufactures LCD TV and Plasma TV sets in its Kentucky plant. The company makes a profit of $400 on each Plasma TV and $300 on each LCD TV set. The production process has a capacity of 30,000 machine-hours. It takes 3 machine-hours to produce a unit of Plasma TV and 1 machine-hour to produce a unit of LCD TV. After a market research survey by a well-known research firm, it is concluded that no more than 8,000 Plasma and 12,000 LCD TVs could be sold.

a. *Formulate the LP model.*

b. *Solve this problem graphically. Do not use Excel Solver.*

What is the optimal product mix?

What is the maximum profit?

*For parts c–e, set up a spreadsheet model and use Solver to find the optimal solution. Use the Solver output and sensitivity reports to answer the questions. Answer d and e independent of each other without resolving the problem. Turn in your spreadsheet model and reports.*

c. What is the optimal product mix?

What is the maximum profit?

d. Capacity can be increased by 1,000 machine-hours for a cost of $100,000. Should the company increase the capacity? Justify your answer.

e. There was an error in the market research report and the actual demand for Plasma TV is less than 8,000.

If the demand is 6,000 would it change the optimum solution? How would this affect the profit?

What if it is 5,000? What would be the impact on the production plan and total profit?

12. A nutritionist recommends his patient take a daily supplement containing four vitamins. The patient may purchase two different supplements and add them to a drink to meet the minimum vitamin recommendation. The vitamin content per ounce in each supplement is as follows:

| VITAMIN | SUPPLEMENT X | SUPPLEMENT Y |
|---------|--------------|--------------|
| A | 100 units | 100 units |
| B | 250 units | 100 units |
| C | 350 units | 200 units |
| D | 50 units | 250 units |

Supplement X costs $3 per ounce and supplement Y costs $4 per ounce. The daily requirement is a minimum of 125 units of Vitamin D, 500 units of Vitamin B, 400 units of Vitamin A, and 900 units of Vitamin C.

a. How many ounces of each should the patient use to minimize the cost per day?

Formulate the LP model.

b. Solve this problem graphically. Do not use Excel Solver.

How much of each supplement should be bought per day?

What is the minimum cost per day?

c. Which vitamins form the binding constraints in the mixture?

13. Ames Manufacturing Plant produces two different replacement parts for dishwashers. During a normal shift, they have 7 hours of time available on their main fabrication machine. The machine will process 40 of Part X in an hour and 25 of Part Y. Each Part X requires 0.5 hours to assemble and each Part Y requires 0.4 hours. Ames has 64 hours of labor available on this line each shift. The painting booth can handle 40 parts per hour and can be used a maximum of 6 hours per shift. Ames has a $45 profit margin for Part X and $40 for Part Y. Below you can see the spreadsheet model with the optimal profit maximizing production plan and the sensitivity analysis. Answer the questions based on this output.

|  | A | B | C | D | E |
|---|---|---|---|---|---|
| 1 | **Ames Manufacturing Plant** | | | | |
| 2 | | | | | |
| 3 | | | Time (in hours) | | |
| 4 | Activity | Part X | Part Y | Available | |
| 5 | Machining | 0.03 | 0.04 | 7 | |
| 6 | Labor | 0.50 | 0.40 | 64 | |
| 7 | Painting | 0.03 | 0.03 | 6 | |
| 8 | Unit Profit | $45 | $40 | | |
| 9 | | | | | |
| 10 | Production Plan | 0 | 160 | | |
| 11 | | | | | |
| 12 | | LHS | | RHS | |
| 13 | Machining | 6.4 <= | | 7 | |
| 14 | Labor | 64 <= | | 64 | |
| 15 | Painting | 4 <= | | 6 | |
| 16 | | | | | |
| 17 | Total profit | 6400 | | | |
| 18 | | | | | |

Adjustable Cells

| Cell | Name | Final Value | Reduced Cost | Objective Coefficient | Allowable Increase | Allowable Decrease |
|---|---|---|---|---|---|---|
| $B$10 | Production Plan Part X | 0 | -5 | 45 | 5 | 1E+30 |
| $C$10 | Production Plan Part Y | 160 | 0 | 40 | 1E+30 | 4 |

Constraints

| Cell | Name | Final Value | Shadow Price | Constraint R.H. Side | Allowable Increase | Allowable Decrease |
|---|---|---|---|---|---|---|
| $B$13 | Machining LHS | 6.4 | 0 | 7 | 1E+30 | 0.6 |
| $B$14 | Labor LHS | 64 | 100 | 64 | 6 | 64 |
| $B$15 | Painting LHS | 4 | 0 | 6 | 1E+30 | 2 |

Answer each part independently of the others. Show your calculations.

a. What is the optimal solution?

b. What is the optimal value?

c. At what minimum Unit Profit would Ames consider manufacturing Part X?

d. The materials requirements for Part Y changed increasing its cost of production by $2 per unit. What impact will this have on the production plan and profit?

e. The materials requirements for Part Y changed increasing its cost of production by $5 per unit. What impact will this have on the production plan and profit?

f. Which constraints are binding?

g. Machining time can be increased by a maximum of 4 hours at a cost of $90 per hour. Should they add any machine time? If so, how many hours?

h. Ames uses overtime to add up to 4 additional hours for assembly. Overtime hours cost the company $50 per hour. How many hours of overtime should they add? Why?

i. Ames uses overtime to add up to 16 additional hours for assembly. Overtime hours cost the company $50 per hour. How many hours of overtime should they add? Why?

14. Interpreting Sensitivity Reports

Adjustable Cells

| Cell | Name | Final Value | Reduced Cost | Objective Coefficient | Allowable Increase | Allowable Decrease |
|---|---|---|---|---|---|---|
| $G$17 | Product X | 120 | 0 | 40 | 13.33333333 | 0 |
| $H$17 | Product Y | 80 | 0 | 40 | 0 | 10 |

Constraints

| Cell | Name | Final Value | Shadow Price | Constraint R.H. Side | Allowable Increase | Allowable Decrease |
|---|---|---|---|---|---|---|
| $I$18 | Machining | 6.2 | 0 | 7 | 1E+30 | 0.8 |
| $I$19 | Labor | 10 | 80 | 10 | 4.70588235 | 1 |
| $I$20 | Painting | 6 | 0 | 6 | 0.666666667 | 0.444444444 |

a. If profit margin for X is increased by 10, what would be the change in optimum value? What if it is increased by 15?

b. If profit margin for Y is decreased to 30, what would be the change in optimum value?

c. If 3 hours of extra labor can be provided for a total cost of $200, should the company do it?

   Why or why not?

d. The machining availability has dropped from 7 to 6.5. What impact will this have on the optimal solution and the optimal value?

e. The painting availability has dropped from 6 to 5.5. What impact will this have on the optimal solution and the optimal value?

15. Lal Inc. manufactures two grades of steel pipes: Standard and Stainless. There is unlimited demand for both of these types in market. Each type of pipe has to go through four processes: heat treating, molding, smearing, and finishing. The table below shows Profit is $400 per pallet for standard and $500 per pallet for stainless.

| | HEAT TREATING | MOLDING | SMEARING | FINISHING |
|---|---|---|---|---|
| STANDARD (PALLET) | 96 minutes | 4 hours | 80 minutes | 10 hours |
| STAINLESS (PALLET) | 146 minutes | 6 hours | 240 minutes | 8 hours |
| CAPACITY (HOURS) | 32 | 60 | 32 | 28 |

a. Formulate an LP to maximize the total profit.

b. Create a spreadsheet model of your LP and use Solver to find the optimal solution. Attach your spreadsheet model and sensitivity reports to your homework.

What is the optimal solution?

What is the maximum total profit?

c. How much excess capacity does Lal have for each process?

Heat treating:                          Molding:

Smearing:                               Finishing:

*Use your sensitivity reports only without resolving to answer parts d and e. Consider each question independent of the other.*

d. The price of a pallet of stainless pipe has dropped by $100 due to a glut in the market. Will the production plan change?

How will this affect the total profit?

e. The price of a pallet of standard pipe has dropped by $100 due to a glut in the market. Will the production plan change?

How will this affect the total profit?

16. Use the graphical method to answer questions regarding the following LP model.

Max $30x_1 + 20x_2$
s.t.

$$x_1 + x_2 \leq 10$$
$$2x_1 + x_2 \leq 14$$
$$5x_1 + x_2 \geq 5$$
$$x_2 \leq 8$$
$$x_1, x_2 \geq 0$$

a. Sketch the feasible region on the plot.

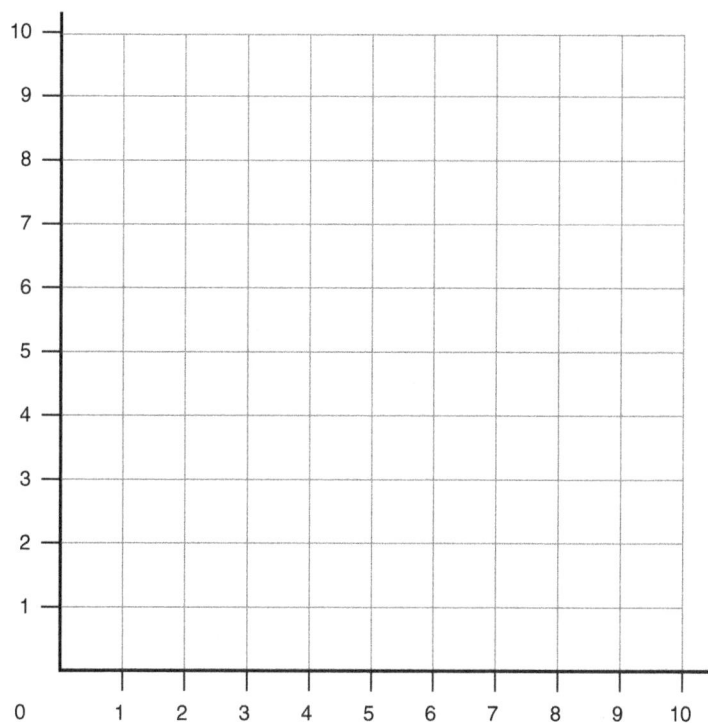

b. What is the optimal solution and optimal value of this LP?

c. This LP has an:

❏ Infeasible Solution

❏ Unique Optimal Solution

❏ Alternate Optimal Solution

❏ Unbounded Optimal Solution

d. If the objective function is changed from **Max** $30x_1 + 20x_2$ to **Min** $30x_1 + 6x_2$. What type of solution will it have?

❑ Infeasible Solution

❑ Unique Optimal Solution

❑ Alternate Optimal Solution

❑ Unbounded Optimal Solution

Input the LP model into the Excel worksheet and use Excel Solver to find the optimal solution to the original problem.

e. What is the optimal solution?

What is the optimal value?

f. What's the range of optimality for each coefficient?

g. What's the range of feasibility for each constraint?

17. The Top-Humid Company wants to find the best product mix. The LP model and the graph are given as follows:

Let $x$ equal the number of humidifiers the company produced.

Let $y$ equal the number of vaporizers the company produced.

Objective Function

$\quad$ Max $15x + 23y$

s.t.

| | |
|---|---|
| $5x + 12y \leq 900$ | Blending hours constraint |
| $2.5x + 3y \leq 300$ | Molding hours constraint |
| $x \geq 40$ | Minimum number of humidifiers constraint |
| $y \geq 20$ | Minimum number of vaporizers constraint |
| $x, y \geq 0$ | Nonnegativity constraint |

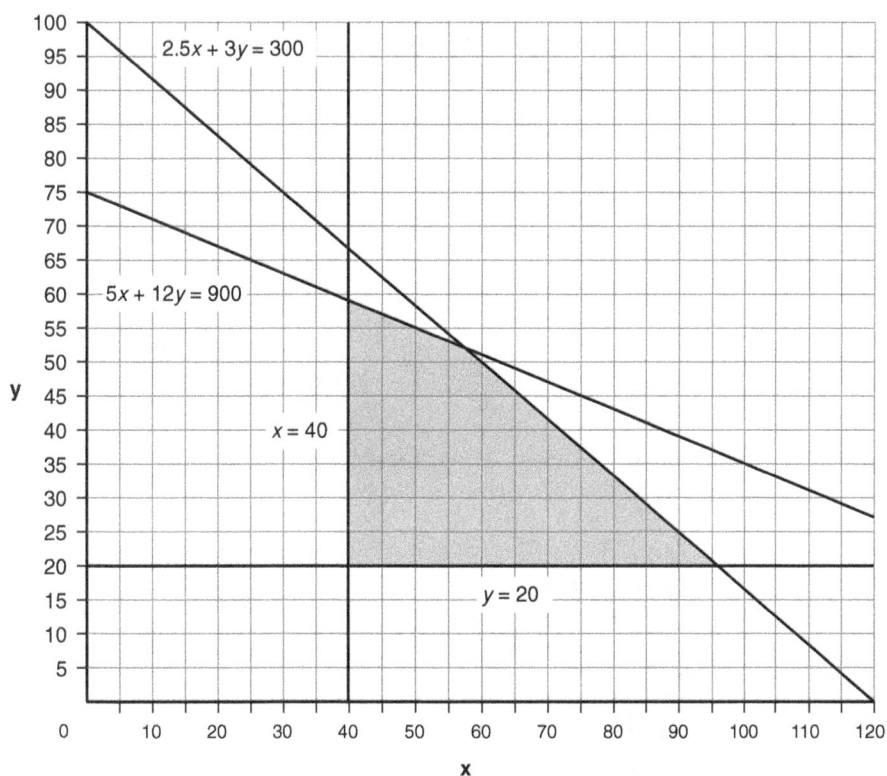

a. Draw a isoprofit line through (40,40). What's the objective function value for this line?

b. Draw a isoprofit line through (60,60). What's the objective function value for this line?

c. In what direction does the isoprofit line improve in its objective function value?

d. Draw a isoprofit line through the optimal solution. What's the optimal solution? What is the optimal value?

Use the graph on the previous page to answer the following questions. Each question should be answered independently.

e. If the company decided to make at least 80 humidifiers, how would the optimal value change?

f. If the company decided it should increase the minimum number of vaporizers to 40 because of the increased demand, how would the optimal value change?

g. The available blending hours is decreased because one of the blending machines broke. The feasible region would become
    i. Larger
    ii. Smaller
    iii. Remain unchanged

The optimal value would
    iv. Stay the same
    v. Increase
    vi. Decrease

18. Odie Dumon raises grapes to sell to wine makers. He just purchased an 80-acre plot on which he intends to plant grape vines. Although the species are the same, the size of the grapes can be controlled to be either large or small through different branch pruning methods and fertilizers.

   On average, an acre of large grapes will yield 120 kilograms and require 3 labor hours to harvest. An acre of small grapes will yield 200 kilograms of small grapes with 4.5 labor hours to harvest. Odie can sell a kilogram of large grapes for $5.50. Small grapes bring $3.80 per kilogram of small grapes to wine makers. He has 260 labor hours for harvest available.

   a. Formulate a linear program model to help Odie Duman know how many acres of small and large grapes to produce in order to maximize his profit. (Define decision variables and write the objective function and constraints.)

   b. Solve graphically.

# CHAPTER 4

# Optimization Applications

- Expand skills in building business optimization models.
- Work with a variety of common optimization applications.
- Recognize problem types and apply standard formulation to solve them.
- Apply optimization to multi-period production and inventory planning, employee scheduling, and marketing research problems.

## Introduction

Linear programming optimization has been used successfully in all areas of business. This chapter will explore three different linear programming applications to problems commonly encountered. If a business situation can be identified as one of these types of problems, then there is often a standard notation and set of decision variables and structured set of constraints that if applied make modeling a simple task. These models have been used in industry to manage their businesses better and achieve superior financial results.

## Multi-Period Production and Inventory Planning

The variation in demand for goods is a challenge for the production planner. Some variation can be forecast such as seasonal demands for lawnmowers, bicycles, skis, and toys. Other demand variations are less predictable. Companies often produce extra items to place in inventory to handle seasonal variations or for immediate shipment to provide good service when there is unforeseen variation in demand. Carrying inventory is not free and the cost of capital and storage must be taken into consideration. There is also a desire to have stable production levels. Major changes in production schedules can lead to additional labor and capacity costs. The multi-period production planning model is used to set production and inventory levels to smooth production schedules and minimize the total labor, capacity, and holding costs.

### Example: Prometheus Grills

Prometheus Grills makes high-end gas grills. Prometheus uses a 6-month planning horizon to decide how many grills to produce each month. They have the capacity to produce 375 grills per month and storage space for 250 grills. It costs Prometheus $220 to manufacture a grill. That cost is expected to remain stable for the next three months and rise to $250 after that. For each grill remaining in inventory at the end of the month, Prometheus will incur a **carrying cost** of 3% of the production cost in capital and storage expenses. They have 40 grills in inventory now and would like to have at least 30 in inventory at the end of six months. The projected six-month demand is shown in Table 4.1. How many grills should Prometheus produce and hold in inventory each month to minimize their total production and holding costs?

☐ TABLE 4.1   Projected Demand at Prometheus Grills

| MONTH | 1 | 2 | 3 | 4 | 5 | 6 |
|--------|-----|-----|-----|-----|-----|-----|
| DEMAND | 100 | 250 | 500 | 500 | 300 | 100 |

## Solution

Decision Variables: In a multi-period production planning problem like this, the company has two decisions to make each month: how many grills to produce and how many to hold in inventory at the end of the month. Using subscript notation, we can quickly define our decision variables:

> Let $P_i$ = the number of grills produced in month $i$.
> Let $I_i$ = the number of grills kept in inventory at the end of month $i$.
>     $i = 1, 2, ..., 6$

Note: Often the company will be planning the production schedule for many items at the same time. The notation used then will be $P_{ij}$ and $I_{ij}$ where $i$ will refer to the item and $j$ will refer to the month.

> Objective Function: Minimize Total Production and Carrying Costs
> MIN: $220P_1 + 220P_2 + 220P_3 + 250P_4 + 250P_5 + 250P_6 + 220*(0.03)I_1 + 220*(0.03)I_2 + 220*(0.03)I_3 + 250*(0.03)I_4 + 250*(0.03)I_5 + 250*(0.03)I_6$

> Constraints: The number of grills produced each month and the number left in inventory are related by this equation:

| $P_i$ | + | $I_{i-1}$ | − | $I_i$ | = | Demand in $i$ |
|-------|---|-----------|---|-------|---|---------------|
| Production in Month $i$ | | Ending Inventory in $i-1$ | | Ending Inventory in Month $i$ | | |

This gives the following six constraints:

$$
\begin{array}{llll}
P_1 & + 40 & - I_1 & = 100 \quad \text{Month 1} \\
P_2 & + I_1 & - I_2 & = 250 \quad \text{Month 2} \\
P_3 & + I_2 & - I_3 & = 500 \quad \text{Month 3} \\
P_4 & + I_3 & - I_4 & = 500 \quad \text{Month 4} \\
P_5 & + I_4 & - I_5 & = 300 \quad \text{Month 5} \\
P_6 & + I_5 & - I_6 & = 100 \quad \text{Month 6}
\end{array}
$$

The constraint to have at least 30 grills in inventory at the end of six months is:

$$ I_6 \qquad\qquad \geq 30 \qquad\qquad \text{Ending Inventory Requirement} $$

Prometheus has the capacity to manufacture 375 grills a month giving the following six constraints:

| | | |
|---|---|---|
| $P_1$ | $\leq 375$ | Capacity Month 1 |
| $P_2$ | $\leq 375$ | Capacity Month 2 |
| $P_3$ | $\leq 375$ | Capacity Month 3 |
| $P_4$ | $\leq 375$ | Capacity Month 4 |
| $P_5$ | $\leq 375$ | Capacity Month 5 |
| $P_6$ | $\leq 375$ | Capacity Month 6 |

The limited storage space yields the following set of constraints:

| | | |
|---|---|---|
| $I_1$ | $\leq 250$ | Inventory Month 1 |
| $I_2$ | $\leq 250$ | Inventory Month 2 |
| $I_3$ | $\leq 250$ | Inventory Month 3 |
| $I_4$ | $\leq 250$ | Inventory Month 4 |
| $I_5$ | $\leq 250$ | Inventory Month 5 |
| $I_6$ | $\leq 250$ | Inventory Month 6 |

Finally, the non-negativity constraints are:

$$P_i, I_i \geq 0, \text{ for } i = 1, 2, \ldots, 6$$

The final model for Prometheus is:

Let $P_i$ = the number of grills produced in month $i$.
Let $I_i$ = the number of grills kept in inventory at the end of month $i$.
$i = 1, 2, \ldots, 6$

MIN: Total Cost = $220P_1 + 220P_2 + 220P_3 + 250P_4 + 250P_5 + 250P_6 +$
$220*(0.03)I_1 + 220*(0.03)I_2 + 220*(0.03)I_3 + 250*(0.03)I_4 +$
$250*(0.03)I_5 + 250*(0.03)I_6$

s.t.

| | | | | |
|---|---|---|---|---|
| $P_1$ | | $- I_1$ | $= 60$ | Month 1 |
| $P_2$ | $+ I_1$ | $- I_2$ | $= 250$ | Month 2 |
| $P_3$ | $+ I_2$ | $- I_3$ | $= 500$ | Month 3 |
| $P_4$ | $+ I_3$ | $- I_4$ | $= 500$ | Month 4 |
| $P_5$ | $+ I_4$ | $- I_6$ | $= 300$ | Month 5 |
| $P_6$ | $+ I_5$ | $- I_6$ | $= 100$ | Month 6 |
| $I_6$ | | | $\geq 30$ | Ending Inventory Requirement |
| $P_1$ | | | $\leq 375$ | Capacity Month 1 |
| $P_2$ | | | $\leq 375$ | Capacity Month 2 |
| $P_3$ | | | $\leq 375$ | Capacity Month 3 |
| $P_4$ | | | $\leq 375$ | Capacity Month 4 |
| $P_5$ | | | $\leq 375$ | Capacity Month 5 |
| $P_6$ | | | $\leq 375$ | Capacity Month 6 |
| $I_1$ | | | $\leq 250$ | Inventory Month 1 |
| $I_2$ | | | $\leq 250$ | Inventory Month 2 |
| $I_3$ | | | $\leq 250$ | Inventory Month 3 |
| $I_4$ | | | $\leq 250$ | Inventory Month 4 |
| $I_5$ | | | $\leq 250$ | Inventory Month 5 |

$$I_6 \leq 250 \quad \text{Inventory Month 6}$$
$$P_i, I_i \geq 0 \quad \text{Non-negativity for } i = 1, 2, ..., 6$$

The Prometheus Grills multiple period production planning problem can be optimally solved using Solver as shown in the spreadsheet in Exhibit 4.1.

## Variations to the Multiple Period Production and Inventory Planning Problem

Many variations exist to the basic scheduling problem. Companies use overtime, part-time, and subcontracted (temporary) labor to meet its labor demands without hiring permanent full-time employees. A linear program handling these alternate sources of labor can be easily formulated by adding decision variables representing each shift of an additional labor source.

**EXHIBIT 4.1**

Prometheus Grills Spreadsheet Model with Optimal Solution

### Prometheus Grills Six Month Production Plan

| | | | | | | | |
|---|---|---|---|---|---|---|---|
| Initial Inventory | 40 | | | | | | |
| Minimum Final Inventory | 30 | | | | | | |
| Inventory Capacity | 250 | | | | | | |
| Production Capacity | 375 | | | | | | |
| Holding Cost | 3% | (% of Production Cost) | | | | | |

| Month | 1 | 2 | 3 | 4 | 5 | 6 |
|---|---|---|---|---|---|---|
| Unit Production Costs | $ 220 | $ 220 | $ 220 | $ 250 | $ 250 | $ 250 |
| Demand | 100 | 250 | 500 | 500 | 300 | 100 |

#### Production Plan

| Month | 1 | 2 | 3 | 4 | 5 | 6 | 1 | 2 | 3 | 4 | 5 | 6 | | |
|---|---|---|---|---|---|---|---|---|---|---|---|---|---|---|
| | $P_1$ | $P_2$ | $P_3$ | $P_4$ | $P_5$ | $P_6$ | $I_1$ | $I_2$ | $I_3$ | $I_4$ | $I_5$ | $I_6$ | | |
| Month 1 Demand | 1 | | | | | | -1 | | | | | | | 60 |
| Month 2 Demand | | 1 | | | | | 1 | -1 | | | | | | 250 |
| Month 3 Demand | | | 1 | | | | | 1 | -1 | | | | | 500 |
| Month 4 Demand | | | | 1 | | | | | 1 | -1 | | | | 500 |
| Month 5 Demand | | | | | 1 | | | | | 1 | -1 | | | 300 |
| Month 6 Demand | | | | | | 1 | | | | | 1 | -1 | | 100 |
| Final Inventory | | | | | | | | | | | | 1 | | 30 |
| Prod. Capacity Month 1 | 1 | | | | | | | | | | | | | 375 |
| Prod. Capacity Month 2 | | 1 | | | | | | | | | | | | 375 |
| Prod. Capacity Month 3 | | | 1 | | | | | | | | | | | 375 |
| Prod. Capacity Month 4 | | | | 1 | | | | | | | | | | 375 |
| Prod. Capacity Month 5 | | | | | 1 | | | | | | | | | 375 |
| Prod. Capacity Month 6 | | | | | | 1 | | | | | | | | 375 |
| Inventory Limit Month 1 | | | | | | | 1 | | | | | | | 250 |
| Inventory Limit Month 2 | | | | | | | | 1 | | | | | | 250 |
| Inventory Limit Month 3 | | | | | | | | | 1 | | | | | 250 |
| Inventory Limit Month 4 | | | | | | | | | | 1 | | | | 250 |
| Inventory Limit Month 5 | | | | | | | | | | | 1 | | | 250 |
| Inventory Limit Month 6 | | | | | | | | | | | | 1 | | 250 |
| Costs | $ 40,700 | $ 82,500 | $ 82,500 | $ 93,750 | $ 75,000 | $ 32,500 | 825 | 1650 | 825 | 0 | 0 | 225 | | |

| | 1 | 2 | 3 | 4 | 5 | 6 | 1 | 2 | 3 | 4 | 5 | 6 |
|---|---|---|---|---|---|---|---|---|---|---|---|---|
| Units producted | 185 | 375 | 375 | 375 | 300 | 130 | 125 | 250 | 125 | 0 | 0 | 30 |

Constraints

| LHS | | RHS |
|---|---|---|
| 60 | = | 60 |
| 250 | = | 250 |
| 500 | = | 500 |
| 500 | = | 500 |
| 300 | = | 300 |
| 100 | = | 100 |
| 30 | >= | 30 |
| 185 | <= | 375 |
| 375 | <= | 375 |
| 375 | <= | 375 |
| 375 | <= | 375 |
| 300 | <= | 375 |
| 130 | <= | 375 |
| 125 | <= | 250 |
| 250 | <= | 250 |
| 125 | <= | 250 |
| 0 | <= | 250 |
| 0 | <= | 250 |
| 30 | <= | 250 |

| Total Costs | $ 408,711.00 |
|---|---|

# Marketing Research

Companies conduct surveys to understand the needs and buying characteristics of their consumers for improved product planning and better forecasting of the demand for their goods. One of the first steps in carrying out a survey is the design phase. During design phase, the company selects the desired target population and number of respondents needed. It then determines the methods needed to reach the target population at a minimum cost. These methods may include direct mail, phone interviews, and face to face interviews to name a few. Costs can vary greatly depending on the method. We will develop a linear program to meet the requirements of the survey at the lowest total cost.

## Example: Tourism Research Inc.

Tourism Research Inc. specializes in surveys of people's desire to travel. The Indiana Tourism Council has commissioned them to gather information about the public awareness of a variety of attractions in the state of Indiana and the desires of households to visit them. They have divided households into four categories for this study.

- Households containing a single adult with no children under the age of 18.
- Households containing a single adult with children under the age of 18.
- Households containing a married couple with no children under the age of 18.
- Households containing a married couple with children under the age of 18.

It was decided to use a combination of direct mail surveys and phone interviews. Tourism Research will mail out 20,000 surveys and conduct 1,000 phone interviews. Direct mail surveys have an advantage in being cheaper per survey mailed out but have a low response rate. Phone interviews are more expensive because of the personnel time involved. The questionnaire for households with children is longer and costs more in printing and postage costs. It costs $1.40 per letter mailed to a household with children and $1.10 per letter to a household without children. The cost of conducting a phone interview is proportional to the time it takes to complete the interview. Interviews of single adult households with children cost $13 to conduct. Households with single adults without children are the cheapest and cost $9 per interview. Households with married couples are more expensive at $16 for those with children and $12 for those without children.

The Indiana Tourism Council has imposed the following restrictions on the research study:

- At least 25% of those contacted by phone must be married households with children.
- At least 50% of those mailed questionnaires must be households with children.
- At most 20% of those contacted in the study can be single adult households without children.
- The same number of married households with children must be contacted as the married households without children.

How many surveys will have to be mailed out and phone interviews conducted in each category in order to minimize the overall cost of the study?

## Decision Variables

Proper selection of decision variables can make a problem easier to formulate. Marketing research problems need a decision variable for each category and method combination. In this problem, Tourism Research has four categories and two methods of reaching them, requiring the use of eight decision variables.

Let $M_{ij}$ = number of mailed questionnaires to group $ij$, where $i = S$ for a single adult household and $M$ for a married couple household and $j = C$ for a household with children and $N$ for a household without children.

Let $P_{ij}$ = number of phone interviews for group $ij$ where $i = S$ for a single adult household and $M$ for a married couple household and $j = C$ for a household with children and $N$ for a household without children.

## Objective Function

Minimize Total Survey Cost

$$\text{MIN: } 1.40M_{SC} + 1.10M_{SN} + 1.40M_{MC} + 1.10M_{MN} + 13.00P_{SC} + 9.00P_{SN} + 16.00P_{MC} + 12.00P_{MN}$$

## Constraints

The constraints for the required number of questionnaires and phone interviews are straightforward:

$$M_{SC} + M_{SN} + M_{MC} + M_{MN} \quad = 20{,}000 \qquad \text{20,000 mailed questionnaires}$$
$$P_{SC} + P_{SN} + P_{MC} + P_{MN} \quad = 1{,}000 \qquad \text{1,000 phone interviews}$$

The restriction that a required percentage of those contacted come from a particular subpopulation are a little trickier and it might be easier to break up the writing of these constraints into two steps. Looking at the first restriction that requires at least 25% of those contacted by phone be married households with children, first identify the population of people that the 25% comes from. In this case the group is those contacted by phone which can be written algebraically as $P_{SC} + P_{SN} + P_{MC} + P_{MN}$ and the subset is married households with children contacted by phone, $P_{MC}$. So $P_{MC}$ must be at least 25% of $P_{SC} + P_{SN} + P_{MC} + P_{MN}$ which can be written as:

$$P_{MC} \quad \geqslant \quad 0.25(P_{SC} + P_{SN} + P_{MC} + P_{MN})$$

Putting this in standard form gives:

$$-0.25P_{SC} - 0.25P_{SN} + 0.75P_{MC} - 0.25P_{MN} \quad \geqslant \quad 0 \quad \text{Restriction 1}$$

Restriction 2. At least 50% of those mailed questionnaires must be households with children. Algebraically, the number of mailed questionnaires can be written as $M_{SC} + M_{SN} + M_{MC} + M_{MN}$. Households with children who were mailed questionnaires can be written as $M_{SC} + M_{MC}$. The constraint is:

$$M_{SC} + M_{MC} \quad \geqslant \quad 0.5(M_{SC} + M_{SN} + M_{MC} + M_{MN})$$

and putting it in standard form gives:

$$0.5M_{SC} - 0.5M_{SN} + 0.5M_{MC} - 0.5M_{MN} \geq 0 \quad \text{Restriction 2}$$

Restriction 3. At most 20% of those contacted in the study can be single households without children.

$$M_{SN} + P_{SN} \leq 0.2(M_{SC} + M_{SN} + M_{MC} + M_{MN} + P_{SC} + P_{SN} + P_{MC} + P_{MN})$$

in standard form is:

$$-0.2M_{SC} + 0.8M_{SN} - 0.2M_{MC} - 0.2M_{MN} - 0.2P_{SC} + 0.8P_{SN} - 0.2P_{MC} - 0.2P_{MN} \leq 0$$
$$\text{Restriction 3}$$

Restriction 4. The same number of married households with children must be contacted as the married households without children.

$$M_{MC} + P_{MC} = M_{MN} + P_{MN}$$

in standard form is:

$$M_{MC} - M_{MN} + P_{MC} - P_{MN} = 0 \quad \text{Restriction 4}$$

Non-negativity constraints are needed also.

$$M_{SC}, M_{SN}, M_{MC}, M_{MN}, P_{SC}, P_{SN}, P_{MC}, P_{MN} \geq 0 \quad \text{Non-negativity}$$

## Summary of LP Formulation

Let $M_{ij}$ = number of mailed questionnaires to group $ij$, where $i = S$ for a single adult household and $M$ for a married couple household, and $j = C$ for a household with children and $N$ for a household without children.

Let $P_{ij}$ = number of phone questionnaires to group $ij$, where $i = S$ for a single adult household and $M$ for a married couple household, and $j = C$ for a household with children and $N$ for a household without children.

MIN: Total Survey Cost = $1.40M_{SC} + 1.10M_{SN} + 1.40M_{MC} + 1.10M_{MN} + 13.00P_{SC} + 9.00P_{SN} + 16.00P_{MC} + 12.00P_{MN}$

s.t.
$$
\begin{aligned}
M_{SC} + M_{SN} + M_{MC} + M_{MN} &= 20{,}000 \quad \text{Mailed questionnaires}\\
P_{SC} + P_{SN} + P_{MC} + P_{MN} &= 1{,}000 \quad \text{Phone interviews}\\[6pt]
-0.25P_{SC} - 0.25P_{SN} + 0.75P_{MC} - 0.25P_{MN} &\geq 0 \quad \text{Restrictions 1–4}\\
0.5M_{SC} - 0.5M_{SN} + 0.5M_{MC} - 0.5M_{MN} &\geq 0\\
-0.2M_{SC} + 0.8M_{SN} - 0.2M_{MC} - 0.2M_{MN} - &\\
0.2P_{SC} + 0.8P_{SN} - 0.2P_{MC} - 0.2P_{MN} &\leq 0\\
M_{MC} - M_{MN} + P_{MC} - P_{MN} &= 0
\end{aligned}
$$

$$M_{SC}, M_{SN}, M_{MC}, M_{MN}, P_{SC}, P_{SN}, P_{MC}, P_{MN} \geq 0 \quad \text{Non-negativity}$$

Exhibit 4.2 shows the spreadsheet model for the Tourism Research problem with its optimal solution.

| | A | B | C | D | E | F | G | H | I | J |
|---|---|---|---|---|---|---|---|---|---|---|
| 1 | Tourism Research Inc | | | | | | | | | |
| 2 | | | | | | | | | | |
| 3 | | | Mailed Questionnaires | | | | Phone Interviews | | | |
| 4 | | | Single Households | | Married Households | | Single Households | | Married Households | |
| 5 | | | Children | No Children | Children | No Children | Children | No Children | Children | No Children |
| 6 | | | MSC | MSN | MMC | MMN | PSC | PSN | PMC | PMN | RHS |
| 7 | 20,000 Mailed | 1 | 1 | 1 | 1 | | | | | 20000 |
| 8 | 1,000 Phone | | | | | 1 | 1 | 1 | 1 | 1000 |
| 9 | Restriction 1 | | | | | -0.25 | -0.25 | 0.75 | -0.25 | 0 |
| 10 | Restriction 2 | 0.5 | -0.5 | 0.5 | -0.5 | | | | | 0 |
| 11 | Restriction 3 | -0.2 | 0.8 | -0.2 | -0.02 | -0.2 | 0.8 | -0.2 | -0.2 | 0 |
| 12 | Restriction 4 | | | 1 | -1 | | | 1 | -1 | 0 |
| 13 | Cost (dollars) | 1.4 | 1.1 | 1.4 | 1.1 | 13 | 9 | 16 | 12 | |
| 14 | | | | | | | | | | |
| 15 | Number Surveyed | 250 | 0 | 9750 | 10000 | 0 | 750 | 250 | 0 | |
| 16 | | | | | | | | | | |
| 17 | | LHS | | Sign | RHS | | | | | |
| 18 | 20,000 Mailed | 20000 | | = | 20000 | | | | | |
| 19 | 1,000 Phone | 1000 | | = | 1000 | | | | | |
| 20 | Restriction 1 | 0 | | >= | 0 | | | | | |
| 21 | Restriction 2 | 0 | | >= | 0 | | | | | |
| 22 | Restriction 3 | -1650 | | <= | 0 | | | | | |
| 23 | Restriction 4 | 0 | | = | 0 | | | | | |
| 24 | | | | | | | | | | |
| 25 | Total Cost | $ 35,750 | | | | | | | | |
| 26 | | | | | | | | | | |

Formulation / Sheet2 / Sheet3

# Workforce Scheduling

Properly scheduling employees is important to every company. In particular, it is vital
to service sector businesses where the bulk of business comes in peaks. Scheduling to
handle the peaks is an essential skill for providing excellent service and containing
costs. Building a schedule starts with projecting the daily or hourly need for employees. Historical information generally used to create the projection of labor requirements. This information is used to match staffing levels to expected demand. Union
rules, labor agreements, governmental regulations, and company policies often limit
staffing options.

## Staffing at National Express Shipping

The New Haven branch of National Express Shipping handles packages for delivery
throughout the country seven days a week. The volume of packages varies from day to
day so the number of employees needed to handle the pickup, shipment, and delivery
varies as well. The staffing requirements to handle the weekly demand can be seen in
Table 4.2 below:

□TABLE 4.2  Daily Staffing Requirements at National Express

| DAY | MONDAY | TUESDAY | WEDNESDAY | THURSDAY | FRIDAY | SATURDAY | SUNDAY |
|---|---|---|---|---|---|---|---|
| Employees Required | 19 | 14 | 12 | 12 | 16 | 9 | 6 |

The National Express staff is unionized and work rules state that all full-time employees work 5 days straight with two consecutive days off. Employees earn a base pay of $540 a week. Employees who work on Saturday or Sunday earn an additional $54 per weekend day worked. National Express would like to minimize their staffing costs.

Proper selection of decision variables can make problems quicker and easier to format. In a scheduling problem, the best approach is to identify each possible work schedule (shift) and assign it a number. This number can then be used with a subscript notation as follows:

Let $X_i$ be the number of employees assigned to shift $i$.

In this case, the National Express employees can be divided into seven separate shifts (see Table 4.3) which can be designated by the day of the week they start their five consecutive days of work. The weekly pay is calculated for each shift and is the coefficient for it in the objective function. In this case the objective function is:

MIN: Weekly Payroll Cost = $540X_1 + 594X_2 + 648X_3 + 648X_4 + 648X_5 + 648X_6 + 594X_7$

### ☐ TABLE 4.3 National Express Shift Information

| SHIFT | DAYS WORKED | DAYS OFF | WEEKLY PAY |
|-------|-------------|----------|------------|
| 1 | Monday, Tuesday, Wednesday, Thursday, Friday | Saturday, Sunday | $540 |
| 2 | Tuesday, Wednesday, Thursday, Friday, Saturday | Sunday, Monday | $594 |
| 3 | Wednesday, Thursday, Friday, Saturday, Sunday | Monday, Tuesday | $648 |
| 4 | Monday, Thursday, Friday, Saturday, Sunday | Tuesday, Wednesday | $648 |
| 5 | Monday, Tuesday, Friday, Saturday, Sunday | Wednesday, Thursday | $648 |
| 6 | Monday, Tuesday, Wednesday, Saturday, Sunday | Thursday, Friday | $648 |
| 7 | Monday, Tuesday, Wednesday, Thursday, Sunday | Friday, Saturday | $594 |

One constraint will be needed for each time period that a worker requirement is given. In this problem there is a daily requirement provided. However in many businesses hourly requirements are used in scheduling.

On Monday, 19 workers are needed. Shifts 1, 4, 5, 6, and 7 work on Mondays. The constraint for Monday is:

$$X_1 \qquad\qquad + X_4 \; + X_5 \; + X_6 \; + X_7 \; \geq 19 \quad \text{Monday}$$

Shifts 1, 2, 5, 6, and 7 work on Tuesdays. The constraint for Tuesday is:

$$X_1 \; + X_2 \qquad\qquad + X_5 \; + X_6 \; + X_7 \; \geq 14 \quad \text{Tuesday}$$

Similarly the rest of the week can be handled and the constraints for these days are:

$$
\begin{array}{llllllllll}
X_1 & + X_2 & + X_3 & & & + X_6 & + X_7 & \geqslant 12 & \text{Wednesday} \\
X_1 & + X_2 & + X_3 & + X_4 & & & + X_7 & \geqslant 12 & \text{Thursday} \\
X_1 & + X_2 & + X_3 & + X_4 & + X_5 & & & \geqslant 16 & \text{Friday} \\
& + X_2 & + X_3 & + X_4 & + X_5 & + X_6 & & \geqslant \;\,9 & \text{Saturday} \\
& & + X_3 & + X_4 & + X_5 & + X_6 & + X_7 & \geqslant \;\,6 & \text{Sunday}
\end{array}
$$

A non-negativity constraint is also needed. The full linear program formulation follows.

$$
x_1 \qquad\qquad\qquad\qquad\qquad\qquad \geqslant \;\,0 \quad \text{Non-negativity}
$$

## Linear Programming Formulation for National Express Shipping

Let $X_i$ be the number of employees assigned to shift $i$.

MIN: Payroll cost $= 540X_1 + 594X_2 + 648X_3 + 648X_4 + 648X_5 + 648X_6 + 594X_7$

Subject to:

$$
\begin{array}{llllllllll}
X_1 & & & + X_4 & + X_5 & + X_6 & + X_7 & \geqslant 19 & \text{Monday} \\
X_1 & + X_2 & & & + X_5 & + X_6 & + X_7 & \geqslant 14 & \text{Tuesday} \\
X_1 & + X_2 & + X_3 & & & + X_6 & + X_7 & \geqslant 12 & \text{Wednesday} \\
X_1 & + X_2 & + X_3 & + X_4 & & & + X_7 & \geqslant 12 & \text{Thursday} \\
X_1 & + X_2 & + X_3 & + X_4 & + X_5 & & & \geqslant 16 & \text{Friday} \\
& + X_2 & + X_3 & + X_4 & + X_5 & + X_6 & & \geqslant \;\,9 & \text{Saturday} \\
& & + X_3 & + X_4 & + X_5 & + X_6 & + X_7 & \geqslant \;\,6 & \text{Sunday} \\
X_i & & & & & & & \geqslant \;\,0 & \text{Non-negativity}
\end{array}
$$

## National Express Shipping Spreadsheet Model

The Excel spreadsheet showing an optimal solution can be seen in Exhibit 4.3. There are other worker schedules that have this same optimal cost of $11,232 per week.

## Common Variations to the Workforce Schedule Problem

Many variations exist to the basic scheduling problem. Companies use overtime, part-time, and subcontracted (temporary) labor to meet its labor demands without hiring permanent full-time employees. A linear program handling these alternate sources of labor can be easily formulated by adding decision variables representing each shift of an additional labor source.

| | A | B | C | D | E | F | G | H | I |
|---|---|---|---|---|---|---|---|---|---|
| 1 | National Express Shipping | | | | | | | | |
| 2 | | | | | | | | | |
| 3 | | Shift 1 | Shift 2 | Shift 3 | Shift 4 | Shift 5 | Shift 6 | Shift 7 | |
| 4 | | X1 | X2 | X3 | X4 | X5 | X6 | X7 | Requirements |
| 5 | Monday | 1 | | | 1 | 1 | 1 | 1 | 19 |
| 6 | Tuesday | 1 | 1 | | | 1 | 1 | 1 | 14 |
| 7 | Wednesday | 1 | 1 | 1 | | | 1 | 1 | 12 |
| 8 | Thursday | 1 | 1 | 1 | 1 | | | 1 | 12 |
| 9 | Friday | 1 | 1 | 1 | 1 | 1 | | | 16 |
| 10 | Saturday | | 1 | 1 | 1 | 1 | 1 | | 9 |
| 11 | Sunday | | | 1 | 1 | 1 | 1 | 1 | 6 |
| 12 | Payroll Cost | 540 | 594 | 648 | 648 | 648 | 648 | 594 | |
| 13 | | | | | | | | | |
| 14 | Workers | 10 | 0 | 0 | 4 | 2 | 3 | 0 | |
| 15 | | | | | | | | | |
| 16 | | LHS | | | RHS | | | | |
| 17 | | Workers | | | Requirements | | | | |
| 18 | Monday | 19 | >= | | 19 | | | | |
| 19 | Tuesday | 15 | >= | | 14 | | | | |
| 20 | Wednesday | 13 | >= | | 12 | | | | |
| 21 | Thursday | 14 | >= | | 12 | | | | |
| 22 | Friday | 16 | >= | | 16 | | | | |
| 23 | Saturday | 9 | >= | | 9 | | | | |
| 24 | Sunday | 9 | >= | | 6 | | | | |
| 25 | | | | | | | | | |
| 26 | Payroll Cost | $11,232 | | | | | | | |
| 27 | | | | | | | | | |

Model / Sheet2 / Sheet3

**EXHIBIT 4.3**

National Express Employee Scheduling Spreadsheet Model

## SUMMARY

In this chapter, we looked at just a few of the many types of problems that have been formulated using linear programming and solved using spreadsheet modeling. Optimization is used in virtually all areas of business to reduce costs, increase profits, and improve productivity. Many problems have formulations that share common structure. If you can identify a business situation as a particular type of problem, the common structure will make the problem easier to model.

## KEY TERMS

**Carrying Cost** The cost keeping one unit in inventory for one period of time is called the carrying or holding cost.

# EXERCISES

1. Honeydew Chemical's Chief Operating Officer, Ash Molinaro, needs to plan their production for the next three months. Honeydew Chemicals produces a single product—liquid fertilizer—for which the following relevant information for the next 3 periods (months) is available.

| PERIOD | PRODUCTION COST PER LITER ($) | DEMAND | INVENTORY HOLDING COST CHARGED AT THE END OF A PERIOD PER LITER ($) | PRODUCTION CAPACITY |
|--------|------|------|------|------|
| 1 | 2.40 | 500 | 0.20 | 600 |
| 2 | 2.50 | 300 | 0.25 | 400 |
| 3 | 2.80 | 500 | 0.20 | 300 |

The company has an initial inventory of 100 liters at the beginning of period 1, and is required to hold a minimum inventory of at least 50 liters at the end of period 3.

a. Formulate a linear program, clearly defining all variables used, to determine the production and inventory in each period that minimizes the total cost for Honeydew over the 3 periods, while meeting its demand requirements.

b. Use Solver to find the optimal solution to the linear program from part a. Turn in the spreadsheet model with solution.

c. The company has an option to use overtime to increase its production capacity in each of the 3 periods. The overtime manufacturing cost per liter is 10% higher than the normal manufacturing cost per liter, for each period. The overtime capacity for each of the 3 periods is as follows:

| PERIOD | OVERTIME CAPACITY (LITERS) |
|--------|----------------------------|
| 1      | 50                         |
| 2      | 80                         |
| 3      | 60                         |

Formulate a linear program, clearly defining all variables used, to determine the regular and overtime production and inventory in each period that minimizes the total cost for Honeydew over the 3 periods, while meeting its demand requirements. You only need to show any changes to part a.

d. Use Solver to find the optimal solution to the linear program from part c.

2. ITG is an electronic company which developed a new MP3 player and plans to do consumer research by collecting surveys. To fully draw statistically valid results, it must fulfill the following requirements:

1) survey at least 4,000 customers in total,
2) survey at least 2,000 customers who are 25 years of age or younger,
3) survey at least 1,200 customers who are 25 and 40 years of age,
3) survey at least 800 customers who are 40 years of age or older,
4) ensure that at least 40% of those surveyed customers are male,
5) ensure that at most 100 of those surveyed male customers are older than 40 years of age.

ITG estimates that the costs of reaching people in each age and gender category are as follows:

| GENDER | COST PER PERSON SURVEYED ($) | | |
|--------|------------|------------|------------|
|        | AGE < 25   | AGE 25–40  | AGE > 40   |
| Male   | $4.50      | $3.50      | $5.00      |
| Female | $3.80      | $4.20      | $5.40      |

Apply linear programming to model this marketing research problem to minimize the interview cost in total. (Define decision variables and write the objective function and constraints.)

a. Formulate this as a Linear Program.

b. Solve this program. What is the optimal solution? What is the total cost?

3. The Big Motor Works (BMW) is considering a production schedule for cars and trucks over the next two months. They must deliver on time 400 trucks and 800 cars in month one. In month two, their demand is 300 trucks and 300 cars. During each month, at most 1,000 vehicles can be built. Each truck uses two tons of steel and each car uses one ton of steel. During the first month, the steel cost will be $400 per ton. During the second month the cost of steel will go up to $600 per ton. At most 2,500 tons of steel can be purchased in each month. (Steel can only be used in the month it is purchased.) At the beginning of month one, 100 trucks and 200 cars are in inventory. At the beginning of each month a holding cost of $150 per vehicle is assessed. Each car gets 30 mpg, and each truck gets 20 mpg. To meet fuel economy regulations, the vehicles produced each month must average at least 26 mpg. The company wants to minimize its total costs.

a. Formulate a linear program to help BMW determine how many cars and trucks it should produce each month and how many it should keep in inventory each month.

b. Use Solver to find the optimal solution to the linear program from part a.

*Using a sensitivity report from the Solver solution in part b, answer questions c–g.*

c. How many trucks and how many cars should be produced in each month?

d. Suppose the price of steel fell by $25 per ton. What would be the total impact on optimal solution and optimal value?

e. The company just got notified the supply of steel has decreased from 2,500 tons to 2,000 tons. What impact will this have on their production plans?

f. The company is able to add overtime at a cost of $900 per car to increase total production in either month. Should they add overtime in either month? Why or why not?

g. The constraint average mpg obtained in month one is shown to be binding. What does that tell us about this constraint?

4. Rachel Nolan surveyed her employee schedule for In a Day Drycleaners. She was having trouble keeping labor costs down while meeting demand. In a Day Drycleaners guarantees to have their customer's clothes cleaned within 24 hours. This means that their drop-off locations and cleaning facility must be staffed 7 days a week. The business has extended hours to permit their customers to drop off and pick up clothes early in the morning and later on their way home. The management has worked out a deal with employees in which they work four consecutive days of 10 hours long and then get off three consecutive days. Base pay is $10 per hour. Hours worked on Saturday earn a 25% premium and hours worked on Sunday earn a 50% premium.

| DAY | MONDAY | TUESDAY | WEDNESDAY | THURSDAY | FRIDAY | SATURDAY | SUNDAY |
|---|---|---|---|---|---|---|---|
| Employees Required | 14 | 12 | 12 | 14 | 16 | 12 | 5 |

a. Given the worker requirements listed in the table above, formulate a linear program to help them minimize their labor costs.

b. Use Solver to determine an optimal work schedule.

5. Market Research Associates (MRA) is a marketing and consumer research firm based in Hannover that handles customer surveys. One of its clients is a national press service that periodically conducts political polls on issues of widespread interest. In a survey for the press service, MRA determines that it must fulfill several requirements in order to draw statistically valid conclusions on the sensitive issue of German immigration policy. These are:

- Survey at least 2,300 German households in total
- Survey at least 900 households whose heads are under 30 years of age
- Survey at least 800 households whose heads are between 30 and 50 years of age
- Ensure that at least 20% of those surveyed live in Bavaria
- Ensure that no more than 15% of those surveyed who are over 50 years of age live in Bavaria

MRA decides that all surveys should be conducted in person. It estimates that the costs of reaching people of each age are: $9.80 (under 30 years), $7.40 (between 30–50) and $5.50 (over 50). Because of the travel distances involved, surveying anyone from Bavaria will add an extra $4 to the costs. MRA wishes to meet all survey requirements for the lowest possible cost. (Note: Bavaria is a state in Germany.)

a. Formulate this as a Linear Program.

b. Solve this program. What is the optimal solution? What is the total cost?

6. The Sixth Sin Chocolate Company has come out with a new chocolate soft drink that they named Gula Cola. Sarah Hopkinson, Director of Marketing Research, has indicated that test market sales of Gula have been brisk and she projects demand for the next 3 months in thousands of gallons to be 100, 140, and 190. They expect their production costs to go down as they gain experience and economies of scale. The costs are reflected in the table below. They currently have production capacity of 160 thousand gallons per month.

| PERIOD | PRODUCTION COST ($/1,000 GAL) | INVENTORY HOLDING COST CHARGED AT THE END OF THE MONTH ($/1,000 GAL) |
|--------|-------------------------------|----------------------------------------------------------------------|
| 1 | 260 | 20 |
| 2 | 250 | 25 |
| 3 | 240 | 28 |

The company has an initial inventory of 10 thousand gallons at the beginning of period 1, and would like to hold a minimum inventory of at least 25 thousand gallons at the end of month 3 to handle any variation in demand.

a. Formulate a linear program, clearly defining all variables used, to determine the production and inventory in each period that minimizes the total cost for The Sixth Sin over the 3 periods, while meeting its demand requirements.

b. Use Solver to find the optimal solution to the linear program from part a.

c. The company has the option to use another production line to expand capacity. There would be a one-time setup cost of $3,000 to refit the production line if they use it. As the line uses older technology, production costs will be 10% higher than the normal manufacturing cost per gallon, for each month. This production line can produce a maximum of 20 thousand gallons per month. Formulate a linear program, to minimize the total cost for The Sixth Sin over the 3 months, while meeting its demand requirements. Modify your formulation in part a to reflect this change.

7. Andrew Dwyer is planning his campaign budget for an upcoming election. He has $90,000 to spend. His political consultants have provided him with the following estimates of additional votes as a result of advertising effort:

- For every thousand bumper stickers placed on a car he will garner 10 additional votes.
- For every hundred personal mailings to registered voters he will get 40 additional votes.
- For every ad heard daily on the radio in the last month before the election, he will get 490 additional votes.

The costs for each of these advertising devices, along with the practical minimum and maximum that should be planned for each are shown in the table below.

| ADVERTISING DEVICE | COST | MINIMUM | MAXIMUM |
|---|---|---|---|
| Bumper Stickers | $50 (per thousand) | 40,000 | 100,000 |
| Personal Mailings | $112 (per hundred) | 50,000 | 80,000 |
| Daily Radio Ads | $2,000 | 3 | 12 |

The politician believes personal mailings are more effective than daily radio ads and has decided that he wants to spend money on personal mailings twice as that on daily radio ads.

a. Formulate this as a Linear Program.

b. Solve this program. What is the optimal solution? What is the number of votes?

8. A polling service is being hired to interview registered voters in a district to gain insight into their opinions about certain issues. Each person is to be interviewed in person. From experience the service knows that the cost of interviewing different types of voters vary throughout the population. The costs to interview males are $4 per Democrat, $3 per Republican, and $6 per Independent. The costs to interview females are $5, $4, and $6, respectively for Democrats, Republicans, and Independents. The polling service has been given certain criteria to which it must adhere:

- There must be at least 4,000 interviews.
- At least 700 Independent voters must be interviewed.
- No more than 2,000 Republicans can be interviewed.
- At least 1,900 Democrats must be interviewed.
- Between 1,800 and 2,200 women must be interviewed.
- The total number of Democratic and Republican men interviewed must not exceed 2,000.
- At least 30% of the Republicans interviewed must be women.

a. Formulate a linear program to find the minimum cost sampling plan. (Define decision variables and write the objective function and constraints.)

b. Use Solver on the formulation in part a to find the optimal solution and value.

*For part c, modify your formulation in part a to add these guidelines. (You just need to write down any new variables, changed or added constraints, or changed or added objective function.)*

c. Before they started their interviews they were instructed to include members of the Green Party in their interviews. Interviewing men in the Green Party will cost $7. Interviewing women in the Green Party will cost $7. The following limitations were also added.

- At least 10% of those polled must come from each of the four political parties.

- Up to 75 Green Party members can be counted toward the requirement that at least 700 Independent Party members are interviewed. Green Party members counted toward this requirement still count toward the Green Party in the 10% constraint (previous bullet point).

9. Jessica Lyell of Action Video Games has received a contract to produce and manufacture two new games for the Wii platform. The first, Downhill Adventure, allows simulating skiing down a variety of slopes against a friend or the clock using a pair of ski pole controllers. The second game, En Guarde, allows players to engage in swordplay using a sword-like controller. Action Video Games wants to plan its production schedule for the next three months for these two games.

| GAME | BEGINNING INVENTORY | POUNDS OF PLASTIC PER GAME | PRODUCTION (GAMES PER HOUR) | PRODUCTION COST PER GAME | INVENTORY COST PER GAME |
|---|---|---|---|---|---|
| Downhill Adventure | 500 | 3 | 15 | $18 | $1.2 |
| En Garde | 750 | 2 | 20 | $14 | $1 |

| SCHEDULE | PLASTIC AVAILABLE (POUNDS) | TIME AVAILABLE (HOURS) | MONTHLY DEMAND DOWNHILL ADVENTURE | MONTHLY DEMAND EN GUARDE |
|---|---|---|---|---|
| January | 20,000 | 500 | 2,200 | 4,500 |
| February | 20,000 | 500 | 3,500 | 6,000 |
| March | 20,000 | 500 | 2,500 | 5,000 |

a. Develop a **linear programming model** that would tell Jessica how many of each game to produce and inventory level each month to minimize the total cost. Clearly define all variables used. Inventory cost will be levied on any items in inventory at the end of each month, after demand for the month has been satisfied. The company wants to end the three-month period with 1,500 Downhill Adventure games and 1,000 En Guarde games in inventory.

b. Use Solver to find the optimal solution to the linear program from part a.

c. Action Video has the option of adding overtime hours in each month to expand production. Each hour of overtime costs them $60 and they can expand their production time by a maximum of 100 hours in each month. Formulate a new linear programming model for Action Video.

10. Lucas Donia is a general manager for a local supermarket, Z-mart, open from 8:00 A.M. to 10:00 P.M. every day. Lucas finds that Z-mart lacks employees on weekends. Lucas plans to hire some part-time employees to help the full-time employees on Saturday and Sunday. Lucas understands that a full-time employee can work a consecutive time of 8 hours with a payroll of $20/per hour and a part-time employee can work a consecutive time of 4 hours with a payroll of $16/per hour. For any hour, there should be at least 8 full-time employees. The total required number of employees are listed as the following table:

| Time | 8:00–9:00 | 9:00–10:00 | 10:00–11:00 | 11:00–12:00 | 12:00–13:00 |
|---|---|---|---|---|---|
| Employees Required | 25 | 30 | 30 | 32 | 28 |
| Time | 13:00–14:00 | 14:00–15:00 | 15:00–16:00 | 16:00–17:00 | 17:00–18:00 |
| Employees Required | 28 | 30 | 32 | 32 | 30 |
| Time | 18:00–19:00 | 19:00–20:00 | 20:00–21:00 | 21:00–22:00 | |
| Employees Required | 36 | 40 | 40 | 36 | |

Lucas wants you to find the best employee scheduling strategy to solve the problem. *Formulate a linear program and use Solver to find the optimal schedule.*

11. Natasha Fernandez is planning to invest her savings of $30,000 into stocks, CDs, and bonds. For each dollar invested in stocks, CDs, and bonds, she can get an 8 percents return, 5 percents return, and 6 percents return, respectively. Natasha's portfolio management policy is that (1) at least 25% of all money invested must be in CDs; (2) at most $14,000 is invested into stocks; and (3) the amount of money invested in bonds is at most twice the amount of money invested in CDs. Formulate an LP to maximize the total annual income from Natasha's investments. (Define decision variables and write the objective function and constraints.)

12. A company wants to plan production and inventory levels for its new product for the next 4 months so as to minimize the inventory holding and production costs. Demand is anticipated to be 130, 160, 270, and 150, respectively. The product is manufactured at the cost of $32 per unit. The cost of carrying one unit of inventory at the end of the month is $4. The inventory level at the beginning of the first month is 10 units and inventory required at the end is at least 20 units. Other information is given below:

| MONTH | PRODUCTION CAPACITY |
|-------|---------------------|
| 1 | 160 |
| 2 | 200 |
| 3 | 210 |
| 4 | 160 |

a. Formulate a linear program, clearly defining all variables used, to determine the production and inventory in each period that minimizes the total cost.

b. Use Solver to find the optimal solution to the linear program from part a.

c. Overtime can be added as given:

| MONTH | ADDITIONAL PRODUCTION UNITS OF CAPACITY |
|-------|------------------------------------------|
| 1 | 20 |
| 2 | 20 |
| 3 | 40 |
| 4 | 20 |

Overtime costs are $6 extra per unit.

Formulate a linear program, clearly defining all variables used, to determine the regular and overtime production and inventory in each period that minimizes the total cost.

d. Use Solver to find the optimum solution to c.

13. Carter Inc. is planning to launch an energy bar in two flavors, demand of which has been determined by a research firm for the next 3 months as shown. Each bar is made from peanuts and a variety of flavors and fillers. The peanut requirements for each bar and baking time are shown below along with associated costs and capacities.

| Demand | Month 1 | Month 2 | Month 3 |
|---|---|---|---|
| Peanut Power | 30,000 | 50,000 | 40,000 |
| Peanut Crunch | 80,000 | 100,000 | 70,000 |

| | PEANUTS REQUIRED (PER BAR) | BAKING HRS REQUIRED (PER BAR) | COST | INVENTORY HOLDING COST | INITIAL INVENTORY |
|---|---|---|---|---|---|
| PEANUT POWER | 60 grams | 0.01 | $2 | $.10 | 10,000 |
| PEANUT CRUNCH | 40 grams | 0.015 | $2.5 | $.15 | 20,000 |

| | PEANUTS AVAILABLE (KILOGRAMS) | BAKING HOURS AVAILABLE |
|---|---|---|
| Month 1 | 5,000 | 1,500 |
| Month 2 | 6,000 | 2,000 |
| Month 3 | 7,000 | 2,000 |

a. Formulate a linear program, clearly defining all variables used, to determine the production and inventory in each month that minimizes the total cost. Ending inventory of each bar at the end of Month 3 should be the same as initial inventory.

b. Set up a spreadsheet model and use Solver to find the optimal production and inventory schedule. Turn in your spreadsheet with the optimal solution.

14. A market research firm needs to conduct a survey for different geographic regions and different ages to test the reaction to a newly developed delicacy.

| | COST OF SURVEY (PER PERSON) | | | | |
|---|---|---|---|---|---|
| AGE | WEST | EAST | MIDWEST | NORTHEAST | SOUTH |
| <20 | $5 | $6 | $4 | $3 | $2 |
| 20–40 | $3 | $4 | $2 | $1 | $1 |
| >40 | $4 | $5 | $4 | $2 | $2 |

The following conditions must be met:

- The total number of people surveyed in each age category should be at least 1,000.

- The total number of people surveyed in each region should be at least 1,000.

- The total number of people surveyed in East and West regions combined should be at least the total for the other three geographical regions combined.

- Total number of people, of age group <20, surveyed in West and East regions should be at least that of the total 20–40-year-olds in those regions.

- People of age group <20 in total should be at least that of all other age groups combined.

- In South at least 500 people of <20 group should be interviewed.

Help the firm design an optimum interview schedule for different age groups and different regions using LP.

a. Formulate a linear programming model.

b. Use Solver to find the minimal cost interview plan. What would be the minimum possible cost of the survey? Turn in your spreadsheet model showing the optimal solution with your homework.

15. The operation manager of EasyCool Co., a manufacturer of air conditioners, is now scheduling the production plan for the next four months. They will incur an inventory cost for each unsold air conditioner at the end of every month. The company now has 150 air conditioners available and is required to hold at least 80 air conditioners at the end of month 4. Information for the next four months is given as follows:

| PRODUCTION MONTH | PRODUCTION COST PER AIR CONDITIONER | PRODUCTION CAPACITY | ESTIMATED DEMANDS | HOLDING COST PER AIR CONDITIONER |
|---|---|---|---|---|
| 1 | $500 | 650 | 600 | $10 |
| 2 | $550 | 650 | 700 | $12 |
| 3 | $520 | 750 | 900 | $15 |
| 4 | $500 | 800 | 550 | $12 |

a. Formulate an LP model for this problem.

b. Construct an Excel Spreadsheet and use Solver to solve this problem.

What is the optimal production and inventory plan?

| | MONTH 1 | MONTH 2 | MONTH 3 | MONTH 4 |
|---|---|---|---|---|
| PRODUCTION | | | | |
| ENDING INVENTORY | | | | |

c. What is the total cost of this plan?

d. Using the sensitivity report, if the company is able to rent extra storage room, which month should it do so? What is the most the company should pay per unit in this period?

The company is able to increase the production capacities by using overtime. Production costs per air conditioner are 8% higher than the normal production costs. The overtime capacities are given as follows:

| PRODUCTION PERIOD | OVERTIME CAPACITY |
|:---:|:---:|
| 1 | 50 |
| 2 | 80 |
| 3 | 70 |
| 4 | 100 |

e. Reformulate your LP in model to allow for overtime. (Hint: new decision variables may be needed.)

f. Use Solver to find the optimal solution for the LP model in e.

| | MONTH 1 | MONTH 2 | MONTH 3 | MONTH 4 |
|---|---|---|---|---|
| REGULAR PRODUCTION | | | | |
| OVERTIME PRODUCTION | | | | |
| ENDING INVENTORY | | | | |

g. What is the total cost of this plan?

16. The Indiana Farmers Association is planning a market research project to obtain information to address several important issues in the agricultural industry. There are nearly 15,000 farmers in Indiana but only 5,000 of them are members of the Association. The Association plans to conduct the survey in three different ways: face-to-face interview, phone interview, and mailing survey. The estimated costs of interviewing people by different methods are as follows:

| TYPE OF FARMER | FACE-TO-FACE PER FARMER | PHONE INTERVIEW PER FARMER | MAILING SURVEY PER MAIL |
|---|---|---|---|
| MEMBER | $50 | $10 | $5 |
| NON-MEMBER | $60 | $15 | $8 |

To fully draw statistically valid results, this research must satisfy the following requirements:

1. At least 900 farmers must be surveyed.

2. At most 50% of surveyed farmers are members of the Association.

3. At least 35% of surveyed farmers are surveyed face-to-face.

4. At least 25% of surveyed farmers are surveyed by phone interviews.

5. Between 40% and 60% of the mail surveys should be sent to Association members.

a. Formulate this problem as a linear program to minimize the total survey cost.

b. Solve this program via Excel Solver. What's the optimal solution?

| TYPE OF FARMER | FACE-TO-FACE PER FARMER | PHONE INTERVIEW PER FARMER | MAILING SURVEY PER MAIL |
|---|---|---|---|
| MEMBER | | | |
| NON-MEMBER | | | |

What's the total cost?

Use the sensitivity report to answer the following questions independently of each other.

c. According to the sensitivity report, at what maximum cost would the Association survey non-member farmers using a face-to-face survey?

d. What impact would increasing the survey size to 1,000 have on the total cost?

e. If the cost of surveying members by mail was actually $6 per survey, would this change the current survey plan?

   What impact would it have on the total cost?

f. If the cost of conducting a phone interview with a non-member farmer went down to $11, would this change the current survey plan?

   What impact would it have on the total cost?

17. Market Research Institute (MRI) conducts marketing and consumer research for its client. One of its clients, the Kentucky state government, wants to conduct a political poll about the minimum legal driving age. MRI estimates the costs of interviewing different types of people as in the table below.

| GENDER | AGE <30 | $30 \leq AGE \leq 55$ | AGE > 55 |
|---|---|---|---|
| MALE | $5.5 | $6 | $4.5 |
| FEMALE | $5.8 | $5.5 | $4.8 |

To draw valid statistical conclusions, this poll must fulfill the following requirements:

(1) Survey at least 500 people.

(2) Survey at least 100 people who are under age 30.

(3) Survey at least 150 people whose age is 30 to 55.

(4) Survey at least 50 but no more than 120 people who are over age 55.

(5) At most 45% of surveyed people can be male.

(6) At least 40% of surveyed people with age under 30 and over 55 must be women.

a. Formulate a linear program to find the minimum cost sampling plan. (Define Decision variables and write the objective function and constraints.)

b. Use Solver to find the optimal solution.

| GENDER | AGE <30 | $30 \leq AGE \leq 55$ | AGE > 55 |
|---|---|---|---|
| MALE | | | |
| FEMALE | | | |

What is the total cost of the survey?

18. The VeryNice Co. is about to launch a new brand of anti-bacteria detergent and wants to test the market and draw the attention of potential customers. It hired a marketing research company to provide some suggestions on planning its $100,000 marketing budget. The consultants, according to their experience, provided the following suggestions:

1. The most effective way, but also most expensive, of advertising is to provide free samples and coupons. Every free sample plus coupon given would attract roughly 0.5 customers.

2. TV ads were proved to be a useful way to increase exposure in introducing new launching products. Every TV ad would garner about 600 customers.

3. Ads in magazines are also an option. Every magazine ad would bring in around 32 customers.

The cost and practical limitations for each of these advertising methods are shown in the table below:

| ADVERTISING METHOD | COST | MINIMUM # | MAXIMUM # |
|---|---|---|---|
| FREE SAMPLE + COUPON | $5/sample | 3,000 | 12,000 |
| TV ADS | $10,000/per ad | 3 | 8 |
| MAGAZINE ADS | $300/per ad | 20 | 600 |

The manager of VeryNice prefers TV ads than the magazine ads and decides that the budget spent on TV ads should be at least twice the budget spent on magazine ads.

a. Formulate an LP model to maximize the number of new customers.

b. Use Solver to find the optimal solution and optimal value.

# of samples:          # of TV Ads:          # of Magazine Ads:
# of customers:

19. Payless Grocery Store is open from 6 A.M. to midnight each day and requires a different number of workers for every two-hour block of time for weekdays based on the requirements shown below:

| FROM | TO | NO. OF WORKERS REQ. | $ PER WORKER PER 2 HRS |
|---|---|---|---|
| 6 A.M. | 8 A.M. | 16 | 18 |
| 8 A.M. | 10 A.M. | 14 | 16 |
| 10 A.M. | 12 Noon | 8 | 16 |
| 12 Noon | 2 P.M. | 22 | 16 |
| 2 P.M. | 4 P.M. | 20 | 16 |
| 4 P.M. | 6 P.M. | 12 | 15 |
| 6 P.M. | 8 P.M. | 24 | 15 |
| 8 P.M. | 10 P.M. | 26 | 16 |
| 10 P.M. | 12 Midnight | 18 | 18 |

There are different shifts in a day every 2 hours starting from 6 A.M. Each shift is for 8 consecutive hours (4 two-hour blocks). As they have difficulty attracting workers to less desirable hours, some two-hour time blocks pay more than others. Management is trying to minimize their total labor cost.

Formulate an ILP to help the management schedule the weekday workers in shifts to minimize the cost.

20. The Persistent Marketing Corporation needs telemarketers every day of the week. Full-time employees work for any five consecutive days and part-time employees work for any three consecutive days. Salary for full-time employees is $100 a day and for that of part-time employees is $90 per day. The minimum daily workforce requirements are shown in the table.

|  | MONDAY | TUESDAY | WEDNESDAY | THURSDAY | FRIDAY | SATURDAY | SUNDAY |
|---|---|---|---|---|---|---|---|
| Telemarketers needed | 50 | 60 | 45 | 40 | 35 | 30 | 45 |

Also, there must be a minimum of 40 full-time employees.

Formulate an LP to help the company decide how many full-time and part-time employees to hire for each shift of 5 consecutive days (for full-time) and 3 consecutive days (for part-time).

# CHAPTER 5

# Non-Linear Optimization

☐CHAPTER OBJECTIVES

- Identify situations where a non-linear model is appropriate.
- Understand the concepts of convexity and concavity.
- Formulate a non-linear model.
- Create and solve non-linear spreadsheet models.
- Apply modeling techniques to the following problem types:
  - Optimal Pricing
  - Portfolio Selection
  - Location Analysis

## Introduction

It can be reasonably argued that linear models are just approximations of non-linear models. If linear programs are only approximations, why do we use them? Linear models are desirable for several reasons. First they are easy to understand and explain. Second, the Simplex method used to solve them runs very fast on the computer. Finally, the optimal solution can be reliably found with a linear model.

However, some business problems would not make sense or generate invalid results if we tried to model them in a linear fashion. Consider the following business concepts which are clearly nonlinear functions:

- decreasing marginal returns from advertising dollars,
- price elasticity,
- time value of money,
- portfolio variance,
- economies of scale, and
- revenue as a function of price.

To build more realistic models incorporating these concepts and others like them, we may need to formulate an objective function or constraints that are not in a linear format. These formulas tend to be more complex and difficult to model. Finding the optimal solution becomes more challenging also as the Simplex method will not work with nonlinear models.

In this chapter we will:

- Discuss the mathematical formulation and solving of nonlinear models.
- Differentiate between global and local optimal solutions.

- Identify when Solver can find the global optimal solution to a nonlinear program.
- Formulate mathematical and spreadsheet models for several common applications.

# Formulation of a Nonlinear Program (NLP)

The formulation of a nonlinear program can look very similar to a linear program. In both you need to define the decision variables that compose the objective function, and formulate the constraints. The main difference is the objective function or one or more of the constraints are not linear equations. The equation may require the multiplying of two variables together, raising a variable to a power, taking the natural log of a variable or some other function that would cause the graph of the equation to be non-linear. These non-linear equations pose extra challenges when we build spreadsheet models which we will discuss in several examples in this chapter.

# Global and Local Optimal Solutions

One of the challenges of solving a nonlinear program is that the feasible region may include both global and local maximums and minimums. A **local maximum** is higher than all nearby points. The highest point in the feasible region is called the **global maximum.** (See Exhibit 5.1.) To illustrate the difference between local and global optimal maximums, suppose we wanted to be at the highest point in the world. If we were at the top of Hoosier Hill, we would be at the highest point in Indiana at 1,257 feet above sea level. No matter which direction you would go it would be downhill, so Hoosier Hill is a local optimal solution. If, instead, we were at the top of Mount McKinley in Alaska, once again no matter which direction we would go it would be downhill. Mount McKinley is a local optimal solution. At 20,320 feet above sea level, it is the highest point in North America, but not the global optimal solution. The global maximum is Mount Everest in Asia at 29,029 feet. Mount Everest is also a local maximum.

### Conditions for Solver to find the Optimal Solution

For some nonlinear programs, Excel Solver can stop at a local optimal solution and never find the global optimal solution. Solver uses an algorithm much like one we might use to find the highest point. Go outside and pick any place to start. At that location, determine which direction has the steepest uphill gradient and go that direction until you start to go downhill. Check again for the steepest uphill gradient at this point and once again go that direction until you start to go downhill. Keep repeating until all directions are downhill from your location. It should be obvious that where you start has a big impact on where you end up. This gives insight into one strategy for finding the optimal solution—try several different starting points and choose the solution with the best value. Good starting points are more likely to result in a better solution so use any information you have to select starting values for your decision variables. While some researchers have developed complex algorithms for selecting a starting point, here are a couple suggestions that you can use.

- Avoid the origin as starting point (all variables at 0).
- Select values that are close in magnitude to what the optimal solution might be.

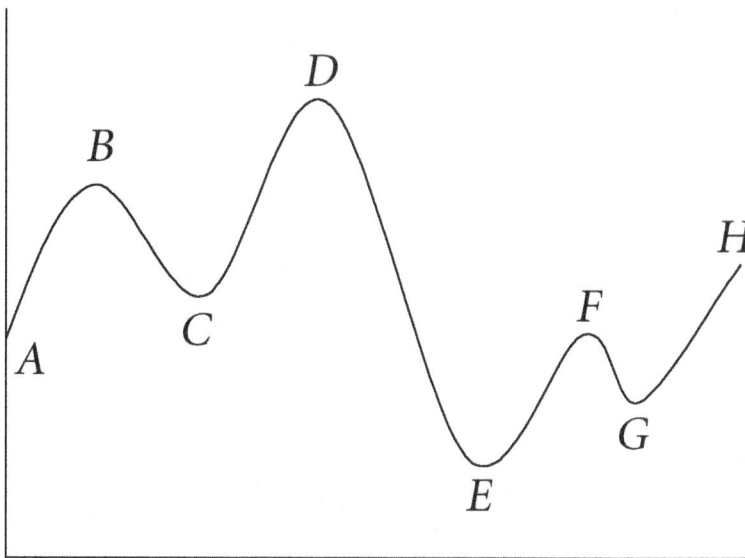

■ EXHIBIT 5.1

**Local and Global Maximums and Minimums**

Points A, C, E, and G are all local minimums. E is the global minimum. B, D, F, and H are all local maximums. D is the global maximum.

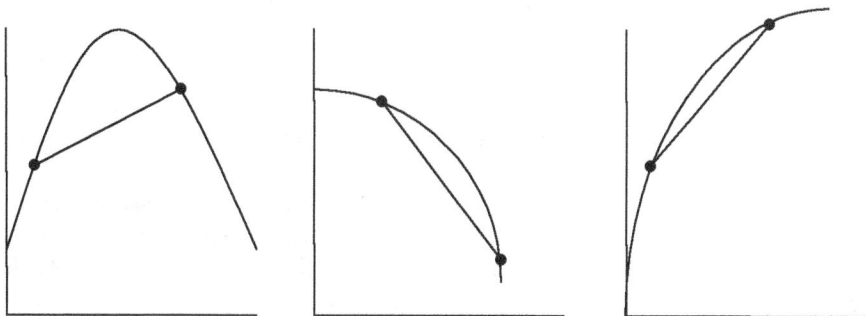

■ EXHIBIT 5.2

Concave Functions

There are two situations where Solver will always find the optimal solution to an NLP. Solver will always find the optimal solution to a maximization problem when:

1. The objective function is concave.
2. All constraints are linear.

Solver will always find the optimal solution to a minimization NLP problem when:

1. The objective function is convex.
2. All constraints are linear.

**Concave Functions**  A function is concave if its slope is always non-increasing. (See Exhibit 5.2.) Concave functions also have another characteristic that can be used to identify them. If you connect any two points on a concave function with a straight line, the line joining them will never go above the function.

**Convex Functions**  A function is convex if its slope is always non-decreasing. (See Exhibit 5.3.) Any two points on a convex function can be joined with a straight line that will never go below the curve of the function.

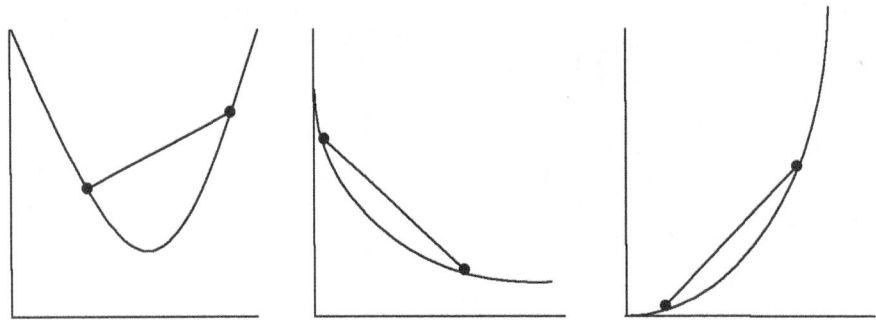

# Applications

There are many business problems that are modeled using non-linear programming. We will look at three common problems that have had valuable applications in business. First, we will see how a NLP can be used to find the price that will maximize the profit for a product. Next, we will explore how NLP can be used in determining the best location to place facilities. Finally, we will examine how non-linear programming is used to find the optimal allocations of assets in a portfolio.

## Optimal Pricing

One of the generally accepted principles of economics is that demand will go down as price of an item goes up. However, the relationship between price and demand is not linear and can be measured using the **elasticity of demand** which measures the sensitivity of demand to changes in price. The elasticity of demand is the percent change in demand that results from a 1% increase in an item's price. A very high price elasticity suggests that when the price of a good goes up, consumers will buy a much smaller amount and when the price goes down they will buy a much larger amount. A very low price elasticity implies that the amount sold will not be influenced much by the price. Fresh fruit, vegetables, restaurant meals, and airline pleasure travel have elastic demands. Cigarettes, gasoline, salt, bread, and rice are products with relatively inelastic demands.

This principle has major impact when determining the price to sell an item. The quantity sold ($Q$) is a function of a constant ($a$), the price ($P$), and the elasticity of demand ($E_d$).

$$Q = aP^{E_d}$$

If the unit cost of an item is $c$, the general form of the nonlinear program maximize profit is:

$$\text{Maximize: Profit} = (P - c)aP^{E_d}$$

subject to:

$$P \geq c \quad \text{Minimum price constraint}$$

## Example: Pricing Peas at Value Fair Foods

Value Fair Foods has an opportunity to purchase up to 300,000 pounds of fresh peas at $0.57 per pound. Research by the U.S. Department of Agriculture found the price elasticity of fresh peas to be –2.8. Value Fair Foods determined that they could estimate demand using the following equation:

$$Q = 54000P^{-2.8}$$

What price should Value Fair Foods set on fresh peas in order to maximize their profit?

Let $P$ = the sales price of fresh peas.
Maximize Profit = (Price – Unit Cost) * Quantity = $(P - 0.57) * (54000P^{-2.8})$

Subject to:

$$\begin{array}{lll} P & \geqslant 0.57 & \text{Minimum price} \\ 54000P^{-2.8} & \leqslant 80000 & \text{Maximum supply} \\ P & \geqslant 0 & \text{Non-negativity} \end{array}$$

**Spreadsheet Model**  The spreadsheet model can be seen in Exhibit 5.4. With regular linear programs, the SUMPRODUCT function was used extensively in the construction for the model. As you can see in Exhibit 5.5, the formulas in this model have to be entered one at a time and the SUMPRODUCT function could not be used. Cell B19 is the objective function cell and B11 is the changing cell. Exhibit 5.6 shows how the model was set up in Solver. The model shows that the optimal price for fresh peas is $0.89 per pound. Value Fair will sell 75,625 pounds at this price and earn a total profit of $23,948.

| | A | B | C | D | E |
|---|---|---|---|---|---|
| 1 | **Pricing Peas at Value Fair Foods** | | | | |
| 2 | | | | | |
| 3 | Unit cost | $0.57 | | | |
| 4 | Availability (lbs) | 80,000 | | | |
| 5 | | | | | |
| 6 | **Parameters of demand function** | | | | |
| 7 | | Constant | Elasticity | | |
| 8 | | 54,000 | -2.800 | | |
| 9 | | | | | |
| 10 | **Pricing model** | | | | |
| 11 | Price | $0.89 | | | |
| 12 | Demand | 75,625 | | | |
| 13 | | | | | |
| 14 | **Constraints:** | | | | |
| 15 | | LHS | Sign | RHS | |
| 16 | Price | $0.89 | >= | $0.57 | |
| 17 | Available | 75,625 | <= | 80,000 | |
| 18 | | | | | |
| 19 | Profit | $23,948 | | | |
| 20 | | | | | |

**EXHIBIT 5.4**

Spreadsheet Model for Value Fair Foods

The spreadsheet shows that the optimal price to sell peas is $.089 per pound.

EXHIBIT 5.5

Formulas for Value Fair
Foods Spreadsheet Model

| | A | B | C | D | E |
|---|---|---|---|---|---|
| 10 | **Pricing model** | | | | |
| 11 | Price | 0.886666664721 | | | |
| 12 | Demand | =B8*B11^C8 | | | |
| 13 | | | | | |
| 14 | **Constraints:** | | | | |
| 15 | | LHS | Sign | RHS | |
| 16 | Price | =B11 | >= | =B3 | |
| 17 | Available | =B12 | <= | =B4 | |
| 18 | | | | | |
| 19 | Profit | =(B11-B3)*B12 | | | |
| 20 | | | | | |

EXHIBIT 5.6

Solver Parameters for Value
Fair Foods Spreadsheet
Model

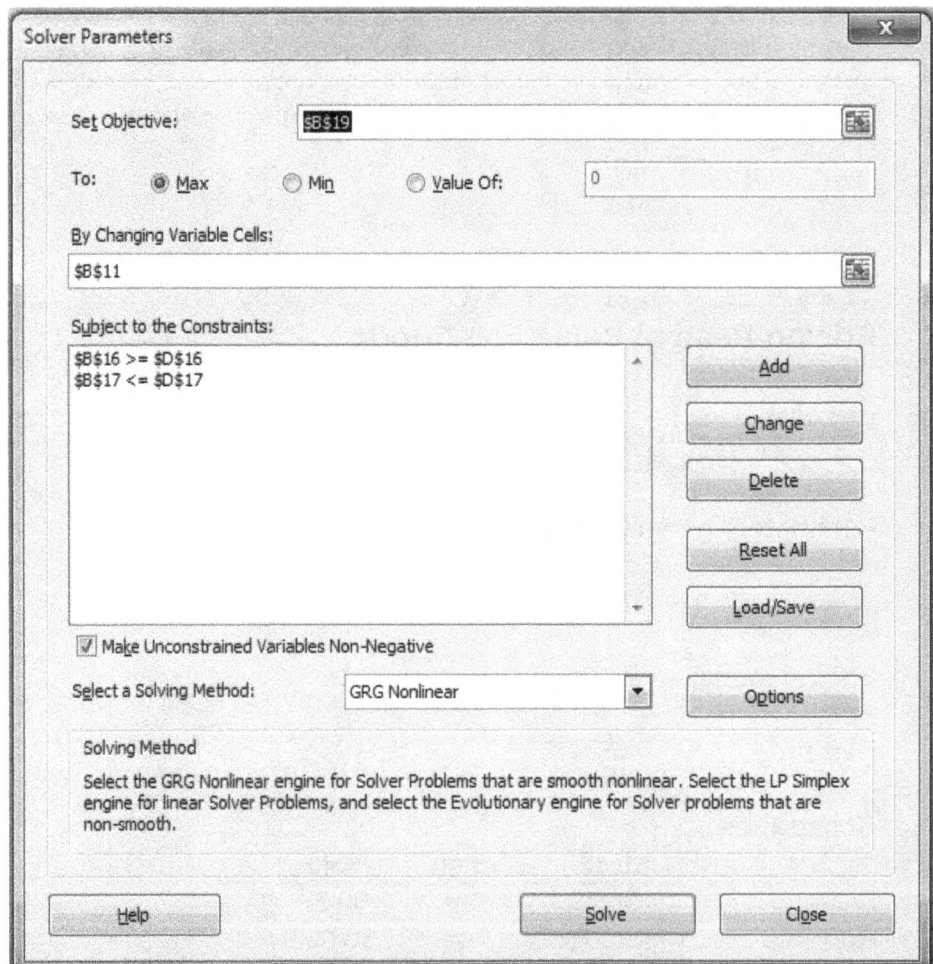

**Solver Parameters**

Se̲t Objective:    `$B$19`

To:    ⦿ M̲ax    ◯ Mi̲n    ◯ V̲alue Of:    `0`

B̲y Changing Variable Cells:

`$B$11`

Su̲bject to the Constraints:

```
$B$16 >= $D$16
$B$17 <= $D$17
```

[ A̲dd ]
[ C̲hange ]
[ D̲elete ]
[ R̲eset All ]
[ L̲oad/Save ]

☑ Ma̲ke Unconstrained Variables Non-Negative

S̲elect a Solving Method:    GRG Nonlinear ▾    [ Op̲tions ]

Solving Method

Select the GRG Nonlinear engine for Solver Problems that are smooth nonlinear. Select the LP Simplex engine for linear Solver Problems, and select the Evolutionary engine for Solver problems that are non-smooth.

[ He̲lp ]    [ S̲olve ]    [ Close ]

## Using Solver

While the formulas in a spreadsheet model are much more complicated when doing non-linear programming, setting up the problem in Solver should be familiar to you (Exhibit 5.6). The objective cell, changing cells, and the constraints are entered in Solver just as they were done in previous chapters. The main difference is that you select the **Generalized Reduced Gradient (GRG) algorithm** instead of the Simplex method to search for the optimal solution. The GRG algorithm is slower and finding an optimal solution takes longer and becomes more challenging in this situation. In fact, Solver may get stuck at a non-optimal solution and never generate the optimal solution. Note that GRG could be used to find the optimal solution for linear programs but it is slower than the Simplex method and will not produce the sensitivity reports containing all of the information that the Simplex method provides.

**Confirmation of Optimal Price**     Exhibit 5.7 shows a graph of the relationship between the price of peas and the profit. It can quickly be seen that this is a concave objective function with a single peak. Since all of the constraints are linear, Solver can find the optimal solution.

### More Complex Optimal Pricing Models

The example we just looked at focused on just a single item. More complex models may seek to optimally price several items that the retailer sells. The price of each item may have a positive or negative effect on the quantity of the other items sold. For example, if a company sells several cell phones, raising the price of one phone could increase the quantity sold of other phones.

## Location Analysis

Real estate agents tout, "Location, location, location," as being the three most important factors in the value of a piece of land. The careful location of a facility will not only help draw customers but also reduce costs and help provide quality service. One of the more common facility location problems is determining where to locate a warehouse. The distribution of goods to customers in a timely and cost effective fashion is an important issue in supply chain management. In 2010, logistics costs were 8.3% of the US GDP. The typical warehouse location problem seeks to find the location that minimizes the total distance traveled by its delivery vehicles.

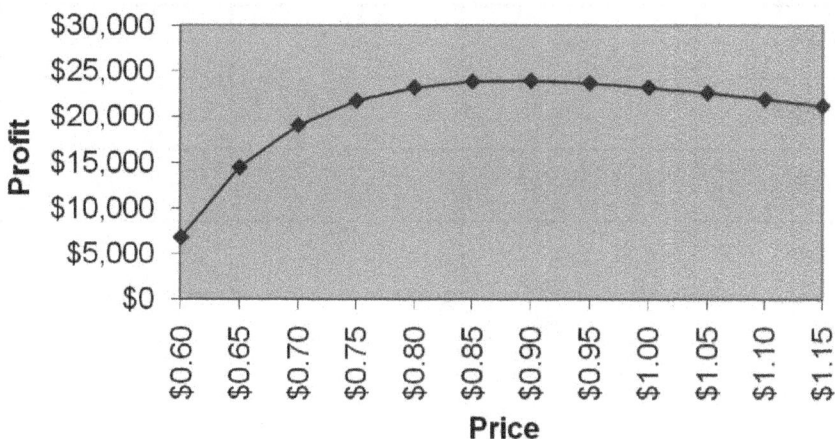

□ EXHIBIT 5.7

Price vs. Profit Graph for Fresh Peas

The challenge of locations analysis problems comes from two dimensional aspects of maps. X-Y (longitude and latitude) coordinate systems are used to define the location of facilities. Suppose facility 1 was located at (6,8) and facility 2 was located at (3,4). What is the distance between these two sites?

The X-Y coordinate system gives us two sides of a right triangle and the Pythagorean Theorem can be used to give us the distance between the facilities. It states that $a^2 + b^2 = c^2$ or the distance, $c = \sqrt{a^2 + b^2}$. The distance in the X direction is the difference in the X coordinates for each site or (6 – 3). The distance in the Y direction would be (8 – 4). Therefore the distance, $c$, between facility 1 and facility 2 is: $c = \sqrt{(6-3)^2 + (8-4)^2} = \sqrt{9 + 16} = 5$.

In the facility location problem, our decision variables will be:

Let X = the X coordinate of the warehouse.
Let Y = the Y coordinate of the warehouse.

The objective function is to minimize the total distance traveled by its delivery vehicles.

Min: 2(number of trips to facilty $i$)(distance to a facility $i$) for all facilities, $i$.

Since coordinate systems may have negative values, there are no constraints in the base model.

## Example: The Three Dollar Store

The Three Dollar Store Company can no longer supply its 5 stores from the small warehouse located next to store number 1. They would like to build a centrally located warehouse to supply all of the stores. Table 5.1 shows the map coordinates (in miles) for each store and the estimated number of deliveries that need to be made to each store each year. Exhibit 5.8 displays a map of the store locations. With the increasing costs of transporting goods, they would like to choose a location that will minimize the total miles driven by their trucks each year.

▢ **TABLE 5.1**

Three Dollar Store Locations and Annual Deliveries

| | MAP COORDINATES | | |
|---|---|---|---|
| | X | Y | ANNUAL TRIPS |
| STORE 1 | 0 | 0 | 100 |
| STORE 2 | –5 | 20 | 200 |
| STORE 3 | 25 | 6 | 100 |
| STORE 4 | 18 | 15 | 200 |
| STORE 5 | 15 | –4 | 150 |

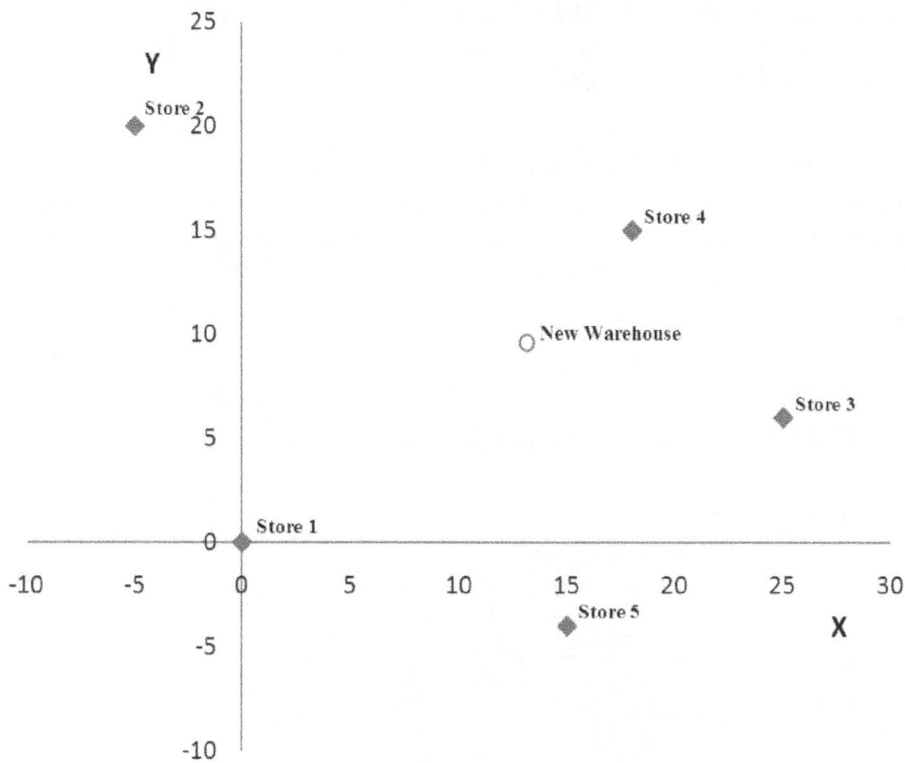

## NLP Fomulation

Let X = the X coordinate of the warehouse.
Let Y = the Y coordinate of the warehouse.

Objective Function
Minimize: the total distance traveled by its delivery vehicles.

Min: $2*\Big(100\sqrt{(0-X)^2 + (0-Y)^2} + 200\sqrt{(-5-X)^2 + (20-Y)^2} +$

$+100\sqrt{(25-X)^2 + (6-Y)^2} + 200\sqrt{(18-X)^2 + (15-Y)^2} +$

$150\sqrt{(15-X)^2 + (-4-Y)^2}\Big)$

subject to:

No constraints.

**Warehouse Location Spreadsheet Model**   The spreadsheet model with the optimal solution can be seen in Exhibit 5.9. Its formulas are in Exhibit 5.10. Exhibit 5.11 shows the Solve Parameters dialogue box. The optimal location for the warehouse on the map (Exhibit 5.8) is (13.1, 9.9).

## Practical Interpretation of Location Analysis Results

The manager gets the optimal mathematical location for the warehouse from the model. However it may not always be the best location from a practical sense. It may want to place the new facility in a residentially zoned area, at the site of an existing

▣ EXHIBIT 5.9

Spreadsheet Model Showing
Optimal Solution

|  | A | B | C | D | E | F |
|---|---|---|---|---|---|---|
| 1 | **The Three Dollar Store Warehouse Location** | | | | | |
| 2 | | | | | | |
| 3 | **Store Locations** | | | | | |
| 4 | | **Map Coordinates** | | | | |
| 5 | | **X** | **Y** | **Annual Trips** | | |
| 6 | Store 1 | 0 | 0 | 100 | | |
| 7 | Store 2 | -5 | 20 | 200 | | |
| 8 | Store 3 | 25 | 6 | 100 | | |
| 9 | Store 4 | 18 | 15 | 200 | | |
| 10 | Store 5 | 15 | -4 | 150 | | |
| 11 | | | | | | |
| 12 | Warehouse | 13.0978 | 9.94963 | | | |
| 13 | | | | | | |
| 14 | Distance | Miles | | | | |
| 15 | Store 1 | 16.45 | | | | |
| 16 | Store 2 | 20.70 | | | | |
| 17 | Store 3 | 12.54 | | | | |
| 18 | Store 4 | 7.04 | | | | |
| 19 | Store 5 | 14.08 | | | | |
| 20 | | | | | | |
| 21 | Total Annual Miles | | 21117.2 | | | |
| 22 | | | | | | |

▣ EXHIBIT 5.10

Warehouse Location
Spreadsheet Formulas

|  | A | B | C | D |
|---|---|---|---|---|
| 14 | Distance | Miles | | |
| 15 | Store 1 | =SQRT((B6-$B$12)^2+(C6-$C$12)^2) | | |
| 16 | Store 2 | =SQRT((B7-$B$12)^2+(C7-$C$12)^2) | | |
| 17 | Store 3 | =SQRT((B8-$B$12)^2+(C8-$C$12)^2) | | |
| 18 | Store 4 | =SQRT((B9-$B$12)^2+(C9-$C$12)^2) | | |
| 19 | Store 5 | =SQRT((B10-$B$12)^2+(C10-$C$12)^2) | | |
| 20 | | | | |
| 21 | **Total Annual Miles** | | =2*SUMPRODUCT(D6:D10,B15:B19) | |
| 22 | | | | |

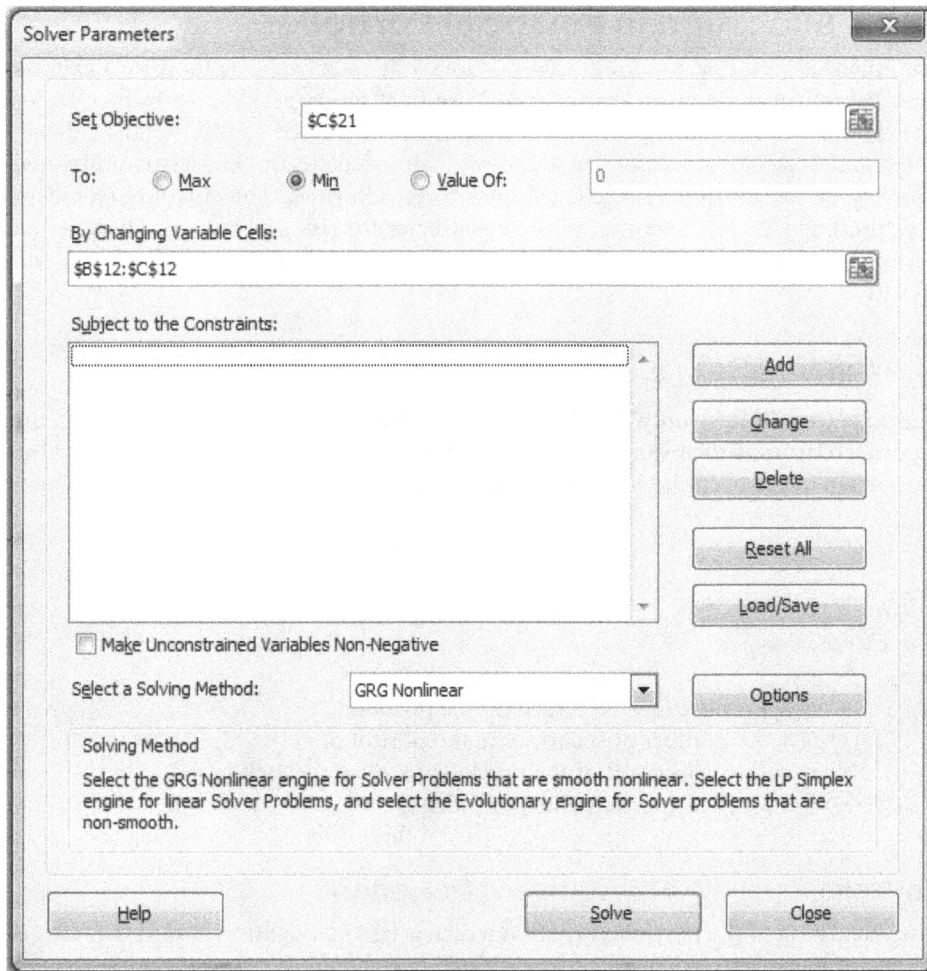

☐ EXHIBIT 5.11

Solver Dialogue Box for the
Warehouse Location Model

building, or in the middle of a park or lake. It does give the manager a good starting
point for identifying possible locations to minimize transportation costs.

## Other Objective Functions in Location Analysis Models

Location analysis models are also used in determining the best place to build fire and
emergency services stations, cell phone towers, and manufacturing plants. Depending
on the situation it may be more desirable to have a different objective function. Some
alternatives are:

- Minimize the maximum distance or time.
- Minimize the average distance or time.
- Minimize the number of facilities placed.

In the Three Dollar Store Warehouse Location Example, if the objective function had
been changed to minimize the maximum distance to a store, the formula in cell C21,
would have been '=MAX(B14:B18)' and the optimal solution would have been
(9.36,11.63) with an optimal value of 16.82 miles. If, instead, our goal was to minimize
the average distance to our stores, the formula in cells C21 would have been
=AVERAGE(B14:B18) with an optimal location of (12.99, 6.45) and an average distance of 13.92 miles.

# Asset Allocation in Financial Portfolios

The financial industry has long used portfolios of assets as a method to maximize expected returns for a given level of risk. If we treat single-period returns for various securities as random variables, we can assign them expected values, standard deviations, and correlations. Based on these, we can calculate the expected return and volatility of any portfolio constructed with those securities. The volatility (standard deviation) and expected return are used as proxies for risk and reward. There are an infinite number of possible portfolios but certain ones will optimally balance risk and reward.

## Portfolio Expected Return Calculation

The **Expected Return on a Portfolio** is computed as the weighted average of the expected returns on the securities which comprise the portfolio. The weights reflect the proportion of the portfolio invested in the securities. This can be expressed as follows:

$$E(R_p) = \sum_{i=1}^{N} w_i E(R_i)$$

where

- $E(R_p)$ = the expected return on the portfolio,
- $N$ = the number of securities in the portfolio,
- $w_i$ = the proportion of the portfolio invested in stock $i$, and
- $E(R_i)$ = the expected return on stock $i$.

## Portfolio Variance and Standard Deviation

The calculation of the portfolio expected return is fairly straightforward. If the returns on investments were independent of each other, we could calculate the variance of a portfolio by taking the weighted average of the variances of the individual investments. But the calculation of the standard deviation and variance of the portfolio is more complicated because the returns on investments are not independent. The variance/standard deviation of a portfolio reflects not only the variance/standard deviation of the securities that make up the portfolio but also how the returns on the assets which comprise the portfolio vary together. **Diversification,** an important portfolio asset allocation concept, reduces the volatility of the portfolio, by the inclusion of a variety of investments which are unlikely to move in the same direction. A decrease in the value of one asset may be compensated by the increase in value of another. Two measures of how the returns on a pair of securities vary together are the covariance and the correlation coefficient.

The variance of two random variables is a function of the variance of each variable and the covariance between the variables. This relationship directly applies in calculating the variance of a two asset portfolio as follows:

$$\sigma_P^2 = w_1^2 \sigma_1^2 + w_2^2 \sigma_2^2 + 2w_1 w_2 \rho_{12} \sigma_1 \sigma_2$$

where $w_i$ is the weight (proportion) of asset $i$ in the portfolio and $\rho_{12}$ is the correlation between asset 1 and 2. The covariance between the two assets, $\sigma_{12}$, is:

$$\sigma_{P12} = \rho_{12} \sigma_1 \sigma_2.$$

The variance of the portfolio return is more complicated to express in a simple equation when there are more than two assets. Fortunately it can be easily expressed using matrices:

$$\sigma_P^2 = (S \cdot W) \cdot R \cdot (S \cdot W)'$$

where $S$ is the standard deviation matrix, $W$ is the asset weight matrix, and $R$ is the correlation matrix. The linear algebra is shown below for the two asset case.

$$\sigma_P^2 = [w_1\sigma_1 \quad w_2\sigma_2] \begin{bmatrix} 1 & r_{12} \\ r_{12} & 1 \end{bmatrix} \begin{bmatrix} w_1\sigma_1 \\ w_2\sigma_2 \end{bmatrix} = w_1^2\sigma_1^2 + w_2^2\sigma_2^2 + 2w_1w_2\rho_{12}\sigma_1\sigma_2$$

The ease of using matrices in Excel greatly simplifies the calculation of a portfolio's variance as shown in the following example.

## Example: Rose Investments Portfolio

David Rose, president of Rose Investments would like to put together a portfolio from a selection of four stocks: IBM, Weyer, Delta, and Gerber. He would like a minimum monthly return of 1% from this portfolio and would like no more than 40% of the portfolio in any one stock. What proportions should he put in each stock to minimize his risk?

Ten years of monthly return data was collected for each stock. Table 5.2 shows the monthly returns and standard deviations of returns for the time period. Table 5.3 shows the correlations in returns between the stocks during this time period.

If we let $w_i$ be the proportion of each stock in the portfolio, we get the following objective function:

$$\text{Min Var}: \sigma_P^2 = \begin{bmatrix} 0.08597w_1 \dots 0.08774w_4 \end{bmatrix} \begin{bmatrix} 1 & \cdots & 0.2972 \\ \vdots & \ddots & \vdots \\ 0.2972 & \cdots & 1 \end{bmatrix} \cdot \begin{bmatrix} 0.08597w_1 \\ \vdots \\ 0.08774w_4 \end{bmatrix}$$

| STOCK DATA (MONTHLY) | IBM | WEYER | DELTA | GERBER |
|---|---|---|---|---|
| MEAN RETURN | 0.00962 | 0.0096 | 0.0117 | 0.0164 |
| STDEV OF RETURN ($\sigma$) | 0.08507 | 0.096 | 0.0959 | 0.08774 |

TABLE 5.2

Monthly Stock Returns and Standard Deviations

| CORRELATIONS (R) | IBM | WEYER | DELTA | GERBER |
|---|---|---|---|---|
| IBM | 1 | 0.4918 | 0.3364 | 0.2972 |
| WEYER | 0.4918 | 1 | 0.49 | 0.2776 |
| DELTA | 0.3364 | 0.49 | 1 | 0.1915 |
| GERBER | 0.2972 | 0.2776 | 0.1915 | 1 |

TABLE 5.3

Stock Correlations

Subject to:

| | | |
|---|---|---|
| $w_1 + w_2 + w_3 + w_4$ | $= 1$ | All money invested. |
| $0.00962w_1 + 0.0096w_2 +$ $0.0117w_3 + 0.0164w_4$ | $\geq 0.01$ | Minimum Expected Return |
| $w_i$ | $\leq 0.40$ for $i = 1, 2, 3, 4$ | Max amount in each stock |
| $w_i$ | $\geq 0$ for $i = 1, 2, 3, 4$ | Non-negativity |

The spreadsheet model for this problem can be seen in Exhibit 5.12. Exhibit 5.13 shows the formulas used in the spreadsheet. The **MMULT** function in Excel allows us to multiply two matrices together. In this case, the MMULT function multiplies the $1 \times 4$ containing the standard deviations multiplied by the weights by the $4 \times 4$ correlation matrix yielding a $1 \times 4$ matrix. You could use the MMULT function again for the final matrix multiplication with the TRANSPOSE function or use the SUMPRODUCT function that we are familiar with. Exhibit 5.14 shows how this spreadsheet model is entered in Solver.

■ EXHIBIT 5.12

Spreadsheet Model for Rose
Investments Showing
Optimal Solution

| | A | B | C | D | E | F |
|---|---|---|---|---|---|---|
| 1 | **Rose Investments Portfolio Optimization** | | | | | |
| 2 | | | | | | |
| 3 | **Stock Data (monthly)** | IBM | WEYER | DELTA | GERBER | |
| 4 | Mean return | 0.009617 | 0.00963 | 0.011692 | 0.0164 | |
| 5 | StDev of return (σ) | 0.08507 | 0.095962 | 0.095932 | 0.087738 | |
| 6 | | | | | | |
| 7 | **Correlations (R)** | IBM | WEYER | DELTA | GERBER | |
| 8 | IBM | 1 | 0.4918 | 0.3364 | 0.2972 | |
| 9 | WEYER | 0.4918 | 1 | 0.49 | 0.2776 | |
| 10 | DELTA | 0.3364 | 0.49 | 1 | 0.1915 | |
| 11 | GERBER | 0.2972 | 0.2776 | 0.1915 | 1 | |
| 12 | | | | | | |
| 13 | Min Monthly Return | 1% | | | | |
| 14 | | | | | | |
| 15 | | IBM | WEYER | DELTA | GERBER | |
| 16 | **Fractions to invest (w)** | 40.0% | 15.8% | 39.6% | 4.6% | |
| 17 | | | | | | |
| 18 | **Constraints** | | | | | |
| 19 | | LHS | | RHS | | |
| 20 | Fully Invested | 100% | = | 100% | | |
| 21 | Min. E(Monthly Return) | 0.01 | >= | 0.01 | | |
| 22 | Max IBM | 40.0% | <= | 40% | | |
| 23 | Max WEYER | 15.8% | <= | 40% | | |
| 24 | Max DELTA | 39.6% | <= | 40% | | |
| 25 | Max GERBER | 4.6% | <= | 40% | | |
| 26 | | | | | | |
| 27 | σ ° w | 0.03403 | 0.01512 | 0.03804 | 0.00403 | |
| 28 | | | | | | |
| 29 | **Portfolio variance** | 0.0050 | | | | |
| 30 | **Portfolio Std Dev** | 0.070456761 | | | | |
| 31 | | | | | | |

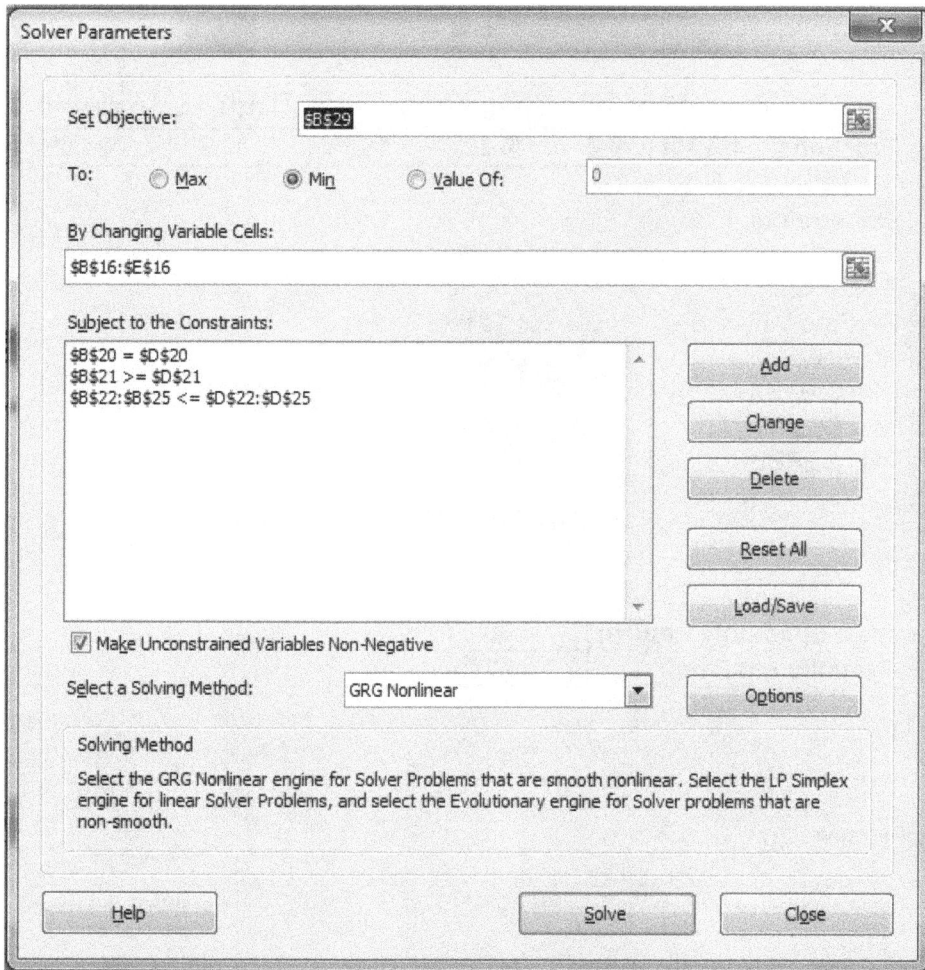

**Optimal Solution** The optimal solution shown in Exhibit 5.15 indicates that 40%
of the investment should be in IBM, 15.8% in Weyer, 39.6% in Delta, and 4.6% in
Gerber. The portfolio achieves the desired goal of 1% per month return and its standard deviation is lower than any of the stocks individually.

**Maximizing Return in a Portfolio for a Given Risk** Suppose instead that Rose
Investments wanted to maximize expected return for a given risk level. Exhibit 5.15
and Exhibit 5.16 show how the spreadsheet could be modified to find the solution to
this problem. Exhibit 5.17 shows the Solver dialogue box for this problem.

■ EXHIBIT 5.15

Portfolio Investment
Spreadsheet for Maximizing
Expected Monthly Return for
a Given Level of Risk

The target cell becomes the
monthly return (B30) and a
constraint is added restricting
the level of risk permitted.

| | A | B | C | D | E | F |
|---|---|---|---|---|---|---|
| 1 | **Rose Investments Portfolio Optimization** | | | | | |
| 2 | | | | | | |
| 3 | **Stock Data (monthly)** | IBM | WEYER | DELTA | GERBER | |
| 4 | Mean return | 0.009617 | 0.00963 | 0.011692 | 0.0164 | |
| 5 | StDev of return (σ) | 0.08507 | 0.095962 | 0.095932 | 0.087738 | |
| 6 | | | | | | |
| 7 | **Correlations (R)** | IBM | WEYER | DELTA | GERBER | |
| 8 | IBM | 1 | 0.4918 | 0.3364 | 0.2972 | |
| 9 | WEYER | 0.4918 | 1 | 0.49 | 0.2776 | |
| 10 | DELTA | 0.3364 | 0.49 | 1 | 0.1915 | |
| 11 | GERBER | 0.2972 | 0.2776 | 0.1915 | 1 | |
| 12 | | | | | | |
| 13 | Max Std Dev Desired | 0.065 | | | | |
| 14 | | | | | | |
| 15 | | IBM | WEYER | DELTA | GERBER | |
| 16 | **Fractions to invest (w)** | 36.2% | 11.7% | 30.2% | 21.9% | |
| 17 | | | | | | |
| 18 | **Constraints** | | | | | |
| 19 | | LHS | | RHS | | |
| 20 | Fully Invested | 100% | = | 100% | | |
| 21 | Portfolio Variance | 0% | <= | 0.00 | | |
| 22 | Max IBM | 36.2% | <= | 40% | | |
| 23 | Max WEYER | 11.7% | <= | 40% | | |
| 24 | Max DELTA | 30.2% | <= | 40% | | |
| 25 | Max GERBER | 21.9% | <= | 40% | | |
| 26 | | | | | | |
| 27 | σ ° W | 0.030778 | 0.011245 | 0.028946 | 0.01924 | |
| 28 | | | | | | |
| 29 | | | | | | |
| 30 | **Max. E(Monthly Return)** | 0.0081 | | | | |
| 31 | **Portfolio Std Dev** | 0.0650 | | | | |
| 32 | | | | | | |

■ EXHIBIT 5.16

Formulas for Maximum
Expected Return Spreadsheet

| | A | B | C | D | E | F |
|---|---|---|---|---|---|---|
| 18 | **Constraints** | | | | | |
| 19 | | | LHS | | RHS | |
| 20 | Fully Invested | =SUM(B16:E16) | = | 1 | | |
| 21 | Portfolio Variance | =SUMPRODUCT(MMULT(B27:E27,B8:E11),B27:E27) | <= | =B13^2 | | |
| 22 | Max IBM | =B16 | <= | 0.4 | | |
| 23 | Max WEYER | =C16 | <= | 0.4 | | |
| 24 | Max DELTA | =D16 | <= | 0.4 | | |
| 25 | Max GERBER | =E16 | <= | 0.4 | | |
| 26 | | | | | | |
| 27 | σ ° W | =B16*B5 | | =C16*C5 | =D16*D5 | =E16*E5 |
| 28 | | | | | | |
| 29 | | | | | | |
| 30 | Max. E(Monthly Return) | =SUMPRODUCT(B4:D4,B16:D16) | | | | |
| 31 | Portfolio Std Dev | =SQRT(B21) | | | | |
| 32 | | | | | | |

## Summary

Non-linear programming allows us to build more realistic models in many situations. But NLP has several disadvantages compared to linear programming. The formulas are more complicated and more difficult to incorporate into a spreadsheet model. The generalized reduced gradient algorithm used to solve NLPs is slower than the simplex method and does not always find the optimal solution.

## KEY TERMS

**Concave** A function is concave if its slope is always non-increasing. If any two points on a concave function are connected with a straight line, the line joining them will never go above the function.

**Convex** A function is convex if its slope is always non-decreasing. Any two points on a convex function can be joined with a straight line that will never go below the curve of the function.

**Diversification** A strategy designed to reduce the risk in a portfolio by combining a variety of investments, such as stocks, bonds, and real estate, which are unlikely to all move in the same direction.

**Generalized Reduced Gradient (GRG) algorithm** Solver uses the Generalized Reduced Gradient algorithm to find the solution to non-linear programs.

**Global optimal solution** The global optimal solution is the best solution to an optimization model. The global optimal solution is also a local optimal solution.

**Local optimal solution** A local optimal solution is a solution to an optimization model that is better than a nearby solution.

**Non-linear program (NLP)** An optimization model which contains one or more equations that are not in a linear format.

## EXERCISES

1. Terri's Town Pump Restaurant would like to run a Tuesday night steak special. Terri has been able to work out a deal with his suppliers so he can serve a New York strip steak, potato, salad, and dessert for a total cost of $3.65. In a recent restaurant journal she read that the demand for restaurant meals is elastic and can be defined by the equation: $Q = 23{,}652P^{-2.5}$. Surveying her kitchen capacity, she estimates that they can prepare a maximum of 100 steak meals on a Tuesday night. What price should Terri charge for a New York strip steak dinner in order to maximize her profit?

   a. Formulate an NLP to determine the optimal price for a steak dinner.

   b. Create a spreadsheet model to find the optimal price. Turn in your spreadsheet model with your homework.

   Optimal Price:                 Optimal Profit:

2. David Roberts started a small business buying tomatoes from growers in central Indiana and delivering them to a farmer's market in downtown Chicago each week. He purchases tomatoes for $0.50 per pound. The demand for fresh tomatoes is highly elastic with a coefficient of 4.6. The demand for fresh tomatoes can be defined by the equation: $Q = 3600P^{-4.6}$. He can haul a maximum of 8,000 pounds in his truck. At what price should David sell his tomatoes in order to maximize his profit?

   a. Formulate an NLP to determine the optimal price for fresh tomatoes.

   b. Create a spreadsheet model to find the optimal price. Turn in your spreadsheet model with your homework.

   Optimal Price:                 Optimal Profit:

3. Jack Watson builds custom golf clubs which he sells to pros and serious amateurs. As each club is specially built for each customer and hand machined, it cost $142 in time and material for each club and Jack is limited to building 160 clubs per year. The demand equation for custom golf clubs is: $Q = 4,061,158P^{-1.6}$. At what price should Jack sell a custom golf club in order to maximize his profit?

   a. Formulate an NLP to determine the optimal price for a custom golf club.

   b. Create a spreadsheet model to find the optimal price. Turn in your spreadsheet model with your homework.

      Optimal Price:                    Optimal Profit:

4. Sharon Stout is a sales representative for a pharmaceutical firm who has been assigned a territory in central Iowa. Throughout the year she has to make visits to doctors, pharmacists, and hospitals in her area. She is thinking about buying a home in Des Moines since she has many customers there. However, it is at the corner of her territory and she wonders if she could cut down on the total number of miles she would have to drive each year if she lived in another location. The table below shows each of the cities in her area, their location, and her expected number of trips per year there.

| CITY | X-COORDINATE | Y-COORDINATE | TRIPS PER YEAR |
|------|--------------|--------------|----------------|
| Des Moines | 0 | 0 | 62 |
| Newton | 40 | 8 | 12 |
| Iowa City | 108 | 5 | 39 |
| Cedar Rapids | 97 | 22 | 36 |
| Ames | 0 | 30 | 18 |
| Waterloo | 67 | 62 | 40 |

   a. Formulate an NLP that would determine the home location that would minimize her total annual driving.

   b. Prepare a spreadsheet model and use Solver to find the optimal location. Turn in your spreadsheet model with your homework.

      X-coordinate:          Y-coordinate:          Total annual driving:

   c. How many driving miles does she save in the new location compared to Des Moines?

5. Titus Logistics has secured a long-term contract to transport grain from five farm cooperatives to processing mills. The table shown here provides information on the location and estimated number of truck loads per year from each.

| COOPERATIVE | X-COORDINATE | Y-COORDINATE | LOADS PER YEAR |
|---|---|---|---|
| ASHCROFT | -12 | 11 | 700 |
| BURR OAK | 57 | 37 | 400 |
| MEYER | 19 | -30 | 250 |
| NEW HAVEN | -35 | -17 | 600 |
| ST. MARTINS | 3 | 33 | 350 |

With the cost of diesel fuel making up a large portion of their annual budget, they have decided to construct a depot on the rail line where they will transfer the grain from their trucks to rail cars. The rail line runs straight east and west at $Y = 5$ as shown in the map below.

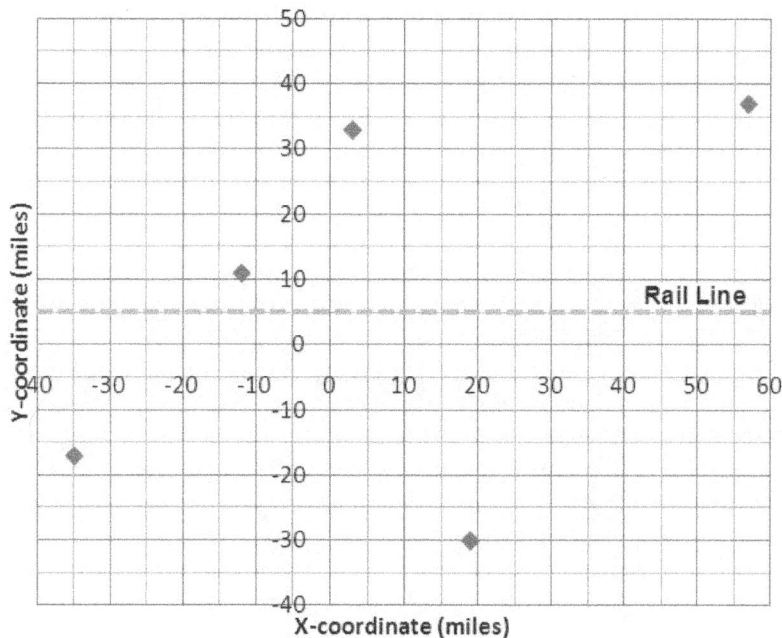

a. Formulate a linear program to determine the best location for the rail depot to help Titus Logistics minimize the total miles driven per year.

b. Create a spreadsheet model and use Solver to find the optimal location for the rail depot. Turn in your spreadsheet model with your homework.

X-coordinate:                 Y-coordinate: 5                 Total annual driving:

6. New Hampshire Bagels would like to construct five new stores that would be supplied from a central bakery. Each store will get a daily (365 days a year) delivery of a variety of bagels that will be reheated in the store before the bagels are sold. The map coordinates of each store can be found in the following table.

| CITY | X-COORDINATE | Y-COORDINATE |
|---|---|---|
| AUBURY | -6 | 10 |
| CANTERBURY | 23 | 11 |
| DORCHESTER | 9 | -5 |
| NEW CASTLE | 22 | 27 |
| YORK | 0 | 24 |

a. Formulate an NLP that would determine the main bakery location that would minimize the total annual driving.

b. Prepare a spreadsheet model and use Solver to find the optimal location. Turn in your spreadsheet model with your homework.

X-coordinate:        Y-coordinate:        Total annual driving:

7. Herbert Investments wants to prepare a portfolio comprising three stocks. They would like to earn at least a 9% return at lowest possible risk.

| | LLR | LZR | TFE |
|---|---|---|---|
| MEAN RETURN | 0.07 | 0.09 | 0.1 |
| STDEV OF RETURN ($\sigma$) | 0.05 | 0.15 | 0.18 |

| CORRELATIONS (R) | LLR | LZR | TFE |
|---|---|---|---|
| LLR | 1 | 0.7 | 0.3 |
| LZR | 0.7 | 1 | 0.5 |
| TFE | 0.3 | 0.5 | 1 |

a. Find the optimal solution using an Excel spreadsheet model and Solver. Attach your spreadsheet model with the optimal solution.

LLR: %        LZR: %        TFE: %

Portfolio standard deviation:

b. Suppose instead that they wanted to maximize the return for a portfolio with a maximum portfolio standard deviation of 0.11. Find the optimal solution using an Excel spreadsheet model and Solver. Attach your spreadsheet model with the optimal solution.

LLR: %        LZR: %        TFE: %

Portfolio return:

8. Herbert Investments wants to prepare a portfolio made up of four stocks. They would like to earn at least a 10.3% return at lowest possible risk.

|  | BBX | DOB | RST | ZTR |
|---|---|---|---|---|
| MEAN RETURN | 0.049 | 0.094 | 0.126 | 0.107 |
| STDEV OF RETURN ($\sigma$) | 0.011 | 0.150 | 0.189 | 0.163 |

| CORRELATIONS (R) | BBX | DOB | RST | ZTR |
|---|---|---|---|---|
| BBX | 1 | 0.12 | 0.09 | 0.18 |
| DOB | 0.12 | 1 | 0.29 | 0.67 |
| RST | 0.09 | 0.29 | 1 | 0.43 |
| ZTR | 0.18 | 0.67 | 0.43 | 1 |

a. Find the optimal solution using an Excel spreadsheet model and Solver. Attach your spreadsheet model with the optimal solution.

BBX: _____ %

DOB: _____ %

RST: _____ %

ZTR: _____ %

Portfolio standard deviation:

9. Herbert Investments wants to prepare a portfolio made up of five stocks. They would like to have at least 10% of the portfolio in each stock and earn at least a 9.7% return at lowest possible risk.

|  | BBX | GTR | HCT | MMC | PLB |
|---|---|---|---|---|---|
| MEAN RETURN | 0.07 | 0.09 | 0.1 | 0.095 | 0.12 |
| STDEV OF RETURN (σ) | 0.05 | 0.15 | 0.18 | 0.16 | 0.20 |

| CORRELATIONS (R) | BBX | GTR | HCT | MMC | PLB |
|---|---|---|---|---|---|
| BBX | 1 | 0.62 | 0.41 | 0.16 | 0.33 |
| GTR | 0.62 | 1 | 0.51 | 0.67 | 0.29 |
| HCT | 0.41 | 0.51 | 1 | 0.36 | 0.27 |
| MMC | 0.16 | 0.67 | 0.36 | 1 | 0.42 |
| PLB | 0.33 | 0.29 | 0.27 | 0.42 | 1 |

a. Find the optimal solution using an Excel spreadsheet model and Solver. Attach your spreadsheet model with the optimal solution.

BBX:         %

GTR:         %

HCT:         %

MMC:         %

PLB:         %

Portfolio standard deviation:

# Integer Modeling and Applications

- Derive a basic understanding of the added complexity in solving a linear program with integer constraints.
- Use integer constraints in the formulation of problems where a fractional value for a decision variable is not reasonable.
- Learn how to construct constraints with binary variables to represent logical conditions.
- Develop skills in writing integer linear programs to model the following business problems:
  - Personnel Assignment
  - Capital Budgeting
  - Fixed Costs
- Create and solve integer linear program spreadsheet models using Solver.

## Introduction

Many times, the solution to a linear program yields a fractional value for decision variables. While it may be reasonable in some problems, fractional values do not always make sense. For example, a production plan that indicates that you should build 2.75 airplanes or a capital budgeting plan that suggests that we should fund only 50% of a project would not be realistic solutions. In this chapter we will see how complex business problems can be modeled using integer and binary (0 or 1) variables.

## Integer and Binary Constraints

Formulating an integer constraint is a straightforward process. Suppose you worked for a ship builder and were devising the production plan. You would not want to have a production plan that would tell you to build half of a tugboat or a third of a yacht. In this linear program, if $X_1$ is the number of tugboats produced and $X_2$ the number of yachts produced, the integer constraint is usually combined with the non-negativity constraint and written as such:

$$X_1, X_2 \geq 0 \text{ and integer} \qquad \text{Non-negativity and integer constraint.}$$

Binary variables are a special case of integer variables that are restricted to having a value of 0 or 1. These variables take on a value of 1 if an event occurs and a 0 otherwise. Some examples would be whether or not a project is financed, a product is produced, or a person is assigned to a task. Binary variables also are frequently used in logical constraints involving IF–THEN statements which will be explored later in this chapter. Suppose you wanted to define a decision variable representing whether or not the company would build a new assembly line. The variable would be defined in the following manner:

$$Y = \begin{cases} 1 \text{ if the assembly line is built} \\ 0 \text{ otherwise} \end{cases}$$

It would be formulated in the constraints part of the ILP as:

$$Y \text{ is binary.}$$

Note that since binary variables can only take on values of 0 and 1 there is no need to include them in the non-negativity and integer constraints.

## Formulating Integer Linear Programs

Linear programs with one or more integer constraints are referred to as **integer linear programming (ILP)** or **integer programming (IP)** models. Model builders will generally try to avoid adding integer constraints whenever possible as these constraints add significantly to the time it takes for Solver to arrive at a solution or cause Solver to indicate that there is not a feasible integer solution when there really is one. Solver uses an efficient algorithm called the **simplex method** to solve linear programs without integer constraints. The simplex method allows Solver to consider only a very small fraction of the potential optimal solutions. When an integer constraint is added, this is no longer possible and Solver uses a technique called **branch and bound** to search for the optimal solution. The branch and bound algorithm involves the successive identification of subsets of possible solutions (branches) and the determining of the limits on the objective function value (bounds) for each solution. An ILP may require hundreds or thousands of branch and bound steps to find a solution. The exact mechanism of both the simplex and branch and bound methods are beyond the scope of this course but we discuss them to help make sense of the dialogue boxes in Solver.

## LP Relaxation

From a practical standpoint, when faced with an ILP, it is often reasonable to simply relax (remove) the integer constraint and find the optimal solution to the resulting LP. This is called **LP relaxation**. This objective function value of the relaxed problem will be at least as good as value of the optimal solution to the original ILP. In the case of a maximization objective function, the optimal value from the LP relaxation will be greater than or equal to the optimal value to the ILP. A minimization problem will have an optimal value to the LP relaxation that is less than or equal to the original ILP. This should not be surprising. In Chapter 3, we looked at what happens when a constraint was removed from a linear program and found that the feasible region stayed the same or got larger and the optimal value stayed the same or improved. In relaxing the integer constraint, we have removed it and the same thing happens to the set of feasible solutions and the optimal value.

LP relaxation can be used to provide a bound or limit on the optimal value of an integer linear program. The optimal value of the LP relaxation gives us an upper bound on the optimal value for a maximization problem and a lower bound for a minimization problem. The branch and bound algorithm used to solve integer linear programs can be quite time consuming. Therefore, it is tempting to take the solution to the relaxed LP and round the decision variables to integer values and use these values as a solution to the problem. A solution found in this fashion is either:

1. not a feasible solution,
2. a feasible solution but not the optimal solution, or
3. the optimal solution to the original ILP.

So while the solution to the relaxed LP may not always be directly useful, the bounds generated by this method can be used to find the solution though the branch and bound technique discussed earlier. The options dialogue box in Solver uses these bounds to help determine a stopping point in its algorithm. This will be discussed in more detail in the next section.

## Example: Sandschloss Rentals

Sam Sandschloss inherited some money from his Aunt Gertrude and has decided to move out of Indiana and live by the ocean. To support himself, he has planned to buy dune buggies and motor scooters to rent out to tourists. After he bought a storage building with 10 parking spaces to house his business, he has $40,000 left to spend on dune buggies and motor scooters. Dune buggies cost $5,300 each and motor scooters cost $1,800 each. Each dune buggy fills one parking space but he can put two motor scooters in one parking space. He has decided he wants to buy at least two dune buggies. He estimates he can make $275 profit per week on a dune buggy and $100 each week on a motor scooter. Formulate a linear program to help Sam determine how many dune buggies and motor scooters to buy in order to maximize weekly profit.

**Solution** We can formulate this problem as follows without the integer constraint:

Let $D$ be the number of dune buggies purchased.
Let $M$ be the number of motor scooters purchased.

$$\text{MAX: Weekly Profit} = 275D + 100M$$

s.t.

| | | | | | |
|---|---|---|---|---|---|
| $5{,}300D$ | | $+\ 1{,}800M$ | $\leq$ | 40,000 | Budget Constraint |
| $1D$ | | $+\ 0.5M$ | $\leq$ | 10 | Parking Spaces |
| $1D$ | | | $\geq$ | 2 | Buggy Minimum |
| | $D,\ M$ | | $\geq$ | 0 | Non-negativity |

Setting up this problem in Excel and solving with the integer constraint relaxed gives an optimal solution to buy 2.35 dune buggies and 15.29 motor scooters with a weekly profit of $2176.47. See Exhibit 6.1. Obviously, it makes no sense to buy a fraction of a dune buggy or a motor scooter. However, this solution does provide an upper bound on the profit to the integer linear program that we need to solve. Suppose Sam decides to round the decision variables to the nearest integer; he would buy 2 dune buggies and 15 motor scooters and earn a weekly profit of $2,050. While this is a feasible solution, it is not necessarily the optimal solution.

**Adding the Integer Constraint** As it does not make sense to buy a fraction of a dune buggy or motor scooter, we add the following constraint to the formulation of the problem:

$$D, M \text{ are integers}$$

Let's take a look at how to add the integer constraint in Solver. First, we set up the problem in Excel just as we have in the past. The range, B10:C10, containing the decision variables has been named "**Purchase.**" The integer constraints are included in the model in the Solver through the Add Constraint dialogue box. See Exhibit 6.2. Select

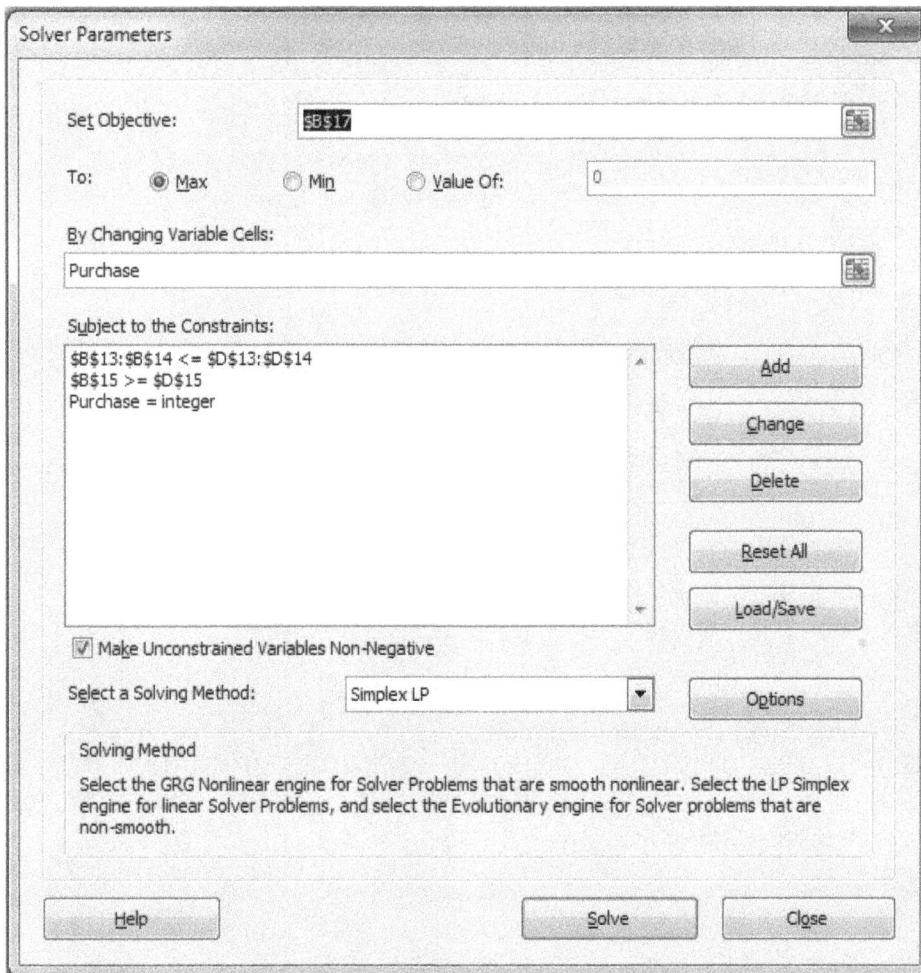

the changing cells that should be integers. Then use the pull-down menu to select "int" as shown. Note that these cells must be identified as changing cells before the integer constraint can be added or you will get an error message.

The Solver Parameters dialogue box (Exhibit 6.3) shows the model with the integer constraint added.

## Solver Options with Integer Linear Programs

The Solver Options dialogue box (Exhibit 6.4) provides a variety of options to tell the program when to quit. These are of special importance in integer linear programs because of the often-slow branch and bound algorithm used. The Max Time default will let the algorithm run for 100 seconds before stopping with its current best solution. The Iterations default would allow 100 branch and bound iterations to occur before stopping the program. In the section of the dialogue box labeled **Solving with Integer Constraints** we will unselect the box **Ignore Integer Constraints** and set the **Integer Optimality (%):** to 0. This will ensure that the optimal solution is found. Since the problems we are working with in this book are relatively small, they can be solved to optimality in a reasonable time period. The integer linear programs found in industry may contain hundreds or thousands of variables and constraints, so having stopping points allows good—although perhaps not optimal—solutions to problems in a reasonable length of time. Solver is ready to run now.

☐ **EXHIBIT 6.4**

**Solver Options Dialogue Settings for the ILP**
The tolerance has been set to 0% to ensure an optimal solution.

| Options | ? X |
| --- | --- |

**All Methods** | GRG Nonlinear | Evolutionary |

Constraint Precision:   `0.000001`

☐ Use Automatic Scaling

☐ Show Iteration Results

Solving with Integer Constraints

☐ Ignore Integer Constraints

Integer Optimality (%):   `0`

Solving Limits

Max Time (Seconds):   `100`

Iterations:   `100`

Evolutionary and Integer Constraints:

Max Subproblems:   ☐

Max Feasible Solutions:   ☐

[ OK ]     [ Cancel ]

## Solver Results

The Solver Results dialogue box (Exhibit 6.5) indicates that it was able to find an optimal solution that satisfied all of the constraints. Request the Answer Report. Since we used the Simplex LP Method, an optimal solution has been found.

## Sandschloss Rentals Solution

The optimal solution to the integer linear program (Exhibit 6.6) shows that Sam can maximize his weekly profit by buying 2 dune buggies and 16 motor scooters. His profit will be $2,150 per week. It can be seen that this solution is superior to the solution we arrived at by rounding the numbers.

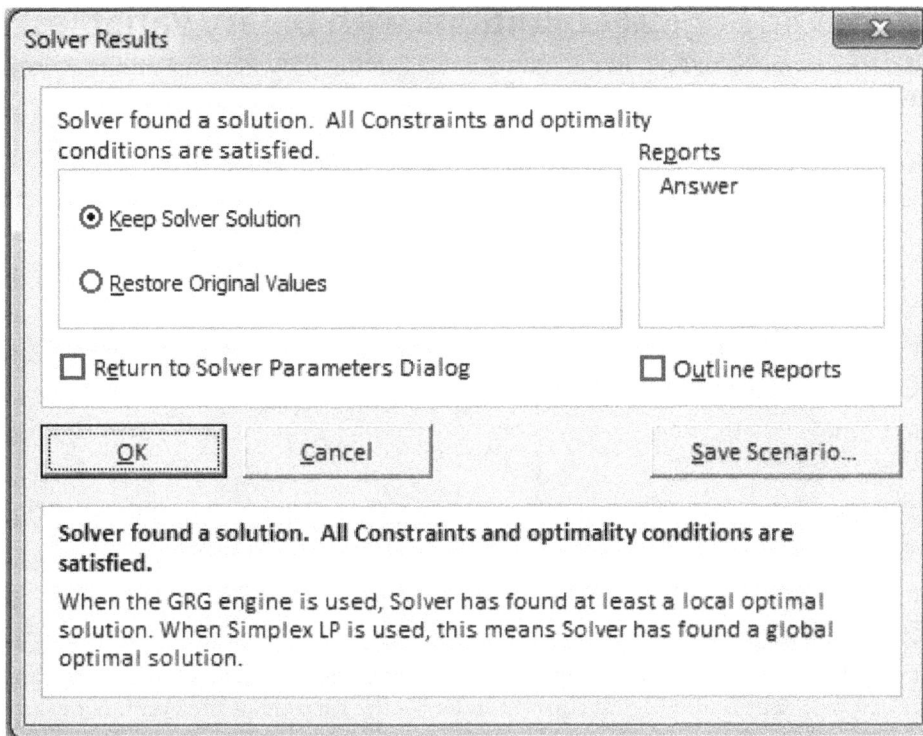

■ EXHIBIT 6.5

Solver Results Dialogue Box

■ EXHIBIT 6.6

Optimal Solution for
Sandschloss Rentals
The model indicates that the
weekly profit can be maximized
by buying 2 dune buggies and
16 motor scooters.

# Modeling Logical Conditions with Binary Variables

In the following set of logical conditions we will use the following binary decision variables.

A is a binary variable with a value of 1 if event A occurs and 0 otherwise.

B is a binary variable with a value of 1 if event B occurs and 0 otherwise.

## Simple IF-THEN Conditions

If A happens, then B happens (A is conditional on B):

$$A \leq B$$

Note that the IF part of the conditional statement is less than or equal to the THEN part.

## Complement Events

If we refer to an event not happening, it is considered the complement of an event, and we can represent it into logical constraints as 1—the variable of the event. For example, event A does not happen would be written as 1-A.

If A happens, then B does not happen:

$$A \leq 1 - B \text{ (same as } A + B \leq 1)$$

If A does not happen, then B happens:

$$1 - A \leq B \text{ (same as } A + B \geq 1)$$

## Compound IF-THEN Conditions

There will be many situations where there will be more than two events that will be in a linear program using an IF-THEN clause with either an AND or an OR. We will use the following decision variables to look at these logical situations.

A is a binary variable with a value of 1 if event A occurs and 0 otherwise.

B is a binary variable with a value of 1 if event B occurs and 0 otherwise.

C is a binary variable with a value of 1 if event C occurs and 0 otherwise.

## An OR in the IF Clause

We can split a compound logical statement into two simple IF-THEN statements if we have an "or" in the "if clause." The compound statement can be modeled with two constraints.

If A or B happens, then C happens. This is equivalent to the following two statements:

If A happens, then C happens; and if B happens, then C happens:

$$A \leqslant C, B \leqslant C$$

Alternatively it can be formulated as:

$$A + B \leqslant 2C$$

## An AND in the THEN Clause

If we have an "and" in the "then clause," the logical statement can be split into two simple IF-THEN statements which are then modeled with two constraints.

If A happens, then B and C happen. This is equivalent to the following two statements:

If A happens, then B happens; and if A happens, then C happens:

$$A \leqslant B, A \leqslant C$$

Alternatively it can be formulated as:

$$2A \leqslant B + C$$

## An AND in the IF Clause

In this situation, the conditional statement cannot be split into two simple conditional statements. Instead it can be modeled as follows:

If A and B happen, then C happens:

$$A + B \leqslant C + 1$$

## An OR in the THEN Clause

This is another situation where the conditional statement cannot be split into two conditional statements. It is modeled in the following manner:

If A happens, then B or C happens:

$$A \leqslant B + C$$

## IF AND ONLY IF

A happens if and only if B happens (A is a co-requisite for B):

$$A = B$$

A happens if and only if B does not happen:

$$A = 1 - B$$

## Other Common Constraints

A and B do not happen at the same time (A and B are mutually exclusive):

$$A + B \leq 1$$

At most one of A and B happens:

$$A + B \leq 1$$

At least one of A and B happens (A or B happens):

$$A + B \geq 1$$

# Integer Linear Programming Applications

Integer and binary variables are used in many optimization models. In the remainder of this chapter we will explore three common applications and discuss how to define the decision variables and formulate the problems in each case. As with the applications from Chapter 4, if we recognize a business situation as fitting a particular type of problem, it will share common structure in constraints, objective function, and constraints that will make it easier to formulate. We will be examining personnel assignment, capital budgeting, and fixed cost problems.

## Assignment Linear Programs

A common decision in Human Resource Management is how to allocate people to various jobs. People have a variety of skills sets and abilities that cause them to complete tasks in different times and levels of quality. An **assignment linear program** can be used to find the optimal way to make one to one assignments of people to tasks. Assignment linear programs are also used in production to assign jobs to machines or assembly lines.

**Defining the Decision Variables** Binary variables are ideal for this type of application. Either a person is assigned to a task or they are not. A double subscript notation is used with the first subscript indicating the person and the second indicating the job as follows:

Let $X_{ij}$ equal 1 if worker $i$ is assigned to task $j$, and 0, otherwise.

**The Objective Function** The objective function can be to either maximize the value of the assignment or to minimize the costs. If the $c_{ij}$ is the objective function coefficient for variable $X_{ij}$, the objective function can be written as:

$$\text{MAX: } \Sigma_{i,j} \, c_{ij} X_{ij}$$

or

$$\text{MIN: } \Sigma_{i,j} \, c_{ij} X_{ij}$$

**Constraints** One of the nice features of using the subscript notation is the ability to write constraints in a very compact fashion. If the number of people equals the number of jobs, each person will be assigned exactly one job. This can be written as:

$$\sum_j X_{ij} = 1 \text{ for each person } i$$

Likewise, the constraints for ensuring each task is assigned to exactly one person can be written in one line.

$$\sum_i X_{ij} = 1 \text{ for each job } j$$

Finally, add the binary constraint. As binary variables have the values 0 and 1, the non-negativity constraint is not required.

$$X_{ij} \text{ is Binary for } i = \text{A, B, C, D, and } j = 1, 2, 3, 4$$

## Example: Andrews Consulting Project Assignments

The Director of Consulting Services at Andrews Consulting has four projects to assign to four new employees. Each project requires a different combination of skills to complete. Based on their resumes, she has estimated the number of days it would take each of the employees to complete each project. Her estimates can be found in Table 6.1.

**TABLE 6.1**  Estimated Project Completion Times

|           | PROJECT 1 | PROJECT 2 | PROJECT 3 | PROJECT 4 |
|-----------|-----------|-----------|-----------|-----------|
| Alexander | 20        | 22        | 30        | 16        |
| Barclay   | 18        | 17        | 24        | 17        |
| Cooper    | 23        | 22        | 26        | 18        |
| Davis     | 19        | 17        | 23        | 21        |

She would like to assign the project so as to minimize the total of the workdays needed to complete the four projects.

**Decision Variables for Andrews Consulting** Let $X_{ij}$ equal 1 if employee $i$ is assigned to project $j$ where $i = $ A, B, C, D and $j = 1, 2, 3, 4$ and 0, otherwise.

(A, B, C, and D represent the first letter of each person's last name.)

**Objective Function for Andrews Consulting** As the goal is to minimize the total workdays the objective function can be written as:

$$\text{MIN: } \sum_{i,j} c_{ij} X_{ij} = 20X_{A1} + 22X_{A2} + 30X_{A3} + 16X_{A4} + 18X_{B1} + 17X_{B2} + 24X_{B3} + 17X_{B4} + 23X_{C1} + 22X_{C2} + 26X_{C3} + 18X_{C4} + 19X_{D1} + 17X_{D2} + 23X_{D3} + 21X_{D4}$$

where $c_{ij}$ equals the time for person $i$ to do project $j$.

**Personnel Constraints** Since the number of projects equals the number of people and each person is assigned exactly one project, these constraints can be written in their compact form as:

$$\sum_{j} X_{ij} = 1 \text{ for each person } i$$

This compact formulation represents the following four constraints:

$$X_{A1} + X_{A2} + X_{A3} + X_{A4} = 1 \qquad \text{Alexander}$$

$$X_{B11} + X_{B2} + X_{B3} + X_{B4} = 1 \qquad \text{Barclay}$$

$$X_{C1} + X_{C2} + X_{C3} + X_{C4} = 1 \qquad \text{Cooper}$$

$$X_{D1} + X_{D2} + X_{D3} + X_{D4} = 1 \qquad \text{Davis}$$

**Task Constraints** Likewise, the constraints for ensuring each project is assigned to exactly one person can be written in compact form as:

$$\sum_{i} X_{ij} = 1 \text{ for each job } j$$

where the compact formulation represents the following four constraints:

$$X_{A1} + X_{B1} + X_{C1} + X_{D1} = 1 \qquad \text{Project 1}$$

$$X_{A2} + X_{B2} + X_{C2} + X_{D2} = 1 \qquad \text{Project 2}$$

$$X_{A3} + X_{B3} + X_{C3} + X_{D3} = 1 \qquad \text{Project 3}$$

$$X_{A4} + X_{B4} + X_{C4} + X_{D4} = 1 \qquad \text{Project 4}$$

**Binary Constraints** Finally, add the binary constraint. As binary variables have the values 0 and 1, the non-negativity constraint is not required.

$$X_{ij} \text{ is Binary for } i = A, B, C, D, \text{ and } j = 1, 2, 3, 4$$

To summarize, the final model is:

Let $X_{ij}$ equal 1 if worker $i$ is assigned to task $j$ where $i = A, B, C, D$ and $j = 1, 2, 3, 4$ and 0, otherwise.

(A, B, C, and D represent the first letter of each person's last name.)

$$\text{MIN: } 20X_{A1} + 22X_{A2} + 30X_{A3} + 16X_{A4} + 18X_{B1} + 17X_{B2} + 24X_{B3} + 17X_{B4} + 23X_{C1} + 22X_{C2} + 26X_{C3} + 18X_{C4} + 19X_{D1} + 17X_{D2} + 23X_{D3} + 21X_{D4}$$

subject to:

$$\sum_j X_{ij} = 1 \text{ for each person } i$$

$$\sum_i X_{ij} = 1 \text{ for each job } j$$

$X_{ij}$ is Binary for $i$ = A, B, C, D, and $j$ = 1, 2, 3, 4

**Spreadsheet Model for Andrews Consulting** The Andrews Consulting spreadsheet model can be seen in Exhibit 6.7. Exhibit 6.8 shows the formulas used in this spreadsheet model. Note that a binary constraint has been added to the changing cells as shown in the Solver dialogue box. See Exhibit 6.9. As the sums of each row and each column are used as the LHS of constraints, it is more convenient to use the layout shown instead of the 1 column for each variable format.

**Optimal Solution** The optimal solution has Alexander assigned to Project 4, Barclay to Project 1, Cooper to Project 3, and Davis assigned to Project 2. The total number of work days to complete the four projects is 77.

**Problem Variations** There are three common variations to the assignment problem.

- Unacceptable assignments
- Number of tasks is not equal to the number of people to assign to them
- A maximization objective function

We will briefly discuss each variation.

**☐ EXHIBIT 6.7**

Andrews Consulting Spreadsheet Model. The optimal is shown here. A 1 in the project assignment section of the spreadsheet indicates that person was assigned to that project.

■ EXHIBIT 6.8

Andrews Consulting
Spreadsheet Model with
Formulas

| | A | B | C | D | E | F | G | H |
|---|---|---|---|---|---|---|---|---|
| 1 | **Andrews Consulting Project Assignments** | | | | | | | |
| 2 | | | | | | | | |
| 3 | **Estimated Completion Times (Days)** | | | | | | | |
| 4 | | Project 1 | Project 2 | Project 3 | Project 4 | | | |
| 5 | Alexander | 20 | 22 | 30 | 16 | | | |
| 6 | Barclay | 18 | 17 | 24 | 17 | | | |
| 7 | Cooper | 23 | 22 | 26 | 18 | | | |
| 8 | Davis | 19 | 17 | 23 | 21 | | | |
| 9 | | | | | | | | |
| 10 | | | | | | | | |
| 11 | Project Assignment | Project 1 | Project 2 | Project 3 | Project 4 | Projects per Person | | Projects Required |
| 12 | Alexander | 0 | 0 | 0 | 1 | =SUM(B12:E12) | = | 1 |
| 13 | Barclay | 1 | 0 | 0 | 0 | =SUM(B13:E13) | = | 1 |
| 14 | Cooper | 0 | 0 | 1 | 0 | =SUM(B14:E14) | = | 1 |
| 15 | Davis | 0 | 1 | 0 | 0 | =SUM(B15:E15) | = | 1 |
| 16 | People per Project | =SUM(B12:B15) | =SUM(C12:C15) | =SUM(D12:D15) | =SUM(E12:E15) | | | |
| 17 | | = | = | = | = | | | |
| 18 | People Required | 1 | 1 | 1 | 1 | | | |
| 19 | | | | | | | | |
| 20 | Total Days | =SUMPRODUCT(B5:E8,B12:E15) | | | | | | |
| 21 | | | | | | | | |
| 22 | | | | | | | | |
| 23 | **Range Names Used** | | | | | | | |
| 24 | Assignments | =Assignments!$B$12:$E$15 | | | | | | |
| 25 | People_per_Project | =Assignments!$B$16:$E$16 | | | | | | |
| 26 | People_Required | =Assignments!$B$18:$E$18 | | | | | | |
| 27 | Projects_per_Person | =Assignments!$F$12:$F$15 | | | | | | |
| 28 | Projects_Required | =Assignments!$H$12:$H$15 | | | | | | |
| 29 | Times | =Assignments!$B$5:$E$8 | | | | | | |
| 30 | Total_Days | =Assignments!$B$20 | | | | | | |
| 31 | | | | | | | | |

H ◄ ► H   Answer Report 1 / **Assignments** / Sheet2 / Sheet3 / ʞ⌐

■ EXHIBIT 6.9

Solver Dialogue Box for
Andrews Consulting Model

**Solver Parameters**

Se_t Objective:     Total_Days

To:    ○ Max    ● Mi_n    ○ _Value Of:    0

_By Changing Variable Cells:

Assignments

Su_bject to the Constraints:

People_per_Project = People_Required
Assignments = binary
Projects_per_Person = Projects_Required

[ Add ]
[ Change ]
[ Delete ]
[ Reset All ]
[ Load/Save ]

☑ Ma_ke Unconstrained Variables Non-Negative

S_elect a Solving Method:    Simplex LP ▼    [ Options ]

Solving Method

Select the GRG Nonlinear engine for Solver Problems that are smooth nonlinear. Select the LP Simplex engine for linear Solver Problems, and select the Evolutionary engine for Solver problems that are non-smooth.

[ Help ]    [ Solve ]    [ Close ]

**Unacceptable Assignments**  There will be situations where an assignment may not be acceptable. Perhaps a machine is not capable of making a part, an employee does not have the security clearance for a government contract, or a task is beyond the skill level of an employee. Considering the Andrew's Consulting example, suppose Barclay has a conflict of interest with the client for project 3 and cannot be assigned to that project. There are three ways of modifying the model to handle this situation. The first is to leave the variable $X_{B3}$ out of the objective function and all of the constraints in the model. This solution, however, reduces our ability to use the compact notation allowed by the use of subscripts. A more simple way of dealing with unacceptable assignments is to set the variable equal to 0 in the constraints. The model would look like this:

Let $X_{ij}$ equal 1 if worker $i$ is assigned to task $j$ where $i$ = A, B, C, D, and $j$ = 1, 2, 3, 4 and 0, otherwise.

(A, B, C, and D represent the first letter of each person's last name.)

MIN: $20X_{A1} + 22X_{A2} + 30X_{A3} + 16X_{A4} + 18X_{B1} + 17X_{B2} + 24X_{B3} + 17X_{B4} + 23X_{C1} + 22X_{C2} + 26X_{C3} + 18X_{C4} + 19X_{D1} + 17X_{D2} + 23X_{D3} + 21X_{D4}$

subject to:

$\sum_{j} X_{ij} = 1$ for each person $i$

$\sum_{i} X_{ij} = 1$ for each job $j$

$X_{B3} = 0$                 Unacceptable Assignment Constraint

$X_{ij}$ is Binary for $i$ = A, B, C, D, and $j$ = 1, 2, 3, 4

The third method to prohibit an assignment is to give that assignment an extremely high cost. In this example the value of $C_{B3}$ could be changed from 24 to 1000 in the objective function.

**Unequal Number of Tasks to People**  In many situations the groups are not the same size. Either the number of tasks exceeds the personnel or machines available, or there are more resources than there are tasks to assign. Models can be adapted to handle this variation replacing the equals sign with a less than or equal to sign for the larger group constraints. Using the Andrew's Consulting example, suppose project 4 was canceled. Each of the three remaining projects has to be assigned to one of the employees. Since the number of employees exceeds the number of jobs, one of them will not be assigned a project. For whichever group is larger, the constraint will change from equals 1 to less than or equal to 1. For this example, the new model would be:

Let $X_{ij}$ equal 1 if worker $i$ is assigned to task $j$ where $i$ = A, B, C, D and $j$ = 1, 2, 3 and 0, otherwise.

(A, B, C, and D represent the first letter of each person's last name.)

MIN: $20X_{A1} + 22X_{A2} + 30X_{A3} + 18X_{B1} + 17X_{B2} + 24X_{B3} + 23X_{C1} + 22X_{C2} + 26X_{C3} + 19X_{D1} + 17X_{D2} + 23X_{D3}$

subject to:

$$\sum_j X_{ij} \le 1 \text{ for each person } i$$

$$\sum_i X_{ij} = 1 \text{ for each job } j$$

$X_{ij}$ is Binary for $i$ = A, B, C, D, and $j$ = 1, 2, 3, 4

Exhibit 6.10 shows the spreadsheet model with the optimal solution to this variation. In it, Alexander is assigned to Project 1, Barclay to Project 2, and Davis is assigned to Project 3. Cooper is not assigned to any project. The total number of work days to complete the three projects is 60.

**Assignment Problem with a Maximization Objective Function** This is the easiest variation to handle. The only change to the formulation is the changing of the objective function from maximize to minimize. The decision variables and all of the constraints are unchanged.

# Capital Budgeting

☐ EXHIBIT 6.10

Assignment Problem with
Unequal Group Sizes

| | A | B | C | D | E | F | G | H |
|---|---|---|---|---|---|---|---|---|
| 1 | **Andrews Consulting Project Assignments** | | | | | | | |
| 2 | | | | | | | | |
| 3 | **Estimated Completion Times (Days)** | | | | | | | |
| 4 | | Project 1 | Project 2 | Project 3 | | | | |
| 5 | Alexander | 20 | 22 | 30 | | | | |
| 6 | Barclay | 18 | 17 | 24 | | | | |
| 7 | Cooper | 23 | 22 | 26 | | | | |
| 8 | Davis | 19 | 17 | 23 | | | | |
| 9 | | | | | | | | |
| 10 | | | | | | | | |
| 11 | Project Assignment | Project 1 | Project 2 | Project 3 | Projects per Person | | Maximum Projects | |
| 12 | Alexander | 1 | 0 | 0 | 1 | <= | 1 | |
| 13 | Barclay | 0 | 1 | 0 | 1 | <= | 1 | |
| 14 | Cooper | 0 | 0 | 0 | 0 | <= | 1 | |
| 15 | Davis | 0 | 0 | 1 | 1 | <= | 1 | |
| 16 | People per Project | 1 | 1 | 1 | | | | |
| 17 | | = | = | = | | | | |
| 18 | People Required | 1 | 1 | 1 | | | | |
| 19 | | | | | | | | |
| 20 | Total Days | 60 | | | | | | |
| 21 | | | | | | | | |

Answer Report 1 / Assignments / Sheet2 / Sh

A **capital budgeting model** can be used when there is the option of several very large investments that either the company fully funds a particular investment or not at all with the intent of maximizing the net present value (NPV) or minimizing the net present cost. Binary variables are perfect for a problem like this. Typically these variables will be defined as such:

Let $X_i$ equal 1 if project $i$ is funded and 0, otherwise.

We will look at an example to see how it is formulated as an ILP and solved as a spreadsheet model.

## Example: Capital Budgeting at Meyer Industries

Meyer Industries recycles used plastic bottles and containers to produce synthetic planks for the construction of playgrounds and decks. It has a contract with six Indiana counties to handle all of their plastic recycling. With government regulations and an increase in people's desires to reduce waste, it needs to expand recycling capacity to at least 240 tons per year. The layout in its current facility is outdated and it must renovate it, build a completely new facility at the same site, or expand the current facility with an improved layout. It also may build a new plant in Monticello or Delphi, but not both. It also has an option of buying a competitor's plant in order to expand capacity. The capacity and net present cost of each option is found in Table 6.2. Meyer Industries would like to expand its capacity at the lowest cost.

TABLE 6.2   Project Capacities and Costs

| COST | | PROJECT (TONS PER YEAR) | CAPACITY (MILLIONS OF $) |
|---|---|---|---|
| 1 | Renovate current facility | 120 | 1.2 |
| 2 | Demolish current facility and rebuild on site | 160 | 3.6 |
| 3 | Expand current facility | 140 | 2.2 |
| 4 | Build new plant in Monticello | 100 | 2.0 |
| 5 | Build new plant in Delphi | 80 | 1.9 |
| 6 | Buy Competitor's Plant | 50 | 0.7 |

**Formulation**

Let $X_i$ equal 1 if project $i$ is chosen and 0, otherwise for $i = 1, 2, 3, \ldots, 6$

MIN: $1.2X_1 + 3.6X_2 + 2.2X_3 + 2.0X_4 + 1.9X_5 + 0.7X_6$

s.t.

$$120X_1 + 160X_2 + 140X_3 + 100X_4 + 80X_5 + 50X_6 \geq 240 \quad \text{Capacity Requirement}$$

$$X_1 + X_2 + X_3 = 1 \quad \text{Current Site Options}$$

$$X_4 + X_5 \leq 1 \quad \text{Monticello or Delphi}$$

$X_i$ is Binary for $i = 1, 2, 3, \ldots, 6$        Binary

## Spreadsheet Model

Figure 6.11 shows the spreadsheet model for Meyer Industries capital planning problem with the optimal solution. It indicates that the minimum cost solution is to renovate the current facility, build a new plant in Monticello, and purchase their competitor. This will cost $3.8 million and generate capacity of 250 tons per year.

## Fixed Cost Problems

☐ EXHIBIT 6.11

Capital Budgeting at Meyer Industries

The optimal solution shows that Meyer Industries should renmovate their current facility, build in Monticello, and purchase their competitor.

| | A | B | C | D | E | F | G | H | I |
|---|---|---|---|---|---|---|---|---|---|
| 1 | **Meyer Industries Capacity Planning** | | | | | | | | |
| 2 | | | | | | | | | |
| 3 | **Project** | **1** | **2** | **3** | **4** | **5** | **6** | | |
| 4 | | Renovate current | Rebuild on site | Expand current | Build in Monticello | Build in Delphi | Purchase Competitor | | |
| 5 | **Capacity (tons/year)** | 120 | 160 | 140 | 100 | 80 | 50 | 240 | |
| 6 | **Current Site Options** | 1 | 1 | 1 | | | | 1 | |
| 7 | **Monticello or Delphi** | | | | 1 | 1 | | 1 | |
| 8 | **Net Present Cost (millions of $)** | 1.2 | 3.6 | 2.2 | 2 | 1.9 | 0.7 | | |
| 9 | | | | | | | | | |
| 10 | **Project Selected (1 = Yes, 0 = No)** | 1 | 0 | 0 | 0 | 1 | 1 | | |
| 11 | | | | | | | | | |
| 12 | **Constraints** | LHS | sign | RHS | | | | | |
| 13 | Capacity (tons/year) | 250 | ≥ | 240 | | | | | |
| 14 | Current Site Options | 1 | = | 1 | | | | | |
| 15 | Monticello or Delphi | 1 | ≤ | 1 | | | | | |
| 16 | | | | | | | | | |
| 17 | Total Net Present Cost | 3.8 | | | | | | | |
| 18 | (Millions of Dollars) | | | | | | | | |
| 19 | | | | | | | | | |

Many business situations involve both fixed and variable costs. A company incurs set-up or change-over costs that are fixed and independent of quantity of that item that it produces. A credit card can have an annual fee that is independent of the amount it is used. There is often a cost for placing an order that is incurred that is separate from the quantity ordered. Binary variables are a valuable tool in modeling problems where fixed costs occur. **Fixed Cost Linear Programs** pose a special problem in modeling. There needs to be a link between the action that incurs a fixed cost and it causing the binary fixed cost variable assuming the value of 1.

The fixed cost can be modeled by defining a binary variable that has a value of $i$ if the conditions for the fixed cost occur and 0 otherwise. Let's say that we want to model a fixed cost setting up an assembly line that is independent of the number of a particular item we manufacture. Our decision variables would be:

Let $X_i$ be the number of item $i$ that is produced.

Let $Y_i$ equal 1 if item $i$ is produced, and 0 otherwise.

The value of the fixed cost variable for an item needs to be set to 1 if the item is produced. At first glance it would seem easy to do in a spreadsheet model. Simply use the IF function giving $Y_1$ a value of 1 if $X_1$ is greater than 0. However, Solver does not handle IF functions reliably. As a consequence, linear constraints need to be formulated to connect the incurrence of the fixed cost when an item is produced. These are called **fixed cost constraints** or **linking constraints.** The fixed cost constraint for a product $i$ takes the form of:

$$X_i \leq M_i Y_i$$

where $M_i$ has a value with a minimum value of the maximum units of $i$ that can be produced. If the $M_i$ is set any smaller than this value, it would limit the number of this item that could be produced more than the other constraint would permit. These linking constraints are vital for these models to function correctly. Modeling these fixed cost constraints will be discussed and demonstrated in the following example.

## Example: Bullfrog Investments

Bullfrog Investment Group is considering the purchase of the patent rights of several new products that they think will do well in the coming year. If they purchase the rights to an item, they can produce as much as they want for the United States market. They have a production facility in Battle Ground with excess capacity they would like to use. They have up to 1,000 hours of machine time available to fabricate the new products. Because of the effort needed for each new item, they have decided to introduce no more than two new products. Bullfrog would like to maximize their net profit. Table 6.3 provides information on the cost, demand, and production time for each product.

TABLE 6.3   Item Production and Cost Information

| UNIT | | ITEM RIGHTS | PATENT TIME (MINUTES) | MACHINE MAXIMUM DEMAND | ESTIMATED PROFIT |
|---|---|---|---|---|---|
| 1 | Electric Spaghetti Fork | $5,000 | 3 | 4,000 | $1.50 |
| 2 | Subsonic Cat Whistle | $7,500 | 3 | 5,000 | $0.50 |
| 3 | Breathalyzer Keychain | $25,000 | 4 | 10,000 | $4.00 |
| 4 | Flying Alarm Clock | $15,000 | 5 | 8,000 | $5.00 |
| | | | | | |

**Decision Variables for Bullfrog Investments** In this case there is a fixed cost of the patent rights incurred if Bullfrog produces at least one of an item. The fixed cost of an item can be modeled by defining a binary variable that has a value of $i$ if the patent rights are purchased and 0 otherwise. So in this example, our decision variables are:

Let $X_i$ be the number of item $i$ that is produced. $i = 1, 2, 3, 4$

Let $Y_i$ equal 1 if the patent rights to item $i$ are purchased, 0 otherwise

**Objective Function** The goal is to maximize net profit which the profit from the units sold minus the cost of acquiring the patent rights. The objective function in this problem is:

$$\text{MAX: } 1.5X_1 + 0.5X_2 + 5X_3 + 5X_4 - 5000Y_1 - 7500Y_2 - 25000Y_3 - 15000Y_4$$

**Capacity and Demand Constraints** The capacity constraint in this problem serves as a reminder that we need to keep track of the units information is provided in. Bullfrog has 1000 machine hours to use to produce new products. The production time per item is given in minutes. Consistent units must be used throughout a constraint. The capacity constraint can be in either minutes or hours as follows:

$$3X_1 + 3X_2 + 4X_3 + 5X_4 \leq 60000 \quad \text{Machine Minutes Available}$$
$$\text{or} \quad 3/60X_1 + 3/60X_2 + 4/60X_3 + 5/60X_4 \leq 1000 \quad \text{Machine Hours Available}$$

The demand constraints can be formulated as follows:

$$X_1 \leq 4000 \quad \text{Maximum Demand for Item 1}$$
$$X_2 \leq 5000 \quad \text{Maximum Demand for Item 2}$$
$$X_3 \leq 10000 \quad \text{Maximum Demand for Item 3}$$
$$X_4 \leq 8000 \quad \text{Maximum Demand for Item 4}$$

**Fixed Cost Constraints** We need to link the events of manufacturing a product with the event of paying for the patent rights. Recalling our discussion of these linking constraints, we first need to determine $M_i$, the maximum number of product $i$ that we could produce. For product 1, if all of the machine time was used to make this item, a maximum of 60,000/3 or 20,000 could be made. Our demand constraint indicates a maximum of 4,000 units. If the coefficient with $Y_1$ in this constraint was any smaller than 4,000, it would limit the number of this item that could be produced more than the capacity or demand constraint would permit. Hence, our linking constraint for the first product is:

$$X_1 \leq 4000Y_1$$

Let's see how this constraint works. The objective function contains the term, $-5000Y_1$. As the objective function is to maximize and $Y_1$ is a binary variable, the objective function will make $Y_1$ equal 0 unless there is a constraint that forces it to take on the value of 1. If we do not produce any of product 1, $X_1 = 0$ and $Y_1$ will take the value of 0. If even one of product 1 is manufactured, then the LHS of the constraint will be greater than 0 which will force $Y_1$ to take on the value of 1.

For products 2, 3, and 4:

$$M_2 = \text{Minimum}(60000/3, 5000) = 5000$$
$$M_3 = \text{Minimum}(60000/4, 10000) = 10000$$
$$M_4 = \text{Minimum}(60000/5, 8000) = 8000$$

Giving the linking constraints of:

$$X_2 \leq 5000Y_2$$
$$X_3 \leq 10000Y_3$$
$$X_4 \leq 8000Y_4$$

**Other Constraints** Bullfrog wants to bring out no more than two new products so the following constraint needs to be added:

$$Y_1 + Y_2 + Y_3 + Y_4 \leq 2 \qquad \text{No more than two new products.}$$

Finally, we need to include the non-negativity, integer, and binary constraints.

$$X_1, X_2, X_3, X_4 \geq 0 \text{ and integer} \quad \text{Non-negativity and integer constraints}$$
$$Y_1, Y_2, Y_3, Y_4 \text{ are binary.} \qquad \text{Binary constraints.}$$

**Complete Formulation** The final complete formulation for the Bullfrog Investment Group example is:

Let $X_i$ be the number of item $i$ produced next year.
Let $Y_i = 1$ if the patent rights to item $i$ are purchased, 0 otherwise

MAX: $1.5X_1 + 0.5X_2 + 5X_3 + 5X_4 - 5000Y_1 - 7500Y_2 - 25000Y_3 - 15000Y_4$

s.t.

| | | | |
|---|---|---|---|
| $3X_1 + 3X_2 + 4X_3 + 5X_4$ | $\leq$ | 60000 | Machine Minutes Available |
| $X_1$ | $\leq$ | 4000 | Maximum Demand Constraints |
| $X_2$ | $\leq$ | 5000 | |
| $X_3$ | $\leq$ | 10000 | |
| $X_4$ | $\leq$ | 8000 | |
| $Y_1 + Y_2 + Y_3 + Y_4$ | $\leq$ | 2 | No more than two new products |
| $X_1$ | $\leq$ | $4000Y_1$ | Linking Constraints |

$$X_2 \leq 5000\,Y_2$$
$$X_3 \leq 10000\,Y_3$$
$$X_4 \leq 8000\,Y_4$$
$$X_1, X_2, X_3, X_4 \geq 0 \text{ and integer} \qquad \text{Non-negativity and Integer}$$
$$Y_1, Y_2, Y_3, Y_4 \text{ are binary.} \qquad \text{Binary constraints.}$$

It can be noted with this example that the fixed cost constraints provide the same limit as the maximum demand constraints. As such, the maximum demand constraints could have been left out of the model. This will not always be the case with fixed cost problems though.

Exhibit 6.12 shows the spreadsheet model for this example with the optimal solution. The model indicates that the optimal solution is for Bullfrog to acquire the rights to the electric spaghetti fork and the flying alarm clock for a total of $20,000. The optimal production plan is to produce 4,000 of the electric spaghetti forks and 8,000 flying alarm clocks generating a net profit of $26,000.

# SUMMARY

**EXHIBIT 6.12**

Bullfrog Investment
Spreadsheet Model with
Optimal Solution

| | A | B | C | D | E | F | G | H | I | J | K |
|---|---|---|---|---|---|---|---|---|---|---|---|
| 1 | **Bullfrog Investment Group** | | | | | | | | | | |
| 2 | | | | | | | | | | | |
| 3 | | | **Patent Rights** | | | | **Production Plan** | | | | |
| 4 | | Fork | Whistle | Keychain | Clock | Fork | Whistle | Keychain | Clock | | |
| 5 | Machine Time (minutes) | | | | | 3 | 3 | 4 | 5 | 60000 | |
| 6 | Max Demand Fork | | | | | 1 | | | | 4000 | |
| 7 | Max Demand Whistle | | | | | | 1 | | | 5000 | |
| 8 | Max Demand Keychain | | | | | | | 1 | | 10000 | |
| 9 | Max Demand Clock | | | | | | | | 1 | 8000 | |
| 10 | Max 2 New Products | 1 | 1 | 1 | 1 | | | | | 2 | |
| 11 | Fixed Cost Fork | -4000 | | | | 1 | | | | 0 | |
| 12 | Fixed Cost Whistle | | -5000 | | | | 1 | | | 0 | |
| 13 | Fixed Cost Keychain | | | -10000 | | | | 1 | | 0 | |
| 14 | Fixed Cost Clock | | | | -8000 | | | | 1 | 0 | |
| 15 | Profit Contribution | ($5,000) | ($7,500) | ($25,000) | ($15,000) | $1.50 | $0.50 | $4.00 | $5.00 | | |
| 16 | | | | | | | | | | | |
| 17 | **Production and Patent Purchase Plan** | | | | | | | | | | |
| 18 | | | Patent Rights (1 = Yes, 0 = No) | | | | Production Plan (Units) | | | | |
| 19 | | Fork | Whistle | Keychain | Clock | Fork | Whistle | Keychain | Clock | | |
| 20 | | 1 | 0 | 0 | 1 | 4000 | 0 | 0 | 8000 | | |
| 21 | | | | | | | | | | | |
| 22 | Constraints | LHS | sign | RHS | | | | | | | |
| 23 | Machine Time (minutes) | 52000 | ≤ | 60000 | | | | | | | |
| 24 | Max Demand Fork | 4000 | ≤ | 4000 | | | | | | | |
| 25 | Max Demand Whistle | 0 | ≤ | 5000 | | | | | | | |
| 26 | Max Demand Keychain | 0 | ≤ | 10000 | | | | | | | |
| 27 | Max Demand Clock | 8000 | ≤ | 8000 | | | | | | | |
| 28 | Max 2 New Products | 2 | ≤ | 2 | | | | | | | |
| 29 | Fixed Cost Fork | 0 | ≤ | 0 | | | | | | | |
| 30 | Fixed Cost Whistle | 0 | ≤ | 0 | | | | | | | |
| 31 | Fixed Cost Keychain | 0 | ≤ | 0 | | | | | | | |
| 32 | Fixed Cost Clock | 0 | ≤ | 0 | | | | | | | |
| 33 | | | | | | | | | | | |
| 34 | Net Profit | $ 26,000 | | | | | | | | | |
| 35 | | | | | | | | | | | |

We often add integer constraints to linear programs when fractional values do not make sense for the decision variables. One consequence of this is that the branch and bound algorithms used to solve ILPs are slower than the simplex method used with regular LPs. Binary variables are useful when we need to model logical conditions. Some problems regularly faced by business analysts follow standard forms that require the use of integer and binary variables.

## KEY TERMS

**Assignment Linear Program** An integer linear program with a standard format used to assign elements of one group to elements of a second group.

**Branch and Bound Technique** An algorithm used to find the solution to an integer linear program.

**Capital Budgeting Problem** An integer linear program using binary variables to determine the best allocation of capital and resources to projects or investments.

**Fixed Cost Linear Programs** An integer linear program which has fixed costs in addition to variable costs.

**Fixed Cost (Linking) Constraint** A constraint which causes a binary variable representing a fixed cost to have the value of 1 when the conditions for incurring that fixed cost happen.

**Integer Linear Programming (ILP)** A linear program with one or more integer constraints is called an integer linear program.

**LP Relaxation** When the integer constraints are relaxed (removed from the ILP) and the resulting LP is solved, it is called an LP relaxation.

**Simplex Method** An algorithm for finding the optimal solution to a linear program.

# EXERCISES

1. Formulate the logical constraints for the following statements (where A, B, C, and D are all binary variables):

   a. If A happens then B or C happens.

   b. If A and B happen then C and D must happen.

   c. If A happens or B does not happen then C or D must happen.

   d. If A happens or B happens then C and D happen.

2. Formulate the logical constraint for the following statements. (Where A, B, C, and D are all binary variables.)

a. If A happens, then both B and C happen.

b. If A does not happen, then both B and C happen.

c. If A does not happen, then neither B nor C happens.

d. If A happens but B does not happen then C and D do not happen.

3. Formulate the constraints for the following statements. (Where A is a binary variable and $x_1$ and $x_2$ are continuous variables.)

a. If A happens then $x_1 + x_2 \leq 50$, else, $x_1 + x_2 \leq 100$.

b. If A does not happen then $x_1 + x_2 \geq 10$, else, $x_1 + x_2 \geq 50$.

4. Orrin Sage is opening a bicycle shop and considering his initial order of bicycles for the coming season. Orrin is considering two different suppliers of bikes—Hoosier Bikes and Albatross Imports. With either supplier, there will be costs associated with setting up the contract. He estimates this cost of being $5,000 with Hoosier Bikes and $6,000 with Albatross Imports.

His entire budget for purchasing bikes is $50,000 (including cost of contracts).

| BIKE COSTS (PER BIKE) | KIDS (K) | MOUNTAIN (M) | COMFORT (C) | ROAD (R) |
|---|---|---|---|---|
| Hoosier Bikes (H) | 45 | 110 | 100 | 400 |
| Albatross Imports (A) | 30 | 130 | 90 | 475 |
| **Selling Price** | **90** | **240** | **190** | **700** |
| **Projected Demand** | **60** | **100** | **80** | **60** |

a. Formulate a linear program to help him maximize his profits.

Use the following decision variables:

for $i$ = H, A, and $j$ = K, M, C, R,

$x_{ij}$: number bikes purchased from supplier $i$ of type $j$;

$y_i$: binary variable of supplier $i$;

i.e., $y_i$ = 1 if Orrin signs a contract with Supplier $i$; $y_i$ = 0, otherwise.

b. Albatross Imports has a special incentive for retailers who sign up to only sell their bikes. If Orrin buys only from them, they will give a rebate of $3,000 at the end of the year on his order. Modify your model from part a. (You may need to add a variable.)

c. Hoosier Bikes are in great demand and the supply is limited for retailers who are not designated as a Hoosier Bikes' Exclusive Dealer. For this year Hoosier Bikes has a limit of 75 of each type of bike for retailers who are not Exclusive Dealers. If Orrin signs up be a Hoosier Bikes' Exclusive Dealer and only buy bikes from them (and none from Albatross), they will supply all of his demand. Modify your model from part a.

5. BeFair Corporation has \$30 million to allocate to the various projects of its three subsidiaries for the next year. BeFair has established that at least one project from each subsidiary must be funded.

The profit (return – investment) at the end of the year and the required investments are given in the table below for each project, where projects 1 to 3 belong to subsidiary 1, projects 4 to 6 belong to subsidiary 2, and the rest belong to subsidiary 3.

| PROJECT | PROFIT (IN MILLION \$) | INVESTMENT (IN MILLION \$) |
|---------|-----------------------|----------------------------|
| 1 | 0.50 | 2 |
| 2 | 1.40 | 5 |
| 3 | 1.70 | 12 |
| 4 | 1.10 | 2 |
| 5 | 4.00 | 15 |
| 6 | 0.60 | 3 |
| 7 | 2.50 | 10 |
| 8 | 1.10 | 1 |

BeFair wants to decide which projects to fund so that the total profit will be maximized. Formulate this problem in the space provided on the answer sheet.

a. Clearly define the decision variables you would use to solve this problem.

b. Formulate an integer linear program for the above problem using only the decision variables defined in a.

c. Formulate the following constraint: BeFair decided to fund at most 2 projects of subsidiary 2.

d. Formulate the following constraint: Project 1 cannot be funded unless projects 4 and 5 are also funded.

e. Projects 5 and 7 share some resources. If both are implemented there will be a combined savings of $2 million in their investment cost. Note that this combined savings is not accounted for in the profit values. (*Just show any new defined decision variable and any modified or added constraints.*)

6. Mellisa Sammut considered her company's expansion plans. They produced computers and were considering opening warehouses in Madrid, Paris, Frankfurt, Milan, and Vienna. The weekly fixed cost for keeping each warehouse open is 400 Euros for Madrid, 800 Euros for Paris, 500 Euros for Frankfurt, 600 Euros for Milan, and 400 Euros for Vienna. Each warehouse can ship up to 100 computers per week. For purposes of calculating shipping costs, she divided Europe up into 2 regions. Region one has a demand of 160 computers per week and region 2 has a demand of 110 computers per week. The table below shows the costs in Euros to ship one unit from a warehouse to a region. There are several restrictions on their plans:

- At most three warehouses can be opened.
- Either Frankfurt or Vienna must be opened.
- If Paris is opened, Madrid cannot be opened.
- If Milan is opened, then Madrid must be opened.

| FROM | TO REGION 1 | TO REGION 2 |
|------|-------------|-------------|
| Madrid | 20 | 70 |
| Paris | 15 | 60 |
| Frankfurt | 25 | 40 |
| Milan | 30 | 40 |
| Vienna | 50 | 30 |

a. Clearly define the decision variables you would use to solve this problem. (Hint: You will need a total of 15 variables.)

b. Formulate this as a Linear Program to minimize cost.

7. Greg Smith would like Lafayette Airlines (LA) to be the next successful low-cost airline. He is considering opening hubs at the following 4 locations: Atlanta, Boston, Chicago, and Detroit. They can open at most one hub at each location. The annual cost of opening and operating a hub at each location, the average revenue from a flight originating from each hub, and the annual maximum flight capacity of each hub are given in the following table:

| LOCATION | HUB OPENING AND OPERATING COST ($) | AVERAGE REVENUE PER FLIGHT ($) | ANNUAL HUB FLIGHT CAPACITY |
|---|---|---|---|
| Atlanta | 2,500,000 | 3,000 | 2,800 |
| Boston | 4,500,000 | 3,800 | 4,000 |
| Chicago | 6,000,000 | 3,500 | 7,000 |
| Detroit | 3,500,000 | 4,000 | 3,500 |

For each location, Greg needs to make two decisions: 1) Whether or not to open a hub at that location, and 2) How many flights per year should be scheduled to originate from that hub. Of course, the annual number of flights originating from each hub must be within the annual flight capacity. Due to financial restrictions, LA would like to open at most 2 hubs. Due to federal regulations, as a start-up airline, they can operate at most 10,000 flights per year. Finally, if they open a hub in Detroit, they wish not to open a hub in Chicago. Formulate a mixed integer programming problem to maximize LA's annual profit (revenue less cost).

a. Clearly define the decision variables you would use to solve this problem.

b. Formulate this as a Linear Program to maximize annual profit.

8. A company manufactures three products: A, B, and C. The company currently has an order for 3 units of product A, 7 units of product B, and 4 units of product C. There is no inventory for any of these products. All three products require special processing that can be done on one of two machines. The cost of producing each product on each machine is summarized in the following table:

### Cost of Producing a Unit of Product

| MACHINE | A | B | C |
|---|---|---|---|
| 1 | $13 | $ 9 | $10 |
| 2 | $11 | $12 | $ 8 |

The time required to produce each product on each machine is summarized in the following table:

### Time (Hours) Needed to Produce a Unit of Product

| Machine | A | B | C |
|---|---|---|---|
| 1 | 0.4 | 1.1 | 0.9 |
| 2 | 0.5 | 1.2 | 1.3 |

Assume machine 1 can be used for eight hours and machine 2 can be used for six hours. Each machine must undergo a special setup operation to prepare it to produce each product. After completing this setup for a product, any number of that product type can be produced. The setup costs for producing each product on each machine are summarized in the following table.

### Setup Costs for Producing a Unit of Product

| MACHINE | A | B | C |
|---|---|---|---|
| 1 | $55 | $93 | $60 |
| 2 | $65 | $58 | $75 |

a. Formulate an ILP model to determine how many units of each product to produce on each machine in order to meet demand at a minimum cost.

b. Implement your model in a spreadsheet and solve it.

c. What is the optimal solution?

9. Purdue women's basketball Head Coach Sharon Versyp is trying to decide the starting lineup for the Lady Boilermakers' first preseason exhibition game. Due to injuries and players' physical conditions, only seven players are available. These players have been rated on a scale of 1 (poor) to 3 (excellent) according to their ball-handling, shooting, rebounding, and defensive abilities. The positions that each player is allowed to play and the players' abilities are listed in the table below.

| PLAYER | POSITION | BALL-HANDLING | SHOOTING | REBOUNDING | DEFENSE |
|--------|----------|---------------|----------|------------|---------|
| 1 | G | 3 | 3 | 1 | 3 |
| 2 | C | 2 | 1 | 3 | 2 |
| 3 | G, F | 2 | 3 | 2 | 2 |
| 4 | F, C | 1 | 3 | 3 | 1 |
| 5 | G, F | 1 | 3 | 1 | 2 |
| 6 | F, C | 3 | 1 | 2 | 3 |
| 7 | G, F | 3 | 2 | 2 | 1 |

The five-player starting line-up must satisfy the following restrictions:

1. At least 2 members must be able to play guard (G), at least 2 members must be able to play forward (F), and at least one member must be able to play center (C).

2. The average ball-handling, shooting, and rebounding level of the starting lineup must each be at least 2.

3. Player 2 or player 3 must start.

4. If player 3 starts, then player 6 cannot start.

5. If player 1 starts, then players 4 and 5 must both start.

6. If player 2 starts, then players 3 or 5 must start.

7. The team will get 2 more defense points in terms of ability if both players 1 and 3 start (*Hint:* define an extra binary variable for whether the team will get 2 more defense points or not).

   Given these constraints, Coach Versyp wants to maximize the total defensive ability of the starting team. Formulate an IP that will help her choose her starting team.

10. Formulate the logic constraint for the following statements. (A, B, C, and D are all binary variables.)

a. A does not happen unless B happens.

b. A and B do not happen unless C happens.

c. A and B do not happen unless C and D happen.

d. Unless A happens, neither does B or C happen.

11. Formulate the logic constraint for the following statements. (A and B are binary variables and $x$ and $y$ are continuouts variables.)

a. If A happens, then $x + y \geq 200$, otherwise $x + y \geq 150$.

b. If A happens, then $x + y \leq 200$, otherwise $x + y \leq 150$.

12. AB Investment Group wishes to invest $10 million in projects marked from A to E with the annual returns as shown:

| PROJECT | PROJECT COST (MILLIONS) | ESTIMATED PERCENT RETURN |
|---------|-------------------------|--------------------------|
| A | 2 | 6 |
| B | 1.5 | 8 |
| C | 2.5 | 10 |
| D | 4 | 12 |
| E | 3 | 7 |
| F | 2 | 9 |

Their client has set the following investment guidelines.

- Any money not invested in one of these projects will be invested in T-Bills paying 4% per year.
- The combined investment amount in A and B may not exceed the total in E and F.
- If they invest in C and D then they cannot invest in F.
- At least one project from C, D, and E must be invested in.
- If they invest in D then at least $1 million has to be invested in T-Bills.

a. Formulate an integer linear programming problem, clearly defining the variables, to help ABI group allocate the funds in order to maximize the return on investment.

b. Use Solver to find the optimal solution.

   How should they allocate their investments?

   What would be the total profit at the end of the year?

13. GuruJi Inc is considering different projects for the next year in order to increase its capacity by at least 100,000 units. It has an option to choose between six different projects. The NPVs and capacities for different projects are given below:

| PROJECT | NPV (IN $) | CAPACITY (UNITS) |
|---------|-----------|------------------|
| 1 | 100,000 | 10,000 |
| 2 | 300,000 | 40,000 |
| 3 | 250,000 | 50,000 |
| 4 | 200,000 | 25,000 |
| 5 | 350,000 | 30,000 |
| 6 | 100,000 | 15,000 |

Also, the following conditions must be met:

- At least one project from 1, 2, and 3 must be selected.
- At least one project from 4, 5, and 6 must be selected.
- If 1 and 2 are selected then 3 cannot be selected.
- If 2 is selected then 5 cannot be selected.
- If 4 is selected then 6 must be selected and vice versa.

a. Formulate an integer linear programming problem clearly defining the variables to maximize the NPV.

b. Use Solver to find the optimal solution.

Which projects should they select?

What is the expected NPV?

14. Indi Inc. is thinking of opening 4 warehouses in four metropolitan areas in India: Delhi, Mumbai, Kolkata, and Chennai. There is a fixed cost associated with operating each warehouse for a week. It is 30,000 rupees for Delhi, 40,000 rupees for Mumbai, 50,000 rupees for Kolkata, and 20,000 rupees for Chennai. Each warehouse can ship a maximum 10,000 units per week. Indi Inc. has identified four regions in India with different demand requirements for each. The requirements for North, South, West, and East India are 5,000, 6,000, 4,000, and 5,000, respectively. The shipping cost per unit is shown below:

|         | NORTH | SOUTH | WEST | EAST |
|---------|-------|-------|------|------|
| DELHI   | 180   | 350   | 250  | 280  |
| MUMBAI  | 320   | 150   | 200  | 275  |
| KOLKATA | 300   | 180   | 250  | 100  |
| CHENNAI | 400   | 80    | 290  | 300  |

Also, the following requirements must be met:

a. If Delhi is opened, Chennai must be opened.

b. If Kolkata and Delhi are opened, Mumbai must not be opened.

c. Either of Delhi or Mumbai must be opened, but not both.

Formulate an integer linear program to supply demand at the lowest total cost.

15. Abracadabra Inc. purchases three types of products: 1, 2, and 3 from two suppliers: A and B. There is a contract cost of $1,000 and $1,500 associated with each supplier, respectively, if any product is purchased from that supplier. The cost and demand matrix is shown below:

| COST (PER UNIT) | 1 | 2 | 3 |
|---|---|---|---|
| A | $15 | $10 | $5 |
| B | $12 | $12 | $6 |
| SELLING PRICE | $19 | $17 | $9 |
| MAXIMUM DEMAND | 900 | 800 | 450 |

Formulate a LP problem to maximize profit. (Hint: Use a binary variable for each supplier with a value of 1 if that supplier is used and a 0 otherwise.)

16. There are 5 machines and 4 jobs to be performed. Each machine can perform only a particular set of jobs and not all jobs. Also, time taken by each machine for each job is different. See the table for hours taken by each machine to do the job. X means the machine can't do that job.

|  | JOB 1 | JOB 2 | JOB 3 | JOB 4 |
|---|---|---|---|---|
| MACHINE 1 | 13 | 12 | X | 15 |
| MACHINE 2 | 12 | X | 12 | 12 |
| MACHINE 3 | X | X | 10 | 10 |
| MACHINE 4 | 10 | 13 | 14 | 11 |
| MACHINE 5 | 9 | 11 | 13 | X |

a. Each machine can do at most one job. Formulate an integer linear program to assign the four jobs to different machines with the goal of minimizing the total time.

b. Find the optimal solution using Solver.

What are the optimal assignments?

What is the total time spent processing the jobs?

17. There are 6 contractors and 5 different tasks. Each contractor charges differently for each task.

|  | Task 1 | Task 2 | Task 3 | Task 4 | Task 5 |
|---|---|---|---|---|---|
| Contractor 1 | 50 | 60 | 55 | 35 | 45 |
| Contractor 2 | 40 | 50 | 60 | 45 | 35 |
| Contractor 3 | 45 | 45 | 45 | 50 | 50 |
| Contractor 4 | 60 | 35 | 35 | 60 | 55 |
| Contractor 5 | 35 | 55 | 40 | 55 | 40 |
| Contractor 6 | 55 | 40 | 65 | 65 | 45 |

a. Formulate an ILP to assign the five tasks to five contractors (each contractor can do only one task) at the lowest total cost.

b. Suppose Contractor 4 cannot do task 1. How would you modify your formulation in part a to handle this situation?

18. FastEngine Co. is the major engine supplier for several car manufacturers. It produces two types of engines, EM1 and EM2. The demands for these two types of engines vary each month because of car demand forecasts and financial issues, etc.

The operation manager of FastEngine Co. is planning the production plan for the next three months to minimize the total production and holding costs.

On average, it takes 5 labor hours to manufacture an EM1 engine and 7 labor hours to manufacture an EM2 engine. Suppose that the holding cost of EM1 and EM2 models are 1.2% and 2.3% of manufacturing costs, respectively. Also, at the end of each month, at most 400 EM1 and 250 EM2 can be stored.

At the beginning of month 1, the company has 140 EM1 and 90 EM2 available. At the end of month 3, the company requires at least 320 EM1 and 150 EM2 in inventories. Other information is given in the following table:

| MONTH | PRODUCTION COST PER EM1 | PRODUCTION COST PER EM2 | DEMANDS FOR EM1 | DEMANDS FOR EM2 | AVAILABLE LABOR HOURS |
|---|---|---|---|---|---|
| 1 | $1,500 | $2,300 | 500 | 260 | 5,300 |
| 2 | $1,700 | $2,100 | 580 | 275 | 5,200 |
| 3 | $1,650 | $2,050 | 560 | 300 | 5,500 |

a. Formulate a linear program to help FastEngine Co. determine how many EM1 and EM2 to produce and hold in inventory in each month.

b. Use Solver to find the optimal solution to the linear program in a.

Using the sensitivity report to answer the following questions:

c. The company is considering hiring temp workers to increase the available labor hours. In which month might this action save money?

For this month, the company could hire two temporary workers. Each temporary worker would increase the labor hours by 160 hours but cost the company $2,000. Should the company do so? Why or why not?

d. The company could pay an extra $10,000 to rent a storage facility and increase the inventory capacity of EM1 from 400 per month to 450 per month. Should the company do so? Why?

e. Suppose the company miscounted their initial inventory level of EM1 and EM2. In fact, they have 200 EM1 and 150 EM2 engines at the beginning of Month 1. How would this affect the optimal value?

19. Anderson's Law Office just received four new legal cases from its clients. Each case is about different legal issues, divorce, bankruptcy, labor and employment, and criminal law. Anderson is assigning these four legal cases to six attorneys in his office. He reviews the past five years' records of each attorney and concludes the winning probabilities of each attorney to each case as follows:

| ATTORNEY/CASE | DIVORCE | BANKRUPTCY | LABOR AND EMPLOYMENT | CRIMINAL LAW |
|---|---|---|---|---|
| 1 | 85% | 70% | 30% | 20% |
| 2 | 35% | 75% | 85% | 15% |
| 3 | 50% | 60% | 25% | 90% |
| 4 | 10% | 55% | 65% | 70% |
| 5 | 45% | 95% | 30% | 65% |
| 6 | 5% | 50% | 60% | 80% |

Anderson is trying to assign these four cases with the following restrictions:

(1) Each attorney should be assigned to at most one case.

(2) One and only one attorney should be assigned to each case.

(3) Attorneys 1 and 6 must be assigned a case.

(4) Attorney 5 cannot be assigned to the Bankruptcy case because of a confliction of interest.

Formulate an integer program model to maximize the total winning probability.

20. Janet Smith is planning to invest her savings of $10,000 into stocks. Her personal financial consultant had suggested her 8 potential stocks from different sectors in the market. For each stock, she needs to make two decisions:

(1) To buy a stock or not? (2) How many shares of stock to buy? Janet would like to diversify her portfolio using the following rules.

- At least one stock of every sector should be purchased.

- At most two stocks in Energy sector would be purchased.

- If PSG is purchased, then BOP will not be in the portfolio.

- The total investment in Biotechnology should be at least $3,000.

| SECTOR | SYMBOL | FIXED INVESTMENT COST | COST PER SHARE | ANNUAL RETURN |
|--------|--------|-----------------------|----------------|---------------|
| ELECTRIC UTILITIES | GREE | $100 | $2.5 | 3.5% |
| | PSG | $150 | $8.3 | 4.5% |
| | BOP | $300 | $12 | 9.5% |
| ENERGY | OTEH | $120 | $3 | 5.6% |
| | FIM | $150 | $6.5 | 6.2% |
| | SUEL | $70 | $1.5 | 2.8% |
| BIOTECHNOLOGY | JHP | $140 | $6 | 6.6% |
| | KIN | $250 | $9 | 7% |

Formulate an integer program to help Janet maximize the value of her investments at the end of one year.

# CHAPTER 7

# Simulation Modeling

- Understand the fundamentals of simulations modeling.
- Identify advantages and disadvantages of a simulation model.
- Construct a simulation model using standard Excel functions.
- Build a simulation model using the simulation software @RISK.

## Introduction

Uncertainty fills the business world. In the optimization models discussed throughout this book, we have used sensitivity analysis to assess the impact of estimated or uncertain probabilities and values on the recommended solution. Simulation modeling allows us to incorporate uncertainty explicitly into a computer model and observe the range of outcomes that result. The ability to see the distribution of results rather than a single bottom line solution and value is a fundamental advantage of a simulation model.

Simulation begins with the generation of random values which are translated into the occurrence of uncertain events. Spreadsheets have made the task of simulating many trials easy with built-in functions and add-ins like @RISK and Crystal Ball. In this chapter, we will learn how to perform simulation using just the built-in functions of Excel and how to use the more sophisticated simulation package called @RISK.

## Deterministic and Stochastic Models

The optimization models like LP and ILP that we have studied so far are **deterministic models.** In a deterministic model, we assume to know what the input values are. A deterministic model will generate the same result each time it is run if the inputs stay the same. Simulation modeling differs from optimization modeling in that it incorporates the natural variation of input values in the model. Each time the model is run, the results of a simulation may never be the same as a previous simulation. A model that relies heavily upon random behavior is referred to as a **stochastic model.** The results generated from a stochastic model are typically analyzed statistically in order to make conclusions regarding the behavior of the system and its outcomes.

## Process for Developing and Using a Simulation Model

1. Select input probability distributions.
2. Build simulation model (write formulas) for a specific decision variable value.
3. Generate outputs from the model.

4. Use a table to simultaneously generate outputs from several decision variable values.
5. Decide a "best" value for the decision variable.

### Probability Distributions for Input Variables

The histograms of variables take on many different shapes. Some variables have discrete distribution with a finite number of distinct values such as a binomial or a Poisson distribution. Other variables may have a continuous distribution with an infinite number of different values like the uniform or normal distribution. The builder of a simulation model will have to decide which inputs should be random and the distribution used to generate values. Historical data allows the inspection of the shape of the distribution to draw insights into which would best represent the input. Finding a good distribution can be a challenge but statistical tests like the chi-squared goodness of fit test can show whether a particular distribution is a good match for the data. @RISK also has a distribution fitting feature that can also help you identify input distributions.

## Simulation with Built-In Excel Functions

### RAND() Function

Simulation of inputs using the functions built into Excel starts with the generation of a random number using the **RAND()** function. The RAND() function generates a random number from a uniform distribution from 0 to 1. Spreadsheets normally recalculate the values in all cells whenever a new entry is made or the F9 key is pressed. This means that every time the sheet recalculates, a new random number will be displayed. With a random value generated by the RAND() function, we can simulate other distributions using a variety of Excel functions.

### Discrete Probability Distributions

A discrete probability distribution can be easily simulated. If the distribution only has two possible values, the IF command can be used to generate values. The syntax for the IF function is:

$$IF(logical\_test, [value\_if\_true], [value\_if\_false])$$

For example, if there was a 70% chance that a project would be done in 2013 and a 30% chance it would be completed in 2014, the following formula could be typed into an Excel spreadsheet to simulate this event:

$$=IF(RAND()<0.7,2013,2014)$$

Up to 64 IF statements could be nested to generate discrete distribution with more than two possible values. However, larger discrete distributions can be simulated easier using the **VLOOKUP or HLOOKUP** functions. The VLOOKUP function works by searching the first column of a table and returns a value from any cell on the same row of the range. The VLOOKUP function has the following syntax:

$$VLOOKUP(lookup\_value, table\_array, col\_index\_num, [range\_lookup])$$

The lookup_value is the value to search in the first column of the table. The values in this row should be entered in ascending value. The table_array directs the function to the range of cells that contain the data. The col_index_num directs the VLOOKUP function to the column containing the data to be returned. Range_lookup is an optional logical argument in this function. If it is left out or set at TRUE, compare the lookup_value with the entries in the first column and it will return the value from the row with highest entry less than or equal to the lookup_value. If it is set to FALSE, it will only return values when there is an exact match. We will not be using the FALSE setting in generating discrete distributions. The VLOOKUP function is demonstrated in Example 7.1. The HLOOKUP function works in a similar fashion with a table that has a horizontal layout.

## Example 7.1 Simulation of Magazine Sales at University Bookstore

The University Bookstore orders Cosmopolitan magazine each month for $2.00 per copy. It sells it for $4.50 per copy. The publisher will buy back any copies that remain unsold at the end of two months for $0.50 a copy. A review of historic sales of the magazine yielded the following discrete probability distribution:

### ▦ TABLE 7.1  Distribution of Demand for Cosmopolitan Magazine

| Demand | 150 | 200 | 250 | 300 | 350 |
|---|---|---|---|---|---|
| Probability | 0.25 | 0.25 | 0.30 | 0.15 | 0.05 |

The University Bookstore would like to maximize its profit. How many magazines should it order?

One approach would be to order the number of magazines to match expected demand. With a discrete probability distribution, the expected value is calculated by the formula: $\sum x^*P(x) = 150^*(0.25) + 200^*(0.25) + 250^*(250) + 300^*(0.15) + 350^*(0.05) = 225$. Using this heuristic, the bookstore would order 225 magazines but is it the best order quantity? We determine the best order quantity using the spreadsheet simulation model.

## Preparing the Spreadsheet

Exhibit 7.1 shows the arrangement of the data used in the simulation model. Of particular note is the table containing the demand distribution. The first column contains the cumulative probability distribution for each level of demand. Note that the cumulative probability column shows the probability the demand is less than the demand in the second column. For the purposes of building the model, any value can be entered for the order quantity.

| | A | B | C | D | E | F | G |
|---|---|---|---|---|---|---|---|
| 1 | Simulation of Magazine Demand at University Bookstore | | | | | | |
| 2 | | | | | | | |
| 3 | Magazine Data | | | Demand distribution | | | |
| 4 | Unit Cost | $2.00 | | Cum Prob | Demand | Probability | |
| 5 | Selling Price | $4.50 | | 0.00 | 150 | 0.25 | |
| 6 | Buyback Price | $0.50 | | 0.25 | 200 | 0.25 | |
| 7 | | | | 0.50 | 250 | 0.30 | |
| 8 | Decision variable | | | 0.80 | 300 | 0.15 | |
| 9 | Order Quantity | 225 | | 0.95 | 350 | 0.05 | |
| 10 | | | | | | | |

Model / Sheet1

## Building the Simulation Model

The simulation model will be built by entering formulas in row 25 of our spreadsheet
(Exhibit 7.2). Table 7.2 shows the formulas used in each cell to build the model. Each
cell and its formula will be discussed in more detail.

| | A | B | C | D | E | F | G | H |
|---|---|---|---|---|---|---|---|---|
| 1 | Simulation of Magazine Demand at University Bookstore | | | | | | | |
| 2 | | | | | | | | |
| 3 | Magazine Data | | | Demand distribution | | | | |
| 4 | Unit Cost | $2.00 | | Cum Prob | Demand | Probability | | |
| 5 | Selling Price | $4.50 | | 0.00 | 150 | 0.25 | | |
| 6 | Buyback Price | $0.50 | | 0.25 | 200 | 0.25 | | |
| 7 | | | | 0.50 | 250 | 0.30 | | |
| 8 | Decision variable | | | 0.80 | 300 | 0.15 | | |
| 9 | Order Quantity | 225 | | 0.95 | 350 | 0.05 | | |
| 10 | | | | | | | | |
| 11 | Summary Measures for Simulated | | | | | | | |
| 12 | Mean Profit | $454.30 | | | | | | |
| 13 | Stdev of Profit | $125.32 | | | | | | |
| 14 | Minimum Profit | $262.50 | | | | | | |
| 15 | Maximum Profit | $562.50 | | Range Name | | Cells | | |
| 16 | | | | Buyback_Price | | =Model!$B$6 | | |
| 17 | Confidence Interval for Mean Profit | | | Demand_Table | | =Model!$D$5:$E$9 | | |
| 18 | Interations | 500 | | Order_Quantity | | =Model!$B$9 | | |
| 19 | Confidence Level | 95% | | Profit | | =Model!$H$25:$H$524 | | |
| 20 | Lower Limit | $443.32 | | Selling_Price | | =Model!$B$5 | | |
| 21 | Upper Limit | $465.28 | | Unit_Cost | | =Model!$B$4 | | |
| 22 | | | | | | | | |
| 23 | Simulation | | | | | | | |
| 24 | Iteration | Random # | Demand | Number Sold | Sales Revenue | Buyback Revenue | Cost | Profit |
| 25 | 1 | 0.2253 | 150 | 150 | $675.00 | $37.50 | $450 | $262.50 |
| 26 | 2 | 0.3262 | 200 | 200 | $900.00 | $12.50 | $450 | $462.50 |
| 27 | 3 | 0.0828 | 150 | 150 | $675.00 | $37.50 | $450 | $262.50 |
| 522 | 498 | 0.2627 | 200 | 200 | $900.00 | $12.50 | $450 | $462.50 |
| 523 | 499 | 0.9335 | 300 | 225 | $1,012.50 | $0.00 | $450 | $562.50 |
| 524 | 500 | 0.4516 | 200 | 200 | $900.00 | $12.50 | $450 | $462.50 |
| 525 | | | | | | | | |

Model / Sheet1

**TABLE 7.2** Formulas Used in Simulation Model

| CELL | CONTENTS | FORMULA |
|------|----------|---------|
| A25 | Iteration Number | 1 |
| B25 | Random # | =RAND() |
| C25 | Simulated Demand | =VLOOKUP(B25,Demand_Table,2) |
| D25 | Number Sold | =MIN(C25,Order_Quantity) |
| E25 | Sales Revenue | =Selling_Price*D25 |
| F25 | Buyback Revenue | =Buyback_Price*(Order_Quantity-D25) |
| G25 | Cost of Magazines | =Order_Quantity*Unit_Cost |
| H25 | Profit | =E25+F25-G25 |

**Cell A25: Iteration Number** Cell A25 contains the trial number. As can be seen, this simulation is set up for 500 repetitions with each row representing a separate scenario.

**Cell B25: Random Value** In cell B25, '=RAND()' is entered to generate a random value between 0 and 1. This value is used in generating the simulated demand in cell C25 using the VLOOKUP function.

**Cell C25: Simulated Demand** Cell C25 contains the formula: '=VLOOKUP (B25,Demand_Table,2)'. This function instructs the spreadsheet to take the random number generated in cell B25 and search the first column of the Demand Distribution table (named Demand_Table) and return a demand value found in the second column of the table.

The VLOOKUP function is ideal for simulating discrete probability distributions. In the University Bookstore example (Exhibit 7.2), the VLOOKUP function will return the value 150 if a random number between 0 and 0.25 is generated, 200 if a random number between 0.25 and 0.50 is generated, 250 for a random number between 0.5 and 0.8, 300 for a random number between 0.8 and 0.95, and 350 if the random number is above 0.95.

**Cell D25 Number Sold** Cell D25 contains the formula: '=MIN(C25,Order_ Quantity)'. The store cannot sell more magazines than it has ordered so the number sold will be the minimum of the order quantity and the demand.

**Cell E25 Sales Revenue** Cell E25 contains the formula: '=Selling_Price*D25'. The sales revenue is the selling price multiplied by quantity sold.

**Cell F25 Buyback Revenue** Cell F25 contains the formula: '=Buyback_ Price*(Order_Quantity – D25)'. The bookstore will sell back the unsold magazines (Order_Quantity – D25).

**Cell G25 Cost** Cell G25 contains the formula: '=Order_Quantity*Unit_Cost'. This cell simply contains the cost of purchasing the magazines from the publisher.

**Cell H25 Profit** Cell H25 contains the formula: '=E25+F25–G25'. E25 and F25 contain the revenue for the magazine minus the cost found in G25 yields the profit.

## Generating Output from the Model

To generate output from the model, the formulas entered in row 25 are copied down the spreadsheet to create 500 repetitions of the model. The range H25:H524 is named 'Profit' for the ease of entering formulas for summary statistics for the model. Exhibit 7.3 shows the formulas used to create summary statistics for the simulation model.

Most of the formulas shown on the top half of Exhibit 7.3 should be fairly familiar. However, the formula for generating a confidence interval for the mean profit is probably not as familiar. The confidence interval is the mean profit ± the margin of error. The function, **CONFIDENCE,** calculates the margin of error for a confidence interval. Its syntax is: CONFIDENCE(alpha,standard_dev,size).

Alpha is the significance level used to compute the confidence level. The confidence level equals 100*(1 – alpha)%, or in other words, a 95 percent confidence level is associated with an alpha of 0.05. Standard_dev is the population standard deviation for the data range that we have estimated with the simulation. Size is the sample size. Cells B20 and B21 contain the formulas for the lower and upper limits for a 95% confidence interval, respectively.

## Using a Data Table to Generate Outputs from Different Decision Variable Values

The simulation model for University Bookstores was constructed using an initial order level of 225 magazines. The simulation run in Exhibit 7.2 has a mean profit for ordering 225 magazines of $467.90. However, it does not provide any information on the profit for other order quantities. We could enter different order quantities into the model and record the summary measures, but there is a faster and easier way to explore different order quantities using the same set of simulated demands. A **Data Table** is a range of cells that shows how changing one or two variables in your formulas will affect the results of those formulas. Data tables provide a shortcut for calculating multiple results in one operation and a way to view and compare the results of all the different variations together on your worksheet.

□ EXHIBIT 7.3

Summary Measure Formulas

|  | A | B |
|---|---|---|
| 11 | Summary Measures for Simulated Profit | |
| 12 | Mean Profit | =AVERAGE(Profit) |
| 13 | Stdev of Profit | =STDEV(Profit) |
| 14 | Minimum Profit | =MIN(Profit) |
| 15 | Maximum Profit | =MAX(Profit) |
| 16 | | |
| 17 | Confidence Interval for Mean Profit | |
| 18 | Interations | 500 |
| 19 | Confidence Level | 0.95 |
| 20 | Lower Limit | =B12-CONFIDENCE(1-B19,B13,B18) |
| 21 | Upper Limit | =B12+CONFIDENCE(1-B19,B13,B18) |
| 22 | | |

◀ ◀ ▶ ▶◀    Model  Sheet1

University Bookstores would like to explore the following order quantities: 175, 200, 225, 250, 275, 300, and 325. For each, they would like to know the mean profit and its 95% confidence interval. The following steps were followed to prepare a data table to collect this information. See Exhibit 7.4.

1. The list of order quantities to be tested was entered in the first column (cells D16:D22) of the data table.

2. The formulas for the output to be collected were entered in the row above and to the right of the order quantities (cells E15:G15). In column E, we want to collect the Mean Profit so the formula '=B12' was entered. To collect the lower and upper limits for the 95% confidence intervals, '=B20' and '=B21' were entered in cells F15 and G15, respectively.

To fill the table with the summary output for each order quantity:

3. Select the range of cells including the column containing the order quantities to be tested, the row containing the formulas, and the body of the table where the output is to be displayed. In this example, the range D15:G22 would be selected.

4. On the **Data** tab, in the **Data Tools** group, click **What-If Analysis,** and then click **Data Table.** A dialogue box as seen in Exhibit 7.5 will appear.

5. Since this data table is set up in a column format, the cell reference, B9, is entered as the Column Input Cell. Cell B9 contains the decision variable, order quantity.

**EXHIBIT 7.4**

Simulation Model with Data Table Prepared

| | A | B | C | D | E | F | G | H |
|---|---|---|---|---|---|---|---|---|
| 1 | Simulation of Magazine Demand at University Bookstore | | | | | | | |
| 2 | | | | | | | | |
| 3 | Magazine Data | | | Demand distribution | | | | |
| 4 | Unit Cost | $2.00 | | Cum Prob | Demand | Probability | | |
| 5 | Selling Price | $4.50 | | 0.00 | 150 | 0.25 | | |
| 6 | Buyback Price | $0.60 | | 0.25 | 200 | 0.25 | | |
| 7 | | | | 0.50 | 250 | 0.30 | | |
| 8 | Decision variable | | | 0.80 | 300 | 0.15 | | |
| 9 | Order Quantity | 225 | | 0.95 | 350 | 0.05 | | |
| 10 | | | | | | | | |
| 11 | Summary Measures for Simulated Profit | | | | | | | |
| 12 | Mean Profit | $462.70 | | Data Table for Various Order Quantities | | | | |
| 13 | Stdev of Profit | $122.19 | | Quantity | Mean | Confidence Interval | | |
| 14 | Minimum Profit | $262.50 | | | Profit | Lower Limit | Upper Limit | |
| 15 | Maximum Profit | $562.50 | | | $462.70 | $451.99 | $473.41 | |
| 16 | | | | 175 | | | | |
| 17 | Confidence Interval for Mean Profit | | | 200 | | | | |
| 18 | Interations | 500 | | 225 | | | | |
| 19 | Confidence Level | 95% | | 250 | | | | |
| 20 | Lower Limit | $451.99 | | 275 | | | | |
| 21 | Upper Limit | $473.41 | | 300 | | | | |
| 22 | | | | 325 | | | | |
| 23 | Simulation | | | | | | | |
| 24 | Iteration | Random # | Demand | Number Sold | Sales Revenue | Buyback Revenue | Cost | Profit |
| 25 | 1 | 0.0381 | 150 | 150 | $675.00 | $37.50 | $450 | $262.50 |
| 26 | 2 | 0.3055 | 200 | 200 | $900.00 | $12.50 | $450 | $462.50 |
| 27 | 3 | 0.5677 | 250 | 225 | $1,012.50 | $0.00 | $450 | $562.50 |
| 28 | 4 | 0.7907 | 250 | 225 | $1,012.50 | $0.00 | $450 | $562.50 |
| 523 | 499 | 0.7842 | 250 | 225 | $1,012.50 | $0.00 | $450 | $562.50 |
| 524 | 500 | 0.2929 | 200 | 200 | $900.00 | $12.50 | $450 | $462.50 |
| 525 | | | | | | | | |

Model / Sheet1

## Selecting the Best Order Quantity for University Bookstores

Exhibit 7.6 shows the spreadsheet model with the data table completed. In comparing the mean profits and confidence intervals for each order quantity, it can be seen that ordering 250 magazines yields the highest mean profit.

## Modeling a Normal Distribution Using Excel

A normal distribution can be simulated easily using Excel functions. Just as with the discrete probability distribution, the simulation starts with the generation of a random value. The normal distribution value is then determined using the NORMINV function. The NORMINV function yields a value of *x* from a normal distribution with a given mean and standard deviation. The syntax is: NORMINV(probability,mean, standard_dev) where *probability* is the probability of an observation being less than or

■ EXHIBIT 7.5

Data Table Dialogue Box

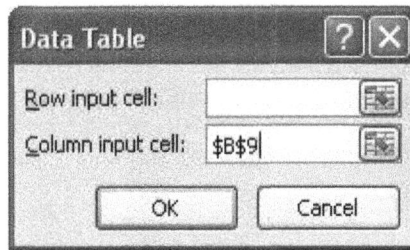

■ EXHIBIT 7.6

University Bookstores Final Model

| | A | B | C | D | E | F | G | H |
|---|---|---|---|---|---|---|---|---|
| 1 | Simulation of Magazine Demand at University Bookstore | | | | | | | |
| 2 | | | | | | | | |
| 3 | Magazine Data | | | Demand distribution | | | | |
| 4 | Unit Cost | $2.00 | | Cum Prob | Demand | Probability | | |
| 5 | Selling Price | $4.50 | | 0.00 | 150 | 0.25 | | |
| 6 | Buyback Price | $0.50 | | 0.25 | 200 | 0.25 | | |
| 7 | | | | 0.50 | 250 | 0.30 | | |
| 8 | Decision variable | | | 0.80 | 300 | 0.15 | | |
| 9 | Order Quantity | 225 | | 0.95 | 350 | 0.05 | | |
| 10 | | | | | | | | |
| 11 | Summary Measures for Simulated Profit | | | | | | | |
| 12 | Mean Profit | $459.10 | | Data Table for Various Order Quantities | | | | |
| 13 | Stdev of Profit | $125.06 | | Quantity | Mean Profit | Confidence Interval | | |
| 14 | Minimum Profit | $262.50 | | | | Lower Limit | Upper Limit | |
| 15 | Maximum Profit | $562.50 | | | $459.10 | $ 448.14 | $470.06 | |
| 16 | | | | 175 | $411.70 | $407.86 | $415.54 | |
| 17 | Confidence Interval for Mean Profit | | | 200 | $452.00 | $444.51 | $459.49 | |
| 18 | Interations | 500 | | 225 | $458.10 | $447.52 | $468.68 | |
| 19 | Confidence Level | 95% | | 250 | $480.60 | $465.95 | $495.25 | |
| 20 | Lower Limit | $448.14 | | 275 | $445.30 | $428.91 | $461.69 | |
| 21 | Upper Limit | $470.06 | | 300 | $439.60 | $420.94 | $458.26 | |
| 22 | | | | 325 | $414.10 | $394.81 | $433.39 | |
| 23 | Simulation | | | | | | | |
| 24 | Iteration | Random # | Demand | Number Sold | Sales Revenue | Buyback Revenue | Cost | Profit |
| 25 | 1 | 0.9529 | 350 | 225 | $1,012.50 | $0.00 | $450 | $562.50 |
| 26 | 2 | 0.6607 | 250 | 225 | $1,012.50 | $0.00 | $450 | $562.50 |
| 27 | 3 | 0.3718 | 200 | 200 | $900.00 | $12.50 | $450 | $462.50 |
| 28 | 4 | 0.0596 | 150 | 150 | $675.00 | $37.50 | $450 | $262.50 |
| 523 | 499 | 0.4247 | 200 | 200 | $900.00 | $12.50 | $450 | $462.50 |
| 524 | 500 | 0.9577 | 350 | 225 | $1,012.50 | $0.00 | $450 | $562.50 |
| 525 | | | | | | | | |

Model / Sheet1

equal to a variable, *x*, in the normal distribution. The *mean* is the arithmetic mean of the distribution and *standard_dev* is the standard deviation of the distribution.

## Example 7.2 Simulation of Magazine Sales at University Bookstore with a Normal Distribution

Changing only the distribution on the University Bookstore example from a discrete probability distribution to a normal distribution with a mean of 240 and standard deviation of 40, we will create the simulation model seen in Exhibit 7.7. The main difference in the formulation of the model is in Demand. The formula entered in cell C25 is '=ROUND(NORMINV(B25,Mean,Std_Dev),0)' where the range name Mean refers to cell E4 and Std_Dev refers to cell E5. The ROUND function ensures that the simulated demand will have an integer value.

## Modeling a Binomial Distribution using Excel

Binomial distributions can be simulated in Excel using the CritBinom and Rand() functions. The CritBinom function returns the smallest value for which the cumulative binomial distribution is greater than or equal to a criterion value. We will use the RAND() to generate the criterion value in a simulation. The syntax for the CritBinom function is:

CRITBINOM(trials,probability_s,alpha) where trials is the sample size, Probability_s is the probability of a success on each trial and alpha is the criterion value.

□ EXHIBIT 7.7

Simulation of Normally Distributed Magazine Demand

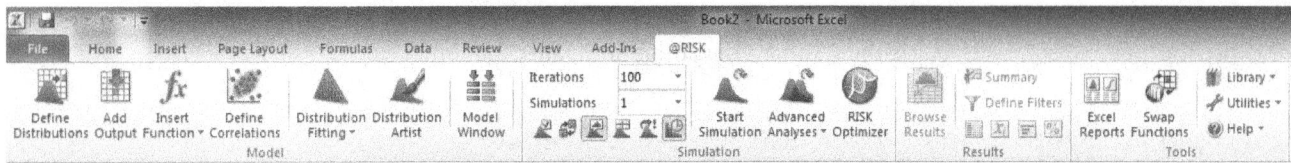

## EXHIBIT 7.8

@RISK Main Menu Bar

This function can be of great use in simulating overbooking policies for hotels and airlines or developing a sampling policy for a quality assurance program. For example, to simulate the number of defective items in samples of 20 with a 10% defect rate, the following formula could be used: '=CritBinom(20,0.1,RAND())'.

## @RISK

While simulation modeling can be done using only Excel functions, it is cumbersome and limited when compared to the distributions and features available in specialized simulation add-ins to Excel like @RISK and Crystal Ball. These add-ins contain built-in functions for many distributions, are easy to use, keeps track of all of the inputs and outputs, and prepares summary statistics for outputs of interest. The @RISK menu bar (Exhibit 7.8) will navigate us through the process of building a model, setting the parameters of the simulation, and analyzing the results. We will demonstrate the use of @RISK with several examples with different distributions. Remember: you need to load @RISK on your computer and add it into Excel to use it.

### Discrete Distributions Using @RISK

Discrete distribution simulations can be generated using the RISKDISCRETE function. The syntax for this function is: RISKDiscrete( *{X1,X2,...,Xn},{p1,p2,...,pn}*) which specifies a discrete distribution with a number of outcomes equaling *n*. Any number of outcomes may be entered. Each outcome has a value *X* and a weight *p* which specifies the outcome's probability of occurrence. Alternatively, the values and their probabilities can be entered in a table and the ranges for the values and probabilities entered in the function.

### Example 7.3: Discrete Distribution Simulation Modeling Using @RISK

To demonstrate spreadsheet model building using @RISK we will use the same problem as in Example 7.1. Recall that the University Bookstore orders Cosmopolitan magazine each month for $2.00 per copy. They sell it for $4.50 per copy. The publisher will buy back any copies that remain unsold at the end of two months for $0.50 a copy. A review of historic sales of the magazine yielded the following discrete probability distribution:

## TABLE 7.3    Historic Magazine Demand at University Bookstore

| Demand | 150 | 200 | 250 | 300 | 350 |
|---|---|---|---|---|---|
| Probability | 0.25 | 0.25 | 0.30 | 0.15 | 0.05 |

## @RISK Spreadsheet Model Design

Looking at Exhibit 7.9, we can see some distinct differences in the spreadsheet design of a simulation model to use with @RISK and without (Exhibit 7.6.) First, there is no need for creating a row for each iteration of the model when using @RISK. @RISK will create and keep the simulated data in another spreadsheet when the model is run. Second, @RISK collects and calculates summary statistics on the profit so these calculations are not included in the @RISK spreadsheet model. Third, @RISK does not use the VLOOKUP so the demand distribution table does not need the cumulative probability column.

**Cell A13: Simulating Magazine Demand**  Cell A13 contains the formula: '=RISKDiscrete(Demand, Probability)'. The range, Demand, contains the possible values for demand. The range, Probability, contains the probabilities associated with each value. The simulated demand function can be typed directly into the cell or entered through @RISK's Define Distributions menu.

**Using the Define Distributions Menu**  To enter a distribution function using the menu, click on the **Define Distribution** button found leftmost in the @RISK menu bar (Exhibit 7.10) to open a window (Exhibit 7.11) displaying the distributions that @RISK has defined in its library. Selecting Discrete will open another window (Exhibit 7.12) that will allow us to enter the parameters for our discrete distribution. The values for X and their probabilities ($p$) can be entered directly or we can click on the **Excel Cell References** to provide the spreadsheet locations of these values. Cell references or

| | A | B | C | D | E | F |
|---|---|---|---|---|---|---|
| 1 | @Risk Simulation of Magazine Demand at University Bookstore | | | | | |
| 2 | | | | | | |
| 3 | Magazine Data | | | Demand Distribution | | |
| 4 | Unit Cost | $2.00 | | Demand | Probability | |
| 5 | Selling Price | $4.50 | | 150 | 0.25 | |
| 6 | Buyback Price | $0.50 | | 200 | 0.25 | |
| 7 | | | | 250 | 0.30 | |
| 8 | Decision variable | | | 300 | 0.15 | |
| 9 | Order Quantity | 225 | | 350 | 0.05 | |
| 10 | | | | | | |
| 11 | Model | | | | | |
| 12 | Demand | Number Sold | Sales Revenue | Buyback Revenue | Cost | Profit |
| 13 | 250 | 225 | $1,012.50 | $0.00 | $450 | $562.50 |
| 14 | | | | | | |
| 15 | | | | | | |
| 16 | Range Names | Cells | | | | |
| 17 | Buyback_Price | =Model!$B$6 | | | | |
| 18 | Demand | =Model!$D$5:$D$9 | | | | |
| 19 | Order_Quantity | =Model!$B$9 | | | | |
| 20 | Probability | =Model!$E$5:$E$9 | | | | |
| 21 | Profit | =Model!$F$13:$F$13 | | | | |
| 22 | Selling_Price | =Model!$B$5 | | | | |
| 23 | Unit_Cost | =Model!$B$4 | | | | |
| 24 | | | | | | |

◻ EXHIBIT 7.9

Modeling Magazine Demand using @RISK's RISKDiscrete Function

◻ EXHIBIT 7.10

@RISK Model Building Menu

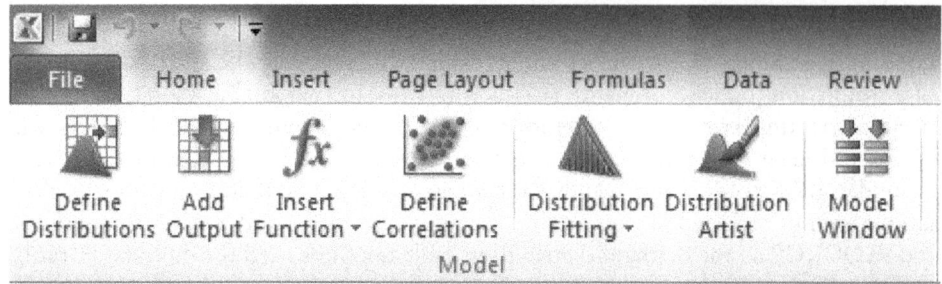

◻ EXHIBIT 7.11

Available Distributions in @Risk

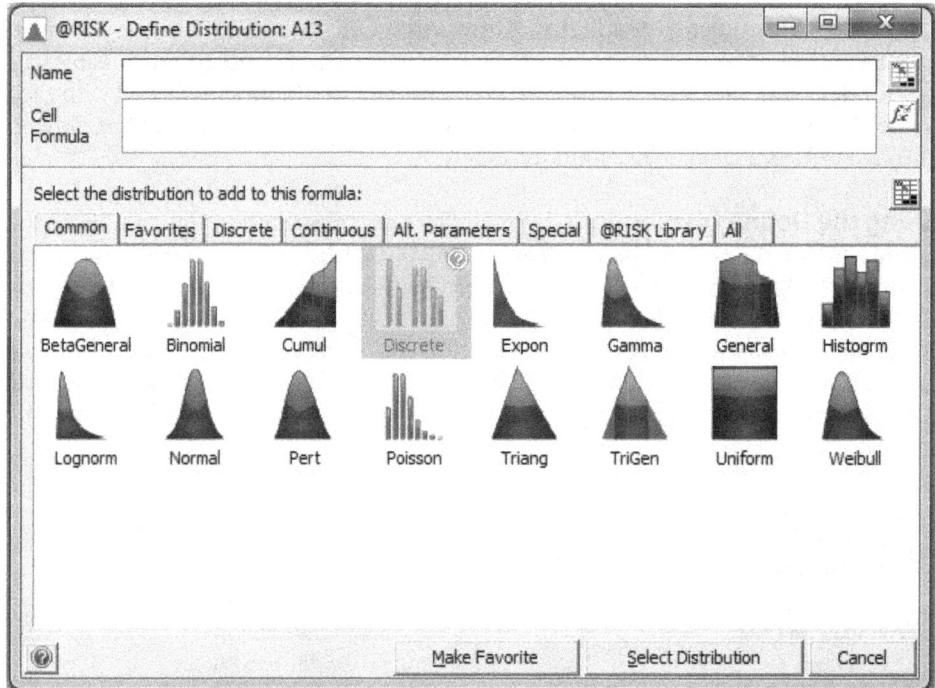

◻ EXHIBIT 7.12

Define Distribution Window

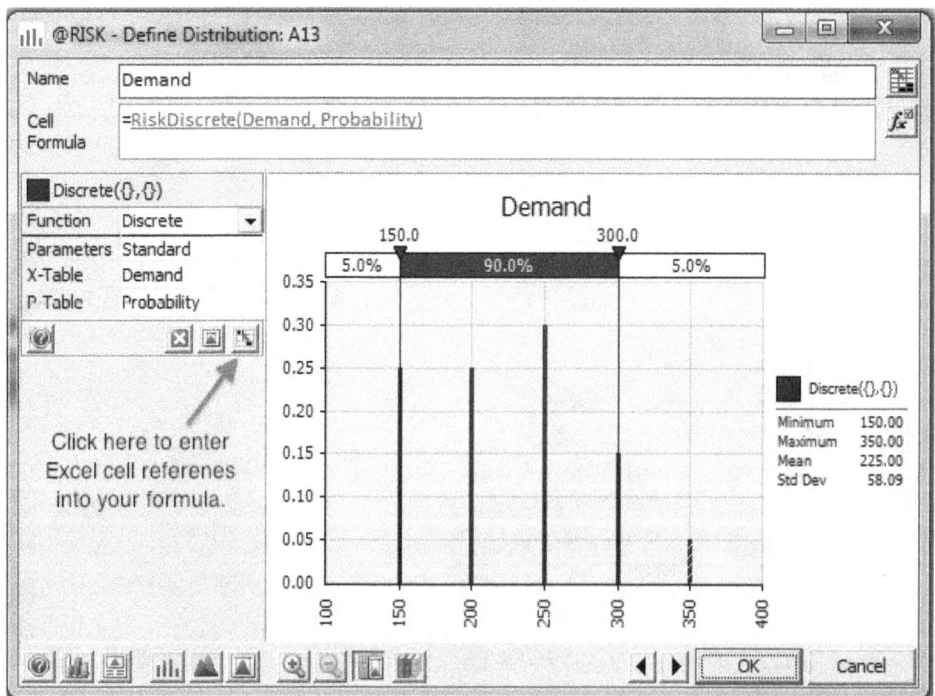

■ EXHIBIT 7.13

Entering a Cell Range or Name to Incorporate Distribution Parameters in the @RISK Function

range names can be used as shown in Exhibit 7.13. A histogram of the distribution and some summary statistics will be displayed. Clicking on the **Okay** button will enter the @RISK formula for this distribution in cell A13.

## The Rest of the @RISK Model

As can be seen in the descriptions of the formula in each of the other cells in row 13, they are essentially identical to the formulas for the Excel model we looked at earlier with the exception of the formula for Profit.

**Cell B13 Number Sold**   Cell B13 contains the formula: '=MIN(A13,Order_Quantity)'. The store cannot sell more magazines than it has ordered so the number sold will be the minimum of the order quantity and the demand.

**Cell C13 Sales Revenue**   Cell C13 contains the formula: '=Selling_Price*B13'. The sales revenue is the selling price multiplied by quantity sold.

**Cell D13 Buyback Revenue**   Cell D13 contains the formula: '=Buyback_Price*(Order_Quantity-B13)'. The bookstore will sell back the unsold magazines (Order_Quantity – B13).

**Cell E13 Cost**   Cell E13 contains the formula: '=Order_Quantity*Unit_Cost'. This cell simply contains the cost of purchasing the magazines from the publisher.

**Cell F13 Profit**   Cell F13 contains the formula: '=RISKOutput() + C13+D13–E13'. The RISKOutput() function identifies the cell as an output cell that we would like the results from tracked and summarized. With the formula, '= C13+D13-E13', in cell F13, select the cell and click on the Add Output button to open the Output Name dialogue box (Exhibit 7.14). The output was named Profit and the OK button was clicked. @RISK will now track the results from this cell.

## Preparing to Run the Simulation

With the model entered into the spreadsheet, we are almost ready to run the simulation. We only need to confirm the simulation settings.

**Simulation Settings**   The **Simulation** segment of the @RISK menu bar (Exhibit 7.15) shows that we are set to do 500 iterations in one simulation. Clicking on **Simulation Settings** button (circled in Exhibit 7.15) opens the Simulation Settings dialogue box (Exhibit 7.16.) The **General** tab shows the basic setting of the simulation.

☐ EXHIBIT 7.14

@RISK Output Name
Dialogue Box

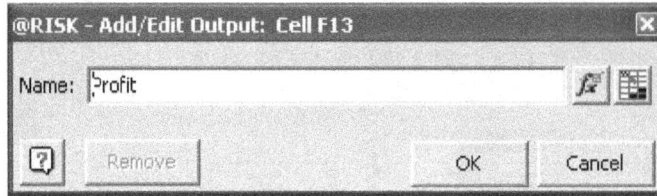

☐ EXHIBIT 7.15

Simulation Menu with
Settings Button Circled

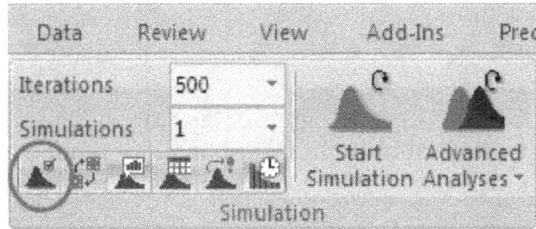

☐ EXHIBIT 7.16

@RISK Simulation Settings

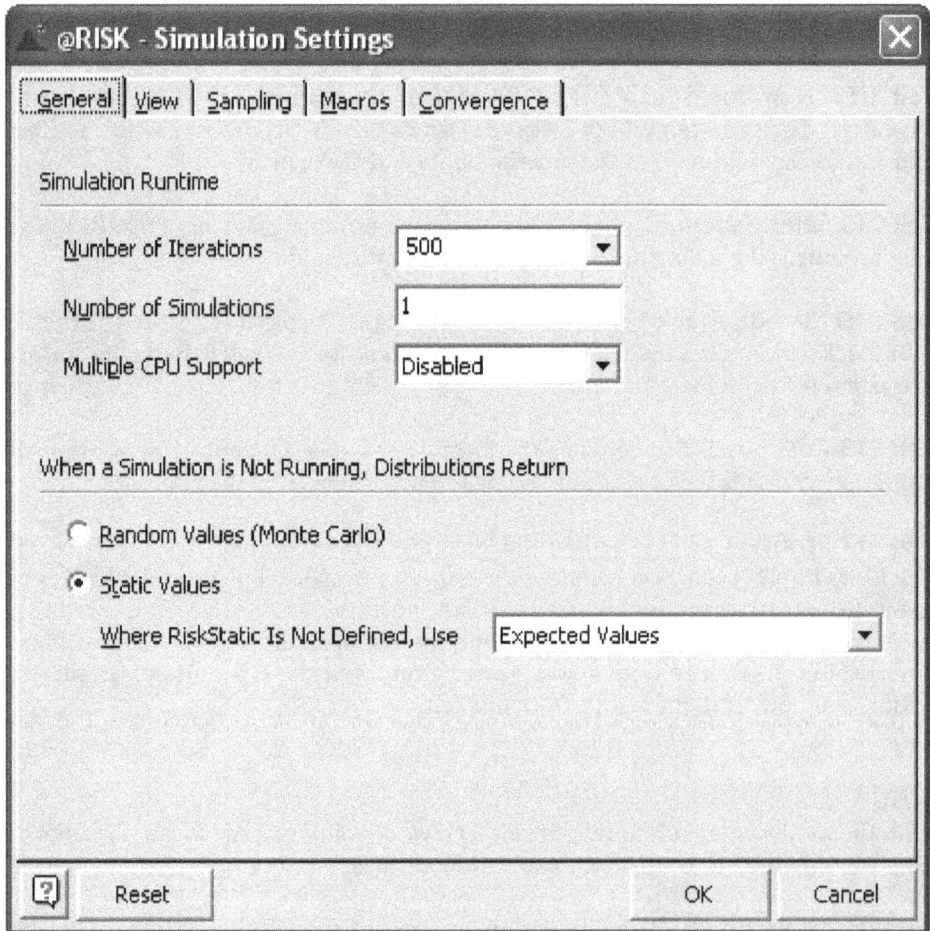

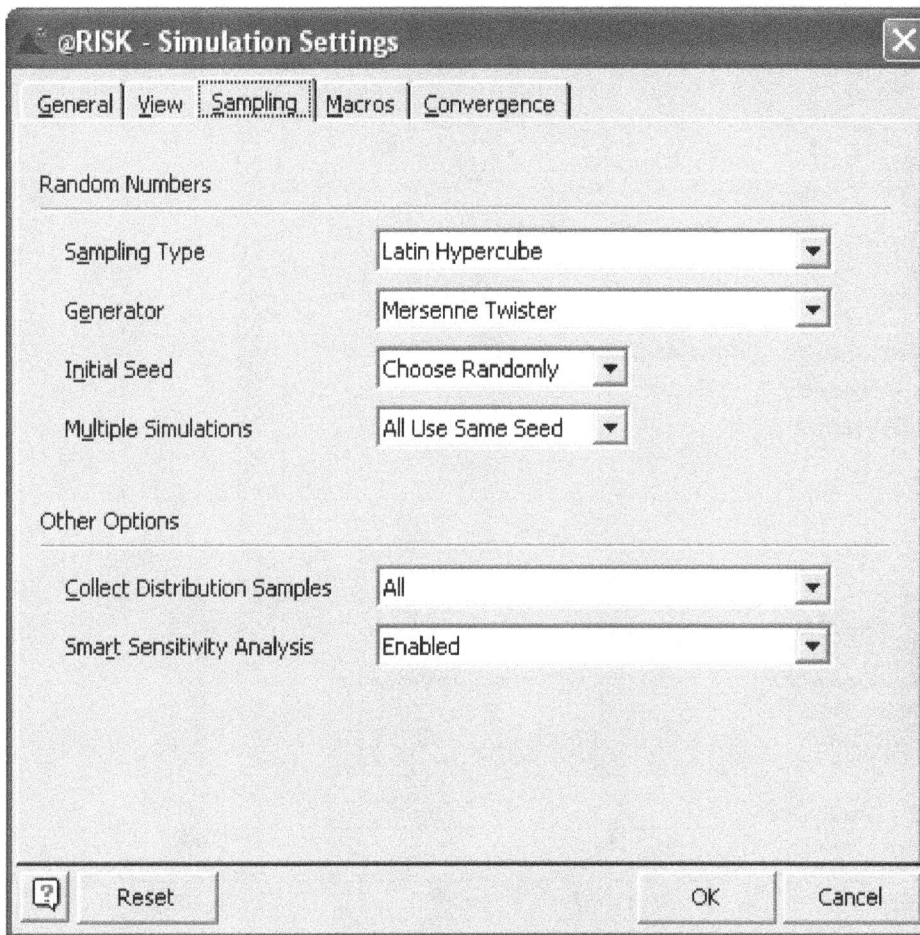

Default Values for Simulation Settings

With **Static Values** selected, the spreadsheet will display the expected values of the simulated distributions in the spreadsheet when the simulation is not running. If you want to check to see if your formulas are working as expected by pressing the F9 key and observing individual scenarios, select Random Values instead. Neither of these settings will have an impact on the values generated by the @RISK simulation.

If we click on the **Sampling** tab we can see the default settings for simulation (Exhibit 7.17.) We will use Latin Hypercube sampling as it has been found to be more efficient than Monte Carlo sampling. We will leave the rest of the settings as shown.

## Running the Simulation

We are now ready to start the simulation. Click the **Start Simulation** button to begin.

## Simulation Output Reports

@RISK gives you different options for examining the results of your simulation. Looking at Exhibit 7.18, we will discuss some of the options displayed there.

**Browse Results**    The leftmost button in the **Results** panel is the **Browse Results** button. It will generate an interactive histogram for any @RISK input or output cell in your spreadsheet model. Exhibit 7.19 shows the histogram for the simulated input distribution in Cell A13. To the right of the histogram will be summary statistics for the

**EXHIBIT 7.18**

@RISK Output Menu Bar

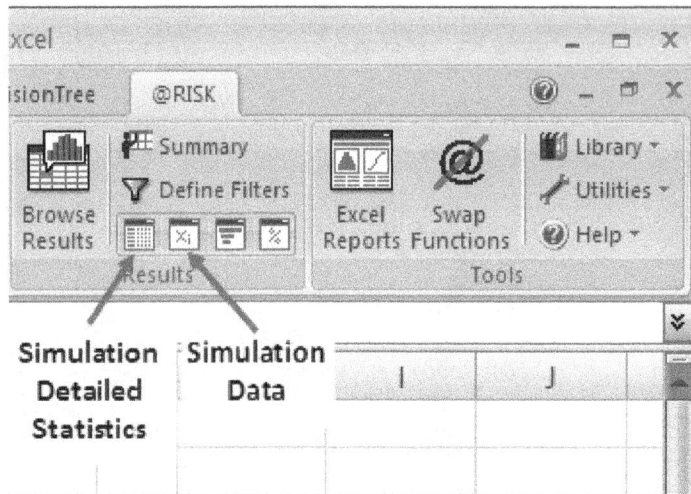

**EXHIBIT 7.19**

Browse Results Screen for the Input Cell A13

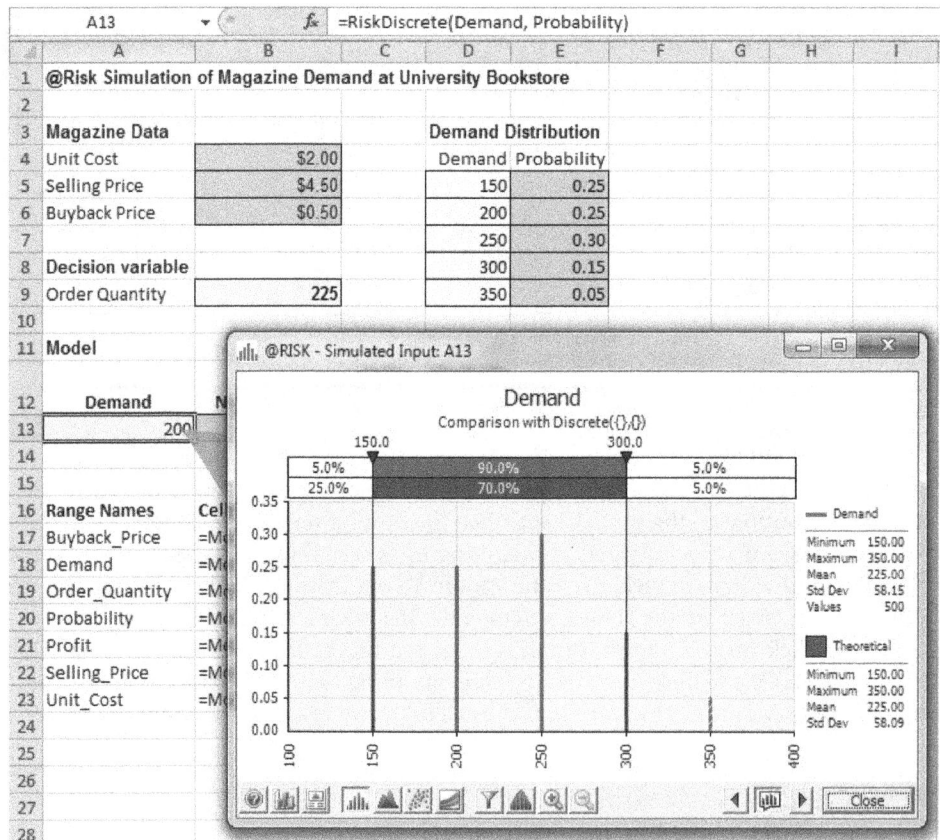

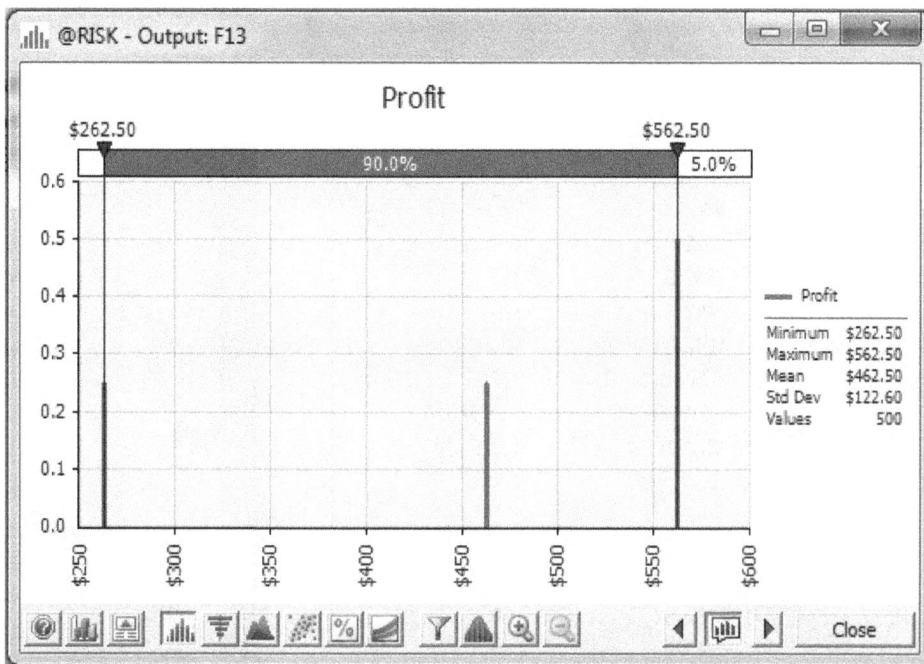

☐ EXHIBIT 7.20

Browse Results Window for
Output Cell F13 (Profit)

distribution. Exhibit 7.20 shows just the window generated by browsing the results of cell F13, Profit. In this exhibit, one of the slider bars has been labeled. These slider bars can be moved using the mouse to display the percent of observations associated with values of the distribution. The slider bars in Exhibit 7.20 indicate that 90% of the observations fall between $262.50 and $562.50.

**Simulated Detailed Statistics**   The **Simulated Detailed Statistics** button is identified in Exhibit 7.18. Clicking on this button will open a window like the one in Exhibit 7.21. In the top part of the window it displays summary statistics including percentiles in 5% increments for both the input and output distributions. The Detailed Statistics window also allows us to request more detailed information about our inputs and outputs in the lower part of the window. Here any target value or percentile can be entered and @RISK calculates the corresponding percentile or value. In Exhibit 7.21, the value of 400 dollars has been entered and the 25th percentile is shown to be associated with it. Just below that, the 33rd percentile has been entered, and a profit of $462.50 is shown to be associated with it.

**Simulation Data**   If you are interested in seeing the data used in the simulation, click on the **Simulation Data** button (Exhibit 7.18) to open a window (Exhibit 7.22) containing all of the simulated values and the outputs associated with them.

# Excel Reports

Clicking on the **Excel Reports** button (Exhibit 7.18) will open a dialogue box (Exhibit 7.23) allowing you to select simulation reports that @RISK will create worksheets in an Excel workbook. Each of the options selected in Exhibit 7.23 will be discussed in this section.

EXHIBIT 7.21

Detailed Statistics Window

@RISK - Detailed Statistics

| Name | Profit | Demand |
|---|---|---|
| Description | Output | RiskDiscrete(D5:D.. |
| Cell | Model!F13 | Model!A13 |
| Minimum | 262.5 | 150 |
| Maximum | 562.5 | 350 |
| Mean | 462.5 | 225 |
| Std Deviation | 122.5971 | 58.15293 |
| Variance | 15030.06 | 3381.763 |
| Skewness | -0.8189555 | 0.2877516 |
| Kurtosis | 2.002024 | 2.205701 |
| Errors | 0 | 0 |
| Mode | 562.5 | 250 |
| 5% Perc | 262.5 | 150 |
| 10% Perc | 262.5 | 150 |
| 15% Perc | 262.5 | 150 |
| 20% Perc | 262.5 | 150 |
| 25% Perc | 262.5 | 150 |
| 30% Perc | 462.5 | 200 |
| 35% Perc | 462.5 | 200 |
| 40% Perc | 462.5 | 200 |
| 45% Perc | 462.5 | 200 |
| 50% Perc | 462.5 | 200 |
| 55% Perc | 562.5 | 250 |
| 60% Perc | 562.5 | 250 |
| 65% Perc | 562.5 | 250 |
| 70% Perc | 562.5 | 250 |
| 75% Perc | 562.5 | 250 |
| 80% Perc | 562.5 | 250 |
| 85% Perc | 562.5 | 300 |
| 90% Perc | 562.5 | 300 |
| 95% Perc | 562.5 | 300 |
| Filter Minimum | | |
| Filter Maximum | | |
| Filter Type | | |
| # Values Filtered | 0 | 0 |
| Target #1 (Value) | | |
| Target #1 (Perc%) | | |
| Target #2 (Value) | 400 | |
| Target #2 (Perc%) | 25% | |
| Target #3 (Value) | 462.5 | |
| Target #3 (Perc%) | 33% | |
| Target #4 (Value) | | |

Close

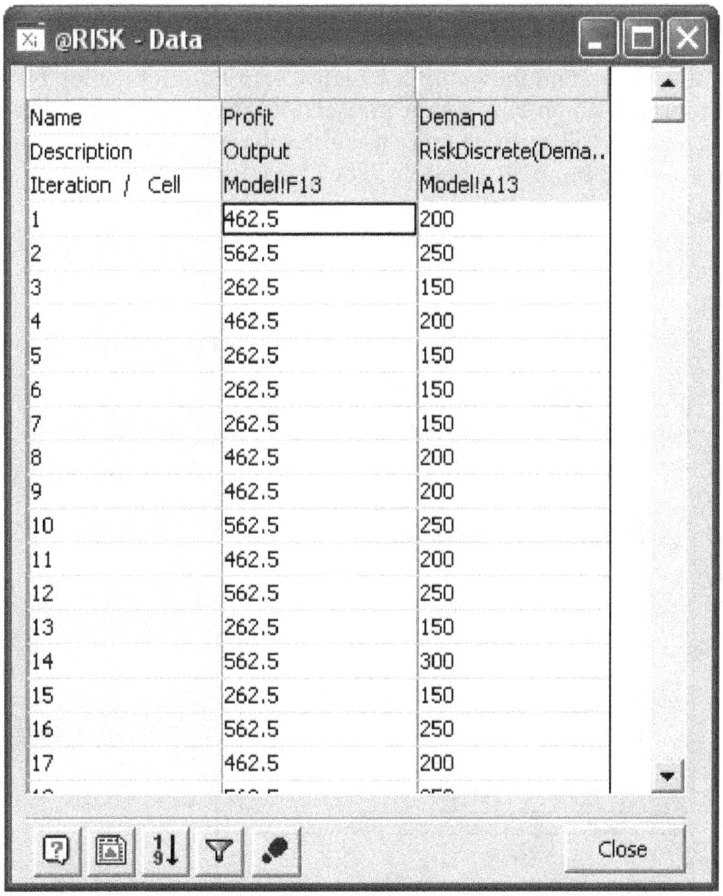

EXHIBIT 7.22

Simulation Data

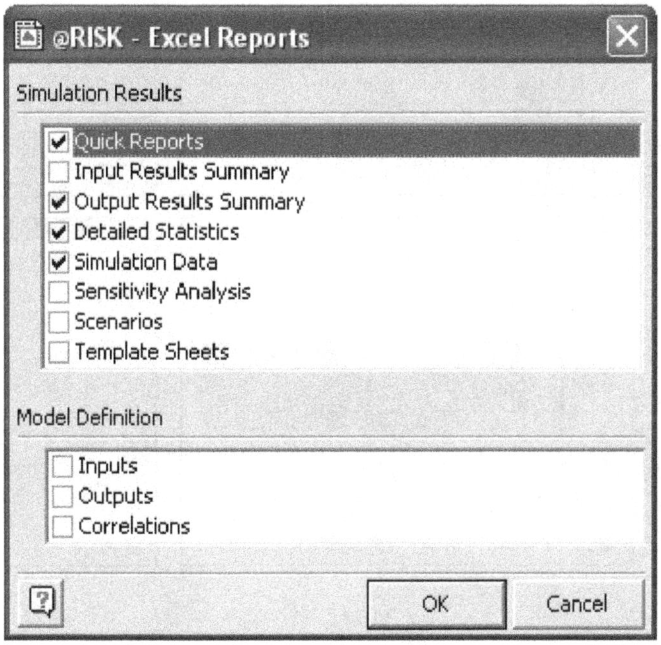

EXHIBIT 7.23

Excel Reports Dialogue Box

**Quick Reports** (Exhibit 7.24)  The Quick Reports option in @RISK generates a worksheet containing three graphs. The first is a histogram of the distribution of the profit. The second shows the cumulative distribution function of the profit. The third is a tornado graph showing the impact of the @RISK inputs on the output, Profit. This third graph will generate more useful results with a more complex model containing two or more input distributions. The Quick Report also provides information regarding the simulation settings and summary statistics.

☐ EXHIBIT 7.24

Excel Quick Reports Spreadsheet

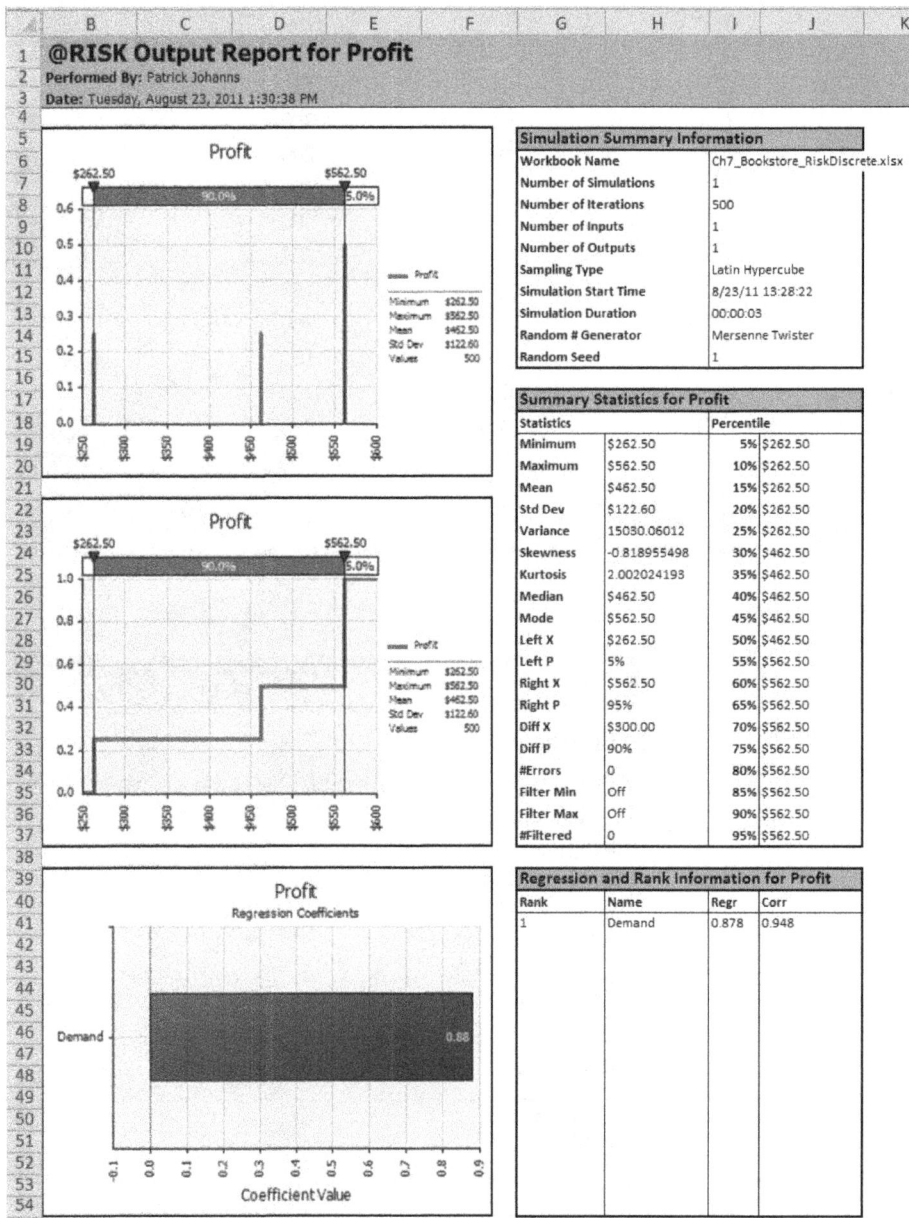

**@RISK Output Report for Profit**
Performed By: Patrick Johanns
Date: Tuesday, August 23, 2011 1:30:38 PM

| Simulation Summary Information | |
| --- | --- |
| Workbook Name | Ch7_Bookstore_RiskDiscrete.xlsx |
| Number of Simulations | 1 |
| Number of Iterations | 500 |
| Number of Inputs | 1 |
| Number of Outputs | 1 |
| Sampling Type | Latin Hypercube |
| Simulation Start Time | 8/23/11 13:28:22 |
| Simulation Duration | 00:00:03 |
| Random # Generator | Mersenne Twister |
| Random Seed | 1 |

| Summary Statistics for Profit | | | |
| --- | --- | --- | --- |
| Statistics | | Percentile | |
| Minimum | $262.50 | 5% | $262.50 |
| Maximum | $562.50 | 10% | $262.50 |
| Mean | $462.50 | 15% | $262.50 |
| Std Dev | $122.60 | 20% | $262.50 |
| Variance | 15030.06012 | 25% | $262.50 |
| Skewness | -0.818955498 | 30% | $462.50 |
| Kurtosis | 2.002024193 | 35% | $462.50 |
| Median | $462.50 | 40% | $462.50 |
| Mode | $562.50 | 45% | $462.50 |
| Left X | $262.50 | 50% | $462.50 |
| Left P | 5% | 55% | $562.50 |
| Right X | $562.50 | 60% | $562.50 |
| Right P | 95% | 65% | $562.50 |
| Diff X | $300.00 | 70% | $562.50 |
| Diff P | 90% | 75% | $562.50 |
| #Errors | 0 | 80% | $562.50 |
| Filter Min | Off | 85% | $562.50 |
| Filter Max | Off | 90% | $562.50 |
| #Filtered | 0 | 95% | $562.50 |

| Regression and Rank Information for Profit | | | |
| --- | --- | --- | --- |
| Rank | Name | Regr | Corr |
| 1 | Demand | 0.878 | 0.948 |

| | Name | Cel | Graph | Min | Mean | Max | 5% | 95% | Errors |
|---|---|---|---|---|---|---|---|---|---|
| | Profit | F13 | 250 ▼ 600 ▼ | $262.50 | $462.50 | $562.50 | $262.50 | $562.50 | 0 |

@RISK Output Results
Performed By: Patrick Johanns
Date: Tuesday, August 23, 2011 2:49:20 PM

▦ EXHIBIT 7.25

Excel Output Results
Summary

**Output Results Summary** (Exhibit 7.25)  This report provides the user with the summary statistics of output variables for the simulation.

**Detailed Statistics** (Exhibit 7.26)  The Detailed Statistics report provides more extensive information regarding the distribution of the input and output variables. It looks like the Detailed Statistics (Exhibit 7.21) within @RISK but is not interactive. Even though it displays the target value labels at the bottom of the report, you cannot type in a value and find out the corresponding percentile or vice versa.

## Multiple Simulations using RiskSimTable

@RISK has a built-in function called RiskSimTable that allows us to test a variety of different decision variable values using the same simulated demand. To use this function we need to modify the spreadsheet model as follows (See Exhibit 7.27):

- The order alternatives are listed in column G.
- In Cell B9, enter the formula: '=RiskSimTable(G4:G9)'. Note: The formula: '=RiskSimTable(200, 225, 250, 275, 300, 325)' would work also.

The simulation settings need to be changed also. Since there are six alternatives we want to test, enter 6 in the simulations setting as shown in Exhibit 7.27. @RISK will run 6 simulations of 1000 each using the same random demands for each of our alternate order quantities when we start the simulation. The results from these simulations can be seen in Exhibit 7.28. The results indicate that an order of 250 will have the highest average profit. The RiskSimTable is a valuable function to help discover the best values for your decision variables.

☐ EXHIBIT 7.26

Excel Detailed Statistics
Report

| | B | C | D | E | F |
|---|---|---|---|---|---|
| 1 | **@RISK Detailed Statistics** | | | | |
| 2 | **Performed By:** Patrick Johanns | | | | |
| 3 | **Date:** Thursday, August 13, 2009 7:24:35 AM | | | | |
| 4 | | | | | |
| 5 | | | | | |
| 6 | Name | Profit | Demand | | |
| 7 | Description | Output | RiskDiscrete(Demand, Probability) | | |
| 8 | Cell | Model!F13 | Model!A13 | | |
| 9 | Minimum | $262.50 | 150 | | |
| 10 | Maximum | $562.50 | 350 | | |
| 11 | Mean | $462.50 | 225 | | |
| 12 | Std Deviation | $122.60 | 58.15293 | | |
| 13 | Variance | 15030.06 | 3381.763 | | |
| 14 | Skewness | -0.8189555 | 0.2877516 | | |
| 15 | Kurtosis | 2.002024 | 2.205701 | | |
| 16 | Errors | 0 | 0 | | |
| 17 | Mode | $562.50 | 250 | | |
| 18 | 5% Perc | $262.50 | 150 | | |
| 19 | 10% Perc | $262.50 | 150 | | |
| 20 | 15% Perc | $262.50 | 150 | | |
| 21 | 20% Perc | $262.50 | 150 | | |
| 22 | 25% Perc | $262.50 | 150 | | |
| 23 | 30% Perc | $462.50 | 200 | | |
| 24 | 35% Perc | $462.50 | 200 | | |
| 25 | 40% Perc | $462.50 | 200 | | |
| 26 | 45% Perc | $462.50 | 200 | | |
| 27 | 50% Perc | $462.50 | 200 | | |
| 28 | 55% Perc | $562.50 | 250 | | |
| 29 | 60% Perc | $562.50 | 250 | | |
| 30 | 65% Perc | $562.50 | 250 | | |
| 31 | 70% Perc | $562.50 | 250 | | |
| 32 | 75% Perc | $562.50 | 250 | | |
| 33 | 80% Perc | $562.50 | 250 | | |
| 34 | 85% Perc | $562.50 | 300 | | |
| 35 | 90% Perc | $562.50 | 300 | | |
| 36 | 95% Perc | $562.50 | 300 | | |
| 37 | Filter Minimum | | | | |
| 38 | Filter Maximum | | | | |
| 39 | Filter Type | | | | |
| 40 | # Values Filtered | 0 | 0 | | |
| 41 | Target #1 (Value) | | | | |
| 42 | Target #1 (Perc%) | | | | |
| 43 | Target #2 (Value) | | | | |
| 44 | Target #2 (Perc%) | | | | |

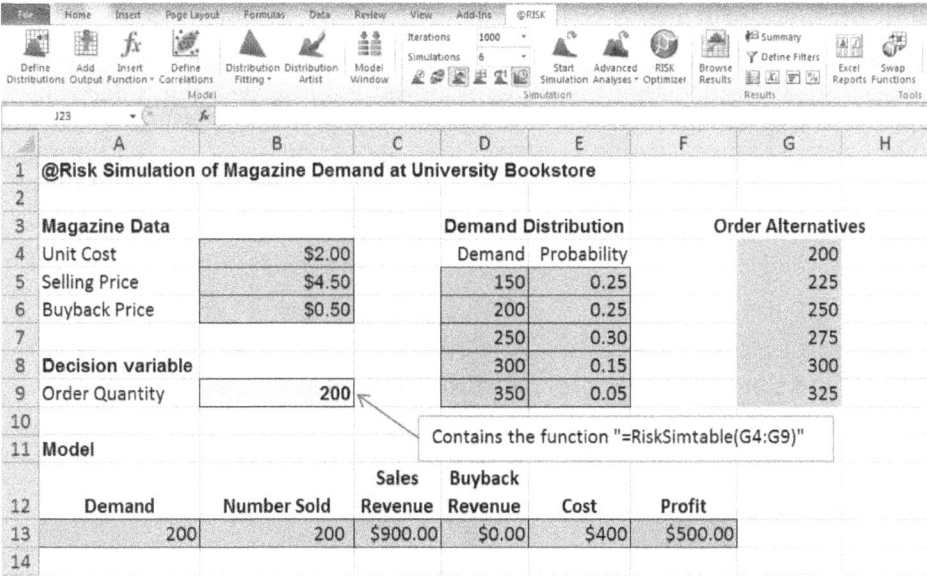

☐ **EXHIBIT 7.27**

**@RISK Spreadsheet Model with RiskSimTable Added**
The number of simulation is set at 6 to match the number of order alternatives.

☐ **EXHIBIT 7.28**

Summary Statistic Output for RiskSimTable. It can be seen that the third simulation (Order 250) yielded the highest mean profit.

| Name | Cell | Sim# | Graph | Min | Mean | Max | 5% | 95% | Errors |
|---|---|---|---|---|---|---|---|---|---|
| Profit | F13 | 1 | | $300.00 | $450.00 | $500.00 | $300.00 | $500.00 | 0 |
| Profit | F13 | 2 | | $262.50 | $462.50 | $562.50 | $262.50 | $562.50 | 0 |
| Profit | F13 | 3 | | $225.00 | $475.00 | $625.00 | $225.00 | $625.00 | 0 |
| Profit | F13 | 4 | | $187.50 | $457.50 | $687.50 | $187.50 | $687.50 | 0 |
| Profit | F13 | 5 | | $150.00 | $440.00 | $750.00 | $150.00 | $750.00 | 0 |
| Profit | F13 | 6 | | $112.50 | $407.50 | $812.50 | $112.50 | $712.50 | 0 |

## @RISK Simulation of a Normal Distribution

A normal distribution can be simulated in @RISK using the formula: '=RiskNormal(Mean,StDev)' where the mean and standard deviation values can be entered directly into the function or referenced to the cell address of these values. The Define Distribution window can also be used. Exhibit 7.29 shows a normal distribution with a mean of 240 and a standard deviation of 40 being entered in Cell A13.

■ EXHIBIT 7.29

A Normal Distribution with Mean of 240 and a Standard Deviation of 40 Being Entered in the Define Distribution Window

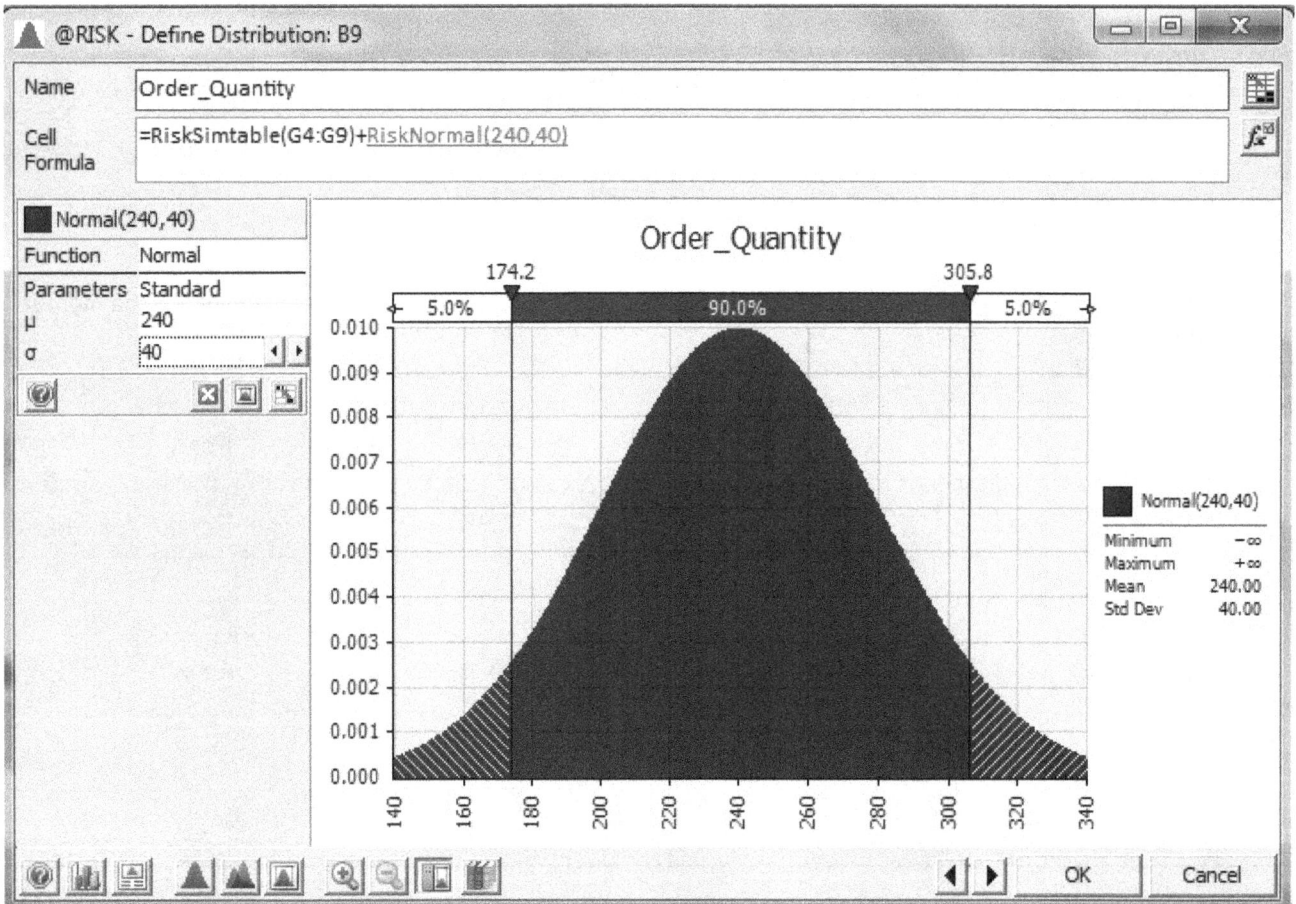

## @RISK Simulation of a Binomial Distribution

Generating a binomial distribution for simulation modeling is a simple process in @RISK. The function RiskBinomial has the following syntax: =RiskBinomial (Trials,probability_s) where Trials is the sample size, n, and probability_s is the probability of success. To create a binomial distribution for samples of 20 with a 10% chance of success, use the formula: '=RiskBinomial(20,0.10) or the Define Distribution window as shown in Exhibit 7.30.

## @RISK Simulation of a Triangular Distribution

The triangular distribution is a continuous distribution sometimes used in simulation. It requires three parameters to define: the minimum, the maximum, and the most likely values. These three values are used for a triangular-shaped distribution for the selection of simulated values. It has appeal in its simplicity to define. It has the syntax: RiskTriang(Minimum_Value, Most_Likely_Value, Maximum_Value). To define a triangular distribution with a minimum of 150, most likely value of 225, and a maximum

◻ EXHIBIT 7.30

Defining Binomial Distributions in @RISK

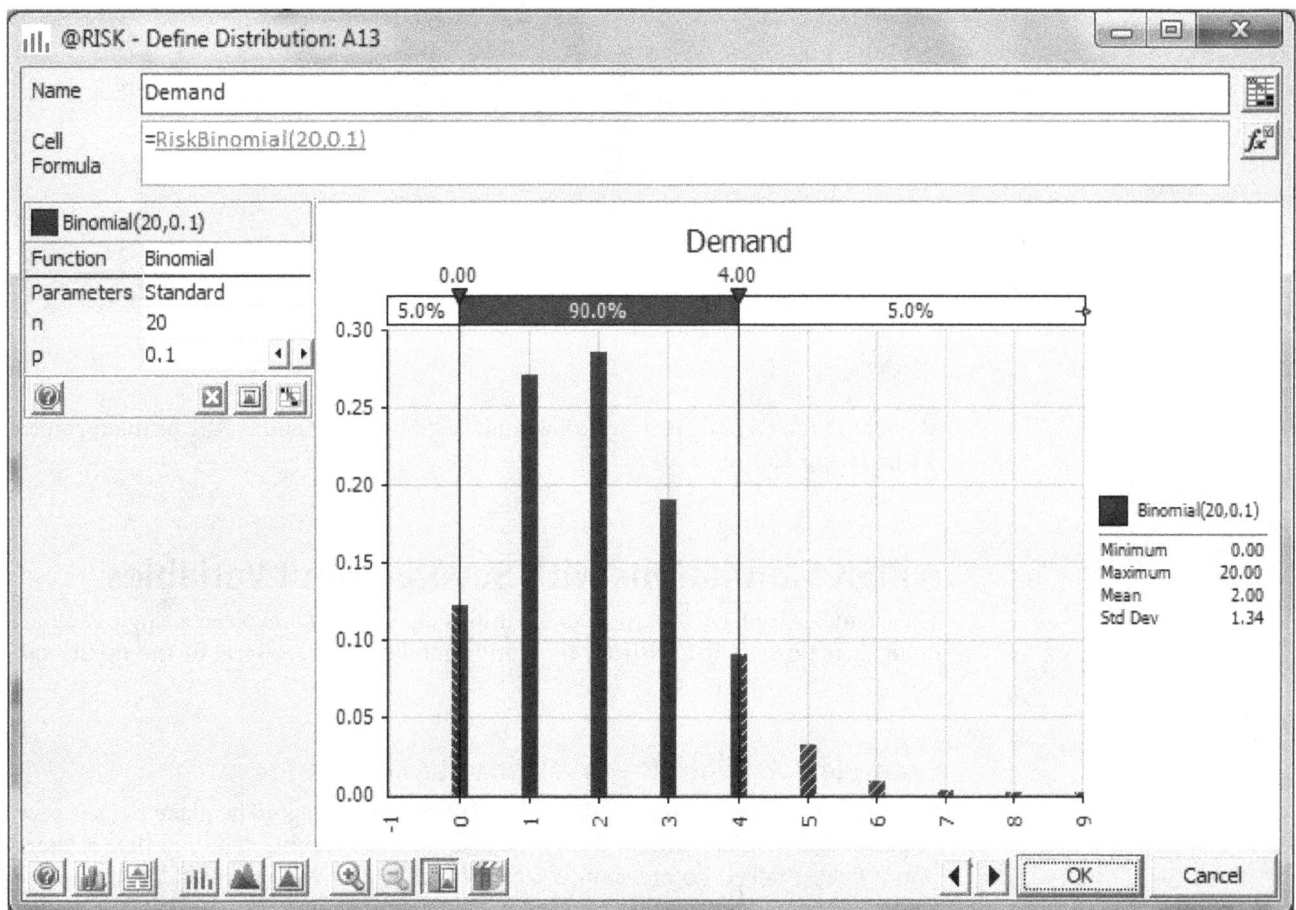

☐ EXHIBIT 7.31

Defining a Triangular Distribution

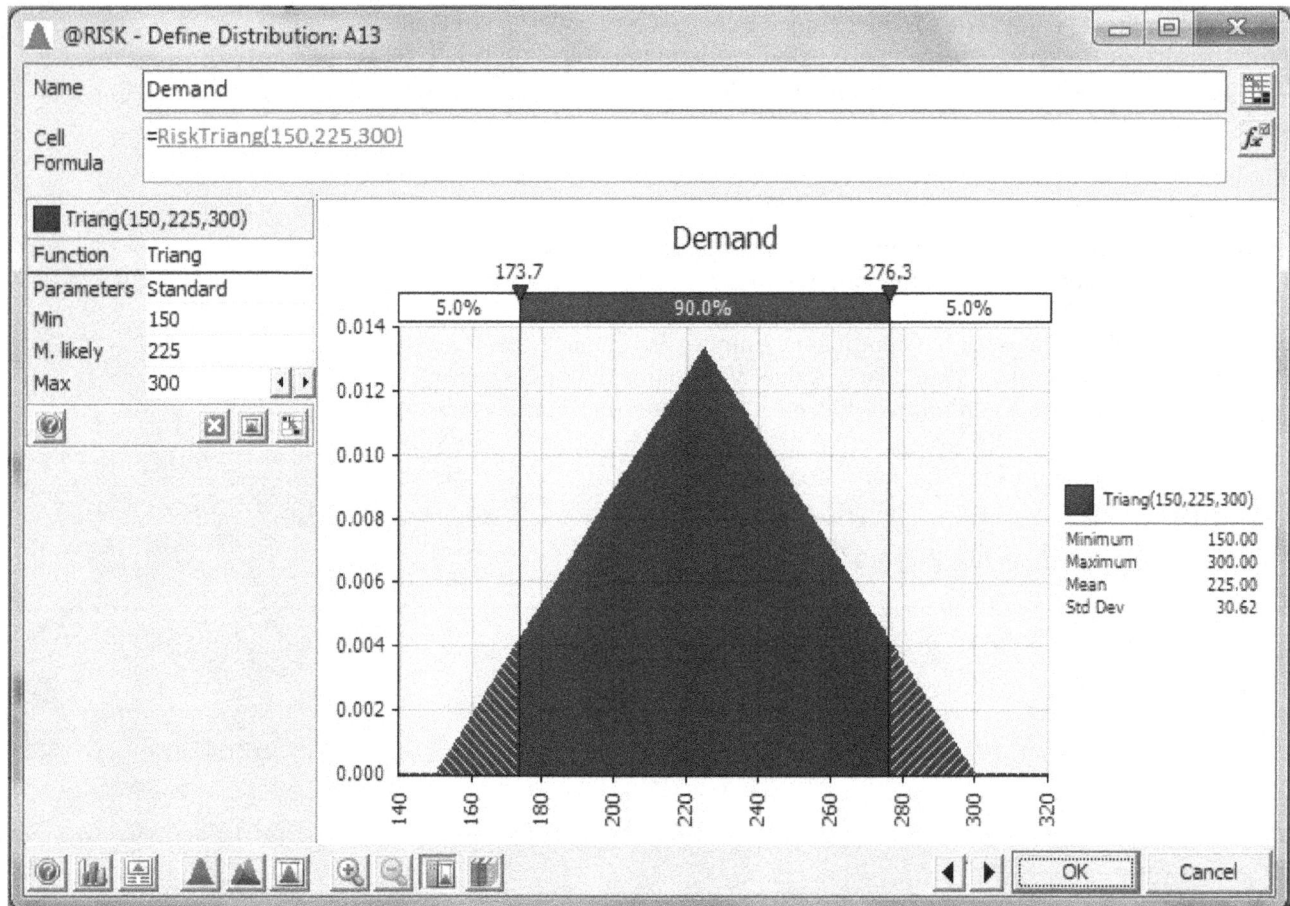

of 350, use the Define Distribution window as shown in Exhibit 7.31 or the formula: '=RiskTriang(150,225,350)'.

## @RISK Simulations with Several Input Variables

The examples we have looked at so far in this chapter have involved a single random input. It is possible to construct simulation models where several of the inputs can vary.

### Example 7.4: Flight Reservations at Midwest Air

Midwest Air runs a commuter flight from Dayton to Chicago. The plane has seats for 21 passengers. It sells nonrefundable tickets for $99 per seat but typically 10% of those who purchase tickets do not show up for the flight. Midwest Air would like to explore the use of an overbooking policy as a method of increasing revenue. While booking extra seats with the anticipation that some tickets would not show up would increase the ticket revenue, it would cause a problem when more ticketed passengers showed up for a flight than there were seats. When a passenger gets bumped from a flight, the airline needs to book them on another flight in addition to providing other compensation that ranges from meals, hotel rooms, and monetary compensation. Midwest has calculated the cost of a bumped passenger to be a normal distribution with a mean of $225 and a standard deviation of $50. A review of historic data indicates that a triangular distribution with a minimum of 15, a most likely value of 23, and a maximum value of 27 is a good fit for the number of seats requested on a flight.

In this simulation model we have three inputs with uncertain distributions: a triangular distribution for seats requested, a binomial distribution for the number of ticketed passengers that show up for a flight, and a normal distribution for the cost of a bumped passenger. The simulation spreadsheet (Exhibit 7.32) has been prepared to run in @RISK.

□ EXHIBIT 7.32

Midwest Air Reservation Model

| | C17 | | | $f_x$ | =RiskSimtable(E4:E9) | | | |
|---|---|---|---|---|---|---|---|---|
| | A | B | C | D | E | F | G | H |
| 1 | **Flight Reservation Policy at Midwest Air** | | | | | | | |
| 2 | | | | | | | | |
| 3 | Seats Available | | 21 | | Reservation Alternatives | | | |
| 4 | Ticket Price | | $99 | | 21 | | | |
| 5 | | | | | 22 | | | |
| 6 | Number of Requested Seats | | | | 23 | | | |
| 7 | Minimum | | 15 | | 24 | | | |
| 8 | Most likely | | 23 | | 25 | | | |
| 9 | Maximum | | 27 | | 26 | | | |
| 10 | | | | | | | | |
| 11 | Cost of Bumping (Per Seat) | | | | | | | |
| 12 | Mean | | $225 | | | | | |
| 13 | Std Dev | | $50 | | | | | |
| 14 | | | | | | | | |
| 15 | Probability of No-Show | | 10% | | | | | |
| 16 | | | | | | | | |
| 17 | Max Reservations | | 21 | | | | | |
| 18 | | | | | | | | |
| 19 | Seats Requested | Tickets Sold | Ticket Revenue | Passengers that Show for Flight | Number Bumped | Cost per Bumped Passenger | Total Cost of Bumping | Net Profit |
| 20 | 22 | 21 | $2,079 | 19 | 0 | $ 225.00 | $ - | $2,079.00 |
| 21 | | | | | | | | |

Reservation Model | Summary Report | Output

**TABLE 7.4    Cell Formulas for Exhibit 7.32**

| CELL | DESCRIPTION | FORMULA |
|------|-------------|---------|
| C17 | Decision Variable | =RiskSimtable(E4:E9) |
| A20 | Seats Requested (rounded to integer) | =ROUND (RiskTriang(C7, C8, C9),0) |
| B20 | Tickets Sold | =MIN(A20,C17) |
| C20 | Ticket Revenue | =B20*C4 |
| D20 | Passengers that Show for Flight | =RiskBinomial(B20, 1–C15) |
| E20 | Number Bumped | =MAX(0,D20–C3) |
| F20 | Cost of Bumped Passenger | =RiskNormal(C12,C13) |
| G20 | Total Cost of Bumping for a Flight | =RiskOutput() + E20*F20 |
| H20 | Net Profit | =RiskOutput() + C20–G20 |

## Results

The summary statistics from running 1,000 iterations for each value for the number of reservations to take are shown in Exhibit 7.33. The highest net profit per flight results from a policy of booking a maximum of 23 seats for a flight. A policy of selling two extra seats per flight will increase the profit per flight from $2,005.15 to $2,062.98.

◻ EXHIBIT 7.33

Midwest Air Reservation Summary Statistics

| Name | Cell | Sim# | Graph | Min | Mean | Max | 5% | 95% | Errors |
|---|---|---|---|---|---|---|---|---|---|
| Total Cost of Bumping | G20 | 1 | | 0 | 0 | 0 | 0 | 0 | 0 |
| Total Cost of Bumping | G20 | 2 | | 0 | 11.5073 | 346.857 | 0 | 122.413 | 0 |
| Total Cost of Bumping | G20 | 3 | | 0 | 38.5964 | 693.713 | 0 | 257.176 | 0 |
| Total Cost of Bumping | G20 | 4 | | 0 | 71.2621 | 957.396 | 0 | 446.379 | 0 |
| Total Cost of Bumping | G20 | 5 | | 0 | 92.2735 | 1276.53 | 0 | 561.927 | 0 |
| Total Cost of Bumping | G20 | 6 | | 0 | 100.898 | 1276.53 | 0 | 605.207 | 0 |
| Net Profit | H20 | 1 | | 1485 | 2005.15 | 2079 | 1683 | 2079 | 0 |
| Net Profit | H20 | 2 | | 1485 | 2049.08 | 2178 | 1683 | 2178 | 0 |
| Net Profit | H20 | 3 | | 1485 | 2062.98 | 2277 | 1683 | 2277 | 0 |
| Net Profit | H20 | 4 | | 1418.6 | 2055.56 | 2376 | 1683 | 2376 | 0 |
| Net Profit | H20 | 5 | | 1198.47 | 2047.51 | 2475 | 1683 | 2376 | 0 |
| Net Profit | H20 | 6 | | 1198.47 | 2043.54 | 2574 | 1683 | 2376 | 0 |

# Summary

Simulation modeling is a powerful tool to aid in managerial decisions that is growing in popularity as the software increases in capability. It allows the analyst to build the uncertainty inherent to systems into the models and consider a wide range of scenarios. These scenarios allow for the consideration of the distribution of outcomes instead of the point estimates generated by optimization modeling.

# Key Terms

**Data Table** A table used in Excel to evaluate different values for the decision variable.
**Deterministic Model** In a deterministic model, it is assumed that all input values are known.

## EXERCISES

1. Jerry is the owner of CarParts Shop and plans to sell a new battery this year. Based on his experience, Jerry knew the return rate of this new battery is binomially distributed with a probability of a return of 12%. The number of batteries he plans to order in each month is shown in the below table. Please help Jerry to estimate how many units of batteries will be returned using simulation modeling. (Hint: Use Excel function, *CRITBINOM*.)

| MONTH | # OF ORDER |
|---|---|
| January | 120 |
| February | 136 |
| March | 98 |
| April | 80 |
| May | 70 |
| June | 65 |
| July | 100 |
| August | 110 |
| September | 72 |
| October | 104 |
| November | 125 |
| December | 148 |

Simulate with 100 iterations the number of batteries returned from each month's order. What is the mean and standard deviation for the total number of batteries ordered for the year. Submit your Excel spreadsheet model showing your simulation. Submit also the formulas used in your spreadsheet. Do not print the entire spreadsheet. One page showing simulation results and one showing the formulas should be submitted.

What is the probability that the returns will be greater than 150 in a year?

2. Bob and Jenny are graduating from Krannert in May and plan to get married in June. One of the challenges facing them is to figure out how many meals to have prepared for the reception. They are inviting 200 people but they have read that not everyone will attend. The best estimate they have is that the number that will attend is binomial distribuition with an N of 200 and p of 0.8. Each meal they reserve for the reception costs them $18. If the reception hall staff has to set up extra tables and serve additional meals that were not planned for, the cost per additional meal is $25. Try values of 140, 145, 150, 155, 160, 165, 170, 175, and 180.

a. Using only Excel functions, use simulation with a minimum of 500 trials to determine the best number of reservations to make.

b. Using @RISK, simulate the number that come to the wedding to determine the best number of reservations to make.

3. The Hata Game Co. orders video games for $20 per copy. They sell it for $39.99 per copy. The supplier will buy back any copies that remain unsold at the end of next year for $4 a copy. A review of historic sales of the series game yielded a normal distribution with a mean of 200 and a standard deviation of 30:

The Hata Game Co. would like to maximize its profit. How many should it order? (*Please simulate and solve the problem in 1,000 iterations in Excel only.*) The alternative order you can consider is listed in the following table:

| Alternatives |
|:---:|
| 150 |
| 175 |
| 200 |
| 225 |
| 250 |
| 275 |

4. Use @Risk to solve Problem 5 with 1000 iterations for 6 alternative orders.

   a. Set up a model under @Risk.

   b. Show the @RISK Output Results.

   c. Show the @RISK Detailed Statistics.

5. KSouth Airline opened a new line from Chicago to Las Vegas and bought a new plane which can offer at most 200 seats. According to the historical data from the last 5 years, some customers do not show up and miss the flight. The number of no-show customers can be considered as a normal distribution with a mean of 3 and a standard deviation of 1.2. KSouth plans to sell more than 200 tickets for $360 per ticket in order to receive more profit. As an example, KSouth may sell 203 tickets per flight and will refund the no-show customers $320. If 201 customers show up for the same flight, KSouth has to rearrange one customer to the other airlines and compensate this customer, which will cost KSouth $480 for one excess customer. The fixed operations cost is $20,000 per flight. KSouth would like to maximize its profit.

a. Determine the best number of reservations to take using Excel functions only. (1000 iterations)

b. Determine the best number of reservations to take using an @RISK model.

c. What is the probability that the profit will exceed $50,000?

6. Kevin is a college junior, majoring in computer science at Purdue University. He made an app, BigTenWinner, and he is selling it for $3 per copy. Kevin finds that 80% of users can successfully open his game after they install it, so he provides two solutions for those users who fail to open the game: 1) refund all the money, or 2) give one alternative game he developed and refund $2. 70% of the users will select the first option and 30% of the users will select the second option. The number of monthly downloads is described as a normal distribution with a mean of 400 and a standard deviation of 50.

a. Set up an @Risk simulation model for monthly downloads and returns and his profit for the year. (Hint: Use a binomial distribution to determine the number who can open the game and the number that seek a refund.)

7. Azzalini and Bowman (1990) analyzed the data of the waiting time (in minutes) of consecutive eruptions of the Old Faithful geyser in Yellowstone National Park. They found that the waiting times can be categorized into two groups in historical data.

- In group 1, the waiting time is normally distributed with mean 54 minutes and standard deviation 2.95.

- In group 2, the waiting time is normally distributed with mean 80 minutes and standard deviation 7.5.

Suppose that there is a 30% chance that the waiting time is from group 1. They want to simulate the waiting time.

a. Use Excel functions only to simulate the waiting time. Your simulations should contain 500 iterations. You need only to turn in one page showing your model and one page displaying the formulas in your model.

b. What is the average waiting time in your simulation?

c. What is the standard deviation of waiting time in your simulation?

d. What is the probability that a person would have to wait more than 1 hour between eruptions?

e. What is the median wait?

8. EasyRent just started its DVD rental business. It charges $3 for overnight rental of new movies and guarantees that every new DVD they have is never out of stock. If a customer is not able to rent a DVD, EasyRent offers three free rentals as compensation. The estimated cost of this compensation is $8. Recently, a new action movie is just about to be launched on DVD. According to historical data about action movies, the daily demand during the first month of release is a normal distribution with mean 125 and standard deviation 15. EasyRent has to pay $60 per copy of DVD for right to rent out the movie. Considering the stock levels of 120, 130, 140, 150, 160, and 170 use simulation approach to decide which stock level EasyRent should have in order to maximize its profit during the first month (30 days).

a. Create an @RISK model for the first month of rentals to simulate net monthly income for the DVD for each stock level.

b. How many copies of the DVD should they stock?

c. Show the @Risk Output Results for the month.

d. Show the @ Risk Detailed Statistics for the month.

e. With a stock level of 130 DVDs, what is probability that they will have a profit of less than $100?

# CHAPTER 8

# Project Management

- Understand how the management of projects differs from the ongoing activities of the organization.
- Apply the Critical Path Method (CPM) to determine the project completion time and the critical activities for its completion.
- Evaluate the likelihood of meeting a deadline using the Program Review and Evaluation Technique (PERT).
- Determine the task starting times and the allocation of additional resources to minimize the cost of meeting a short deadline (Project Crashing).

## Introduction

The activities of a company can generally be thought of as either ongoing functions or projects. Projects differ from the ongoing activities in that they have defined goals with a clear beginning and end. Typical projects that a company may undertake are: developing a new product or marketing campaign, constructing and opening a new store or warehouse, acquisition of another company, adoption of a new software program, etc. These projects are often carried out using cross-functional teams who have broken down the project into a series of tasks. Some tasks can be performed at the same time while others cannot begin until other tasks have been completed. Managing a project requires special skills and tools. This chapter shows how the **Critical Path Method (CPM)** can be used to identify activities that are critical for the timely completion of the project. When there is uncertainty in the task completion times, we can use **Program Review and Evaluation Technique (PERT)** to estimate the probability of completing the project within a deadline. Finally, when the deadline is less than the normal project completion time, we can use a project crashing LP to determine the most economical allocation of additional resources to ensure that the deadline is met.

## Critical Path Method (CPM)

Projects are often large and complex posing many challenges to managing effectively. The Critical Path Method is used in project management to identify which activities are vital to the on-time completion of the project. In CPM, the project is broken down into a list of all of the activities or tasks needed to complete the project. The time to complete each task is estimated as well as the identification of all other tasks that need to be completed before it can be started. Table 8.1 contains a list of six tasks for the start of a new restaurant. The slack for each node will be typically written over the node.

▣ TABLE 8.1   Project Task List for a New Restaurant Opening

| ACTIVITY | NODE ($i$) | IMMEDIATE PREDECESSORS | DURATION IN WEEKS ($t_i$) |
|---|---|---|---|
| Advertise Positions | A | None | 2 |
| Finalize Location | B | None | 3 |
| Hire Employees | C | A | 4 |
| Remodel | D | B | 9 |
| Stock and Train | E | C, D | 3 |
| Health Department Approval | F | D | 2 |

These tasks can be graphically represented using a network flow diagram as seen in Figure 8.1. In this diagram, each task is represented by a node and the precedence relationships between tasks are represented by the arcs between the nodes.

## Critical Path Method Network Diagram

While the diagram in Figure 8.1 gives a visual representation of the project, it does not contain a great deal of information. To make it more useful we will create a Critical Path Method (CPM) diagram in which we expand each node to add information about the activity's duration ($t_i$), **Earliest Start Time (EST), Earliest Finish Time (EFT), Latest Start Time (LST), Latest Finish Time (LFT),** and **Slack**. Figure 8.2 shows an expanded node. A rectangular node is divided into 6 parts. In the upper left hand corner is the activity, below that can be found the activity's duration, $t$. In the top middle box is the earliest starting time for the activity and in the upper right box is the earliest finish time for the activity. In the corresponding bottom boxes are the latest start time and the latest finish time. The slack for each node will be typically written over the node.

▣ FIGURE 8.1

Project Network Diagram

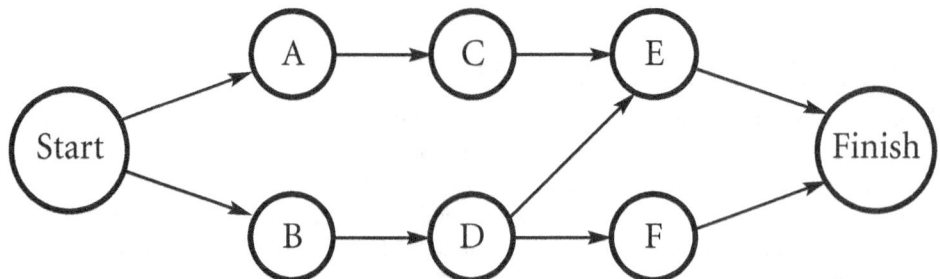

SLACK

| Activity $i$ | Earliest Start Time (EST$_i$) | Earliest Finish Time (EFT$_i$) |
|---|---|---|
| Duration $t_i$ | Latest Start TIme (LST$_i$) | Latest Finish Time (LFT$_i$) |

□ **FIGURE 8.2**

Layout of an Expanded Node for a Project Management Network Diagram

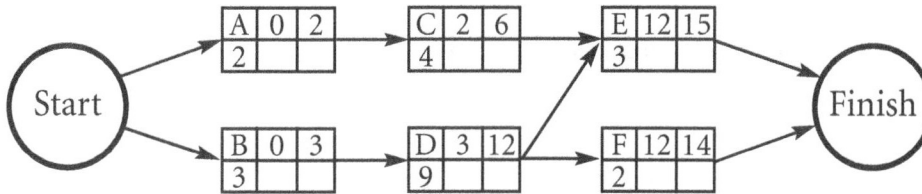

□ **FIGURE 8.3**

Critical Path Method (CPM) Diagram with ESTs and EFTs

## Calculations for the CPM

Step 1: Make a *forward pass* (left to right) through the network as follows. For each activity $i$ beginning at the *Start* node, calculate:

- Earliest Start Time (EST$_i$) = the maximum of the earliest finish times of all activities immediately preceding activity $i$. (This is 0 for an activity with no predecessors.) You cannot calculate the EST for an activity until all of its predecessors are calculated.
- Earliest Finish Time (EFT$_i$) = EST$_i$ + $t_i$.

The project completion time, $T$, is the maximum of the Earliest Finish Times at the Finish node. Table 8.2 contains the calculations for the earliest possible starting times and the earliest possible finishing times for each node. Figure 8.3 shows the CPM diagram at the end of the forward pass. The project completion time ($T$) is maximum EFT and can be seen to be 15 weeks.

□ **Table 8.2**   CPM Forward Pass Calculations for Each Node

| NODE | EST CALCULATIONS | EFT CALCULATIONS |
|---|---|---|
| A | EST$_A$ = 0 | EFT$_A$ = EST$_A$ + $t_A$ = 0 + 2 = 2 |
| B | EST$_B$ = 0 | EFT$_B$ = EST$_B$ + $t_B$ = 0 + 3 = 3 |
| C | EST$_C$ = EFT$_A$ = 2 | EFT$_C$ = EST$_C$ + $t_C$ = 2 + 4 = 6 |
| D | EST$_D$ = EFT$_B$ = 3 | EFT$_D$ = EST$_D$ + $t_D$ = 3 + 9 = 12 |
| E | EST$_E$ = Max(EFT$_C$, EFT$_D$) = Max(6, 12) = 12 | EFT$_E$ = EST$_E$ + $t_E$ = 12 + 3 = 15 |
| F | EST$_F$ = EFT$_D$ = 12 | EFT$_F$ = EST$_F$ + $t_F$ = 12 + 2 = 14 |
| Finish | Project Completion Time (T) = Max(EFT$_E$, EFT$_F$) = Max(15, 14) = 15 | |

Step 2: Make a *backward pass* (right to left) through the network as follows. Move sequentially backward from the *Finish* node to the *Start* node. At a given node $i$, consider all activities succeeding activity $i$:

- **Latest Finish Time (LFT$_i$)** = the minimum of the latest start times of activities immediately succeeding activity $i$. (For nodes with no succeeding activities, this is the project completion time.) You cannot calculate the LFT for a node until the LSTs for all successor activities are calculated.

- **Latest Start Time (LST$_i$)** = LFT$_i$ − t$_i$

**TABLE 8.3   CPM Backward Pass Calculations**

| NODE | LFT CALCULATIONS | LST CALCULATIONS |
|------|------------------|------------------|
| E | $LFT_E = T = 15$ | $LST_E = LFT_E - t_E = 15 - 3 = 12$ |
| F | $LFT_F = T = 15$ | $LST_F = LFT_F - t_F = 15 - 2 = 13$ |
| C | $LFT_C = LST_E = 12$ | $LST_C = LFT_C - t_C = 12 - 4 = 8$ |
| D | $LFT_D = MIN(LST_F, LST_F) =$ $MIN(12, 13) = 12$ | $LST_D = LFT_D - t_D = 12 - 9 = 3$ |
| A | $LFT_A = LST_C = 8$ | $LST_A = LFT_A - t_A = 8 - 2 = 6$ |
| B | $LFT_B = LST_D = 3$ | $LST_B = LFT_B - t_B = 3 - 3 = 0$ |

Table 8.3 contains the calculations for the LFT and LST for each node. Figure 8.4 shows the CPM network diagram with the latest times included.

Step 3:   Calculate the **slack** time for each activity:

$$\underline{Slack} = LST_i - EST_i = LFT_i - EFT_i$$

The slack time calculations can be seen in Table 8.4. A **critical path** is a path of activities from the Start node to the Finish node with 0 slack times. Activities B, D, and E make up the critical path for this example. These activities are called **critical or bottleneck activities** and should be of special interest to the project manager as a delay in any of these activities will delay the completion of the project.

**FIGURE 8.4**

Completed CPM Diagram

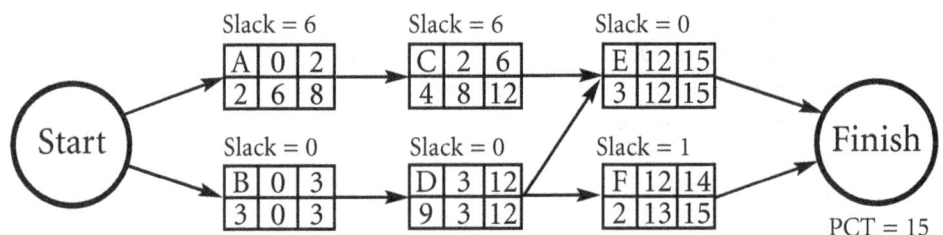

Table 8.4   Calculation of Slack using LST – EST (* denotes Critical Activities)

| NODE($i$) | EST$_i$ | EFT$_i$ | LST$_i$ | LFT$_i$ | SLACK$_i$ |
|-----------|---------|---------|---------|---------|-----------|
| A | 0 | 2 | 6 | 8 | $6 - 0 = 6$ |
| B | 0 | 3 | 0 | 3 | $0 - 0 = 0^*$ |
| C | 2 | 6 | 8 | 12 | $8 - 2 = 6$ |
| D | 3 | 12 | 3 | 12 | $3 - 3 = 0^*$ |
| E | 12 | 15 | 12 | 15 | $12 - 12 = 0^*$ |
| F | 12 | 14 | 12 | 14 | $13 - 12 = 1$ |

# Models with Uncertain Activity Times

In the previous example, it was assumed that the time it took to complete an activity was known with certainty. Of course, it is more often the case that activity times are estimated or uncertain. The Program Review and Evaluation Technique (PERT) is commonly used for projects where there are uncertain activity times to determine the likelihood of on-time completion. It was developed by the U.S. Navy in the 1950s to manage the Polaris submarine missile program.

## Mean Activity Times using a Three Point Estimate

One technique for calculating a value for mean time for an activity commonly used in industry is called a three point estimate. For each task, three values are estimated: an optimistic time (a), a pessimistic time (b), and a most likely time (m). These values are used with the following formulas to generate Beta distribution a mean and standard deviation for activity $i$:

$$E(t_i) = \mu_i = (a_i + 4m_i + b_i)/6$$

and

$$\sigma_i = (b_i - a_i)/6$$

As can be seen, the expected time for activity $i$ is a weighted average of the three estimates with the greatest weight placed on the most likely value. This is called the **PERT 1-4-1 rule.** This is a standard for PERT analysis goes back to a document called the DOD-NASA PERT-Cost Guide of 1962 and even earlier documents. The value for the standard deviation can be traced to the Empirical Rule which states that almost all values will be within plus or minus three standard deviations of the mean. Thus, we divide the difference between the pessimistic and optimistic values by six to calculate a value for one standard deviation.

The expected activity completion times are used in a project network diagram to determine an expected project completion time. The expected project completion time, $E(T)$, is the sum of the expected task times for activities on the critical path.

$$E(T) = \mu_T = \sum_{i^*} E(t_{i^*}) \text{ where } i^* \text{ denotes an activity on the critical path.}$$

The distribution of the mean completion time can be determined by summing the variances of the activities along the critical path.

$$\sigma^2_T = \sum_{i^*} \sigma^2_{ti^*} \text{ where } i^* \text{ denotes an activity on the critical path.}$$

## Determining the Probability that a Project Will Be Completed by a Deadline

The distributions of individual activity completion may vary greatly but if there are many tasks along the critical path, it is reasonable to assume that the project completion time is normally distributed using the Central Limit Theorem. With the mean project completion time and its standard deviation (or variance), we can use a standard normal distribution to determine the likelihood that the project will be completed by a deadline, $D$.

$$P(T \leq D) = P(z \leq (D - \mu_T)/\sigma_T)$$

## Calculation Assumptions

There are three assumptions that must be true for these calculations to be valid.

- The durations of activities on the critical path are independent. This assumption implies that the variance of project completion time = sum of variances of the activity durations on the critical path.
- There is a normal distribution of project completion times. This assumption is reasonable if there are many activities on the critical path (Central Limit Theorem).
- Non-critical activities will not become critical in spite of their uncertain durations.

## Example: Hospital Database Management System Installation

Barbara Kirst, Product Manager for Misys Healthcare Systems, looked over the contract that had just been signed by the CEO of Midwest Health Management. Misys specialized in healthcare databases and an important part of providing quality medical services was maintaining accurate and confidential patient records. Misys customized their basic software for each customer, converted databases to work with their software, and provided training and support. Midwest Health Management was responsible for the smooth operation of three hospitals and fifteen clinics and badly needed to computerize their recordkeeping.

Barbara looked over the time estimates for each task (Table 8.5) in the Midwest Health Management project. She had promised that the conversion would be complete including the Post Transition Assessment in six months (130 working days). Now that she had the estimates, she wanted to determine the probability the project would be completed within the deadline.

Table 8.5 Three Point Estimates for Database Installation (Times in Working Days)

| TASK | CODE | PREDECESSORS | OPTIMISTIC | MOST LIKELY | PESSIMISTIC |
|------|------|--------------|-----------|-------------|-------------|
| Assign Installation Team | A | - | 4 | 7 | 10 |
| Order Hardware | B | - | 6 | 12 | 15 |
| Customize Software | C | A | 20 | 29 | 50 |
| Install Hardware | D | B | 10 | 15 | 26 |
| Test Code | E | C, D | 18 | 24 | 30 |
| Write Manual | F | D | 15 | 21 | 24 |
| Test System | G | E | 10 | 15 | 20 |
| Train Employees | H | F | 10 | 15 | 20 |
| Convert Current Database | I | D | 5 | 10 | 15 |
| Parallel User Test | J | G, H, I | 20 | 20 | 20 |
| Post Transition Assessment | K | J | 20 | 25 | 30 |

**Calculation of Task Completion Time Values** The first step in determining this assessment is to calculate for each activity its mean activity time, standard deviation, and variance.

For activity A:

$$E(t_a) = \mu_a = (a_a + 4m_a + b_a)/6 = (4 + 4(7) + 10)/6 = 7 \text{ days}$$

and

$$\sigma_a = (b_a - a_a)/6 = (10 - 4)/6 = 1 \text{ day.}$$

The variance for activity $a$ is $\sigma_a^2 = 1^2 = 1$.

For activity B:

$$E(t_b) = \mu_b = (a_b + 4m_b + b_b)/6 = (6 + 4(12) + 15)/6 = 11.5 \text{ days}$$

and

$$\sigma_b = (b_b - a_b)/6 = (15 - 6)/6 = 1.5 \text{ days.}$$

The variance for activity $b$ is $\sigma_b^2 = 1.5^2 = 2.25$.

Table 8.6 shows the mean activity times with their standard deviation and variance for the entire project. In Figure 8.2, the mean times have been included in the project network diagram and the EST, EFT, LST, LFT, and slack have been calculated for each activity.

### TABLE 8.6    Activity Mean Times, Standard Deviation, and Variance

| TASK | CODE | OPTIMISTIC | MOST LIKELY | PESSIMISTIC | MEAN | STD DEV | VAR |
|------|------|-----------|-------------|-------------|------|---------|-----|
| Assign Installation Team | A | 4 | 7 | 10 | 7.0 | 1 | 1 |
| Order Hardware | B | 6 | 12 | 15 | 11.5 | 1.5 | 2.25 |
| Customize Software | C | 20 | 29 | 50 | 31.0 | 5 | 25 |
| Install Hardware | D | 10 | 15 | 26 | 16.0 | 2.67 | 7.11 |
| Test Code | E | 18 | 24 | 30 | 24.0 | 2 | 4 |
| Write Manual | F | 15 | 21 | 24 | 20.5 | 1.5 | 2.25 |
| Test System | G | 10 | 15 | 20 | 15.0 | 1.67 | 2.78 |
| Train Employees | H | 10 | 15 | 20 | 15.0 | 1.67 | 2.78 |
| Convert Current Database | I | 5 | 10 | 15 | 10.0 | 1.67 | 2.78 |
| Parallel User Test | J | 20 | 20 | 20 | 20.0 | 0 | 0 |
| Post Transition Assessment | K | 20 | 25 | 30 | 25.0 | 1.67 | 2.78 |

### FIGURE 8.5

Project Network Diagram for the Hospital Database Installation

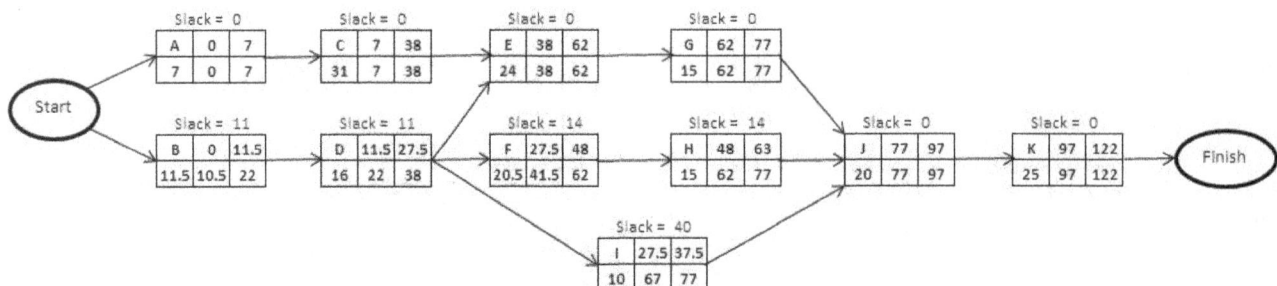

**Critical Path for the Hospital Database Installation** From Figure 8.5 (on previous page), it can be observed that the critical path is A, C, E, G, J, and K. The mean project completion time ($\mu_T$) is 122 days. The variance for the critical path is:

| ACTIVITY | VARIANCE |
|:---:|:---:|
| A | 1.00 |
| C | 25.00 |
| E | 4.00 |
| G | 2.78 |
| J | 0.00 |
| K | 2.78 |
| $\mathrm{Var}(T) =$ | 35.56 |

The standard deviation for the project is: $\sigma_T = \sqrt{35.56} = 5.96$ days.

**Probability of Completion within 130 Days**

$$P(T \leqslant 130) = P(z \leqslant (130 - 122)/5.96) = P(z \leqslant 1.34)$$

From a standard normal table, $P(z \leqslant 1.34) = 0.9099$. There is a 90.99% chance that Misys will complete the database installation within the six month deadline.

# Time-Cost Trade Offs (Project Crashing)

Frequently a project may need to be completed in a shorter time than what is indicated by the Critical Path Method. The project completion times can often be shortened by the commitment of additional resources to them. This is referred to as **crashing** the project. Reducing the time of the project increases the cost of completing the project. Linear programming can be used to identify which tasks should be crashed and by how much to minimize the total crash cost of the project and bring it down to the desired deadline.

For an activity, $i$, the normal time to complete an activity is $t_i$, which can be met at a normal cost $c_i$. Activity $i$ can be crashed at maximum to a reduced time $t_i'$ at a crash cost $c_i'$. Activity $i$'s maximum time reduction, $M_i$, may be calculated by the equation:

$$M_i = t_i - t_i'.$$

The cost per time unit of reduction, $K_i$ is assumed to be linear and is calculated by the equation:

$$K_i = (c_i' - c_i)/M_i.$$

Given a required project completion time (deadline), $D$, a project crashing linear program can be formulated.

## Decision Variables for a Project Crashing LP

Two decision variables are needed for each activity in the project. One decision variable is needed for the time the activity begins and the other for the amount the activity is crashed. For activity $i$ they would be defined as:

$$T_i: \text{time at which activity } i \text{ starts, and}$$

$$C_i: \text{amount of time by which activity } i \text{ is crashed.}$$

## Objective Function for a Project Crashing LP

The goal is to minimize the total cost to crash the project. Thus the objective function takes the form of:

$$\text{MIN: Total Crash Cost} = \sum_i K_i C_i$$

## Constraints for a Project Crashing LP

A constraint is needed for each arc going from one activity to another in the project network diagram. This constraint ensures that the successor activity does not begin before the predecessor activity has been completed. For each arc going from activity $i$ to activity $j$ the following constraint is needed:

$$T_i + t_i - C_i \leq T_j \text{ for each arc } (i, j)$$

Since $t_i$ has a known value in the problem, this constraint written in standard form would be:

$$T_i - T_j - C_i \leq - t_i \text{ for each arc } (i, j)$$

Each activity $i$ which is an immediate predecessor of the finish node needs to have a constraint ensuring it is completed by the deadline, $D$. These constraints can be written as such:

$$T_i + t_i - C \leq D \text{ for every immediate predecessor } i \text{ of the finish node}$$

Written in standard form, this constraint would be:

$$T_i - C_i \leq D - t_i$$

As there is a limit to the extent an activity time can be shortened, a constraint is needed for each activity defining the maximum amount that activity can be crashed. It takes the form:

$$C_i \leq M_i \qquad \text{for each activity } i$$

Finally, non-negativity constraints are needed for all variables:

$$T_i, C_i \geq 0 \qquad \text{for each activity } i$$

## Summary of the Standard Formulation for a Project Crashing LP

Decision Variables

$T_i$: time at which activity $i$ starts.

$C_i$: amount of time by which activity $i$ is crashed.

$$\text{Min } \sum_i K_i C_i$$

s.t.

$T_i - T_j - C_i \leq -t_i$    for each arc $(i, j)$

$T_i - C_i \leq D - t_i$    for every immediate predecessor $i$ of the finish node

$C_i \leq M_i$    for each activity $i$

$T_i, C_i \geq 0$    for each activity $i$

## Example: Project Crashing

Going back to the first example in this chapter, additional information has been provided regarding the amount each activity can be crashed and the cost of crashing in Table 8.7. The project network diagram can be seen in Figure 8.1. The normal project completion time is 15 weeks but the client requires the job to be completed in 15 days. What is the lowest cost plan for finishing the project in 12 weeks?

**TABLE 8.7** Project Crashing Information

| NODE | PREDECESSORS | NORMAL TIME ($t_i$) | CRASH TIME ($t_i'$) | NORMAL COST ($c_i$) | CRASH COST ($c_i'$) | MAX CRASH ($M_i$) | CRASH COST/DAY ($K_i$) |
|------|--------------|---------------------|---------------------|---------------------|---------------------|-------------------|------------------------|
| A | — | 2 | 1 | 400 | 600 | 1 | 200 |
| B | — | 3 | 2 | 600 | 900 | 1 | 300 |
| C | A | 4 | 2 | 1000 | 2000 | 2 | 500 |
| D | B | 9 | 5 | 1400 | 2400 | 4 | 250 |
| E | C, D | 3 | 2 | 1500 | 1850 | 1 | 350 |
| F | D | 2 | 1 | 900 | 1150 | 1 | 250 |

## Linear Program

The LP for this example is:

Decision Variables

$T_i$: time at which activity $i$ starts

$C_i$: amount of time by which activity $i$ is crashed.

$$i = A, B, C, D, E, F$$

$$\text{MIN: } \sum_i K_i C_i = 200C_A + 300C_B + 500C_C + 250C_D + 350C_E + 250C_F$$

s.t.

| | |
|---|---|
| $T_A - T_C - C_A \leq -2$ | Arc A to C |
| $T_B - T_D - C_B \leq -3$ | Arc B to D |
| $T_C - T_E - C_C \leq -4$ | Arc C to E |
| $T_D - T_E - C_D \leq -9$ | Arc D to E |
| $T_D - T_F - C_D \leq -9$ | Arc D to F |
| $T_E - C_E \leq 12 - 3$ | Arc E to Finish |
| $T_F - C_F \leq 12 - 2$ | Arc F to Finish |
| $C_A \leq 1$ | Maximum Crash Amounts |
| $C_B \leq 1$ | |
| $C_C \leq 2$ | |
| $C_D \leq 4$ | |
| $C_E \leq 1$ | |
| $C_F \leq 1$ | |
| $T_i, C_i \geq 0, i = A, B, C, D, E, F$ | Non-Negativity |

## Spreadsheet Model for Project Crashing

This linear program can be constructed into a spreadsheet model as shown in Exhibit 8.1. The optimal solution is to crash activity D by 3 days. The cost of crashing the project is $750.

# SUMMARY

Project management involves a special set of analytical tools to effectively manage the project and complete it on time and in a cost effective manner. The Critical Path Method helps the manager identify activities that require special attention to prevent the delay of the project completion time. When there is uncertainty in the time to complete project tasks, the Program Evaluation and Review Technique (PERT) can be used to determine the likelihood of on-time completion. Frequently, projects need to be completed before their estimated completion times. The project completion time can be shortened through crashing tasks. A crash time linear program can be used to determine the most cost efficient method of meeting the deadline. Being assigned a project team is a frequent occurrence in the working world. Acquisition of project management techniques can help you succeed in these assignments.

**EXHIBIT 8.1**

Spreadsheet Model for Project Crashing

# Restaurant Opening Crash Time Linear Program

| | Task Starting Times | | | | | | Task Crash Amounts | | | | | | |
|---|---|---|---|---|---|---|---|---|---|---|---|---|---|
| | A | B | C | D | E | F | A | B | C | D | E | F | RHS |
| A to C Precedence | 1 | | -1 | | | | -1 | | | | | | -2 |
| B to D Precedence | | 1 | | -1 | | | | -1 | | | | | -3 |
| C to E Precedence | | | 1 | | -1 | | | | -1 | | | | -4 |
| D to E Precedence | | | | 1 | -1 | | | | | -1 | | | -9 |
| D to F Precedence | | | | 1 | | -1 | | | | -1 | | | -9 |
| E to Finish | | | | | 1 | | | | | | -1 | | 9 |
| F to Finish | | | | | | 1 | | | | | | -1 | 10 |
| Max Crash A | | | | | | | 1 | | | | | | 1 |
| Max Crash B | | | | | | | | 1 | | | | | 1 |
| Max Crash C | | | | | | | | | 1 | | | | 2 |
| Max Crash D | | | | | | | | | | 1 | | | 4 |
| Max Crash E | | | | | | | | | | | 1 | | 1 |
| Max Crash F | | | | | | | | | | | | 1 | 1 |
| Crash Cost/Day (Ki) | | | | | | | 200 | 300 | 500 | 250 | 350 | 250 | |

| | Task Starting Times | | | | | | Task Crash Amounts | | | | | |
|---|---|---|---|---|---|---|---|---|---|---|---|---|
| | A | B | C | D | E | F | A | B | C | D | E | F |
| | 0 | 0 | 5 | 3 | 9 | 9 | 0 | 0 | 0 | 3 | 0 | 0 |

Constraints

| | LHS | | RHS |
|---|---|---|---|
| A to C Precedence | -5 | <= | -2 |
| B to D Precedence | -3 | <= | -3 |
| C to E Precedence | -4 | <= | -4 |
| D to E Precedence | -9 | <= | -9 |
| D to F Precedence | -9 | <= | -9 |
| E to Finish | 9 | <= | 9 |
| F to Finish | 9 | <= | 10 |
| Max Crash A | 0 | <= | 1 |
| Max Crash B | 0 | <= | 1 |
| Max Crash C | 0 | <= | 2 |
| Max Crash D | 3 | <= | 4 |
| Max Crash E | 0 | <= | 1 |
| Max Crash F | 0 | <= | 1 |

| | | |
|---|---|---|
| Total Crash Cost | $ 750 | |

## KEY TERMS

**Bottleneck Activity** A bottleneck activity is an activity that must be started and completed on time to ensure the on-time completion of the project. It is also known as a critical activity.

**Critical Activity** An activity that must be started and completed on time to ensure the on-time completion of the project. Critical activities have a slack of 0.

**Critical Path** A critical path is a sequence of project tasks that add up to the longest overall duration. Any delay of an activity on the critical path directly impacts the planned project completion date. All activities along the critical path have a slack of 0.

**Critical Path Method** A technique used in project management to identify which activities are vital to the on-time completion of the project.

**Earliest Finish Time (EFT)** The earliest time a task can be completed. It is calculated by adding the time it takes to complete the task to the earliest start time for that activity.

**Earliest Start Time (EST)** The earliest time a task in a project can be started. It is the maximum of all of the earliest finish times of tasks that immediately precede it.

**Latest Finish Time (LFT)** The latest time a task can be completed without delaying the completion of the project. It is the minimum of latest start times of activities that immediately follow it.

**Latest Start Time (LST)** The latest that a task can start without delaying the completion of a project. It is calculated by subtracting the task duration from its latest finish time.

**Program Review and Evaluation Technique (PERT)** The Program Review and Evaluation Technique (PERT) is commonly used for projects where there are uncertain activity times to determine the likelihood of on-time completion.

**PERT 1-4-1 rule** A method of estimating the mean completion time for a task and its variance using three points. For each task, three values are estimated: an optimistic time (a), a pessimistic time (b), and a most likely time (m). A mean time is calculated using weighted average of these times with the most likely time having a weight of four times the optimistic or pessimistic times.

**Project Crashing** Project crashing is the process of shortening the project completion time by the commitment of additional resources to project tasks.

**Slack** The amount of time a task could start after its earliest start time without delaying the project. It is calculated by subtracting the earliest start time from the latest start time or subtracting the earliest finish time from the latest finish time.

Section # _____          Section # _____

## EXERCISES

1. In a given project network, each activity has the same format (cells) as

| Activity $i$ | Earliest Start Time ($EST_i$) | Earliest Finish Time ($EFT_i$) |
|---|---|---|
| Duration $t_i$ | Latest Start Time ($LST_i$) | Latest Finish Time ($LFT_i$) |

Fill the empty cells in the group below and highlight the critical path.

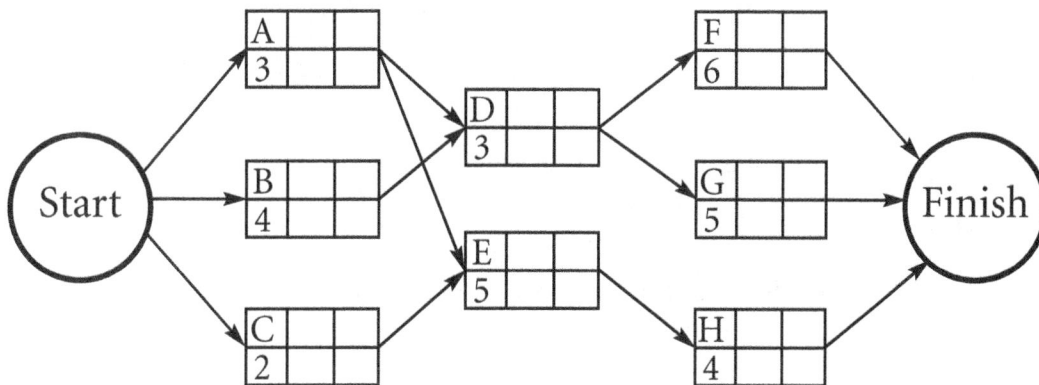

a. What is the project completion time?

b. If activity D finishes at time 8, will the project be delayed?

c. If activity E duration was reduced to 4, would the project completion time decrease?

2. Consider the following project network for the questions. Activity's time (in days) is given below the name in each activity's box.

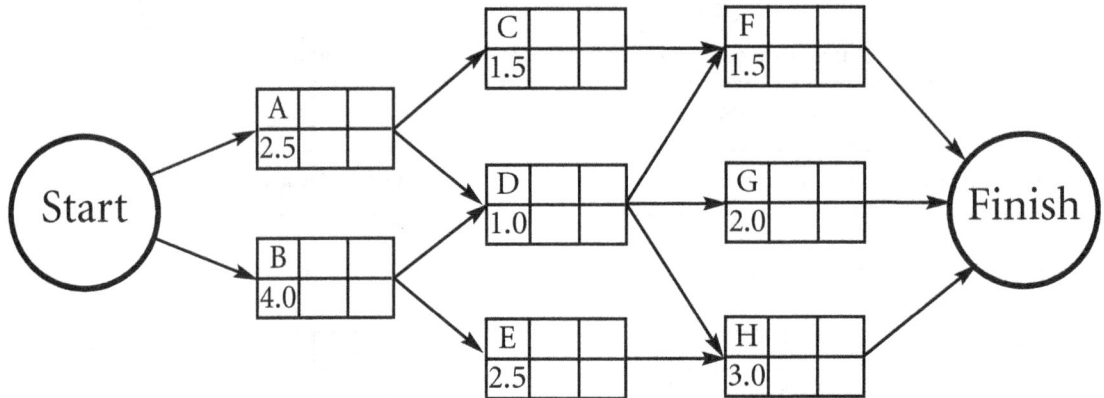

a. What is the project completion time?

b. What is the Latest Finish Time of activity C?

c. What is the Earliest Start Time of activity G?

d. What is the Slack Time for activity A?

e. What is the Slack Time for activity E?

f. What is the Critical Path?

3. The table below contains a list of tasks needed to build a residential home. Draw a Project Network Diagram.

a. What is the project completion time?

b. Which are critical activities?

| CODE | ACTIVITY | DURATION (DAYS) | PREDECESSOR ACTIVITIES |
|------|----------|-----------------|------------------------|
| A | Develop plans with architect | 21 | None |
| B | Sign contract with builder and apply for permits | 1 | A |
| C | Clear lot and install underground utilities | 1 | B |
| D | Pour the foundation | 30 | C |
| E | Frame the walls | 19 | D |
| F | Finish the roof | 7 | E |
| G | Install exterior doors and windows | 3 | F |
| H | Complete exterior siding | 3 | G |
| I | Rough-in plumbing | 6 | E |
| J | String wires for electrical | 5 | E |
| K | String wires and cables for phone, cable, computer, and alarm | 2 | E |
| L | Insulate walls and attic | 9 | H, I, J, K |
| M | Drywall | 10 | L |
| N | Paint and wallpaper | 20 | M |
| O | Install cabinets | 5 | M |
| P | Finish plumbing | 5 | O |
| Q | Finish electrical | 3 | M |
| R | Complete wiring for phone, cable, computer, and alarm | 2 | M |
| S | Lay tile and carpet | 3 | N |
| T | Install appliances | 1 | S |
| U | Landscaping and grounds work | 10 | H |
| V | Final acceptance | 7 | P, Q, R, T, U |
| W | Final inspection for certificate of occupancy | 1 | V |

4. Consider the project in the next page and answer the following questions. Activity's time (in days) is given below the name in each activity's box.

a. What is the project completion time?

b. What is the duration of activity F?

c. What is the critical path?

d. What is the maximum amount of time activity G could be put on hold without delaying the project?

e. By what time could activity B start without delaying the project?

f. Which of the following arcs, if removed, will reduce the project completion time? Why?

   I.   IK.
   II.  HJ.
   III. DF.
   IV.  AE.

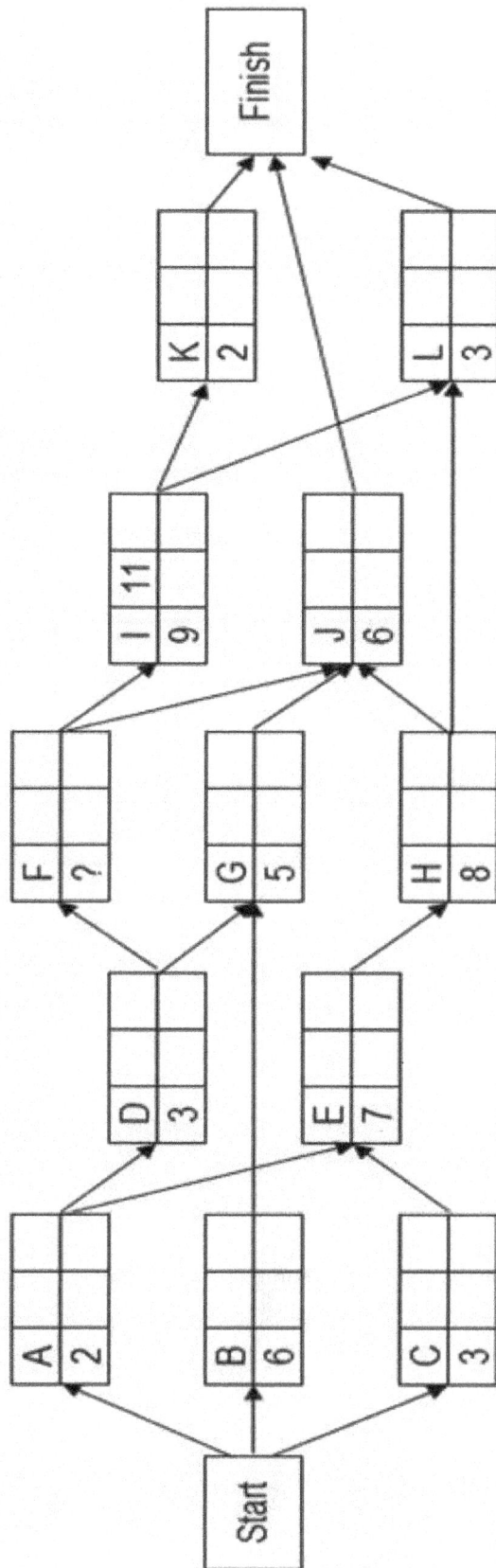

5. Building a bookstore consists of six major activities. According to the knowledge of activities and their immediate predecessors, the project network is drawn below:

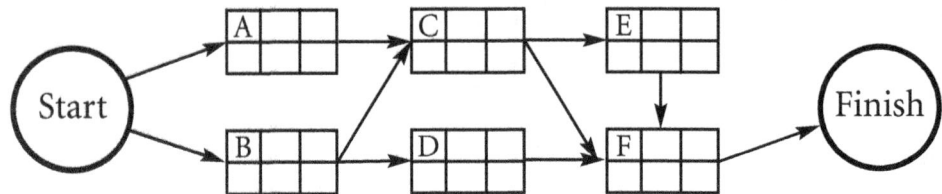

Assume that the activity time estimates (in days) for the bookstore construction project are

| ACTIVITY | OPTIMISTIC | MOST PROBABLE | PESSIMISTIC | EXPECTED TIME | VARIANCE |
|----------|-----------|---------------|-------------|---------------|----------|
| A | hidden | hidden | hidden | 4 | 0.6 |
| B | hidden | hidden | hidden | 5 | 0.5 |
| C | hidden | hidden | hidden | 6 | 0.1 |
| D | hidden | hidden | hidden | 10 | 0.3 |
| E | 2 | 3 | 7 | | |
| F | hidden | hidden | hidden | 8 | 0.2 |

a. What are the expected time and variance for activity E? (fill them into the above table)

b. What are the critical activities?

c. What is the expected time to complete the project?

d. What is the probability that the project is completed in 25 or more days?

6. Building a piano consists of six major activities. According to the knowledge of activities, their immediate predecessors and expected activity times, the project network is drawn below:

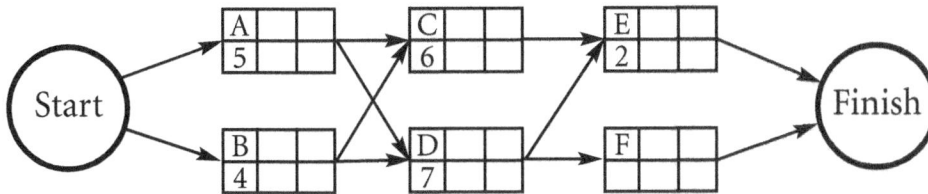

| A 5 | | | C 6 | | | E 2 | | |
|---|---|---|---|---|---|---|---|---|

Start → A, B
B 4 | | | D 7 | | | F | | |

Finish

Assume that the activity time estimates (in days) for the piano production are:

| ACTIVITY | OPTIMISTIC | MOST PROBABLE | PESSIMISTIC | EXPECTED TIME | VARIANCE |
|---|---|---|---|---|---|
| A | hidden | hidden | hidden | 5 | 0.7 |
| B | hidden | hidden | hidden | 4 | 0.6 |
| C | hidden | hidden | hidden | 6 | 0.1 |
| D | hidden | hidden | hidden | 7 | 0.3 |
| E | hidden | hidden | hidden | 2 | 0.11 |
| F | 1 | 2 | 6 | | |

a. What are the **expected time** and **variance** for activity **F**? (keep two decimal precision)

b. What are the critical activities?

c. What is the probability that the project can be completed in 15.5 or fewer days? (Keep two decimal precision throughout your calculation.)

7. The following table describes the various activities of a new drug development in a pharmaceutical company.

| ACTIVITY | NORMAL TIME ($t_i$) WEEKS | CRASH TIME ($t_i'$) | NORMAL COST ($c_i$) | CRASH COST ($c_i'$) | PREDECESSORS |
|----------|---------------------------|---------------------|---------------------|---------------------|--------------|
| A | 4 | 2 | 50000 | 80000 | — |
| B | 11 | 7 | 75000 | 85000 | — |
| C | 9 | 6 | 90000 | 120000 | A |
| D | 7 | 5 | 80000 | 120000 | B |
| E | 12 | 8 | 125000 | 165000 | B |
| F | 8 | 6 | 85000 | 125000 | C, D |
| G | 14 | 10 | 150000 | 200000 | D, E |
| H | 16 | 11 | 180000 | 210000 | C, E |

a. Calculate the crash cost per week for each activity.

b. Formulate an LP program to crash this project to 30 weeks in the space below. Build a spreadsheet model of the project. Use Solver to find the optimal solution. What is the minimum cost plan for crashing the project?

8. SkyEducation will develop a new branch in West Lafayette for J2EE programming training. The information is given in the following table:

| TASK | A | B | C | D | E | F | G |
|---|---|---|---|---|---|---|---|
| Predecessors | - | - | - | A | B | C | D, E |
| Normal Time ($t_i$ weeks) | 2 | 3 | 4 | 7 | 6 | 15 | 10 |
| Crash Time ($t_i'$) | 1 | 1 | 2 | 4 | 3 | 5 | 5 |
| Normal Cost ($c_i$) | 1000 | 2100 | 1500 | 500 | 900 | 800 | 1250 |
| Crash Cost ($c_i'$) | 1200 | 2500 | 1600 | 800 | 1200 | 1300 | 1750 |
| Max Crash($M_i$) | 1 | 2 | 2 | 3 | 3 | 10 | 5 |
| Crash Cost/Weeks ($k_i$) | 200 | 200 | 50 | 100 | 100 | 50 | 100 |

SkyEducation's plan is to open this new branch within 18 weeks.

a. Formulate a linear program to determine the minimum cost plan.

b. Build a spreadsheet model of the project. Use Solver to find the optimal solution. What is the minimum cost plan to crash the project?

9. Referring to the hospital database management system installation example, Barbara has received word from her client that they need the new system completed in 100 workdays. Looking at statistics from other jobs, she has determined the amount each task could be crashed and the cost (See Table 8.8).

■ TABLE 8.8  Database Installation Crash Information

| TASK | CODE | PREDECESSORS | NORMAL TIME ($t_i$) | CRASH TIME($t_i'$) | NORMAL COST ($c_i$) | CRASH COST ($c_i'$) |
|---|---|---|---|---|---|---|
| Assign Installation Team | A | — | 7 | 5 | 3000 | 5000 |
| Order Hardware | B | — | 11.5 | 10 | 5500 | 8500 |
| Customize Software | C | A | 31 | 20 | 60000 | 120000 |
| Install Hardware | D | B | 16 | 10 | 15000 | 25000 |
| Test Code | E | C, D | 24 | 16 | 50000 | 90000 |
| Write Manual | F | D | 20.5 | 15 | 15000 | 25000 |
| Test System | G | E | 15 | 12 | 50000 | 75000 |
| Train Employees | H | F | 15 | 10 | 40000 | 65000 |
| Convert Current Database | I | D | 10 | 5 | 15000 | 35000 |
| Parallel User Test | J | G, H, I | 20 | 20 | 50000 | 50000 |
| Post Transition Assessment | K | J | 25 | 15 | 25000 | 50000 |

a. Formulate a linear program to determine the minimum cost plan to complete the project in 100 days.

b. Build a spreadsheet model of the project. Use solver to find the optimal solution. Which activities should Barbara crash and by how much? What is the total cost?

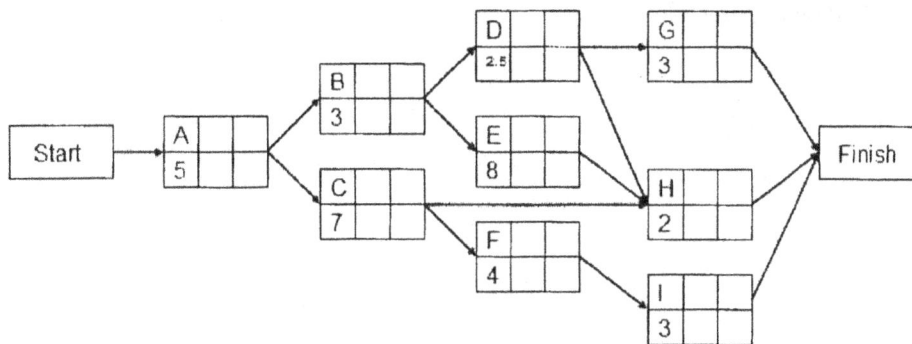

10. Fill the empty cells in the network diagram above and highlight the critical path. Answer the following questions.

   a. What is the project completion time?

   b. What is the latest finish day of activity D?

   c. What is the slack time for activity E?

   d. What is the slack time for activity H?

11. Based on the flow chart given below, answer the following questions.

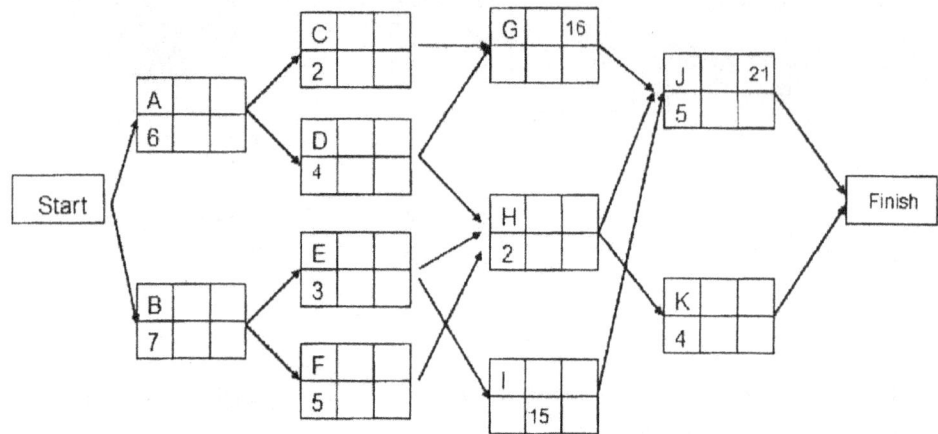

a. What is the project completion time?

b. What is the critical path?

c. What is the earliest starting time of project E?

d. What is the latest starting time of project H?

e. What is the maximum amount of time activity D could be put on hold without delaying the whole project?

f. Which of the arc, if removed, will reduce the project completion time? Why?

• D → G

• E → H

• J → J

• K → Finish

12. A manager of human resource department is in the process of designing a new training program for new recruiters. The program consists of seven major tasks and some of them must be finished before the others are taken. The tasks, task durations, and immediate predecessors appear in the following table:

| TASK | PREDECESSORS | DURATIONS (DAYS) |
|------|--------------|------------------|
| A | - | 3 |
| B | - | 5 |
| C | A | 3 |
| D | A, B | 4 |
| E | C, D | 5 |
| F | D | 2 |
| G | E, F | 2 |

a. Develop a network diagram for this program.

b. What is the project completion time?

c. What is the critical path?

13. Use the network diagram and the table to answer the following questions:

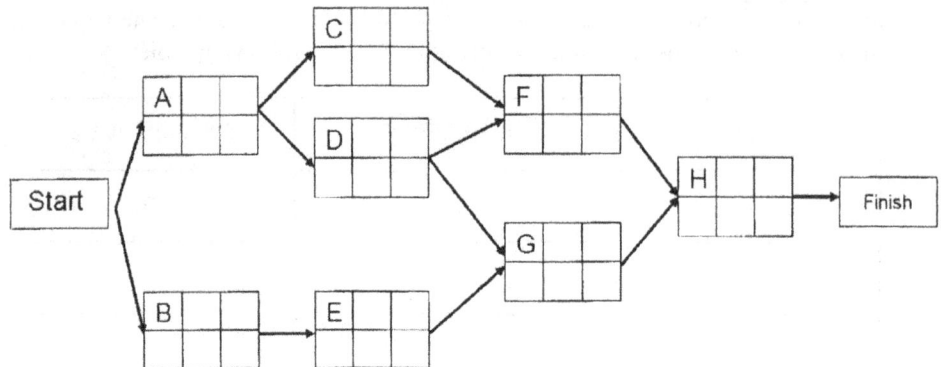

A B C D E F G H Start Finish

| ACTIVITY | OPTIMISTIC | MOST LIKELY | PESSIMISTIC | EXPECTED TIME | VARIANCE |
|---|---|---|---|---|---|
| A | 1 | 2.5 | | | 0.25 |
| B | N/A | N/A | N/A | 3 | 0.5 |
| C | N/A | N/A | N/A | 5 | 0.7 |
| D | N/A | N/A | N/A | 6 | 0.6 |
| E | N/A | N/A | N/A | 2 | 0.6 |
| F | N/A | N/A | N/A | 4.5 | 0.4 |
| G | N/A | N/A | N/A | 2 | 0.8 |
| H | 2 | 5 | 8 | | |

a. Fill the empty cells in the diagram and table.

b. What is the critical path?

c. What is the expected project completion time?

d. What is the variance of project completion time?

e. What is the probability that this project can be completed in 16 or fewer days?

f. What is the probability that this project would be completed in more than 19 days?

14. Use the network diagram and the table to answer the following questions:

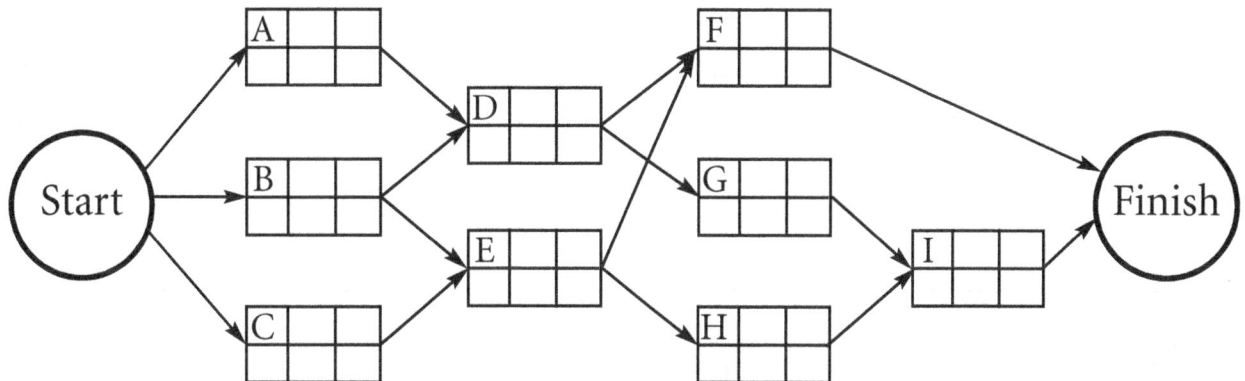

| ACTIVITY | OPTIMISTIC | MOST LIKELY | PESSIMISTIC | EXPECTED TIME | VARIANCE |
|----------|-----------|-------------|-------------|---------------|----------|
| A | N/A | N/A | N/A | 2 | 0.2 |
| B | N/A | N/A | N/A | 3 | 0.8 |
| C | N/A | N/A | N/A | 5 | 0.7 |
| D | N/A | N/A | N/A | 4 | 1.2 |
| E | N/A | N/A | N/A | 2 | 0.6 |
| F | 3 | 4.5 | 9 | | |
| G | N/A | N/A | N/A | 4 | 1 |
| H | 1 | 2 | 3 | | |
| I | NA | N/A | N/A | 14 | 2 |

a. What are the expected durations and variances of activities F and H?

b. What are the critical activities?

c. What is the expected project completion time?

d. What is the variance of project completion time?

e. What is the probability that this project can be complete in fewer than 25 days?

15. Because of the increasing demands of small laptop computers, a manufacturer needs to modify its production process. The following table describes the various activities of this modification.

| ACTIVITY | NORMAL TIME (WEEKS) | CRASH TIME (WEEKS) | NORMAL COST (MILLION) | CRASH COST (MILLION) | PREDECESSORS | $M_I$ | $K_I$ (COST/WEEK) |
|---|---|---|---|---|---|---|---|
| A | 3 | 1 | 1.5 | 3 | — | | |
| B | 4 | 2 | 2 | 4 | — | | |
| C | 4 | 3 | 2 | 2.5 | A, B | | |
| D | 3 | 2 | 4.5 | 6.5 | A | | |
| E | 2 | 1 | 0.8 | 2 | C, D | | |
| F | 4 | 2 | 3 | 4 | E | | |
| G | 6 | 3 | 5 | 8 | E | | |

Follow the instructions given below to build a worksheet of Excel and use Solver to solve this problem.

a. Calculate the maximum crash time ($M_i$) and unit crash cost ($K_i$).

b. Formulate an LP model to crash this project to 12 weeks.

c. Build an Excel spreadsheet model of the project. What is the minimum cost for crashing the project?

d. If the company could extend the due date to 13 weeks by paying a late penalty fee of $0.5 million, should the company pay this penalty to extend the due day? Why?

# Decision Analysis

- Understand the structure of decisions.
- Select and apply decision criteria based on the decision maker's attitude toward risk and the information available.
- Calculate the Expected Value of Perfect Information (EVPI).
- Use decision tree analysis to develop an optimal strategy for a series of interrelated decisions.
- Solve decision trees using the PrecisionTree software.
- Perform sensitivity analysis using PrecisionTree.

## Introduction

We operate in a world of uncertainty. Estimates and forecasts are used in decisions every day. When good historical data is available it can be used in building a decision model. When it is a new product or an unusual situation, managerial judgment is often used to generate inputs to models. In any event, one of the most important skills for a manager is the ability to make good decisions. In this chapter we will explore quantitative decision analysis. We will look at how the decision criteria can affect the selection between alternatives. We will use decision trees to determine the best strategy when faced with a series of related decisions. Decision analysis lets a manager consider the overall impact of a series of decisions and developing a strategy for handling them. Sensitivity Analysis will allow us to see if changes in the probabilities or payoffs in a decision would cause us to change our decision strategy.

## Decision Structure

Decisions are characterized by having a set of decision alternatives to choose from, a set of uncertain future outcomes, estimated payoffs for decisions and outcomes and a goal. Each of these aspects of decision structure will be explored in more detail in this section.

**Decision alternatives** are different courses of action that may be taken. These courses of action should be mutually exclusive and exhaustive. In decision analysis, these alternatives are usually represented by the variables: $d_1, d_2, d_3, \ldots, d_n$.

**States of nature** are the future events that we do not have control over but may be able to assign probabilities regarding the likelihood that they will occur. The set of states of nature should also be mutually exclusive and exhaustive. The states of nature are usually represented by the variables: $s_1, s_2, s_3, \ldots, s_n$.

**Payoffs** are measurable outcomes that are of interest to the decision maker. Payoffs may take the form of profit, cost, time, productivity, market share, or other measures of interest. Payoffs result from the combination of a particular decision alternative and the specific occurrence of a state of nature. **Payoff tables** are typically used to display the results of decisions and the possible states of nature. To generate a payoff table:

1. In the first column, list the decision alternatives.
2. At the top of each column, list a state of nature possible.
3. In each cell of the table, place the payoff expected for that combination of decision and event.

## Example: Seaborg Concessions

Glen Seaborg was trying to decide how many cases of hot dogs with buns to order for his concession stand at the football stadium for the next weekend. Demand for hot dogs was largely dependent on the weather. If the weather was hot, fans wanted ice cream and he would only sell enough hot dogs to use one case. During warm weather, the demand for hot dogs was higher and he could sell two cases. If the weather turned cold, he could sell three cases. Each case of hot dogs with buns cost him $300. Sales of a case of hot dogs would bring in $500 in revenue. Any unsold hot dogs would be donated to the homeless shelter since they would not keep until the next home game. We will prepare a payoff table for Glen's decision.

**List Decision Alternatives** Glen has the option of buying one, two, or three cases of hot dogs with buns. These decisions are listed in the first column of the payoff table as shown in Table 9.1. Note that the decision alternatives are mutually exclusive and contain all of Glen's options.

**List States of Nature Possible** The weather will be hot, warm, or cold this weekend. These states of nature are listed at the top of each column in Table 9.1. The states of nature should be mutually exclusive and exhaustive.

**TABLE 9.1    Seaborg Concessions Empty Profit Payoff Table**

| DECISION ALTERNATIVES | WEATHER (STATES OF NATURE) | | |
|---|---|---|---|
| | HOT ($s_1$) | WARM ($s_2$) | COLD ($s_3$) |
| Buy 1 Case ($d_1$) | | | |
| Buy 2 Cases ($d_2$) | | | |
| Buy 3 Cases ($d_3$) | | | |

**Payoffs for Decision Alternative 1 ($d_1$)** If Glen buys one case of hot dogs with buns, he will spend $300. If the weather is hot, he will sell the case of hot dogs and have revenue of $500 giving him a net profit of $200. This value goes in the cell at the intersection of $d_1$ and $s_1$. If the weather is warm or cold, demand for hot dogs will be higher, but since Glen only has one case of hot dogs, his profit on hot dogs in either of these states of nature will still only be $200 and this value is entered in each cell in the row containing the first decision alternative. See Table 9.2.

**Payoffs for Decision Alternative 2 (d₂)** If Glen buys two cases of hot dogs with buns, he will spend $600. If the weather is hot, he will sell only one case of hot dogs and have revenue of $500 giving him a net loss of $100. If the weather is warm or cold, demand for hot dogs will be higher and Glen will be able to sell both of the cases he has purchased, his profit on hot dogs in either of these states of nature will still only be $400. The calculations for each state of nature for decision alternative 2 are shown below.

|  | Hot ($s_1$) | Warm ($s_2$) | Cold ($s_3$) |
|---|---|---|---|
| **Revenue** | 500 | 1000 | 1000 |
| **– Cost** | –600 | –600 | –600 |
| **Profit** | **–100** | **400** | **400** |

**Payoffs for Decision Alternative 3 (d₃)** If Glen buys three cases of hot dogs with buns, he will spend $900. The weather will dictate how many of these three cases he can sell. The calculations for each state of nature for decision alternative 3 are shown below.

|  | Hot ($s_1$) | Warm ($s_2$) | Cold ($s_3$) |
|---|---|---|---|
| **Revenue** | 500 | 1000 | 1500 |
| **– Cost** | –900 | – 900 | –900 |
| **Profit** | **–400** | **100** | **600** |

■ TABLE 9.2   Seaborg Concessions Payoff Table (Dollars of Profit)

| DECISION ALTERNATIVES | WEATHER (STATES OF NATURE) | | |
|---|---|---|---|
|  | HOT ($s_1$) | WARM ($s_2$) | COLD ($s_3$) |
| Buy 1 Case ($d_1$) | 200 | 200 | 200 |
| Buy 2 Cases ($d_2$) | –100 | 400 | 400 |
| Buy 3 Cases ($d_3$) | –400 | 100 | 600 |

# Decision Criteria

Table 9.2 shows the payoffs for Glen's decision, but it does not tell which is the best decision. In fact there is no one best decision in this example. Decision makers can use a variety of decision criteria to select the decision alternative that fits their goals and their attitude toward risk. The manager's or company's attitude toward risk has a big impact on the decision criteria used and the resulting decision alternative selected. In this section we will examine four different decision criteria and show how the criteria selected has an impact on the decision alternative selected. The four common methods for decision selection are the:

1. optimistic approach,
2. conservative approach,
3. minimax regret approach, and
4. the expected value (EV) approach.

## Optimistic Approach

A decision maker using an optimistic approach considers each decision alternative based on the best possible outcome for that decision. In problems where the maximum value is desirable, the alternative with the highest possible outcome is selected. Table 9.3 shows the maximum payoffs possible for each decision alternative. Selecting the maximum of these indicates that Glen should buy three cases of hot dogs with buns with a maximum profit of $600.

▢ TABLE 9.3   Optimistic Approach using Seaborg Concessions. The optimistic approach indicates that the best decision would be to buy three cases with a maximum payoff of $600.

| DECISION ALTERNATIVES | WEATHER (STATES OF NATURE) | | | |
|---|---|---|---|---|
| | HOT ($s_1$) | WARM ($s_2$) | COLD ($s_3$) | MAXIMUM PAYOFF |
| Buy 1 Case ($d_1$) | 200 | 200 | 200 | 200 |
| Buy 2 Cases ($d_2$) | −100 | 400 | 400 | 400 |
| Buy 3 Cases ($d_3$) | −400 | 100 | 600 | 600 |

The optimistic approach with maximization problems is often called **Maximax Approach.** Likewise, the optimistic approach used with a minimization problem is often the **Minimin Approach.**

## Conservative Approach

A decision maker using a **conservative approach** determines the worst possible outcome for each decision alternative. The alternative that yields the best outcome for the worst case scenario is selected. See Table 9.4. The maximum minimum pay off is to buy 1 case. The conservative approach is sometimes called the Maximin Approach.

TABLE 9.4 Conservative Approach using Seaborg Concessions. The conservative approach indicates that the best decision would be to buy one case of hot dogs with the best worst case profit of $200.

| DECISION ALTERNATIVES | WEATHER (STATES OF NATURE) | | | |
|---|---|---|---|---|
| | HOT ($s_1$) | WARM ($s_2$) | COLD ($s_3$) | MINIMUM PAYOFF |
| Buy 1 Case ($d_1$) | 200 | 200 | 200 | 200 |
| Buy 2 Cases ($d_2$) | –100 | 400 | 400 | –100 |
| Buy 3 Cases ($d_3$) | –400 | 100 | 600 | –400 |

## Minimax Regret Approach

The minimax regret approach to decision making looks at how much regret or opportunity loss would be felt for each decision alternative when state of nature, $s_i$, occurs. The opportunity loss is calculated by comparing the payoff for each decision alternative in a particular state of nature with the best payoff for that state of nature. For example, if the weather was hot, the best decision would have been to buy 1 case of hot dogs. The regret experienced with decision 1 would have been 200 – 200 or 0. If two cases of hot dogs had been purchased, 200 – (– 100) or 300 dollars of regret would have been experienced. If Glen had purchased 3 cases of hot dogs, he would have experienced an opportunity loss of 200 – (–400) or 600 dollars. Exhibit 9.1 and Exhibit 9.2 show the calculation of regret for $s_2$ and $s_3$.

| | Buy 1 Case ($d_1$) | Buy 2 Cases ($d_2$) | Buy 3 Cases ($d_3$) |
|---|---|---|---|
| **Best Decision ($d_2$)** | 400 | 400 | 400 |
| **– Payoff for $d_i$** | – 200 | – 400 | – 100 |
| **Dollars of Regret** | **200** | **0** | **300** |

EXHIBIT 9.1

Regret Calculations for Warm Weather ($s_2$). The best decision would have been to buy 2 cases.

| | Buy 1 Case ($d_1$) | Buy 2 Cases ($d_2$) | Buy 3 Cases ($d_3$) |
|---|---|---|---|
| Best Decision ($d_3$) | 600 | 600 | 600 |
| – Payoff for $d_i$ | – 200 | – 400 | – 600 |
| **Dollars of Regret** | **400** | **200** | **0** |

EXHIBIT 9.2

Regret Calculations for Cold Weather ($s_3$). The best decision in cold weather would have been to buy 3 cases.

The calculations of regret are combined in a **regret table** (Table 9.5) and the maximum potential regret is determined for each decision alternative. Finally, using the minimax regret approach, the decision maker compares the maximum regret values and selects the decision alternative with the minimum value. Using this approach, Glen would buy two cases of hot dogs with buns with a maximum potential regret of 300.

☐ TABLE 9.5     Regret Table for Seaborg Concessions. The Minimax Regret approach would indicate that the best decision is to buy 2 cases.

| DECISION ALTERNATIVES | WEATHER (STATES OF NATURE) | | | OPPORTUNITY LOSS (REGRET) | | | |
|---|---|---|---|---|---|---|---|
| | HOT ($s_1$) | WARM ($s_2$) | COLD ($s_3$) | HOT ($s_1$) | WARM ($s_2$) | COLD ($s_3$) | MAXIMUM REGRET |
| Buy 1 Case ($d_1$) | 200 | 200 | 200 | 0 | 200 | 400 | 400 |
| Buy 2 Cases ($d_2$) | −100 | 400 | 400 | 300 | 0 | 200 | 300 |
| Buy 3 Cases ($d_3$) | −400 | 100 | 600 | 600 | 300 | 0 | 600 |

## Expected Value Approach

The optimistic, conservative, and minimax regret approaches to the selection of decision alternatives do not require knowledge of the probabilities of each state of nature occurring. When a company is developing a new product or process, or otherwise has low confidence in their ability to estimate the likelihood of events happening, these approaches are suitable. However, when the probability of states of natures can be reliably estimated, the **expected value (EV)** approach can be used.

In the EV approach, the expected value of each decision is calculated. The expected value is the sum of the weighted payoffs for each state of nature using the probability of each state of nature as its weight. Note that since the states of nature are mutually exclusive and exhaustive, the sum of the probabilities for all of the states of nature will equal 1.

In the Seaborg Concessions example, the probability of hot weather is estimated to be 0.25, warm weather is estimated to be 0.35, and cold weather is estimated to be 0.40, as shown in Table 9.6. The expected value calculations are shown below.

$$\begin{aligned}
EV(d_1) &= 0.25(200) &&+ 0.35(200) &&+ 0.40(200) &&= 200 \\
EV(d_2) &= 0.25(-100) &&+ 0.35(400) &&+ 0.40(400) &&= 275 \\
EV(d_3) &= 0.25(-400) &&+ 0.35(100) &&+ 0.40(600) &&= 175
\end{aligned}$$

Using the EV approach, the best decision would be to order two cases of hot dogs with buns with an expected value of $275.

**TABLE 9.6** Payoff Table with Expected Value Calculations. The Expected Value criteria indicates that the best decision is to buy 2 cases.

| DECISION ALTERNATIVES | WEATHER (STATES OF NATURE) | | | |
|---|---|---|---|---|
| | HOT ($s_1$) | WARM ($s_2$) | COLD ($s_3$) | EXPECTED VALUE |
| Buy 1 Case ($d_1$) | 200 | 200 | 200 | **200** |
| Buy 2 Cases ($d_2$) | –100 | 400 | 400 | **275** |
| Buy 3 Cases ($d_3$) | –400 | 100 | 600 | **175** |
| Probability of $S_i$ | **0.25** | **0.35** | **0.4** | |

## Good Decisions vs. Good Outcomes

It is worthwhile pointing out that there is a difference between making a good decision and achieving a good outcome. A good decision is not necessarily one that has a good outcome. A good well-considered decision may have an undesirable result. For example, Glen may have ordered two cases of hot dogs given the forecast of warm weather for Saturday's game, but a heat wave rolled in causing Glenn to lose $100.

# Expected Value of Perfect Information (EVPI)

Suppose Glen was able to get a weather forecast that was 100% accurate. How much value would this information have for him? Currently, Glen's optimal strategy is to buy two cases with an expected value of $275. With a 100% accurate forecast, Glen's strategy would change depending on the forecast. With each state of nature forecast, he would examine the payoffs and select the decision associated with the highest payoff for that state of nature. Using these payoff and the probabilities of each of these states of nature occurring, the **Expected Value with Free Perfect Information (EVwPI)** can be calculated. Exhibit 9.3 shows the calculation of EVwPI for Seaborg Concessions.

| STATE OF NATURE FORECASTED | P($s_i$) | STRATEGY | PAYOFF | EV CALCULATION |
|---|---|---|---|---|
| Hot ($s_1$) | 0.25 | Buy 1 Case ($d_1$) | 200 | **0.25(200)** |
| Warm ($s_2$) | 0.35 | Buy 2 Cases ($d_2$) | 400 | **+0.35(400)** |
| Cold ($s_3$) | 0.40 | Buy 3 Cases ($d_3$) | 600 | **+ 0.40(600)** |
| **Expected Value with Free Perfect Information (EVwPI) =** | | | | **$ 430** |

**EXHIBIT 9.3**

Calculation of the Expected Value with Free Perfect Information (EVwPI)

The expected value with perfect information is $430. Glen would expect to earn on average $430 using perfect information compared to $275 without it. The expected value of the perfect information is:

| Expected Value with Free Perfect Information (EVwPI) | $430 |
|---|---|
| – Expected Value without Perfect Information (EVwoPI) | –275 |
| = Expected Value of Perfect Information (EVPI) | $155 |

The EVPI is $155. This is the most Glen would be willing to pay for this information. Note that the EVPI calculation was conducted with the assumption that the information was free, allowing the result to indicate the value of that information and maximum amount that should be paid for it.

While perfect information may be unattainable, companies do conduct surveys, collect research samples, hire consultants, and spend money on other sources to help them assess the likelihood of future events. The EVPI calculation serves as an upper limit on how much a company should be willing to pay for such information.

## Decision Trees

Decision trees are used extensively in business. Corporate lawyers, attorneys, and mediators use decision trees to determine legal strategies and estimate the settlement value of litigation. Government officials and economists assess the effects of different policy decisions through the use of decision trees. Decision trees are also used by the energy and petroleum industries to deal with uncertainties in exploration and drilling and by pharmaceutical companies to determine the cost-effectiveness of research into new products. The medical profession develops protocols for the early identification and treatment of life-threatening conditions by assessing risks and costs/benefits using decision trees. Executives and managers make and support financial and strategic decisions through decision tree analysis.

A **decision tree** is an excellent tool to show the chronological nature of a series of decisions and states of nature. By including probabilities and payoffs, it is also used to develop an optimal strategy for choosing the decision alternatives that yield the highest expected value.

Decision trees are drawn from left to right showing the chronological sequence of decisions and states of nature. Decision trees contain two types of nodes: **decision nodes** and **uncertainty** (or state of nature) **nodes.** Decisions are represented with square nodes. Each branch emanating from a decision node represents a different decision alternative. Uncertainty nodes are circular. Branches leaving each uncertainty node represent different states of nature that could occur. Each branch in the tree is labeled with either the decision alternative or state of nature that it represents. In addition, the branches of uncertainty nodes are labeled with their associated probabilities.

At the end of each limb of the tree are the payoffs associated with the series of decisions and states of nature that it took to get there. These payoffs are called **terminal values.**

Decision analysis using a decision tree can be broken down into the following steps, which will be discussed in more detail using the Seaborg Concessions example:

1. Draw the structure of the tree in chronological order.
2. Place the probabilities on the branches of each uncertainty node. Ensure that the probabilities for the branches from an uncertainty node sum to 1.
3. Calculate and place on your tree the terminal values for each limb.

4. Fold back the tree to determine the optimal strategy. The optimal strategy describes the series of decisions that will be taken considering the resultant states of nature.

5. Conduct a sensitivity analysis to determine which inputs have the greatest impact on the expected value and strategy selected.

## 1. Drawing the Decision Tree Structure for Seaborg Concessions

Drawing the structure of any tree always begins with determining which event happens first. In the Seaborg Concessions problem, the first event is the decision of how many cases to order. This event is represented with a square node as shown in Exhibit 9.4. Each decision alternative branch is labeled.

After this decision is made, then we wait to see what the weather will be. This is represented by a round uncertainty node at the end of each decision branch. Each uncertainty node has three branches coming from it labeled Hot, Warm, and Cold as shown in Exhibit 9.5. As there are no further decisions or uncertain events, this is our complete decision tree structure.

## 2. Place the Probabilities on Each Uncertainty Branch

Above each uncertainty node branch, we write the likelihood of that event happening. Above each Hot branch is written 0.25. Each Warm branch is assigned the probability of 0.35 and each Cold branch has the likelihood of 0.40. Adding 0.25, 0.35, and 0.4, we confirm that they sum to 1.

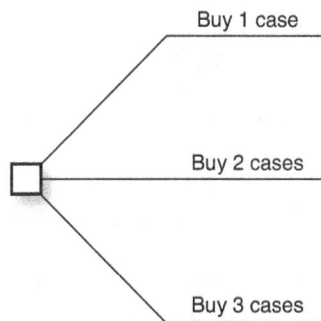

**EXHIBIT 9.4**

Seaborg Concessions
Amount to Buy Node

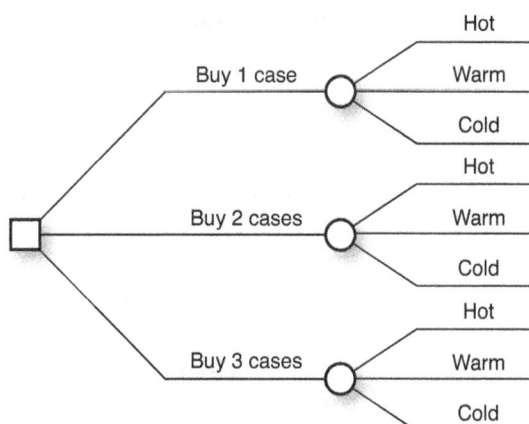

**EXHIBIT 9.5**

Decision Tree Structure for
Seaborg Concessions

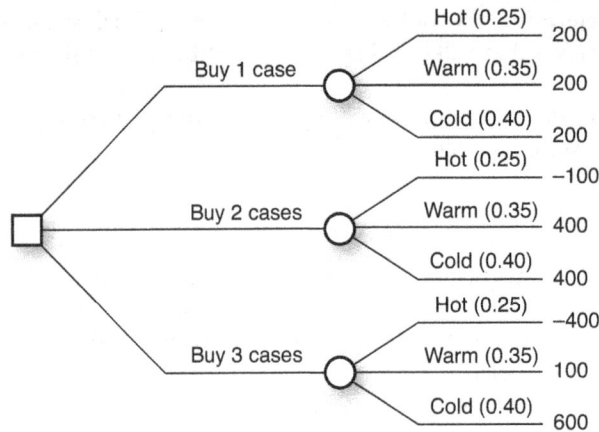

### 3. Terminal Values for Each Seaborg Concessions

We did the calculation of our terminal values when we prepared our payoff table for this example. The probabilities and terminal values have been added to the tree structure and the terminal values for each limb placed on your tree.

### 4. Folding Back the Decision Tree

After the tree is drawn, fold it back to determine the optimal strategy.

- For decision trees, "forward" is left to right, "backward" is right to left.
- When we **fold back** a decision tree, we analyze it from right to left one node at a time.
- For each uncertainty node, calculate the expected value for that node using payoffs and associated probabilities for each of its branches. Write the expected value above the node.
- For each decision node, select the branch with the best expected value and place a line across the other decision alternative branches. Write the expected value of the selected branch above the decision node.
- After the tree is folded back, the optimal strategy describes the decision branches which are not crossed out on the decisions tree.

To fold back the Seaborg Concessions Decision tree, we start with the uncertainty node at the end of the "Buy 1 case" Branch. Its expected value is calculated as follows:

$$EV(d_1) = \quad 0.25(200) \quad + 0.35(200) \quad + 0.40(200) \quad = 200$$

The "Buy 2 cases" and "Buy 3 cases" branches are calculated in a similar fashion:

$$EV(d_2) = \quad 0.25(\text{-}100) \quad + 0.35(400) \quad + 0.40(400) \quad = 275$$
$$EV(d_3) = \quad 0.25(\text{-}400) \quad + 0.35(100) \quad + 0.40(600) \quad = 175$$

Exhibit 9.7 shows the decision tree with the expected values added to the diagram. With the uncertainty nodes calculated, now move to the decision node. As our goal is to maximize our expected value, the "Buy 2 cases" branch with an EV of 275 is preferred over the 200 of the "Buy 1 case" branch and the 175

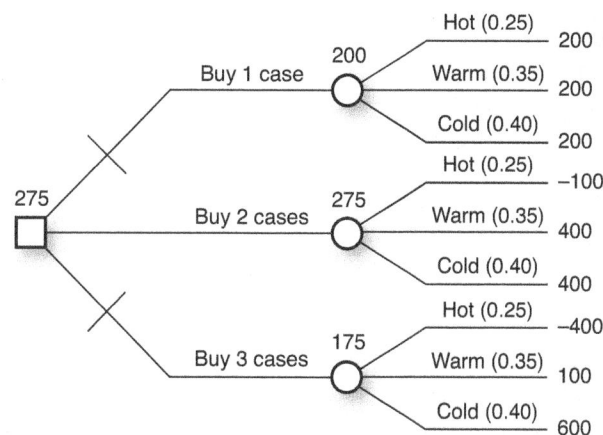

of the "Buy 3 cases" branch. A line is drawn across the branches not selected indicating that they are pruned from our optimal strategy. Exhibit 9.7 shows the final decision tree. The optimal strategy is to buy two cases of hot dogs with buns with an expected value of $275.

## 5. Sensitivity Analysis

Sensitivity analysis in this problem would involve changing the values of the payoffs or probabilities to determine the impact on the optimal strategy and expected value. Decisions that do not change when subjected to large changes in the parameters are called **robust decisions**. Sensitivity analysis can be done by hand but we will focus later in this chapter on how to use PrecisionTree to conduct a sensitivity analysis.

## Risk Analysis

The expected value of the optimal strategy shows the decision maker the long-term average result if they were to make many such decisions following the strategy. Glen would have a long-term average of $275 profit per game if he bought 2 cases of hot dogs with buns under identical conditions. The expected value, however, does not indicate the distribution of actual payoffs that are possible. Risk analysis permits the decision maker to see the difference between the expected value and the payoff that can actually occur. A **risk profile** is a valuable tool to show possible payoffs and their associated probabilities. The risk profile generally takes the form of a table where the first column contains the possible payoffs and the second column indicates the probability of the payoff. Table 9.7 Seaborg Concessions Optimal Strategy Risk Profile shows the risk profile for the optimal strategy for Seaborg Concessions. The risk profile is also frequently displayed in a histogram.

■ TABLE 9.7 Seaborg Concessions Optimal Strategy Risk Profile

| PAYOFF | P(PAYOFF) |
|--------|-----------|
| −100 | 0.25 |
| 400 | 0.75 |

# Decision Analysis Software

While decision trees can be drawn and solved by hand, there are numerous software programs on the market can help you draw and analyze decision trees. They have considerable advantages in sensitivity analysis, allowing the exploration of a variety of changes in the original model. In this book we will use the Excel add-in PrecisionTree. The skills you develop in this software package should quickly allow you to use other decision tree software.

## Using Precision Tree

PrecisionTree is an add-in to Excel and is installed in the same fashion as @Risk. When installed in Excel, a PrecisionTree tab appears on the menu bar as shown in Exhibit 9.8.

To start a new decision tree, simply click on the first button labeled Decision Tree. A dialogue box will appear asking you in which cell you would like to start your tree. After you select the starting cell, the Tree Settings Dialogue box will open as shown in Exhibit 9.9. In it, we give the tree a descriptive name. Next click to open the

☐ EXHIBIT 9.8

PrecisionTree Menu Bar

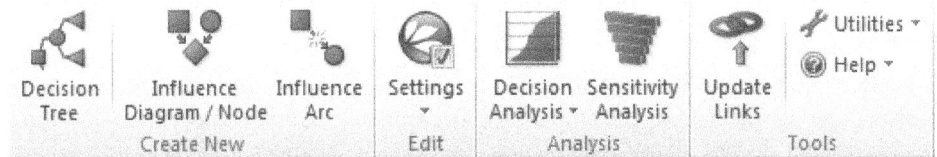

☐ EXHIBIT 9.9

PrecisionTree Settings

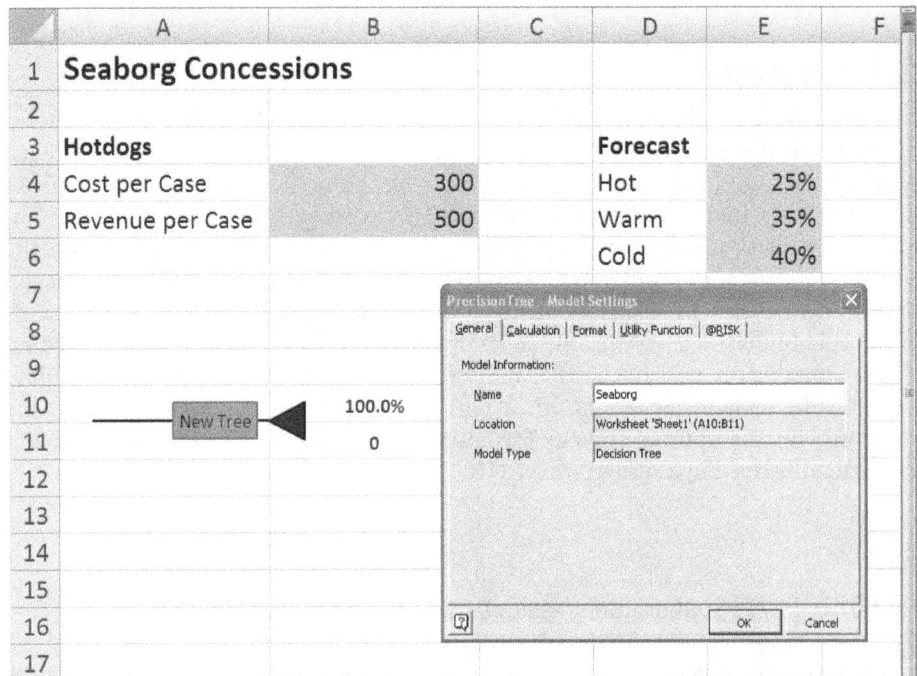

**Calculation** tab (Exhibit 9.10). In this dialogue box we will indicate that we are seeking to maximize the expected cumulative payoff, and then click on the OK button. The other settings in this dialogue box are beyond the scope of this book.

## Adding a Decision Node to the Tree

PrecisionTree adds a blue triangle to the end of each branch. To add the node to our tree, click on this triangle. The Node Settings dialogue box (Exhibit 9.11) will appear where we can select the node type and name the node name. Here, we click on the green square decision node button and give this node the name, "Number of Cases to Purchase." Clicking on the **Branches** tab at the top of the dialogue box will switch the dialogue window (Exhibit 9.12) to allow us to indicate the number of branches to the node, name them, and add any cash flows associated with a particular branch. The branches have been named "Buy 1," "Buy 2," and "Buy 3." In the column labeled "Value" the formulas for the cost of purchasing the cases of hot dogs with buns have been entered. Exhibit 9.13 shows the tree with the added node.

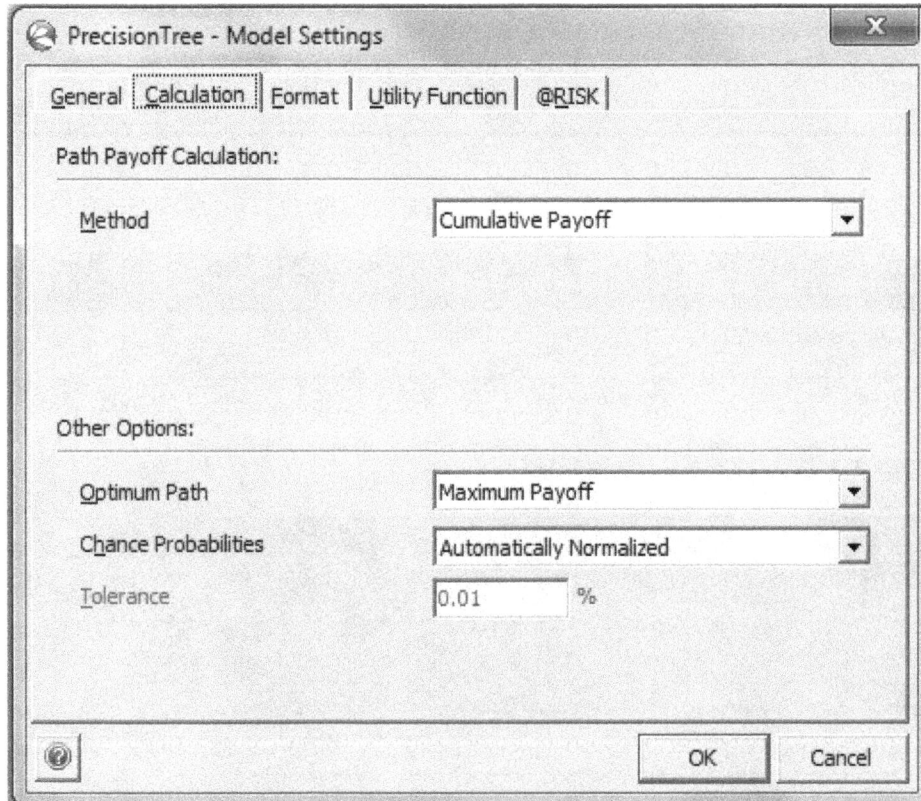

□ EXHIBIT 9.10

Precision Tree Calculation Settings

**EXHIBIT 9.11**

The Node Settings Dialogue Box. It is used to select the node type, insert a node name, and set the number of branches.

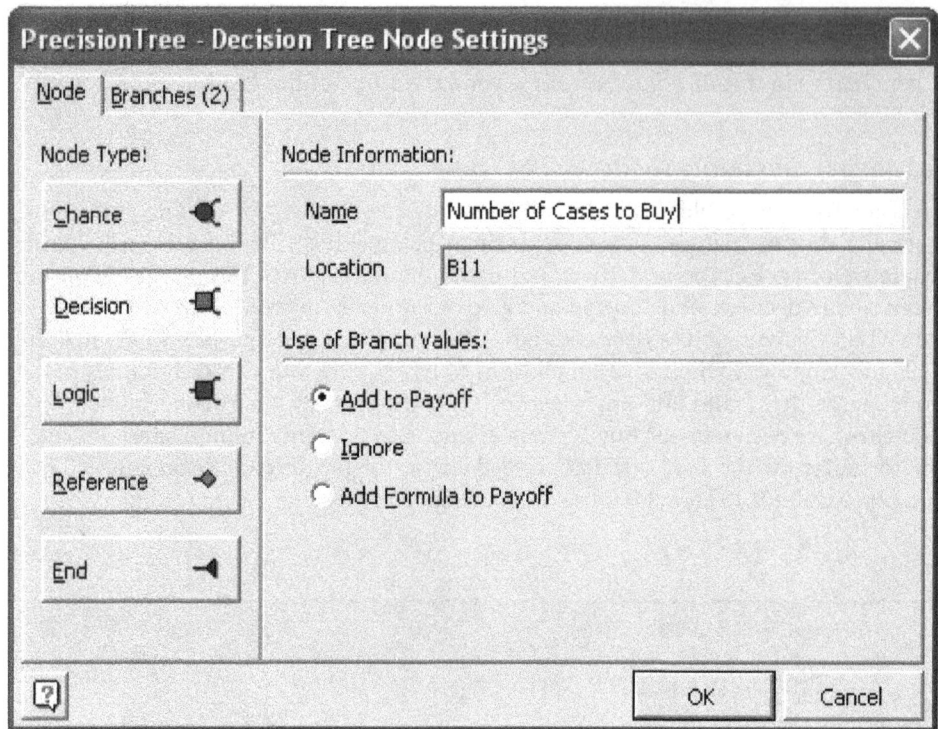

**EXHIBIT 9.12**

Defining the Branches of the Decision Node

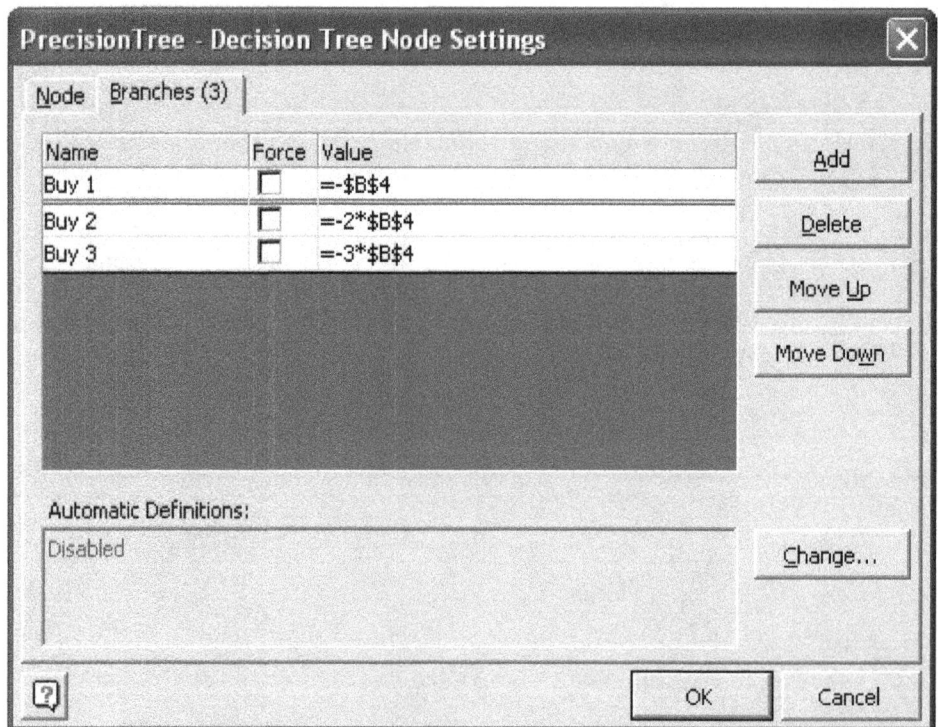

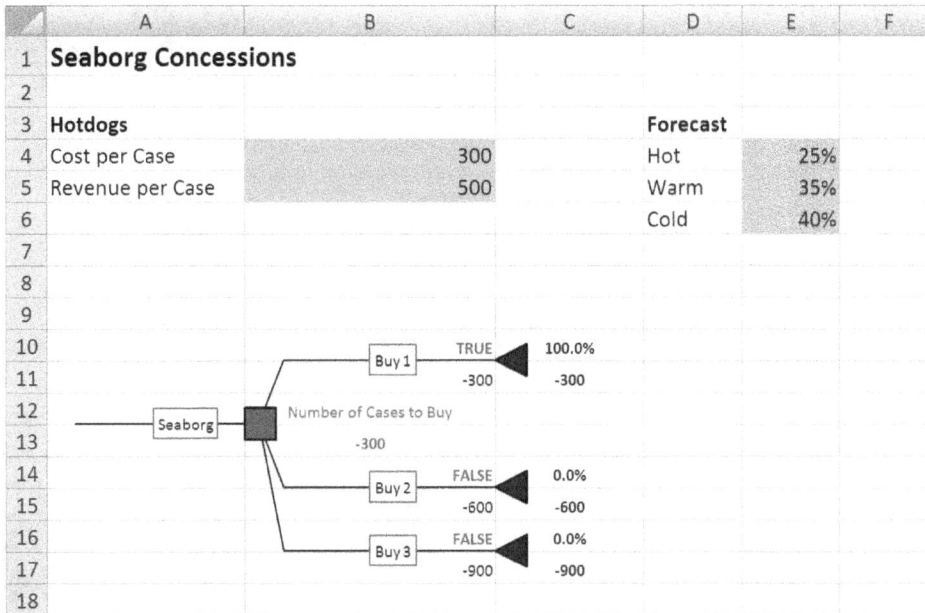

Tree with First Node Added. Note that PrecisionTree automatically calculates the terminal and expected values for the tree.

## Adding the Uncertainty Nodes

Adding an uncertainty node is done just like the decision node. Click on the blue triangle at the end of the branch you want to add. Select the red circular chance node and give the node a name. In this case we will call it "Weather." (See Exhibit 9.14.) In the **Branches** tab a third branch is added and each of the branches named (Exhibit 9.15). In the "Probability" column, cell references are entered containing the likelihood of each weather event. The revenue from selling one case of hot dogs and buns is entered in the "Value" column.

## Copying Subtrees

A node or set of nodes with their branches are referred to as a **Subtree.** Subtrees are often repeated in a decision tree. In the Seaborg Concessions example, the uncertainty nodes are identical except for the payoffs. One of the time-saving aspects of using a software program like PrecisionTree to draw your decision trees is the ability to copy a subtree and paste it in another location in the tree. In this example the uncertainty node is copied by right-clicking on the node and selecting the **Copy Subtree** option on the menu that opens, as shown in Exhibit 9.16. The node is pasted by right-clicking on the triangular nodes at the end of the other branches and selecting **Paste Subtree** option (Exhibit 9.17.) After the subtree is pasted onto the "Buy 2" and "Buy 3" branches, the revenue for the Buy 2 and Buy 3 branches for each branch will have to be updated.

■ EXHIBIT 9.14

Node Settings for an
Uncertainty Node

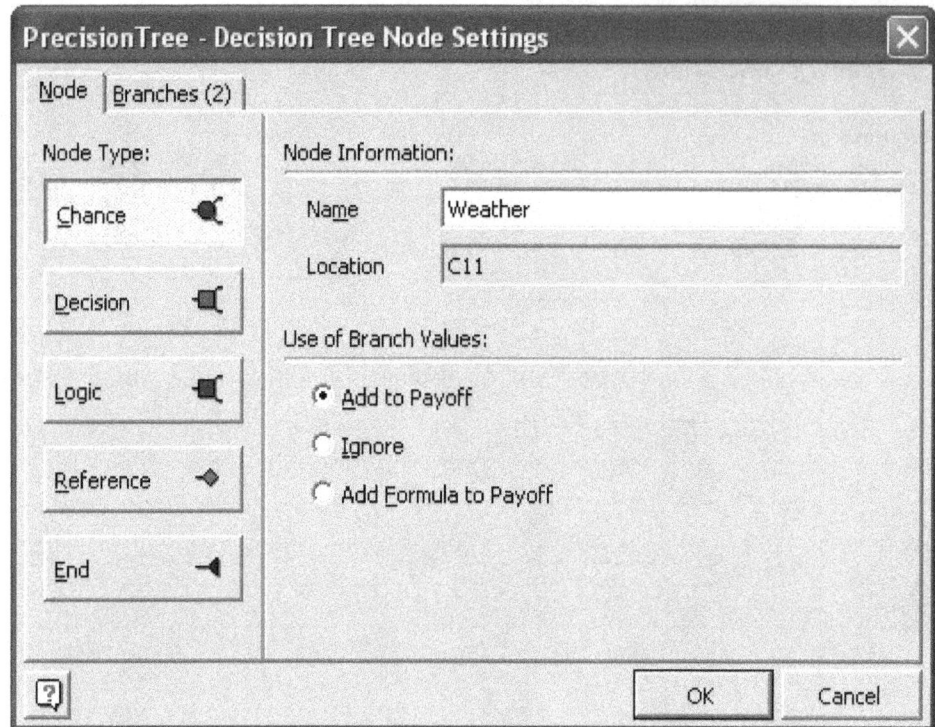

■ EXHIBIT 9.15

Defining the Branches in an
Uncertainty Node

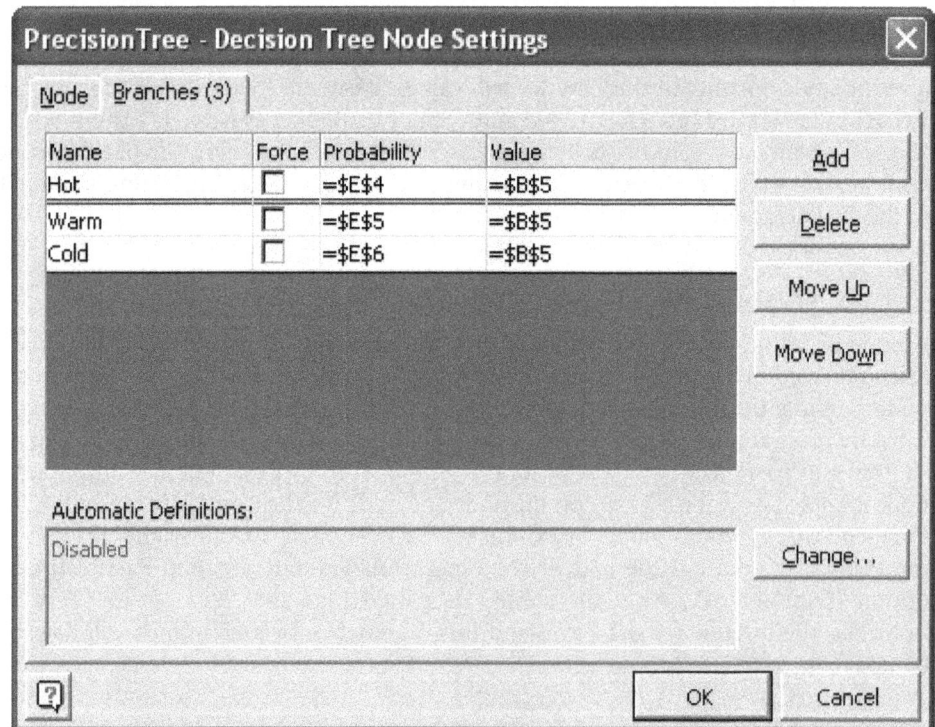

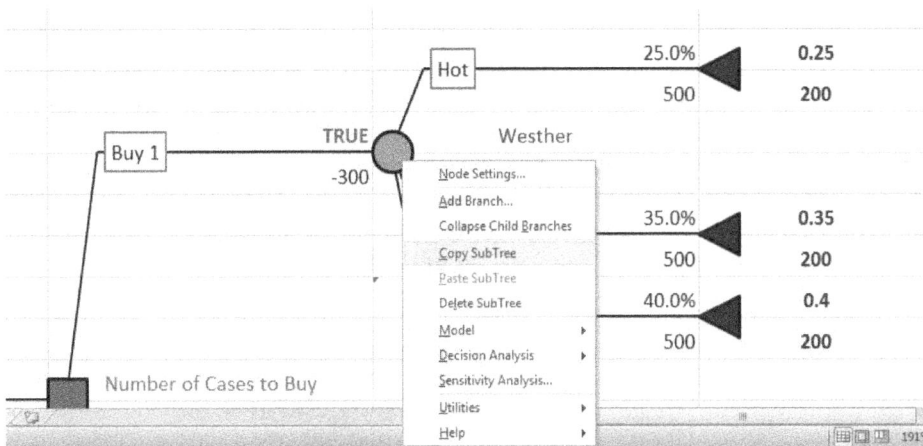

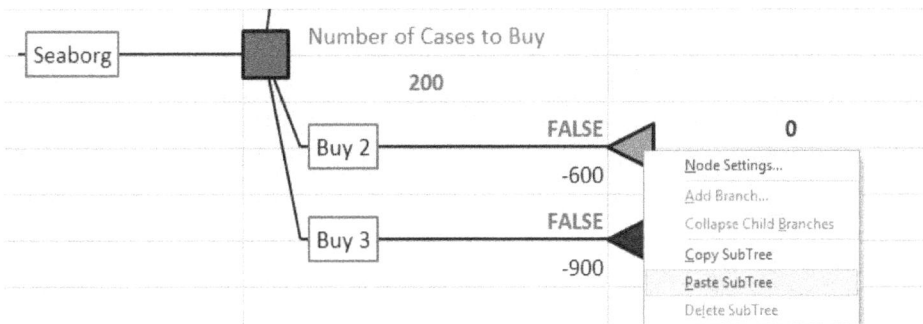

## Changing Probabilities and Values in Trees

With events with the same probabilities appearing in multiple places in the decision tree, it is extremely important to use data tables to record probabilities and data needed to calculate payoffs. The use of range names or absolute addresses for these values will reduce errors that could occur when nodes are copied. After the subtrees are pasted, the formulas for the correct values for the "Warm" and "Cold" branches will have to be entered. They can either be entered by right-clicking on the nodes and changing them in the dialogue window or by directly entering the formulas in the cells below the branches. Table 9.8 shows the cells and the formulas that would have to be entered in them.

■ TABLE 9.8   Formulas for Revenue

|  | CELLS | FORMULAS |
|---|---|---|
| Revenue for selling 2 cases | C25, C27, and C33 | =2*$B$5 |
| Revenue for selling 3 cases | C35 | =3*$B$5 |

## Terminal Values

When constructing a decision tree by hand we had to calculate the terminal values for each terminal limb. PrecisionTree allows the entry of cashflows with the decision or events that occur. These cashflows are shown in the cell underneath the branch they are associated with and terminal values are automatically calculated to reflect the net cashflows along the path from the start of the tree to the end of that limb. To the right of each terminal node, two values can be seen. The first number is the probability of arriving at the end of that limb following the optimal strategy. The value below it is the terminal value for that branch. Exhibit 9.18 shows the completed tree with its terminal values.

## Interpreting the PrecisionTree Diagram (Exhibit 9.18)

The optimal strategy in the tree can be identified by the branches in the tree that are labeled with the word "TRUE" above the branch. Pruned branches are labeled with the word "FALSE." Looking at the final tree, the optimal strategy can be identified as "Buy 2 Cases." PrecisionTree displays the expected value for each node in the diagram in the

### ☐ EXHIBIT 9.18

**Final Decision Tree for Seaborg Concessions**

The optimal decision branch is labeled with TRUE.

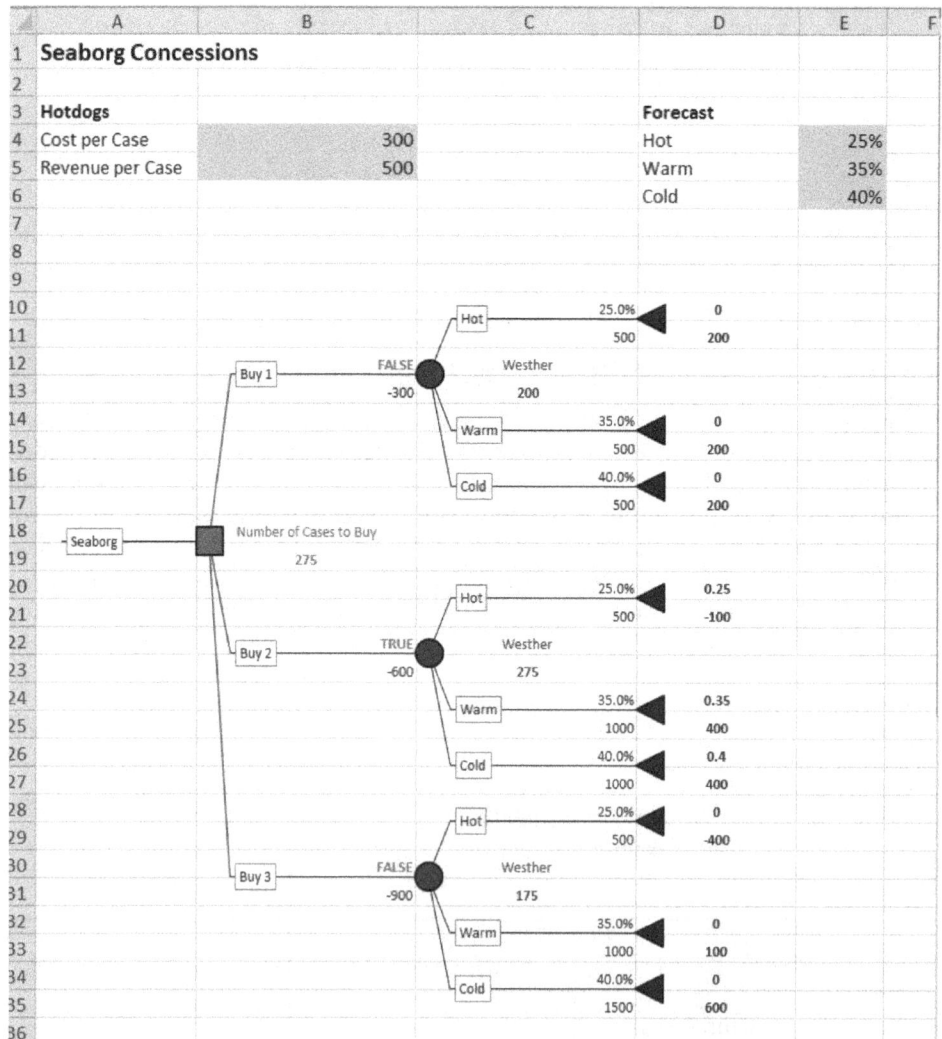

cell to the right of the node. The expected value for following the optimal strategy, found in cell B19, is $275.

Looking at the terminal values, we can see that there is a 0.25 probability of losing $100, and a 0.35 + 0.40 or a 0.75 probability of earning a $400 profit following the optimal strategy.

## Policy Suggestion (Optimal Strategy)

PrecisionTree can generate a variety of reports that help understand the optimal strategy and the returns that can result from following the optimal strategy. To generate the Policy Suggestion report, click on the Decision Analysis button on the PrecisionTree menu (see Exhibit 9.8) and select **Policy Suggestion.** This will open the dialogue box shown in Exhibit 9.19. Make sure the **Optimal Decision Tree** box is ticked and click on **Okay.**

The Policy Suggestion report displays the optimal strategy in tree form. Decisions that were not chosen in the tree have been removed (pruned) from the diagram. This report (Exhibit 9.20) clearly shows that the optimal strategy is to buy 2 cases. Each of the potential payoffs can be seen at the end of the limbs of the tree with their respective probabilities.

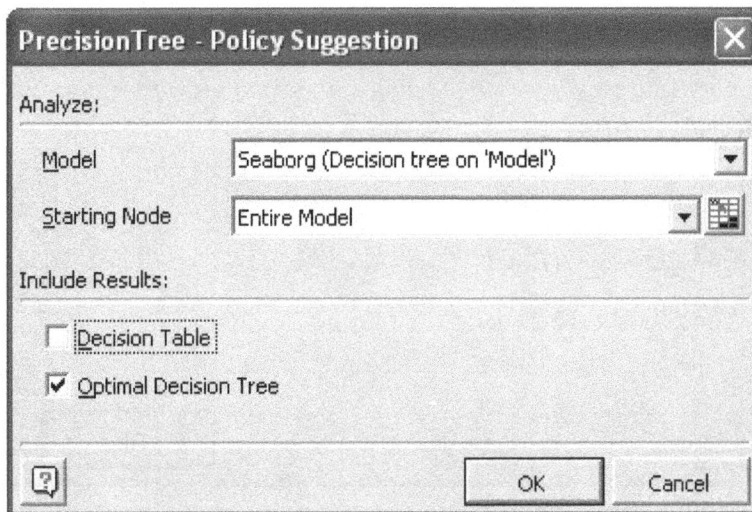

■ EXHIBIT 9.19

Policy Suggestion Dialogue Box

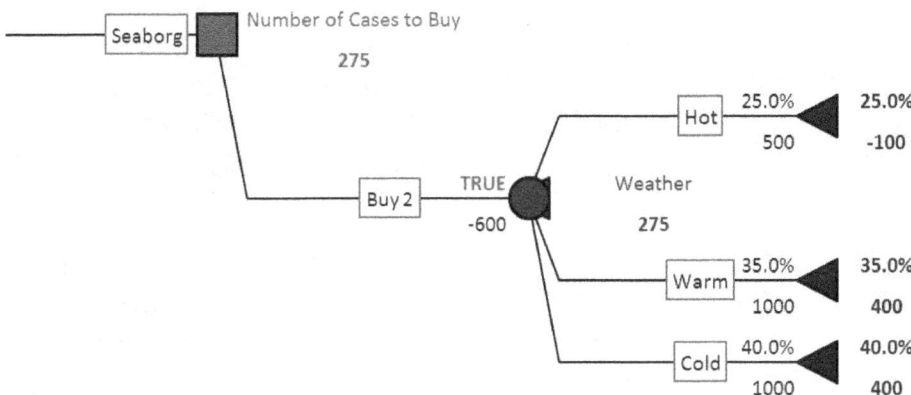

■ EXHIBIT 9.20

Policy Suggestion

PrecisionTree displays the optimal strategy for a decision tree in its Policy Suggestions report. The decision alternative branches that were not selected on the original tree have been pruned off.

## Risk Profile and Statistical Summary

Clicking on **Risk Profile** opens the dialogue box shown in Exhibit 9.21. PrecisionTree will open a new spreadsheet with a tab for each of the options ticked at the bottom of the dialogue box. The **Probability Chart** tab (Exhibit 9.22) contains a spreadsheet showing the risk profiles (probability distributions) for each decision alternative displayed in a different color. The risk of the strategy can be further assessed by looking at the risk profile for each decision alternative printed in table form at the bottom of the sheet. Clicking on the **Statistical Summary** tab (Exhibit 9.23), the user can assess the risk of each decision alternative using the mean and standard deviation and other basic summary statistics provided.

☐ EXHIBIT 9.21

Risk Profile Dialogue Box

☐ EXHIBIT 9.22

Risk Profile Probability Chart Data

The table shows the risk profile for each branch of the decision node.

|  |  | Buy 1 | | Buy 2 | | Buy 3 | |
|---|---|---|---|---|---|---|---|
|  |  | Value | Probability | Value | Probability | Value | Probability |
| 32 | #1 | 200 | 100.0000% | -100 | 25.0000% | -400 | 25.0000% |
| 33 | #2 |  |  | 400 | 75.0000% | 100 | 35.0000% |
| 34 | #3 |  |  |  |  | 600 | 40.0000% |

| Statistics | Buy 1 | Buy 2 | Buy 3 |
|---|---|---|---|
| Mean | 200 | 275 | 175 |
| Minimum | 200 | -100 | -400 |
| Maximum | 200 | 400 | 600 |
| Mode | 200 | 400 | 600 |
| Std. Deviation | 0 | 216.5063509 | 396.0744879 |
| Skewness | N/A | -1.1547 | -0.2731 |
| Kurtosis | N/A | 2.3333 | 1.6412 |

◻ **EXHIBIT 9.23**

PrecisionTree Statistics Report. The Statistics Report provides basic summary statistics for each decision alternative.

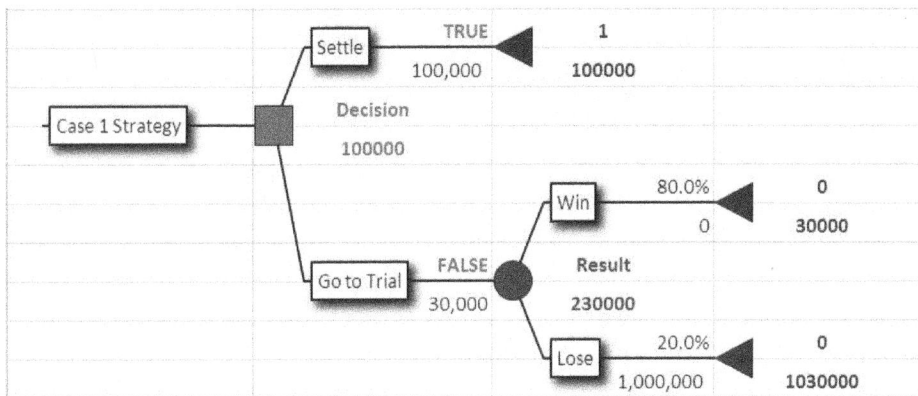

◻ **EXHIBIT 9.24**

Acme Manufacturing Decision Tree for the First Lawsuit

The optimal strategy is the settle the case out of court with an expected cost of $100,000.

## Multiple Stage Decision Trees

The power of decision trees can be seen when there is a need to make a series of inter-related decisions. Often the decisions made early in the process will affect the probabilities of uncertain events at later stages or their payoffs.

## Example: Acme Manufacturing

Sherrie Settle laid out the scenario for her client, Acme Manufacturing. The company was facing two product liability lawsuits. The first case was next month and could be settled out of court with no admission of liability for $100,000. Alternatively, they could fight the case in court. A court battle would incur about $30,000 in legal expenses whether they won or lost. It was a relatively weak case against them and she estimated their chances of winning at 80%. If they won the case, the damages awarded would be zero but if they lost, it would cost them $1,000,000 in damages. A decision tree for this case (Exhibit 9.24) shows that the optimal strategy for the first case is to settle it out of court for $100,000.

The second case was much larger and was scheduled to go to trial in six months. It could be settled out of court for $3,000,000. If it were to go to trial, they would incur about $50,000 in legal expenses whether they won or lost. Sherrie estimated their chances of winning at 60%. If they lose the case, the damages awarded would be $10,000,000. Examining the decision tree for the second case (Exhibit 9.25), the optimal strategy is to settle out of court for a cost of $3,000,000.

Considering the two cases separately indicates that both should be settled out of court for a total cost of $3.1 million. However, a trial decision on the first case would set a legal precedence that would have a big impact on the likelihood of winning and the amount of damages awarded in the second case. The projected outcomes of the second case are summarized in Table 9.9. Acme Manufacturing wants to minimize its total expected costs in settlements, damages, and legal fees. What legal strategy should they follow?

□ **EXHIBIT 9.25**

**Acme Manufacturing Decision Tree for Case 2**

The optimal strategy for the second lawsuit is to settle it out of court with an expected cost of $3,000,000.

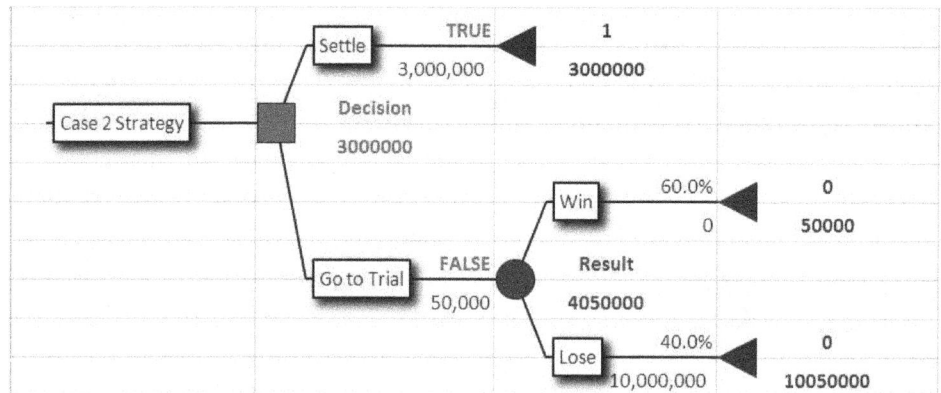

□ TABLE 9.9  Projected Costs and Probabilities

|  | CASE 2 | | |
|---|---|---|---|
|  | CASE 1 SETTLED OUT OF COURT | CASE 1 TRIAL LOST | CASE 1 TRIAL WON |
| COST TO SETTLE OUT OF COURT | 3,000,000 | 6,000,000 | 2,000,000 |
| PROBABILITY OF WINNING | 60% | 30% | 80% |
| ESTIMATED TRIAL DAMAGES IF LOST | 10,000,000 | 14,000,000 | 5,000,000 |
| TRIAL LEGAL PREPARATION COSTS | 50,000 | 50,000 | 50,000 |

Considering these two cases independently ignores the fact that there is a relationship between the two cases. The decision made in the first case and its outcome affects the probabilities and payoffs in the second case. A multistage decision tree is a good tool to visualize and assess this example. Exhibit 9.26 contains the decision tree for Acme Manufacturing.

Exhibit 9.27 shows that when the cases are considered together, the optimal strategy is to go to trial on the first case. If Acme wins, they should go to trial on the second case. If they lose, they should settle the second case out of court before the trial. The expected cost of this strategy is $2,270,000 compared to $3,100,000 when ignoring

## EXHIBIT 9.26

### Acme Manufacturing Decision Tree

The optimal strategy is to go to court with the first case. If Acme wins, go to court with the second case. If they lose, settle the second case.

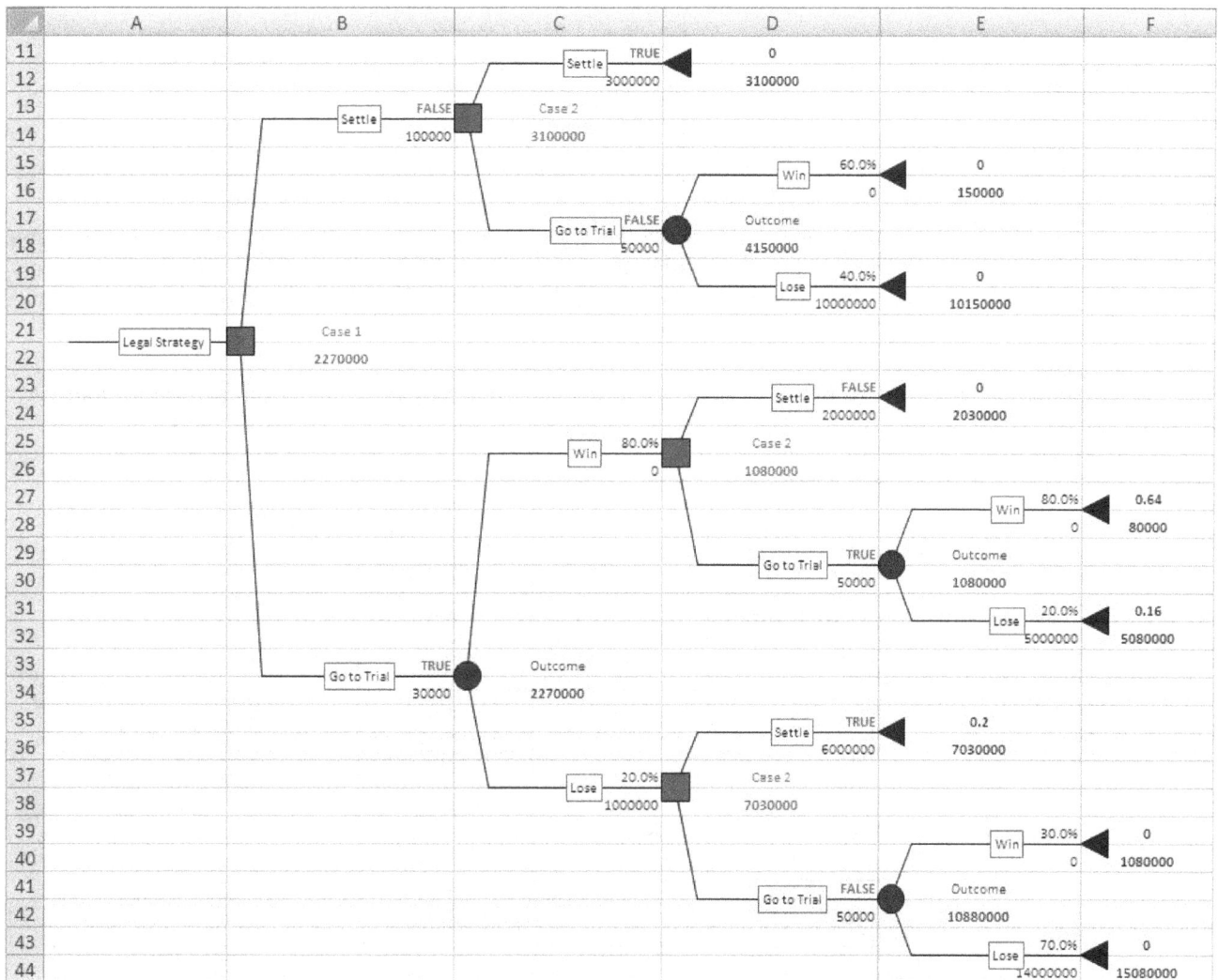

■ EXHIBIT 9.27

Optimal Strategy for Acme
Manufacturing

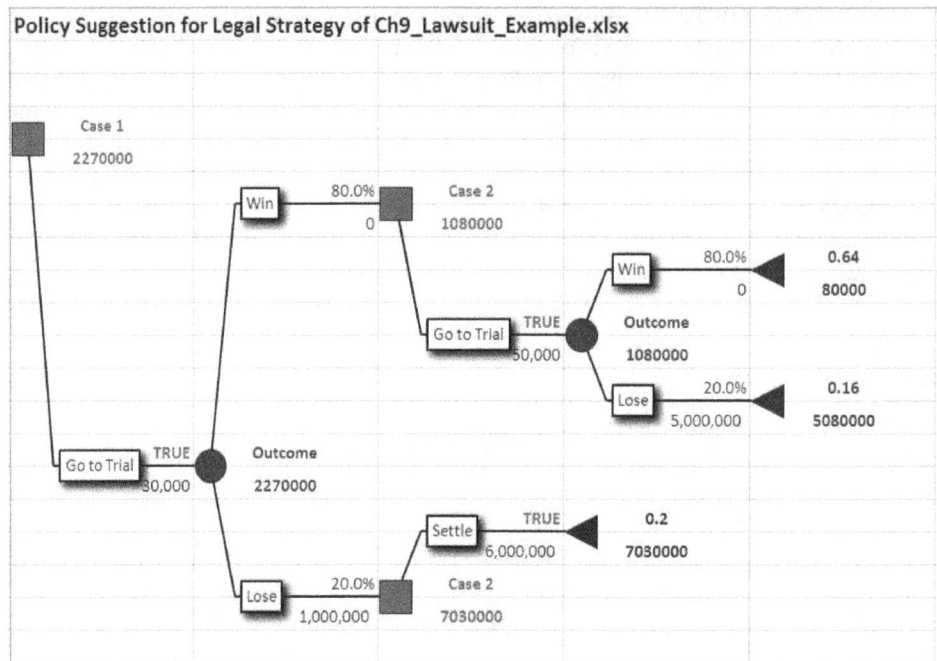

Policy Suggestion for Legal Strategy of Ch9_Lawsuit_Example.xlsx

the connection between the cases. The risk profile (Table 9.10) indicates that there is a 64% chance that Acme will win both cases and have just legal costs of $80,000. There is a 16% chance of costs reaching $5.08 million and a 20% chance they will be $7.03 million if the suggested policy is followed.

■ TABLE 9.10    PrecisionTree Statistics for Acme Manufacturing Legal Strategy

| STATISTICS | SETTLE | GO TO TRIAL |
|---|---|---|
| **Mean** | 3100000 | 2270000 |
| **Minimum** | 3100000 | 80000 |
| **Maximum** | 3100000 | 7030000 |
| **Mode** | 3100000 | 80000 |
| **Std. Deviation** | 0 | 2977314.226 |
| **Skewness** | N/A | 0.6971 |
| **Kurtosis** | N/A | 1.6210 |

| CHART DATA | | | | |
|---|---|---|---|---|
| | SETTLE | | GO TO TRIAL | |
| | VALUE | PROBABILITY | VALUE | PROBABILITY |
| **#1** | 3100000 | 1 | 80000 | 0.64 |
| **#2** | | | 5080000 | 0.16 |
| **#3** | | | 7030000 | 0.2 |

# Sensitivity Analysis using PrecisionTree

As has been observed throughout this book, analysis does not end with finding the optimal solution. Numerical values are estimated and subject to change in dynamic business environments. If the probability of an event changed would it affect our decision? If the estimate of a payoff was a bit too high or low, would the strategy that we had selected still be optimal? Spreadsheets are great tools because we can enter different values in and determine the impact on the strategy and expected outcome.

PrecisionTree gives us the ability to test the impact of changing inputs in a systematic fashion using its sensitivity analysis feature. To activate it, click on the Sensitivity Analysis button on the PrecisionTree menu (Exhibit 9.8.) This will call up a dialogue box like the one in Exhibit 9.28. With it we can analyze the impact of changes on the expected value of the entire tree or on the expected value of any node in the tree.

For this example, we want to explore the impact of changes on the expected value for the entire tree. Using the Input Editor section of the dialogue box, we select inputs to vary and the range of values for each by clicking on the **Add** button found on the right hand side of the dialogue box. In this example we will explore the impact of varying the probability of winning the first case, winning the second case given the first case was won, and the probability of winning the second case given the first case was lost. In addition, we will vary the cost of losing the first case and see if this affects our optimal strategy. The complete tree with cell references can be seen in Exhibit 9.31.

☐ EXHIBIT 9.28

Sensitivity Analysis Dialogue Box

Exhibit 9.29 and Exhibit 9.30 show the dialogue windows for varying the probability of winning the first case (cell B6) and winning the second case given the first case was won (cell E6.) The default setting will be used in each case except for the label for cell E6 which we will add as "P(Win Case 2|Case 1 Won)." Since cell B6 is adjacent to the row labels in column A of the spreadsheet, PrecisionTree is able to generate a meaningful label automatically for it.

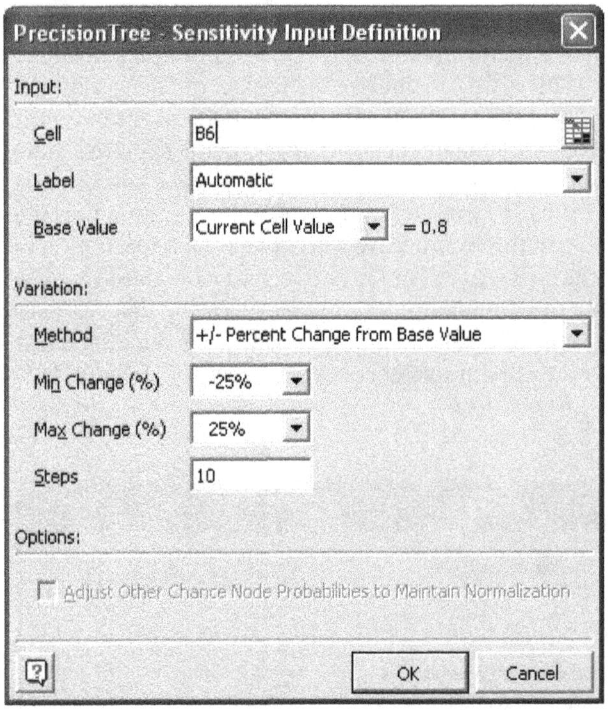

**EXHIBIT 9.29**

Sensitivity Input Definition Window with Default Setting for Cell B6

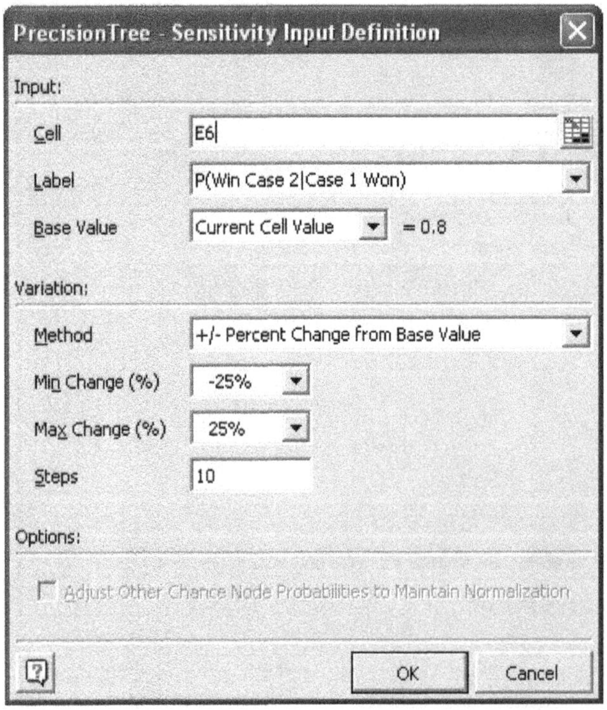

**EXHIBIT 9.30**

Sensitivity Input Definition for Cell E6 with Label Added

When all of the inputs to vary have been added, the **OK** button at the bottom of the window is clicked and PrecisionTree will open a new workbook containing the sensitivity analysis.

⬜ EXHIBIT 9.31

Complete Spreadsheet for Acme Manufacturing

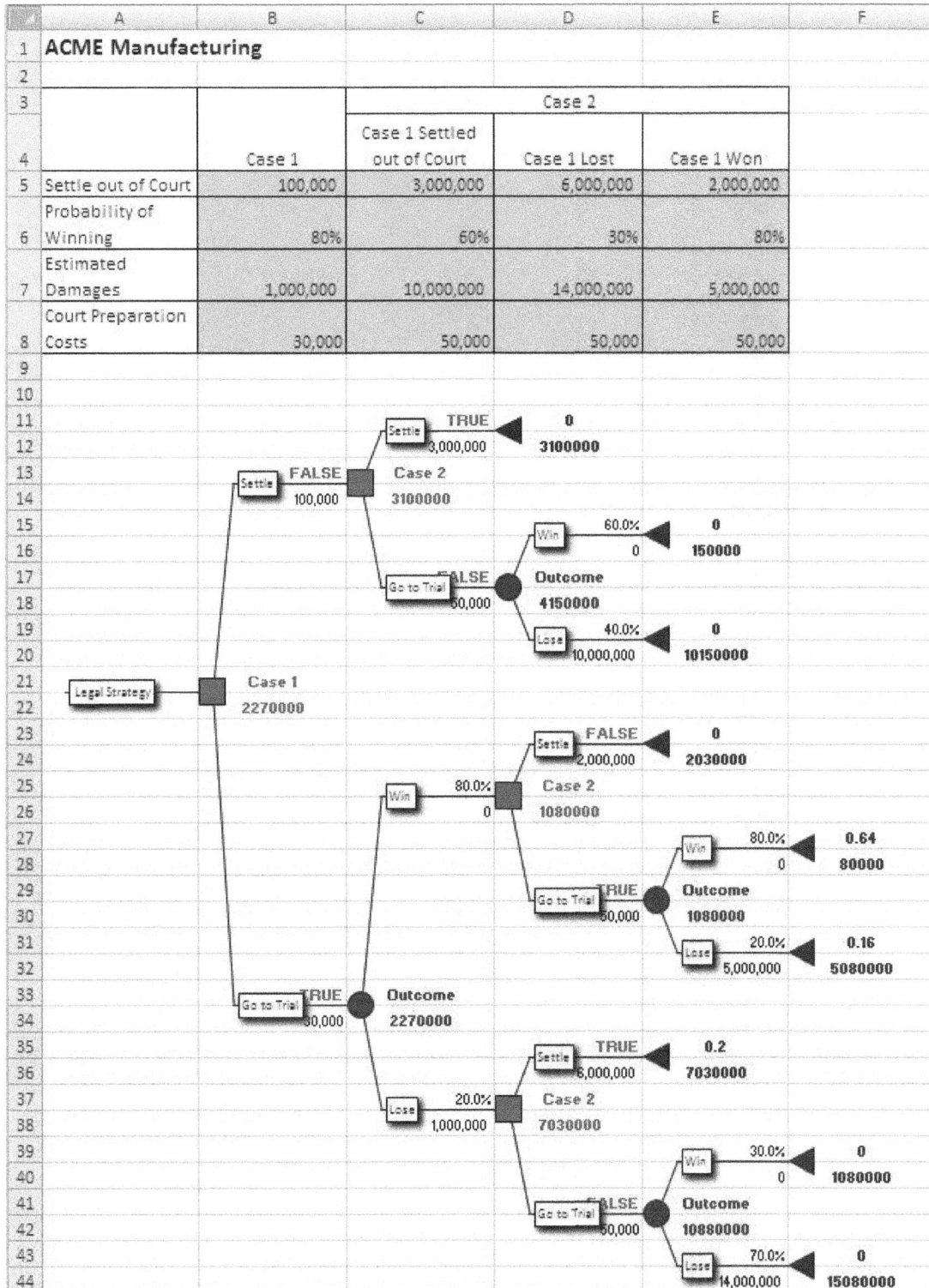

# Interpreting the Sensitivity Analysis Output

PrecisionTree will generate two graphs for each input variable tested. The first, a sensitivity graph (Exhibit 9.32), illustrates how the expected value for the tree changes as the value of the input variable changes. In the graph, we can see that the expected cost is $3,100,000 until the probability of winning exceeds a value between 64 and 69%.

**EXHIBIT 9.32**

Sensitivity Graph for the Probability of Winning Case 1

The graph shows how the expected cost changes as the probability of winning the first case changes.

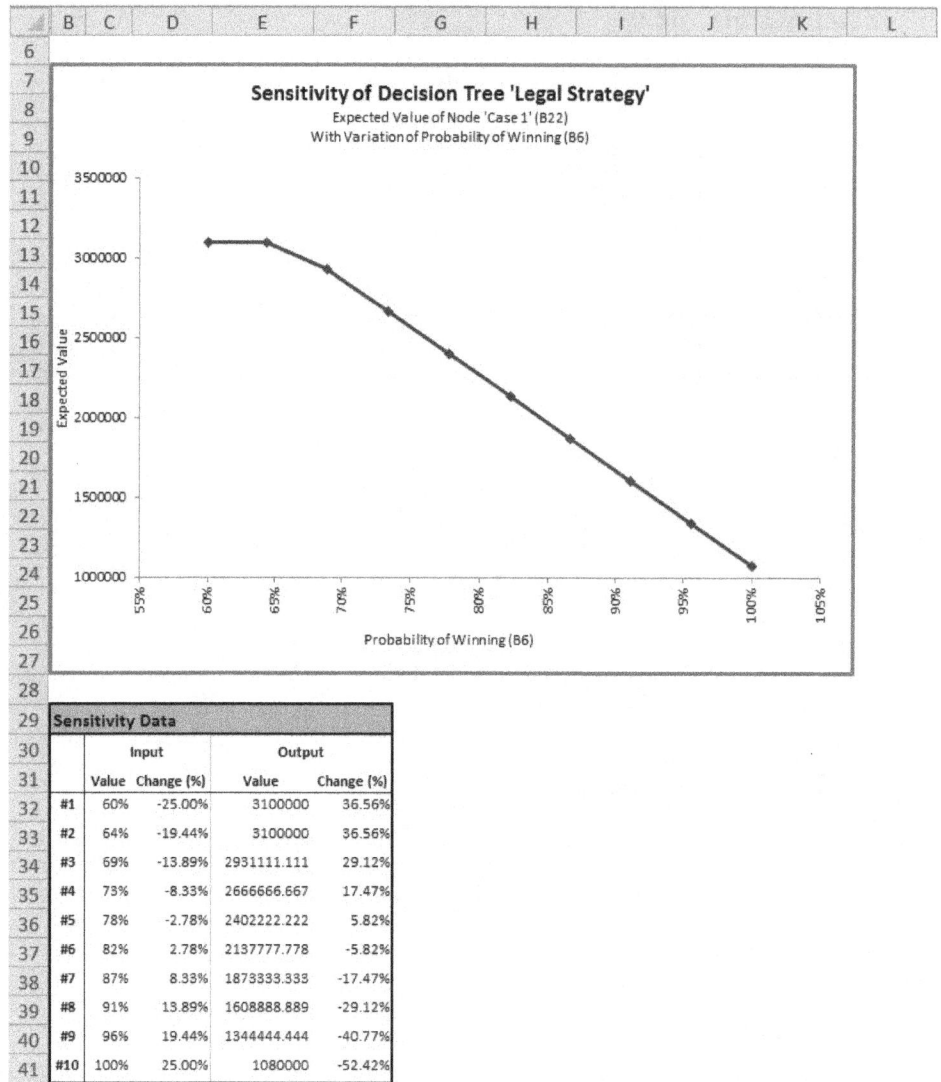

Sensitivity of Decision Tree 'Legal Strategy'
Expected Value of Node 'Case 1' (B22)
With Variation of Probability of Winning (B6)

| Sensitivity Data | | | | | |
|---|---|---|---|---|---|
| | | Input | | Output | |
| | | Value | Change (%) | Value | Change (%) |
| #1 | | 60% | -25.00% | 3100000 | 36.56% |
| #2 | | 64% | -19.44% | 3100000 | 36.56% |
| #3 | | 69% | -13.89% | 2931111.111 | 29.12% |
| #4 | | 73% | -8.33% | 2666666.667 | 17.47% |
| #5 | | 78% | -2.78% | 2402222.222 | 5.82% |
| #6 | | 82% | 2.78% | 2137777.778 | -5.82% |
| #7 | | 87% | 8.33% | 1873333.333 | -17.47% |
| #8 | | 91% | 13.89% | 1608888.889 | -29.12% |
| #9 | | 96% | 19.44% | 1344444.444 | -40.77% |
| #10 | | 100% | 25.00% | 1080000 | -52.42% |

The strategy region graph (Exhibit 9.33) shows expected cost of both branches of the Case 1 decision node, Settle and Go to Trial, as the probability of winning the first case changes. The two lines cross indicating that when the probability of winning the first case falls below 0.67, the optimal strategy is to settle Case 1 out of court. When the probability of winning is 0.67 or higher, the preferred strategy is to go to trial with Case 1.

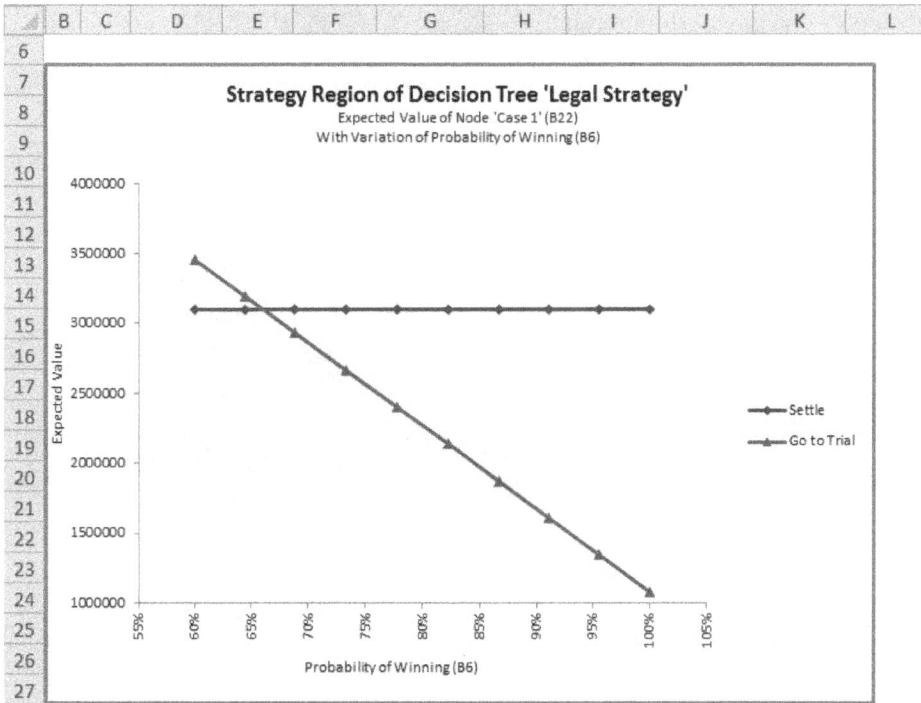

**EXHIBIT 9.33**

Strategy Region Graph—
Expected Cost of Each
Branch of the Case 1
Decision Node as the
Probability of Winning Case
1 Changes

Settling out of court becomes
a superior strategy when the
probability of winning the first
case drops below 0.67.

**Strategy Region Data**

| | Input | | Settle | | Go to Trial | |
|---|---|---|---|---|---|---|
| | Value | Change (%) | Value | Change (%) | Value | Change (%) |
| #1 | 60% | -25.00% | 3100000 | 36.56% | 3460000 | 52.42% |
| #2 | 64% | -19.44% | 3100000 | 36.56% | 3195555.556 | 40.77% |
| #3 | 69% | -13.89% | 3100000 | 36.56% | 2931111.111 | 29.12% |
| #4 | 73% | -8.33% | 3100000 | 36.56% | 2666666.667 | 17.47% |
| #5 | 78% | -2.78% | 3100000 | 36.56% | 2402222.222 | 5.82% |
| #6 | 82% | 2.78% | 3100000 | 36.56% | 2137777.778 | -5.82% |
| #7 | 87% | 8.33% | 3100000 | 36.56% | 1873333.333 | -17.47% |
| #8 | 91% | 13.89% | 3100000 | 36.56% | 1608888.889 | -29.12% |
| #9 | 96% | 19.44% | 3100000 | 36.56% | 1344444.444 | -40.77% |
| #10 | 100% | 25.00% | 3100000 | 36.56% | 1080000 | -52.42% |

# Tornado Chart

When several inputs are varied, PrecisionTree generates a **tornado chart.** The tornado chart shows how sensitive the expected value of the optimal strategy is to changes in each input. The length of each bar shows the percent change in the expected value. Inputs with longer bars have a greater impact on the expected value and are organized in decreasing order. Exhibit 9.34 shows that the probability of winning Case 1 has the largest impact on the expected cost. The cost probability of winning Case 2, given Case 1 was lost, has the smallest impact of the inputs tested. Tornado charts help identify inputs that are most important.

**EXHIBIT 9.34**

**Tornado Graph**

The tornado graph shows which of the analyzed variables has the largest impact on the expected value for the tree.

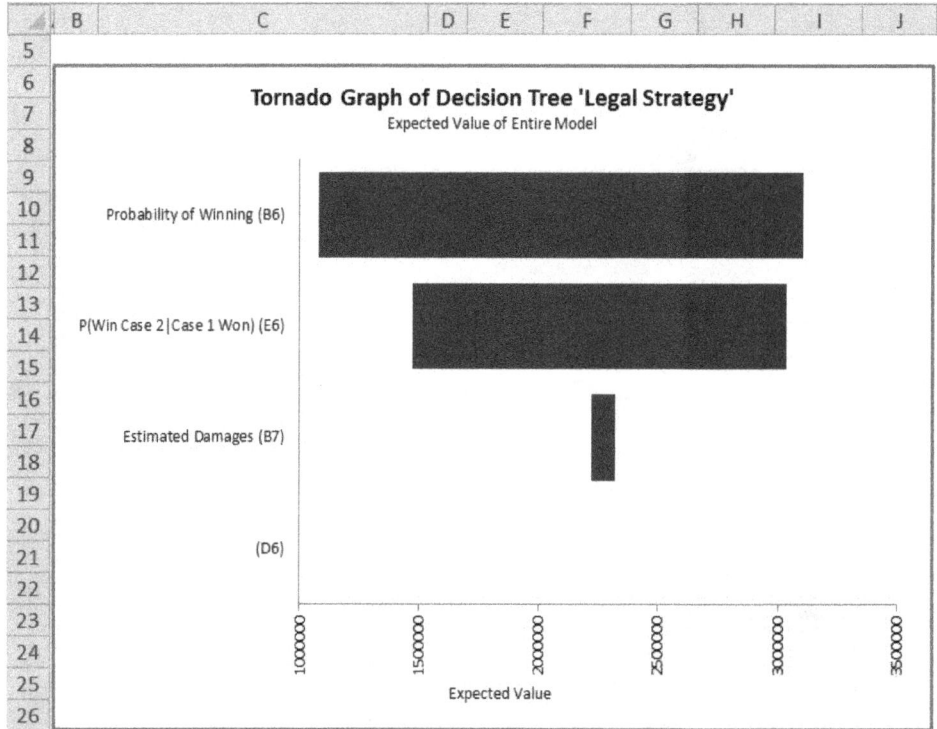

Tornado Graph of Decision Tree 'Legal Strategy'
Expected Value of Entire Model

**Tornado Graph Data**

Decision Tree 'Legal Strategy' (Expected Value of Entire Model)

| Rank | Input Name | Cell | Minimum Output Value | Change (%) | Minimum Input Value | Maximum Output Value | Change (%) | Maximum Input Value |
|---|---|---|---|---|---|---|---|---|
| 1 | Probability of Winning (B6) | B6 | 1080000 | -52.42% | 1 | 3100000 | 36.56% | 0.6 |
| 2 | P(Win Case 2\|Case 1 Won) (E6) | E6 | 1470000 | -35.24% | 1 | 3030000 | 33.48% | 0.6 |
| 3 | Estimated Damages (B7) | B7 | 2220000 | -2.20% | 750000 | 2320000 | 2.20% | 1250000 |
| 4 | (D6) | D6 | 2270000 | 0.00% | 0.225 | 2270000 | 0.00% | 0.225 |

# Summary

Managers make decisions every day. Decision analysis provides structure for the decision making process which is especially helpful in complex decisions. The decision maker can choose decision criteria based on their attitude toward risk and the data available. Decision trees are a valuable tool to structure a series of complex interrelated decisions to determine the optimal strategy and identify the inputs that affect the expected value the greatest amount. Software like PrecisionTree speeds up the process of drawing and analyzing a decision tree.

# Key Terms

**Conservative Approach** Decision making criteria which seeks to minimize the maximum downside of a decision.

**Decision Alternatives** The set of different choices that a decision maker can take.

**Decision Criteria** The method the decision maker uses to select between the decision alternatives.

**Decision Nodes** Square nodes in a decision tree that represent a decision that needs to be made.

**Expected Monetary Value Approach** A decision making criteria that seeks to maximize the expected value for the decision maker.

**Expected Value of Perfect Information (EVPI)** The additional value to decision maker of free perfect information about the state of nature that will occur.

**Folding Back a Tree** The process of determining the optimal strategy in a decision tree.

**MiniMax Regret Approach** A decision making criteria that considers the lost opportunities that would result from each decision alternative and selects the one that minimizes the maximum lost opportunity.

**Optimistic Approach** A decision making criteria that seeks to maximize the upside potential outcome.

**Payoff** The result of the combination of a decision alternative and a state of nature.

**Payoff Table** A table that contains all of the payoffs for a set of decisions and states of nature.

**Regret(Opportunity Loss) Table** A table used in determining the best decision alternative when using the Minimax Regret decision criteria.

**Risk Profile** A table or graph that show the actual payoffs that may occur and their probabilities for a given decision strategy.

**Robust Decision** A decision that does not change when parameters in the problem change substantially.

**States of Nature** Events the decision maker has no control over that can affect the payoffs.

**Terminal Values** The results of a chain of decisions and states of nature in a decision tree.

**Uncertainty Nodes** Circular nodes in a decision tree that represent states of nature that the decision maker does not have control over.

# EXERCISES

1. Tom and Jerry are playing the Rock, Paper, and Scissors game. If Tom wins, he can get a free dinner paid by Jerry, a worth of $10. If Tom loses the game, he will buy Jerry a dinner with the same value. Set up a payoff table for Tom. If there is a tie, no one pays.

   a. Define decision alternatives:

   b. Define states of nature:

   c. Set up payoff table.

2. You have the following payoff table for a decision analysis problem. Payoffs are in units of thousands of dollars of profit.

| | STATE OF NATURE | | |
|---|---|---|---|
| ALTERNATIVES | $s_1$ | $s_2$ | $s_3$ |
| $d_1$ | 3 | 3 | 9 |
| $d_2$ | 4 | 7 | 6 |
| $d_3$ | 2 | 6 | 7 |

a. Which decision alternative would you choose using an optimistic approach?

b. Which decision alternative would you choose using a conservative approach?

c. Which decision alternative would you choose using the Minimax Regret approach?

For parts d and e, assume that $P(s_1) = 0.2$, $P(s_1) = 0.3$, and $P(s_3) = 0.5$.

d. Which decision alternative would you choose using the EV approach?

e. What would be the value of perfect information?

3. You have the following payoff table for a decision analysis problem. Payoffs are in units of thousands of dollars of profit.

| ALTERNATIVES | STATE OF NATURE | | | |
| --- | --- | --- | --- | --- |
| | $s_1$ | $s_2$ | $s_3$ | $s_4$ |
| $d_1$ | 35 | 50 | 45 | 40 |
| $d_2$ | 45 | 40 | 30 | 60 |
| $d_3$ | 20 | 35 | 40 | 80 |

a. Which decision alternative would you choose using an optimistic approach?

b. Which decision alternative would you choose using a conservative approach?

c. Which decision alternative would you choose using the Minimax Regret approach?

For parts d and e, assume that $P(s_1) = 0.2$, $P(s_1) = 0.1$, and $P(s_3) = 0.4$ and $P(s_4) = 0.3$.

d. Which decision alternative would you choose using the EV approach?

e. What would be the value of perfect information?

4. AntiSpyPro, a software company focusing on spyware, is about to launch a new software with P2P techniques and make a price for it. When AntiSpyPro makes a decision on price, it will consider high, medium, and low price and the price set on another competing new spyware software introduced by SpyDoctor. The table below shows the payoff per year for each combination of prices.

| | SPYDOCTOR | | |
|---|---|---|---|
| ANTISPYPRO | LOW ($s_1$) | MEDIUM ($s_2$) | HIGH ($s_3$) |
| LOW ($d_1$) | $20,000 | $25,000 | $30,000 |
| MEDIUM ($d_2$) | -$5,000 | $24,000 | $28,000 |
| HIGH ($d_3$) | -$15,000 | $18,000 | $50,000 |

a. Which price should AntiSpyPro choose if it uses the maximax approach?

b. Which price should AntiSpyPro choose if it uses the maximin approach?

c. Which price should AntiSpyPro choose if it uses the minimax regret approach?

d. Which price should AntiSpyPro choose if it uses the equally likely approach? (Each outcome has the same probability.)

5. University Bookstore is planning to buy back used books and sell them in the next academic year. But the problem is that University Bookstore does not know the real demand. According to past experience, the related profit and probability for different inventory level and demand level is listed in the following table.

| INVENTORY | DEMAND | | |
|---|---|---|---|
| | LOW ($s_1$) | MEDIUM ($s_2$) | HIGH ($s_3$) |
| LOW ($d_1$) | $18,000 | $25,000 | $32,000 |
| MEDIUM ($d_2$) | -$8,000 | $36,000 | $25,000 |
| HIGH ($d_3$) | -$10,000 | -$5,000 | $48,000 |
| PROBABILITY | 30% | 40% | 30% |

a. Find the inventory level for University Bookstore, if it uses the EMV approach.

b. University Bookstore plans to spend $5,000 to do a survey to get the perfect information. Do you think it is a good idea or bad idea?

c. Use PrecisionTree to find the optimal strategy. What is the risk profile for the optimal strategy?

6. Stephanie Mills plans to open a hair salon close to Purdue campus. She has three difference strategies: opening a small-size shop, medium-size shop, and a large-size shop. She estimates the profit and probability for difference favorable markets: Good Market, Fair Market, and Bad Market (refer to the table). Additionally, ZS Consulting Co. offers Stephanie a deal to do a marketing research for her. If Kim pays them $7,000, she can get the perfect information provided by ZS. Do you agree to accept this offer or not?

| | FAVORABLE MARKET | | |
|---|---|---|---|
| SHOP SIZE | GOOD ($s_1$) | FAIR ($s_2$) | BAD ($s_3$) |
| SMALL ($d_1$) | $10,000 | $8,000 | $5,000 |
| MEDIUM ($d_2$) | $30,000 | $20,000 | $0 |
| HIGH ($d_3$) | $50,000 | $10,000 | -$5,000 |
| PROBABILITY | 35% | 40% | 25% |

a. Use PrecisionTree to create a decision tree and find the Optimal Strategy.

b. What is the Policy Suggestion?

c. Change the payoff value for the large-size shop and Good market with a change range from –25% to 25%; Set up 10 iterations; Show the Sensitivity and Strategy Reports.

7. Rebecca Roundtree hung up the phone and pondered her options. A potential client, Ronald Evens, proposed an interesting deal. He had three properties to sell but would only let her list one property at a time to sell. If she could not sell the property in 90 days, the deal was off and she would be out the money she had spent advertising the property. If she took the deal she would have to list the Antioch property first. If she sold it, she could choose between the other two properties which one to list next. She also had the option to quit after selling a property. Rebecca did some research and came up with the values summarized in the table below. Use a commission rate of 4% (If Rebecca sells Antioch she will get $200,000(.004) or $8,000.)

|  | PRICE | ADVERTISING COST | PROBABILITY TO SELL |
|---|---|---|---|
| ANTIOCH | 200,000 | 6,000 | 0.4 |
| BOYLESTON | 500,000 | 8,000 | 0.5 |
| COLFAX | 800,000 | 10,000 | 0.6 |

a. Consider the Antioch property alone in a decision tree. What is her optimal strategy if it were the only property in the deal?

b. Construct a decision tree for the entire deal in PrecisionTree. What is her optimal strategy? What is the EMV? What is the risk profile?

c. At what probability of selling Antioch would she change her mind on this deal?

8. The Eureka Mining and Drilling (EMD) conducts geological explorations for significant petroleum deposits. Currently EMD has an option to purchase outright petroleum rights for a property for $3m. If EMD purchases these rights then it will conduct a geological exploration of the land. Past experience indicates that for the type of geological structure under consideration geological explorations cost approximately $1m and yield significant petroleum deposits as follows:

- natural gas 3% chance

- high quality crude 0.05% chance

- low quality crude 0.2% chance

Past experience has shown that they will not find more than one of these three deposits.

If natural gas is found then the petroleum rights can be sold for $20m, if high quality crude is found then the petroleum rights can be sold for $300m and if low quality crude is found the petroleum rights can be sold for $150m.

EMD has the option to pay $750,000 for the privilege to conduct three days of test drilling before deciding whether to purchase the petroleum rights or not. Such three-day test explorations can only give a preliminary indication of whether significant petroleum deposits are present. The three-day test drilling costs $250,000 and indicates that significant petroleum deposits are present 40% of the time.

If the test drilling indicates significant petroleum deposits then the chances of finding natural gas, high quality crude, and low quality crude increase to 10%, 2%, and 1%, respectively. If the three-day test exploration fails to indicate significant petroleum deposits then the chances of finding natural gas, high quality crude, and low quality crude decrease to 1%, 0.03%, and 0.15%, respectively.

a. What would you recommend EMD should do and why? Construct a decision tree to determine the optimal strategy.

b. At what total cost of conducting the three-day test drilling would they change their decision?

# CHAPTER 10

# Multiple Criteria Decision Analysis

- Apply the concept of dominance to identify the set of Pareto optimal solutions.
- Formulate a goal program for decisions with preemptive priorities.
- Build a spreadsheet model for a goal program and use Solver to find the optimal solution.

## Introduction

In Chapter 9, we looked at decision analysis when there was a single overriding goal that we wanted to achieve, such as maximizing profit or minimizing cost. Not all managerial decisions are this way. Sometimes the decision maker will have several different, and sometimes conflicting, objectives that are important. For example, when purchasing a car you may consider characteristics such as the cost, reliability, gas mileage, horsepower, or towing capacity. Combining these different variables into a single value to maximize or minimize can be a challenge. In this chapter, we explore multiple criteria decisions, the use of trade-off curves, and how to formulate a goal program to find the best solution.

## Domination and Efficient Solutions

In a multiple criteria problem it is possible to find solutions that are **dominated** by other feasible solutions. A solution dominates another solution if it is as least as good as the other solutions on every criteria/criterium and strictly better on at least one criteria/criterium. A solution that is not dominated by any other feasible solution is called an **efficient** or **Pareto optimal solution.** When considering alternative solutions to a problem, it is possible to narrow the choices to the set of efficient solutions.

### Example: Hiring Decision at Peerless Publishing

The selection committee reviewed their interviews and summarized their impressions of each candidate for their management opening in the textbook division. The two most important criteria in their decision were years of experience in publishing and management potential. A candidate's management potential was a subjective judgment of the committee on a scale of 1 to 10 with 10 being the best. Table 10.1 shows the results of their evaluation.

TABLE 10.1   Job Candidate Summary

| CANDIDATE | YEARS OF EXPERIENCE | MANAGEMENT POTENTIAL |
|-----------|--------------------|--------------------|
| A | 8 | 7 |
| B | 5 | 9 |
| C | 10 | 7 |
| D | 10 | 6 |
| E | 12 | 4 |

Using the concept of dominance, they determined that Candidate C dominated Candidate A as they both had a rating of 7 on management potential but C had more years of experience. C also dominated D with a higher management potential rating and the same years of experience. B was not dominated by any other candidate nor was E as they had the best management potential score and highest years of experience, respectively. Candidates B, C, and E are considered efficient solutions as they are not dominated by any others. The selection committee can eliminate A and D from consideration.

The graph of all efficient solutions is called a **trade-off curve** (Exhibit 10.1). This graph of the efficient solutions is also called the **efficient frontier.** The decision maker only needs to consider solutions found on the efficient frontier. As you move along the curve, you trade a better score on one criteria for a better score on the other criteria.

▨ EXHIBIT 10.1

**Efficient Frontier**

The set of Pareto optimal solutions form a trade-off curve when graphed. This trade-off curve is called the efficient frontier.

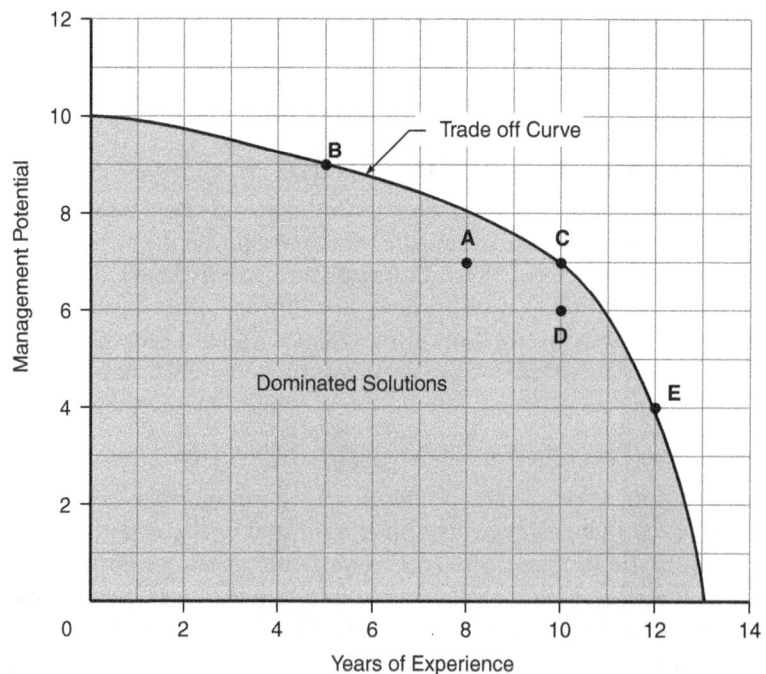

# Goal Programming

**Goal programming** is another tool to use when there are multiple criteria in a decision. It may be impossible to meet all of the goals at the same time. If the objectives can be prioritized, goal programming can be used to optimize each objective in descending order of importance using a concept called **preemptive priorities.** A linear program is used to optimize the first priority with regard to the goal set for it. Then the next priority is optimized in a linear program with a constraint ensuring the achievement of a high priority goal does not suffer in order to achieve a lower priority goal. Each successive priority is tackled in the same fashion; adding a constraint to make sure that the degree that the previous priority was optimized to is not sacrificed in order to reach a lower level goal.

# Frazee Motor Company

The Frazee Motor Car Company (FMC) was planning the release of its new sports car, the E4. They thought it would appeal best to new college graduates and people with high incomes. They set four goals for its ad campaign (listed in descending order of importance):

1. Seen by at least 16 million recently graduated females (RGF)
2. Seen by at least 14 million recently graduated males (RGM)
3. Seen by at least 48 million high income males (HIM)
4. Seen by at least 52 million high income females (HIF)

They have five different types of shows that they can place advertisements in. Table 10.2 shows the views in millions of each demographic and the cost of placing an advertisement.

**TABLE 10.2** Views per Ad (Millions)

| SHOW TYPE | HIM | HIF | RGM | RGF | COST ($1,000) |
|-----------|-----|-----|-----|-----|---------------|
| Drama | 5 | 6 | 1 | 2 | 60 |
| News | 5 | 5 | 1 | 1 | 60 |
| Reality | 3 | 4 | 2 | 1 | 50 |
| Sitcom | 3 | 5 | 2 | 2 | 50 |
| Sports | 6 | 3 | 3 | 1 | 80 |

## Defining the Decision Variables

FMC has to decide how many advertisements to place in each show type. We will use the following decision variables:

Let $D$ represent the number of advertisements placed in dramatic shows.

Let $N$ represent the number of advertisements placed in news shows.

Let $R$ represent the number of advertisements placed in reality shows.

Let $C$ represent the number of advertisements placed in comedy shows.

Let $S$ represent the number of advertisements placed in sports shows.

In addition to these, we need to have two deviation variables for each goal that indicate how much each goal was over- or under-achieved.

Let $d_i^+$ represent the amount goal $i$ was overachieved. $i = 1, 2, 3, 4$.

Let $d_i^-$ represent the amount goal $i$ was underachieved. $i = 1, 2, 3, 4$.

## Objective Functions

In goal programming, you need to solve a linear program for each goal in the order of their priority. Each linear program will have its own objective function. The solution of each objective function will be included in the successive goal programs as constraints. This ensures that higher priority goals will not be sacrificed in order to reach lower priority goals.

| IF THE GOAL IS: | THEN THE OBJECTIVE FUNCTION IS: |
|---|---|
| At least a particular value | Minimize: $d_i^-$ |
| At most a particular value | Minimize: $d_i^+$ |
| To be a particular value | Minimize: $d_i^+ + d_i^-$ |

The first priority goal for FMC is for their advertisement to be seen by at least 16 million recently graduated females (RGF). FMC would like to meet this goal if possible and if not possible to come as close to the goal as it can. Therefore, it wants to minimize the amount it underachieves the goal or:

$$\text{MIN: } d_1^-$$

In the linear program for the second priority goal, FMC would like for its ads to reach at least 14 million recently graduated males (RGM) or barring that come as close to that as possible without sacrificing the level of meeting the first goal. The objective function for the second priority goal is:

$$\text{MIN: } d_2^-$$

Likewise, for the third priority goal to be seen by at least 48 million high income males (HIM), the objective function will be:

$$\text{MIN: } d_3^-$$

The fourth priority goal is for the advertisements to be seen by at least 52 million high income females (HIF). The objective function for this linear program will be:

$$\text{MIN: } d_4^-$$

The objective functions of the linear programs are often summarized in a single line as follows:

$$\text{MIN: } P1(d_1^-) + P2(d_2^-) + P3(d_3^-) + P4(d_4^-)$$

Note that P1, P2, P3, and P4 are not variables but rather short hand notation indicating the objective function for the 4 linear programs.

## Constraints

The constraints in a goal program can be split into two categories: **soft** and **hard constraints.** Soft constraints are also called goal constraints and are used to measure how the solution deviates from the goal. Hard constraints are often called functional constraints and directly limit the values of the decision variables.

**Soft Constraints** A soft constraint is needed for each goal. These constraints are called soft constraints because they do not limit the values of the decision variables but rather measure the difference between value obtained with the solution and the goal value. To do this, each soft constraint, $i$, has two deviation variables, $d_i^+$ and $d_i^-$, which measure the amount the goal is overachieved and underachieved, respectively. The soft constraint for FMC's first priority goal is:

$$2D + 1N + 1R + 2C + 1S = 16 + d_1^+ - d_1^- \qquad \text{Priority 1 goal constraint}$$

This constraint is coupled with the first objective function which minimizes $d_1^-$. If the goal can be met, $d_1^-$ will equal 0. If not, it will have a positive value that tells us how much the goal was underachieved. Soft constraints for other goals are formulated in a similar fashion as follows:

$$1D + 1N + 2R + 2C + 3S = 14 + d_2^+ - d_2^- \qquad \text{Priority 2 goal constraint}$$

$$5D + 5N + 3R + 3C + 6S = 48 + d_3^+ - d_3^- \qquad \text{Priority 3 goal constraint}$$

$$6D + 5N + 4R + 5C + 3S = 52 + d_4^+ - d_4^- \qquad \text{Priority 4 goal constraint}$$

**Hard Constraints** The hard constraints reflect the functional limitations on the problem. FMC has limits on the number of each type of advertisement it can place as well as a budget constraint.

| | | | |
|---|---|---|---|
| $D$ | $\leq 5$ | Maximum Drama Advertisements |
| $N$ | $\leq 5$ | Maximum News Advertisements |
| $R$ | $\leq 5$ | Maximum Reality Advertisements |
| $C$ | $\leq 5$ | Maximum Comedy Advertisements |
| $S$ | $\leq 5$ | Maximum Sports Advertisements |

$$60D + 60N + 50R + 50C + 80S \leq 580 \qquad \text{Budget (in thousands of dollars)}$$

$$D, N, R, C, S, d_i^+, d_i^- \geq 0, \ i = 1, 2, 3, 4 \qquad \text{Non-negativity}$$

### Formulation Summary

The goal program for FMC can be summarized in standard form as follows:

Let $D$ represent the number of advertisements placed in dramatic shows.

Let $N$ represent the number of advertisements placed in news shows.

Let $R$ represent the number of advertisements placed in reality shows.

Let $C$ represent the number of advertisements placed in comedy shows.

Let $S$ represent the number of advertisements placed in sports shows.

Let $d_i^+$ represent the amount goal $i$ was overachieved. $i = 1, 2, 3, 4$.

Let $d_i^-$ represent the amount goal $i$ was underachieved. $i = 1, 2, 3, 4$.

$$\text{MIN: } P1(d_1^-) + P2(d_2^-) + P3(d_3^-) + P4(d_4^-)$$

subject to:

$$2D + 1N + 1R + 2C + 1S - d_1^+ + d_1^- = 16 \quad \text{Priority 1 goal constraint}$$

$$1D + 1N + 2R + 2C + 3S - d_2^+ + d_2^- = 14 \quad \text{Priority 2 goal constraint}$$

$$5D + 5N + 3R + 3C + 6S - d_3^+ + d_3^- = 48 \quad \text{Priority 3 goal constraint}$$

$$6D + 5N + 4R + 5C + 3S - d_4^+ + d_4^- = 52 \quad \text{Priority 4 goal constraint}$$

$$D \qquad\qquad\qquad\qquad\qquad \leq 5 \quad \text{Maximum Drama Advertisements}$$

$$N \qquad\qquad\qquad\qquad \leq 5 \quad \text{Maximum News Advertisements}$$

$$R \qquad\qquad\qquad \leq 5 \quad \text{Maximum Reality Advertisements}$$

$$C \qquad\qquad \leq 5 \quad \text{Maximum Comedy Advertisements}$$

$$S \qquad \leq 5 \quad \text{Maximum Sports Advertisements}$$

$$60D + 60N + 50R + 50C + 80S = 580 \quad \text{Budget (in thousands of dollars)}$$

$$D, N, R, C, S, d_i^+, d_i^- \geq 0, i = 1, 2, 3, 4 \qquad \text{Non-negativity}$$

## Solving the Goal Program

To arrive at the optimal solution to this goal program will require us to solve four linear programs in succession. In the first linear program, the objective function will be:

$$\text{MIN: } d_1^-$$

Exhibit 10.2 shows the spreadsheet model used for this goal program. The initial objective cell is B34 which contains the amount the first goal is underachieved. Exhibit 10.3 shows the Solver Parameters dialogue box used to solve the initial linear program.

| | A | B | C | D | E | F | G | H | I |
|---|---|---|---|---|---|---|---|---|---|
| 1 | **Frazee Auto Ad Campaign** | | | | | | | | |
| 2 | | | | | | | | | |
| 3 | **Show Type** | Drama | News | Reality | Sitcom | Sports | | | |
| 4 | **Drama Max** | 1 | | | | | 5 | | |
| 5 | **News Max** | | 1 | | | | 5 | | |
| 6 | **Reality Max** | | | 1 | | | 5 | | |
| 7 | **Sitcom Max** | | | | 1 | | 5 | | |
| 8 | **Sports Max** | | | | | 1 | 5 | | |
| 9 | **Cost ($1,000)** | 60 | 60 | 50 | 50 | 80 | 580 | | |
| 10 | **RGF** | 2 | 1 | 1 | 2 | 1 | | | |
| 11 | **RGM** | 1 | 1 | 2 | 2 | 3 | | | |
| 12 | **HIM** | 5 | 5 | 3 | 3 | 6 | | | |
| 13 | **HIF** | 6 | 5 | 4 | 5 | 3 | | | |
| 14 | | | | | | | | | |
| 15 | **Number of Ads** | 1 | 2 | 3 | 0 | 0 | | | |
| 16 | | | | | | | | | |
| 17 | **Hard Constraints** | **LHS** | **sign** | **RHS** | | | | | |
| 18 | Drama Max | 1 | <= | 5 | | | | | |
| 19 | News Max | 2 | <= | 5 | | | | | |
| 20 | Reality Max | 3 | <= | 5 | | | | | |
| 21 | Sitcom Max | 0 | <= | 5 | | | | | |
| 22 | Sports Max | 0 | <= | 5 | | | | | |
| 23 | **Cost ($1,000)** | 330 | <= | 580 | | | | | |
| 24 | | | | | | | | | |
| 25 | **Goal Constraints** | | | | | | | | |
| 26 | | **Exposures** | **Over** | **Under** | **LHS** | | **Goal** | | |
| 27 | **RGF** | 7 | 0 | 0 | 7 | = | 16 | | |
| 28 | **RGM** | 9 | 0 | 0 | 9 | = | 14 | | |
| 29 | **HIM** | 24 | 0 | 0 | 24 | = | 48 | | |
| 30 | **HIF** | 28 | 0 | 0 | 28 | = | 52 | | |
| 31 | | | | | | | | | |
| 32 | **Objective Functions** | | | | | | | | |
| 33 | | Deviation Value | | Best | | | | | |
| 34 | **LP1: RGF Under** | 0 | <= | 1000 | | The values for in cells | | | |
| 35 | **LP2: RGM Under** | 0 | <= | 1000 | | D34:D37 are set arbitarily | | | |
| 36 | **LP3: HIM Under** | 0 | <= | 1000 | | high in the initial model and | | | |
| 37 | **LP4: HIF Under** | 0 | <= | 1000 | | changed as each linear | | | |
| 38 | | | | | | | | | |
| 39 | **Range Names** | | | | | | | | |
| 40 | Deviations | ='Goal Program Model'!$C$27:$D$30 | | | | | | | |
| 41 | Num_Ads | ='Goal Program Model'!$B$15:$F$15 | | | | | | | |

■ EXHIBIT 10.2

Frazee Motor Company Advertising Spreadsheet Model

**Solver Parameters**

Set Target Cell:  $B$34

Equal To:  ○ Max  ● Min  ○ Value of:  0

By Changing Cells:

Num_Ads,Deviation

Subject to the Constraints:

$B$12:$B$16 <= $D$12:$D$16
$B$19 <= $D$19
$B$30:$B$33 <= $D$30:$D$33
$E$23:$E$26 = $G$23:$G$26
Num_Ads = integer

[Solve] [Close] [Guess] [Options] [Add] [Change] [Delete] [Reset All] [Help]

■ EXHIBIT 10.3

Solver Parameters for First Linear Program

Looking at Exhibit 10.4 (cell B34), we can see that $d_1^-$ equals 0. For the next three linear programs, the constraint, $d_1^- = 0$, will be added to the formulation. This is done by changing the value in cell D34 to 0 .

**Solver Parameter for the Second Linear Program**
The objective function cell has been set to B35.

| | Exposures | Over | Under | LHS | | Goal |
|---|---|---|---|---|---|---|
| **RGF** | 18 | 2 | 0 | 16 | = | 16 |
| **RGM** | 14 | 0 | 0 | 14 | = | 14 |
| **HIM** | 35 | 0 | 13 | 48 | = | 48 |
| **HIF** | 49 | 0 | 3 | 52 | = | 52 |

**Objective Functions**

| | Deviation Value | | Best | |
|---|---|---|---|---|
| **LP1: RGF Under** | 0 | <= | 0 | The values for in cells D34:D37 are set arbitrarily high in the initial model and changed as each linear |
| **LP2: RGM Under** | 0 | <= | 1000 | |
| **LP3: HIM Under** | 13 | <= | 1000 | |
| **LP4: HIF Under** | 3 | <= | 1000 | |

**Range Names**

| | |
|---|---|
| Deviations | ='Goal Program Model'!$C$27:$D$30 |
| Num_Ads | ='Goal Program Model'!$B$15:$F$15 |

## Solving for the Priority 2 Goal

To solve for the second objective: MIN: $d_2^-$, the target cell is changed to cell B35 in Solver. Exhibit 10.5 shows an optimal solution to the second goal program. The second goal is successfully met as $d_2^-$ equals 0. With the placement of advertisements of 2 in dramas, 3 in news, 4 in comedies, and 1 in sports, there are 16 million views of the advertisements by recently graduated males.

## Solving for the Priority 3 Goal

To solve for the third goal, a constraint is first added to ensure that the second goal of at least 14 million views by recently graduated males is always met. The constraint, $d_2^- = 0$, is added by entering a 0 in cell D35. B36 becomes the new target cell in Solver.

Exhibit 10.5 shows that $d_3^-$ equals 5. The third priority goal was not met. Only 43 million high income males will view the advertisement, 5 million short of the goal of 48 million. The constraint, $d_3^- = 5$, is added to the linear program.

| 14 | | | | | | | | |
|---|---|---|---|---|---|---|---|---|
| 15 | Number of Ads | 2 | 3 | 0 | 4 | 1 | | |
| 16 | | | | | | | | |
| 17 | Hard Constraints | LHS | sign | RHS | | | | |
| 18 | Drama Max | 2 | <= | 5 | | | | |
| 19 | News Max | 3 | <= | 5 | | | | |
| 20 | Reality Max | 0 | <= | 5 | | | | |
| 21 | Sitcom Max | 4 | <= | 5 | | | | |
| 22 | Sports Max | 1 | <= | 5 | | | | |
| 23 | Cost ($1,000) | 580 | <= | 580 | | | | |
| 24 | | | | | | | | |
| 25 | Goal Constraints | | | | | | | |
| 26 | | Exposures | Over | Under | LHS | | Goal | |
| 27 | RGF | 16 | 0 | 0 | 16 | = | 16 | |
| 28 | RGM | 16 | 2 | 0 | 14 | = | 14 | |
| 29 | HIM | 43 | 0 | 5 | 48 | = | 48 | |
| 30 | HIF | 50 | 0 | 2 | 52 | = | 52 | |
| 31 | | | | | | | | |
| 32 | Objective Functions | | | | | | | |
| 33 | | Deviation Value | | Best | | | | |
| 34 | LP1: RGF Under | 0 | <= | 0 | | | | |
| 35 | LP2: RGM Under | 0 | <= | 0 | | | | |
| 36 | LP3: HIM Under | 5 | <= | 5 | | | | |
| 37 | LP4: HIF Under | 2 | <= | 1000 | | | | |
| 38 | | | | | | | | |

The values for in cells D34:D37 are set arbitrarily high in the initial model and changed as each linear

**EXHIBIT 10.5**

Optimal Solution from Second Goal Program

## Solving for the Priority 4 Goal

With cell D36 set to 5 to ensure that the achievement level of priority 3 goal does not deteriorate in the final linear program, Solver is run again with cell B37 as the target cell. Exhibit 10.5 shows the spreadsheet prior to solving the fourth linear program.

## Final Solution

Exhibit 10.6 shows the final solution to the linear program. Placing 4 advertisements in Dramas, 1 in News, 4 in Sitcoms, and 1 in Sports, Frazee can best meet its goals. It actually exceeds goals 1 and 2 while coming up short by 5 million on goal 3. If the goals were ranked differently, a different advertising solution could result.

**EXHIBIT 10.6**

FMC Spreadsheet Model after Solving for the Fourth Goal.

Cell D36 was set to 5 to ensure that the achievement level of priority 3 goal does not deteriorate in the final linear program.

| | A | B | C | D | E | F | G | H |
|---|---|---|---|---|---|---|---|---|
| 14 | | | | | | | | |
| 15 | **Number of Ads** | **4** | **1** | **0** | **4** | **1** | | |
| 16 | | | | | | | | |
| 17 | **Hard Constraints** | **LHS** | sign | **RHS** | | | | |
| 18 | Drama Max | 4 | <= | 5 | | | | |
| 19 | News Max | 1 | <= | 5 | | | | |
| 20 | Reality Max | 0 | <= | 5 | | | | |
| 21 | Sitcom Max | 4 | <= | 5 | | | | |
| 22 | Sports Max | 1 | <= | 5 | | | | |
| 23 | **Cost ($1,000)** | 580 | <= | 580 | | | | |
| 24 | | | | | | | | |
| 25 | **Goal Constraints** | | | | | | | |
| 26 | | **Exposures** | **Over** | **Under** | **LHS** | | **Goal** | |
| 27 | RGF | 18 | 2 | 0 | 16 | = | 16 | |
| 28 | RGM | 16 | 2 | 0 | 14 | = | 14 | |
| 29 | HIM | 43 | 0 | 5 | 48 | = | 48 | |
| 30 | HIF | 52 | 0 | 0 | 52 | = | 52 | |
| 31 | | | | | | | | |
| 32 | **Objective Functions** | | | | | | | |
| 33 | | Deviation Value | | Best | | | | |
| 34 | **LP1: RGF Under** | 0 | <= | 0 | The values for in cells | | | |
| 35 | **LP2: RGM Under** | 0 | <= | 0 | D34:D37 are set arbitarily | | | |
| 36 | **LP3: HIM Under** | 5 | <= | 5 | high in the initial model and | | | |
| 37 | **LP4: HIF Under** | 0 | <= | 1000 | changed as each linear | | | |
| 38 | | | | | | | | |

# SUMMARY

Business managers are often under pressure to achieve goals beyond simply maximizing profit or minimizing cost. They may have several important goals that are sometimes contradictory. They can limit their set of decision alternatives using the concept of dominance to find a set of efficient solutions. They can also use goal programming to find an optimal solution when preemptive priorities exist.

# KEY TERMS

**Dominate** A solution dominates another solution if it is at least as good as the other solutions on every objective and strictly better on at least one objective.

**Efficient Frontier** The graph of all efficient solutions is called the efficient frontier. It is also called a **trade-off curve.**

**Efficient Solution** A solution that is not dominated by any other feasible solution is called an efficient or Pareto optimal solution.

**Goal Programming** Goal programming is an optimization technique that can be used when there are multiple criteria in a decision. The goals are ranked in order of importance. Each goal is optimized using linear programming in descending order of importance.

**Hard Constraint** Hard constraints directly limit the values of the decision variables. They are often called functional constraints.

**Pareto Optimal Solution** A solution that is not dominated by any other feasible solution is called an efficient or Pareto optimal solution.

**Preemptive Priority** When preemptive priorities are used, each objective is considered in descending order of importance. The level of success in achieving a higher ranked priority will not be sacrificed in order to reach a lower level goal.

**Soft Constraint** Soft constraints measure how the solution deviates from each goal. They are also called goal constraints.

**Trade-off Curve** The graph of all efficient solutions is called a **trade-off curve.**

# EXERCISES

1. While researching power saws, you read the following statements in Consumer Reports:

   - **Black & Decker** is cheaper than **SkillSaw** and **Makita.**

   - **SkillSaw** is cheaper than **Makita.**

   - **Makita** has more power than **Black & Decker.**

   - **Makita** has the same power as **SkillSaw.**

   Considering your two objectives (saving money and getting a more powerful saw), which of the following saws can be considered efficient solutions to your power saw purchasing problem?

   I.   Black & Decker
   II.  SkillSaw
   III. Makita


2. With four basketball players being picked, a high school team has the following athletic reports:

   - David Parks runs faster than Scott Thompson and Michael Allen, and Scott Thompson runs faster than Michael Allen. Kent James runs faster than David Parks.

   - Michael Allen is taller than David Parks, and Michael Allen is the same height as Scott Thompson. David Parks is taller than Kent James.

   Considering two objectives (having taller and faster players), which of the following players is (are) efficient solution(s) to the high school player-picking problem?

   I.   David Parks
   II.  Scott Thompson
   III. Michael Allen
   IV.  Kent James

3. Pete was looking for a diamond to give his girlfriend. The jewelry store had hundreds of diamonds. How could he narrow his choices? His research indicated that in picking a diamond he should consider four attributes called the four C's: Cut, Color, Carats, and Clarity. The first one was easy because he knew she liked the round cut.

**Color**—Diamonds that are of the very highest purity are totally colorless, and appear a bright white. Diamonds in the normal color range are graded on various scales developed by internationally recognized laboratories and societies, such as the American Gem Society (AGS). The AGS scale ranges from 0 to 10 with diamonds with a score of 0 being colorless and the most rare (and thus valuable).

**Clarity**—A diamond's clarity is measured by the existence, or absence, of visible flaws, both internal (inclusions) and external (blemishes). The fewer inclusions or blemishes in a diamond, the more desirable it is. A clarity grade is assigned based on the overall appearance of the diamond under 10x magnification. The American Gem Society (AGS) grades clarity on a number scale between 0 and 10 where flawless diamonds are rated a 0. A higher number indicates a more flawed diamond.

**Carat**—The traditional unit of measure for diamonds is the carat (approximately 0.2 grams). In diamonds, bigger is better.

| DIAMOND | COLOR | CLARITY | CARATS |
|---------|-------|---------|--------|
| A | 2 | 3 | 0.5 |
| B | 1 | 3 | 0.4 |
| C | 2 | 2 | 0.5 |
| D | 1 | 3 | 0.3 |
| E | 0 | 3 | 0.4 |

a. Find the dominant relationships. (Which diamonds dominate others?)

b. Find the Efficient Solutions.

4. Rebecca will graduate from Krannert with a major in accounting next semester and has obtained five job offers. The related information is shown in the table below. Rebecca is considering her job offers to make a decision. She would like a high salary, lots of vacation, and a high percentage bonus. Her family is important to her so she would like to be close to them.

| OFFER | SALARY | VACATION (DAY/YEAR) | BONUS (%) | DISTANCE TO FAMILY (MILES) |
|-------|--------|----------------------|-----------|-----------------------------|
| A | 40000 | 15 | 8 | 0 |
| B | 45000 | 10 | 8 | 50 |
| C | 45000 | 12 | 5 | 50 |
| D | 50000 | 10 | 8 | 100 |
| E | 50000 | 9 | 7 | 100 |

Find the Efficient Solutions.

5. Recall our first example, the Down to Earth Pottery case in Chapter 1. The complete LP model for Down to Earth Pottery can be written as: Let V be the number of vases made this week and B be the number of bowl sets to make this week.

$$\text{MAX:} \quad 12V + 15B$$

Subject to:

| | | | | |
|---|---|---|---|---|
| $3V$ | $+\,2B$ | $\leq$ | $60$ | Available clay |
| $1V$ | $+\,1.5B$ | $\leq$ | $40$ | Labor |
| | $B$ | $\geq$ | $8$ | Bowl set order |
| $V,$ | $B$ | $\geq$ | $0$ | Non-negativity |

Suppose Mary Alexander sets the following goals for this week:
Priority 1, Goal 1: make at least $320 in profits
Priority 2, Goal 2: to fully utilize the available clay
Priority 3, Goal 3: to avoid working any overtime
Priority 4, Goal 4: to produce at least 8 bowls

a. Define any additional decision variables to set up a Goal Programming for this case.

b. Formulate the Goal Programming.

c. Solve the goal program using Solver.

6. Superior Office Equipment manufactures scanners and fax machines. All the produced scanners and fax machines can be sold.

| | SCANNER | FAX MACHINE |
|---|---|---|
| Profit per unit | $60 | $25 |
| Labor Hours per unit | 4 | 3 |
| Motors used per unit | 2 | 2 |

Superior Office Equipment has 76 motors available per week. Superior Office Equipment sets the following goals for every week:

Priority 1, Goal 1: produce at least 10 scanners to fulfill a contract
Priority 2, Goal 2: make at least $2,000 in profits
Priority 3, Goal 3: use at most 200 labor hours

Superior Office Equipment develops a goal programming model with the following variables:

$x$ = number of scanners produced.
$y$ = number of fax machines produced.
$d_i^+$ = amount over the target value of goal $i$.
$d_i^-$ = amount below the target value of goal $i$.

a. Formulate the Goal Programming.

b. Solve the goal program using Solver.

7. The LifeFitting Company, a distributor of fitness equipment, wants to decide on how many running machines to order from two of the most popular models. The company has developed the following linear program to maximize its profits. ($x =$ Number of units to be ordered from model 1 and $y =$ Number of units to be ordered from model 2)

$$Max \quad 50x + 30y$$

s.t.

| | | | | | |
|---|---|---|---|---|---|
| Storage constraint | $2x$ | $+$ | $y$ | $\leq$ | 20 |
| Budget constraint | $2x$ | $+$ | $3y$ | $\leq$ | 24 |
| Demand constraint | $x$ | $+$ | $y$ | $\geq$ | 16 |
| | $x,$ | | $y$ | $\geq$ | 0 |

In revision, LifeFitting drops the original objective and establishes the following three goals in order of importance:

Priority 1 with a value of 45, Goal 1: Don't exceed 20 in the storage constraint.

Priority 2 with a value of 30, Goal 2: Don't exceed 24 in the budget constraint.

Priority 3 with a value of 15, Goal 3: Don't fall short of 16 in the demand constraint.

Priority 4 with a value of 10, Goal 4: Make a $300 profit.

Define decision variables and formulate a Goal programming for this problem.

8. iSpeaker is a speaker manufacturer, producing two different speakers for iPod Nano and iPod iTouch. The following goal programming model has been formulated to find the number of each to produce each day to meet its goals:

$x$ = number of iPod Nanos produced.
$y$ = number of iPod iTouch produced.
$d_i^+$ = amount over the target value of goal $i$.
$d_i^-$ = amount below the target value of goal $i$.

MIN: $P1(d_1^-) + P2(d_2^+) + P2(d_3^-)$

$2x + 4y + d_1^- + d_1^+ = 40$

$4x + 9y + d_2^- + d_2^+ = 100$

$x + y + d_3^- + d_3^+ = 30$

$x, y, d_i^-, d_i^+ \geq 0$ for $i = 1, 2, 3$

Solve this problem using Excel Solver. What is the optimal solution? Print and submit your final spreadsheet.

9. Gzen FoF Co. is a fund of hedge funds company which has an asset under management of $10 billion dollars. Gzen invests in a portfolio consisting of hedge funds with different strategies. The expected annual net-of-fee return is listed in the table below.

| HEDGE FUNDS | STRATEGY | NET-OF-FEE RETURN |
|:---:|:---:|:---:|
| A | Emerging market | 15.2% |
| B | Equity Long Short | 11.8% |
| C | Fixed Income | 7.6% |
| D | Equity Long Short | 13.5% |
| E | Fixed Income | 6.8% |
| F | Equity Long Short | 10.4% |
| G | Emerging market | 6% |

The investment goals are ranked based on the weight in parentheses as following:

Goal 1 (35): Maximize the total return with a target of 10%.
Goal 2 (25): At most 25% of AUM invested in Emerging Market.
Goal 3 (20): At least 30% of AUM invested in Equity Long/Short.
Goal 4 (15): No more than 50% of AUM invested in Fixed Income.
Goal 5 (5): No more than 15% of AUM invested in A.

Which hedge funds should be added into the portfolio while meeting these goals?

a. Formulate a Goal Programming for this problem.

b. Solve it with Excel Solver.

10. Consider the Frazee Motor Car Company example. Suppose the goals had the following priorities:

a. Seen by at least 48 million high income males (HIM).

b. Seen by at least 52 million high income females (HIF).

c. Seen by at least 16 million recently graduated females (RGF).

d. Seen by at least 14 million recently graduated males (RGM).

    1. Formulate a set of soft constraints for these goals:

    2. Find the optimal solution to the goal program with these priorities. Show your final Excel spreadsheet with your solution.

# Standard Normal Distribution:
## Table Values Represent AREA to the LEFT of the Z Score

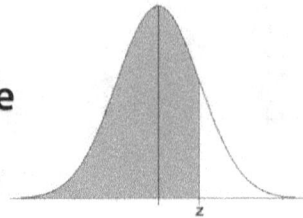

| Z | .00 | .01 | .02 | .03 | .04 | .05 | .06 | .07 | .08 | .09 |
|---|-----|-----|-----|-----|-----|-----|-----|-----|-----|-----|
| −3.9 | .00005 | .00005 | .00004 | .00004 | .00004 | .00004 | .00004 | .00004 | .00003 | .00003 |
| −3.8 | .00007 | .00007 | .00007 | .00006 | .00006 | .00006 | .00006 | .00005 | .00005 | .00005 |
| −3.7 | .00011 | .00010 | .00010 | .00010 | .00009 | .00009 | .00008 | .00008 | .00008 | .00008 |
| −3.6 | .00016 | .00015 | .00015 | .00014 | .00014 | .00013 | .00013 | .00012 | .00012 | .00011 |
| −3.5 | .00023 | .00022 | .00022 | .00021 | .00020 | .00019 | .00019 | .00018 | .00017 | .00017 |
| −3.4 | .00034 | .00032 | .00031 | .00030 | .00029 | .00028 | .00027 | .00026 | .00025 | .00024 |
| −3.3 | .00048 | .00047 | .00045 | .00043 | .00042 | .00040 | .00039 | .00038 | .00036 | .00035 |
| −3.2 | .00069 | .00066 | .00064 | .00062 | .00060 | .00058 | .00056 | .00054 | .00052 | .00050 |
| −3.1 | .00097 | .00094 | .00090 | .00087 | .00084 | .00082 | .00079 | .00076 | .00074 | .00071 |
| −3.0 | .00135 | .00131 | .00126 | .00122 | .00118 | .00114 | .00111 | .00107 | .00104 | .00100 |
| −2.9 | .00187 | .00181 | .00175 | .00169 | .00164 | .00159 | .00154 | .00149 | .00144 | .00139 |
| −2.8 | .00256 | .00248 | .00240 | .00233 | .00226 | .00219 | .00212 | .00205 | .00199 | .00193 |
| −2.7 | .00347 | .00336 | .00326 | .00317 | .00307 | .00298 | .00289 | .00280 | .00272 | .00264 |
| −2.6 | .00466 | .00453 | .00440 | .00427 | .00415 | .00402 | .00391 | .00379 | .00368 | .00357 |
| −2.5 | .00621 | .00604 | .00587 | .00570 | .00554 | .00539 | .00523 | .00508 | .00494 | .00480 |
| −2.4 | .00820 | .00798 | .00776 | .00755 | .00734 | .00714 | .00695 | .00676 | .00657 | .00639 |
| −2.3 | .01072 | .01044 | .01017 | .00990 | .00964 | .00939 | .00914 | .00889 | .00866 | .00842 |
| −2.2 | .01390 | .01355 | .01321 | .01287 | .01255 | .01222 | .01191 | .01160 | .01130 | .01101 |
| −2.1 | .01786 | .01743 | .01700 | .01659 | .01618 | .01578 | .01539 | .01500 | .01463 | .01426 |
| −2.0 | .02275 | .02222 | .02169 | .02118 | .02068 | .02018 | .01970 | .01923 | .01876 | .01831 |
| −1.9 | .02872 | .02807 | .02743 | .02680 | .02619 | .02559 | .02500 | .02442 | .02385 | .02330 |
| −1.8 | .03593 | .03515 | .03438 | .03362 | .03288 | .03216 | .03144 | .03074 | .03005 | .02938 |
| −1.7 | .04457 | .04363 | .04272 | .04182 | .04093 | .04006 | .03920 | .03836 | .03754 | .03673 |
| −1.6 | .05480 | .05370 | .05262 | .05155 | .05050 | .04947 | .04846 | .04746 | .04648 | .04551 |
| −1.5 | .06681 | .06552 | .06426 | .06301 | .06178 | .06057 | .05938 | .05821 | .05705 | .05592 |
| −1.4 | .08076 | .07927 | .07780 | .07636 | .07493 | .07353 | .07215 | .07078 | .06944 | .06811 |
| −1.3 | .09680 | .09510 | .09342 | .09176 | .09012 | .08851 | .08691 | .08534 | .08379 | .08226 |
| −1.2 | .11507 | .11314 | .11123 | .10935 | .10749 | .10565 | .10383 | .10204 | .10027 | .09853 |
| −1.1 | .13567 | .13350 | .13136 | .12924 | .12714 | .12507 | .12302 | .12100 | .11900 | .11702 |
| −1.0 | .15866 | .15625 | .15386 | .15151 | .14917 | .14686 | .14457 | .14231 | .14007 | .13786 |
| −0.9 | .18406 | .18141 | .17879 | .17619 | .17361 | .17106 | .16853 | .16602 | .16354 | .16109 |
| −0.8 | .21186 | .20897 | .20611 | .20327 | .20045 | .19766 | .19489 | .19215 | .18943 | .18673 |
| −0.7 | .24196 | .23885 | .23576 | .23270 | .22965 | .22663 | .22363 | .22065 | .21770 | .21476 |
| −0.6 | .27425 | .27093 | .26763 | .26435 | .26109 | .25785 | .25463 | .25143 | .24825 | .24510 |
| −0.5 | .30854 | .30503 | .30153 | .29806 | .29460 | .29116 | .28774 | .28434 | .28096 | .27760 |
| −0.4 | .34458 | .34090 | .33724 | .33360 | .32997 | .32636 | .32276 | .31918 | .31561 | .31207 |
| −0.3 | .38209 | .37828 | .37448 | .37070 | .36693 | .36317 | .35942 | .35569 | .35197 | .34827 |
| −0.2 | .42074 | .41683 | .41294 | .40905 | .40517 | .40129 | .39743 | .39358 | .38974 | .38591 |
| −0.1 | .46017 | .45620 | .45224 | .44828 | .44433 | .44038 | .43644 | .43251 | .42858 | .42465 |
| −0.0 | .50000 | .49601 | .49202 | .48803 | .48405 | .48006 | .47608 | .47210 | .46812 | .46414 |

| Z | .00 | .01 | .02 | .03 | .04 | .05 | .06 | .07 | .08 | .09 |
|-----|-------|-------|-------|-------|-------|-------|-------|-------|-------|-------|
| 0.0 | .50000 | .50399 | .50798 | .51197 | .51595 | .51994 | .52392 | .52790 | .53188 | .53586 |
| 0.1 | .53983 | .54380 | .54776 | .55172 | .55567 | .55962 | .56356 | .56749 | .57142 | .57535 |
| 0.2 | .57926 | .58317 | .58706 | .59095 | .59483 | .59871 | .60257 | .60642 | .61026 | .61409 |
| 0.3 | .61791 | .62172 | .62552 | .62930 | .63307 | .63683 | .64058 | .64431 | .64803 | .65173 |
| 0.4 | .65542 | .65910 | .66276 | .66640 | .67003 | .67364 | .67724 | .68082 | .68439 | .68793 |
| 0.5 | .69146 | .69497 | .69847 | .70194 | .70540 | .70884 | .71226 | .71566 | .71904 | .72240 |
| 0.6 | .72575 | .72907 | .73237 | .73565 | .73891 | .74215 | .74537 | .74857 | .75175 | .75490 |
| 0.7 | .75804 | .76115 | .76424 | .76730 | .77035 | .77337 | .77637 | .77935 | .78230 | .78524 |
| 0.8 | .78814 | .79103 | .79389 | .79673 | .79955 | .80234 | .80511 | .80785 | .81057 | .81327 |
| 0.9 | .81594 | .81859 | .82121 | .82381 | .82639 | .82894 | .83147 | .83398 | .83646 | .83891 |
| 1.0 | .84134 | .84375 | .84614 | .84849 | .85083 | .85314 | .85543 | .85769 | .85993 | .86214 |
| 1.1 | .86433 | .86650 | .86864 | .87076 | .87286 | .87493 | .87698 | .87900 | .88100 | .88298 |
| 1.2 | .88493 | .88686 | .88877 | .89065 | .89251 | .89435 | .89617 | .89796 | .89973 | .90147 |
| 1.3 | .90320 | .90490 | .90658 | .90824 | .90988 | .91149 | .91309 | .91466 | .91621 | .91774 |
| 1.4 | .91924 | .92073 | .92220 | .92364 | .92507 | .92647 | .92785 | .92922 | .93056 | .93189 |
| 1.5 | .93319 | .93448 | .93574 | .93699 | .93822 | .93943 | .94062 | .94179 | .94295 | .94408 |
| 1.6 | .94520 | .94630 | .94738 | .94845 | .94950 | .95053 | .95154 | .95254 | .95352 | .95449 |
| 1.7 | .95543 | .95637 | .95728 | .95818 | .95907 | .95994 | .96080 | .96164 | .96246 | .96327 |
| 1.8 | .96407 | .96485 | .96562 | .96638 | .96712 | .96784 | .96856 | .96926 | .96995 | .97062 |
| 1.9 | .97128 | .97193 | .97257 | .97320 | .97381 | .97441 | .97500 | .97558 | .97615 | .97670 |
| 2.0 | .97725 | .97778 | .97831 | .97882 | .97932 | .97982 | .98030 | .98077 | .98124 | .98169 |
| 2.1 | .98214 | .98257 | .98300 | .98341 | .98382 | .98422 | .98461 | .98500 | .98537 | .98574 |
| 2.2 | .98610 | .98645 | .98679 | .98713 | .98745 | .98778 | .98809 | .98840 | .98870 | .98899 |
| 2.3 | .98928 | .98956 | .98983 | .99010 | .99036 | .99061 | .99086 | .99111 | .99134 | .99158 |
| 2.4 | .99180 | .99202 | .99224 | .99245 | .99266 | .99286 | .99305 | .99324 | .99343 | .99361 |
| 2.5 | .99379 | .99396 | .99413 | .99430 | .99446 | .99461 | .99477 | .99492 | .99506 | .99520 |
| 2.6 | .99534 | .99547 | .99560 | .99573 | .99585 | .99598 | .99609 | .99621 | .99632 | .99643 |
| 2.7 | .99653 | .99664 | .99674 | .99683 | .99693 | .99702 | .99711 | .99720 | .99728 | .99736 |
| 2.8 | .99744 | .99752 | .99760 | .99767 | .99774 | .99781 | .99788 | .99795 | .99801 | .99807 |
| 2.9 | .99813 | .99819 | .99825 | .99831 | .99836 | .99841 | .99846 | .99851 | .99856 | .99861 |
| 3.0 | .99865 | .99869 | .99874 | .99878 | .99882 | .99886 | .99889 | .99893 | .99896 | .99900 |
| 3.1 | .99903 | .99906 | .99910 | .99913 | .99916 | .99918 | .99921 | .99924 | .99926 | .99929 |
| 3.2 | .99931 | .99934 | .99936 | .99938 | .99940 | .99942 | .99944 | .99946 | .99948 | .99950 |
| 3.3 | .99952 | .99953 | .99955 | .99957 | .99958 | .99960 | .99961 | .99962 | .99964 | .99965 |
| 3.4 | .99966 | .99968 | .99969 | .99970 | .99971 | .99972 | .99973 | .99974 | .99975 | .99976 |
| 3.5 | .99977 | .99978 | .99978 | .99979 | .99980 | .99981 | .99981 | .99982 | .99983 | .99983 |
| 3.6 | .99984 | .99985 | .99985 | .99986 | .99986 | .99987 | .99987 | .99988 | .99988 | .99989 |
| 3.7 | .99989 | .99990 | .99990 | .99990 | .99991 | .99991 | .99992 | .99992 | .99992 | .99992 |
| 3.8 | .99993 | .99993 | .99993 | .99994 | .99994 | .99994 | .99994 | .99995 | .99995 | .99995 |
| 3.9 | .99995 | .99995 | .99996 | .99996 | .99996 | .99996 | .99996 | .99996 | .99997 | .99997 |

# Index

**Note:** Page numbers followed by an italic letter indicates (*f*) figure, (*t*) table, and (*e*) exhibit.